Here and There

Here and There

SITES OF PHILOSOPHY

Stanley Cavell

Edited by Nancy Bauer, Alice Crary, and Sandra Laugier

Harvard University Press

CAMBRIDGE, MASSACHUSETTS

LONDON, ENGLAND

2022

LIBRARY OF CONGRESS CATALOGING-IN-PUBLICATION DATA

Names: Cavell, Stanley, 1926–2018, author. | Bauer, Nancy, 1960– editor. |
    Crary, Alice, 1967– editor. | Laugier, Sandra, editor.
Title: Here and there : sites of philosophy / Stanley Cavell ;
    edited by Nancy Bauer, Alice Crary, and Sandra Laugier.
Description: Cambridge, Massachusetts : Harvard University Press, 2022. |
    Includes bibliographical references and index.
Identifiers: LCCN 2021044220 | ISBN 9780674270480 (cloth)
Subjects: LCSH: Philosophy, Modern. | Criticism (Philosophy) |
    Psychoanalysis and philosophy.
Classification: LCC B945 .C271 2022 | DDC 170—dc23/eng/20211008
LC record available at https://lccn.loc.gov/2021044220

Contents

Here and There

Editors' Introduction

There is the audience of philosophy; but there also, while it lasts, is its performance.

—STANLEY CAVELL, foreword to *Must We Mean What We Say?*

On January 20, 2001, the American philosopher Stanley Cavell drafted a preface to a book he was planning to call *Here and There: Sites of Philosophy*. The book was to consist of unpublished lectures and essays of his reaching back over more than a decade.[1] In his draft preface, Cavell wrote:

> Gathered in this place from here and there are the pieces of work, con-
> centrated within recent years but in a few cases going back to the
> 1980s, that I find worth rescuing either from oblivion or from the eva-
> nescence or specialization of their original locations of publication. . . .
> The idea of a here with a there as sites of philosophy, namely as
> suggesting measures of distance between different philosophical
> projects, but as a sense or measure of the task within each project,
> became explicit in a comparatively recent essay of mine on the
> aesthetics of Wittgenstein's *Philosophical Investigations,* where the or-
> dinary in which we exist and from which we philosophize, and the
> fervor of aspiration with and toward which we philosophize, are pic-
> tured as near and far shores between which the river of philosophy
> has to take and modify its way. It is the peculiarity of this river that it
> is incessantly tempted to deny the necessity of one or other of its
> shores.[2]

Within this brief text, Cavell gives the titular phrase "here and there" a particular inflection. For him, philosophical reflection is a drive of all human

thought. Because philosophy is composed in response to particular circumstances, using the particular words and concepts that happen to be on hand at a particular time, it is inevitably rooted in what Cavell calls "the ordinary in which we exist." This standpoint opposes our "fervor of aspiration" to grasp things as they fundamentally are. Philosophy requires a willingness to navigate, endlessly, between these two shores.

This way of understanding philosophy's aspirations implies that its subject matter is not fixed in advance. It depends on what a thinker cares about enough to reflect on. Cavell's interests were deep and wide, and his writings display an exceptional breadth of range. In the manner of the jazz pianist and composer he had once been, he riffed on the work of others that riveted him, both within and outside of philosophy. His wide range of interests included J. L. Austin, Ludwig Wittgenstein, Ralph Waldo Emerson, Henry David Thoreau, Shakespearean tragedy, Hollywood classic comedies and melodramas, opera, Jane Austen, Edgar Allan Poe, Samuel Beckett—and this is in no way a comprehensive list. Cavell also differed from most professional philosophers of his time insofar as he didn't limit himself to specific areas of philosophy or set out to build a system or endorse a set of philosophical doctrines or methods. What he cared about were the particular audiences to whom he was speaking, a commitment to responsiveness and conversation that is palpable throughout the present collection. Though he often stressed that philosophy is made of "texts, not problems," his work was not primarily exegetical.[3] Instead, he modeled for his audiences how to pay deep critical attention to the things they found themselves caring about—a practice that by definition might lead to having, or wanting, to let certain obsessions go. In this way, his understanding of the work of philosophy bears a resemblance to the practice and theory of psychoanalysis, which aims at self-knowledge as a work of repair.

Cavell wanted to inspire readers to think for themselves, to judge what he wrote and said in reference to their own experience and acts of thinking. As he put it in 1969: "No man is in any better position for knowing than any other man unless wanting to know is a special position. And this discovery about himself is the same as the discovery of philosophy, when it is the effort to find answers, and permit questions, which nobody knows the way to nor the answer to any better than you yourself."[4] The claim that philosophy is concerned with questions of human significance, and that no one is an expert in philosophy so understood, or is otherwise in a special position to address these questions, is an undercurrent of Cavell's work from beginning to end.

Here and There is the first publication from Cavell's *Nachlass*. All of the writings in this book are "occasional" in the sense that they were composed for particular occasions, mostly in response to invitations.[5] Cavell cared about what he saw as an "internal relation between philosophy and sites or spaces that is mostly unthematized in philosophy" (Prologue). For him, words spring to life in concrete places and spaces of speech, a point he flags in the title of the present volume. The circumstances of what we say—to whom, from where— matter as much as the meaning of our words. That the themes of situational responsiveness and of the site-specific power of voice—themes that animate all of his writings—provide this book's organizing principle makes *Here and There* congenial for readers new to Cavell as well as for readers already familiar with his work.

Between 1999 and 2000, Cavell produced four tables of contents for this book. During this period, he repeatedly expressed his sense that the pieces were "too dispersed," "too scattered in too specialized places." He wanted them to be brought together in a way that would "help to organize" his work.[6] The kind of organization he sought was that not of a theoretical edifice but of a set of exercises, whose power as provocations for readers to continue thinking on our own would be enhanced by displaying their essential unity.

No book entitled *Here and There* emerged during Cavell's lifetime. All told, there is no evidence that Cavell made a deliberate decision not to publish the material in the present book and every reason to believe that he simply never got back to it after 2001. In 2003, Cavell published a final, enlarged edition of *Disowning Knowledge.*[7] He gave the scholar David LaRocca permission to edit *Emerson's Transcendental Etudes,* which absorbed the entire contents of one projected part of *Here and There,* a part Cavell had been calling "Mostly Emerson."[8] He also allowed William Rothman, professor of cinema and interactive media at the University of Miami, to publish a number of his essays on film in *Cavell on Film* (2005).[9] Still other writings he had considered including in *Here and There* were published in his collection *Philosophy the Day after Tomorrow* (2006).[10] During this whole period, Cavell was also working steadily on his autobiography, *Little Did I Know,* whose first entries are dated 2003, and which was published in 2010.[11]

When Stanley Cavell died on June 19, 2018, the three most substantial parts of *Here and There*—parts he had labeled "Departures," "Assignments," and "Music"—remained uncollated. This material constitutes the core of the present book. We have curated the writings, leaving out—with one exception—pieces already published in Cavell's other books, and adding a number of thematically congenial pieces written after 2001. These include "Notes Mostly about Empathy" (2009), "Foreword to Veena Das, *Life and Words*" (2007), "Reflections on Wallace Stevens at Mount Holyoke" (2003), "Foreword to *Qu'est-ce que la philosophie américaine?*" (2009), "A Scale of Eternity" (2003), and "Bon Voyage" (1997).[12] The only chapter that appears in another book by Cavell is "The World as Things," which is crucial to the present volume as a reflection on thought as a process of collecting.

Cavell composed almost all of the essays in this book in response to speaking or writing invitations—and they appeared in a wide variety of formats. Some of them, including "The World as Things," the essays on Walter Benjamin, "On a Psychoanalytical Response to Faulkner's Form," and "Reflections on Wallace Stevens at Mount Holyoke," address topics that Cavell does not treat elsewhere.

Cavell's range of philosophical interests was *sui generis* and not typical of his time. He rarely fell in with trends in professional philosophy and instead focused on the particular phenomena—and they could come from any source—that called for his philosophical attention: films of the 1930s and 1940s, Wittgenstein's woodcutters, Emerson's visit to the collections in the Jardin des Plantes in Paris, Walter Benjamin's interest in the Parisian arcades, and the power of women's voices in opera, to name a very few. This is in effect to say that he declined to understand philosophy as a science or a system-building enterprise—though it is not to imply that his work lacks rigor. To the contrary, his capacity to attend carefully and thoroughly to the phenomena that he found engaging, characteristically over many years and in conversation with a wide variety of friends, colleagues, and students, was one of his most striking features. His ability to get in focus and articulate important features of the conditions that we human beings both are subject to and collectively craft for ourselves—conditions that are in plain view but that we ordinarily avoid noticing—was perhaps his most remarkable gift.

As Cavell makes clear in "Notes after Austin" (Chapter 5), a critical turning point in his philosophical development was his first encounter with the work of J. L. Austin, a British philosopher now most often remembered for stressing the capacity of everyday human speech not just to communicate thoughts but to do things. This is the subject of Austin's book *How to Do Things with Words,* which originally took the form of a lecture series given at Harvard in 1955.[13] At the time a dispirited graduate student, Cavell found in Austin's lectures a way forward with his own thinking.[14] Austin's drawing attention to the capacity of words to do things—order lunch, congratulate, marry, rebuke, chasten, hurt, and so on—revealed to Cavell how in speaking and understanding language we are obliged to fall back on our own sensibility, on our feel for the kinds of things words can do. As he writes in "Notes after Austin," "Austin's philosophizing . . . allowed me—demanded of me—the use of myself as the source of its evidence and as an instance of its conclusions. Whatever philosophy's pertinence to me, I felt for the first time my pertinence to philosophy." Here, Cavell is claiming that Austin's philosophical practice depends on our willingness to develop and refine in our lives with language what musicians call an *ear*.

Cavell's new understanding of what philosophy could do and be developed further when, starting in 1959, he began to read Wittgenstein's *Philosophical Investigations*. Although, as Cavell was wont to observe, Austin and Wittgenstein were in many respects very different from one another, he credited both for teaching him to appreciate what he calls "the power of ordinary or so-called natural language."[15] Rather than dissect language at arm's length, these philosophers, each in their own way, demand that we take into account that language is used by individual human beings speaking within what Wittgenstein called a "form of life"—that is, the practices that collect around our words and in which we engage. As Cavell put it in one of his earliest essays—in a passage that has resonance for all of the chapters of the current book and that is discussed explicitly in two of them—developing a life in language is "a matter of our sharing routes of interest and feeling, modes of response, senses of humor and of significance and of fulfillment, of what is outrageous, of what is similar to what else, what a rebuke, what forgiveness."[16]

Austin's and Wittgenstein's conceptions of ordinary language play an organizing role in Cavell's first book, *Must We Mean What We Say?* (1969), which discusses for the first time topics that return in *Here and There*, including poetry, novels, psychoanalysis, and music. Written thirty years later, *Here and There* resolutely broaches anew the topic of the *modern*.[17] This word signaled for Cavell not just a twentieth-century literary and artistic movement, but a moment in which human beings no longer understand tradition as a determinate guide and therefore feel that they must innovate and improvise—while still, at the same time, forging a future that counts as a meaningful continuation of the past.

This understanding of the modern condition structures Cavell's 1979 mono-graph, *The Claim of Reason,* into which, eighteen years after receiving his doctorate in philosophy, he reworked his PhD dissertation. Decades after the book's publication, Cavell said of it, "Everything I have written after its ap-pearance, as well as much before its appearance, is in some way indebted to it" (Chapter 18). *The Claim of Reason* questions the single-minded pursuit in philosophy of absolute "explanations," as though in their absence language can be nothing more than what he calls a "thin net over an abyss."[18] An impor-tant thread winding through the book, as well as Cavell's subsequent writ-ings, is the nature of skepticism—that is, of philosophical doubt about the existence of the world and of other people (or, as philosophers prefer to say, of "other minds").[19] The latter problem is often understood by philosophers to be just an instance of external-world skepticism. For Cavell, however, the problem of other minds is at the heart of our ordinary lives. He regards it as a cover for—a form of denial of—our failure to acknowledge other people's humanity. In Cavell's words: "skepticism concerning other minds is not skep-ticism but tragedy."[20] Indeed, as early as the 1960s, Cavell had been struck by the idea that the skeptical problematic is integral to Shakespeare's tragedies.[21] In Chapter 4 of the present book he characterizes his exploration of skeptical questions as "lead[ing] to my claim of [Wittgenstein's] *Investigations* as a work written not to refute skepticism, but to uncover its possibility, and allure." This allure is what he calls the "truth" of skepticism.[22] For him, the right response to skepticism about other minds—taking the form, say, of another person's claim to be in pain—is not an *argument* attempting to prove that the person is in pain, but an act of *acknowledging* it. Cavell was especially interested in the role of acknowledgment, as well as failures of acknowledgment, in Shake-speare, certain genres of film, and the philosophical works of Emerson and Thoreau.[23]

A further key moment in Cavell's philosophical trajectory was his turning in the late 1970s to Emerson's writings.[24] Though Cavell had been concerned with the nature of morality at least as far back as his first writings, it was only in the wake of rediscovering Emerson that he began gradually to develop a view to counter the idea, ingrained in Anglophone ethics, that the patterns of the moral life are indifferently accessible. He gradually transformed this concern into a view of the ethical life that he called "moral perfectionism," which emphasizes, in his words, "the notion, pervasive in Emerson, of be-coming who you are" (Chapter 9).[25] Cavell worked intensively to refine the contours of moral perfectionism, eventually publishing in quick succession the books *In Quest of the Ordinary* (1988), *This New Yet Unapproachable America* (1989), and *Conditions Handsome and Unhandsome* (1990), as well as a number of freestanding essays.[26] In the late 1980s he developed what became a large and perennially popular undergraduate course at Harvard focused on perfectionist themes. By the 1990s, when he was writing the bulk of the essays in *Here and There,* he was calling his own philosophy "Emersonian Perfectionism." *Here and There* belongs to this transformational moment and epitomizes its new departures and themes. Cavell would later express the ambition of this phase of his work this way: "I hope I am right to see in these texts of mine Emerson's force making itself felt in the way I read Wittgenstein" (Chapter 20, foreword to *Qu'est-ce que la philosophie américaine*).[27] Cavell's Emersonian commitments are evident in the writings collected in the present book. He is especially interested in exploring a new formulation of skepticism—what he called, in a gesture to Freud, "the uncanniness of the ordinary."[28] Discussions of this concept pervade *Here and There* and culminate in the essays on psychoanalysis. In Cavell's words, "The intersection of the familiar and the strange is an experience of the uncanny, an intersection therefore shared by the anthropologist, the psychoanalyst, and the Wittgensteinian (Socratic, Rousseaulike, Thoreau-like, etc.) philosopher" (Chapter 14).

―――――――

Working in the early 2000s on the table of contents of *Here and There,* Cavell envisioned an "opening section, 'Departures,' [that] puts together mostly the longer texts involved, which lay out the general lines of my interests that are mainly new, or newly explicit, and that I expect to motivate further work" (Appendix). This section in the present book includes three of the pieces Cavell originally had in mind for it, followed by two essays that expand the ground from which these longer pieces "depart," expressing Cavell's philosophical debts to Wittgenstein and Austin in personal ways that go beyond his reflections in other published work.[29]

It is worth tracing out a few of the themes that run through the three longer pieces.

"Time after Time" was written for a 1994 forum held in Le Mans, France. The essay contains Cavell's first touching on the idea of "philosophy the day after tomorrow" and is his only foray into environmental issues.[30] In Cavell's vision, which overlaps with the visions of Emerson and Nietzsche, every new step of thought forges fresh links to steps past, creating its own temporal projection, so that "philosophy as such is thinking for the future."

"The World as Things: Collecting Thoughts on Collecting" was written for the catalogue of a 1998 exhibition entitled *Rendezvous,* which was a joint venture of the Guggenheim Museum in New York and the Musée National d'Art Moderne in Paris. Starting from the concept of collecting in its various modalities—rain in pails, one's thoughts, coins, and curiosities—Cavell considers accounts of collecting by different artists, art critics, sociologists, and philosophers. He turns his attention to his own acts of collecting—that is, to what it means for texts, or thoughts, or words to be put together, as a series or collection, thus presenting his own philosophical procedures in a new light.[31] He asks, "Why do we put things together as we do? Why do we put ourselves together with just these things to make a world?" presenting his study as a contribution to human natural history.[32]

"The Division of Talent" contains remarks Cavell delivered at the 1984 meeting of the Association of Departments of English at Yale University, the school that at that time was the epicenter of interest in Derridean deconstructionism in the United States. Cavell took the opportunity to consider a number of then-recent controversies that might betoken a crisis in literary studies, oriented by the observation that these controversies express "arguments about the obligation to literary theory as part of literary study" and, additionally, that "these arguments sometimes take on the color or texture of strong statements of, or against, something called deconstruction." He spells out his concern that deconstruction veers toward retaining aspects of the very positivism it seeks to overcome.[33] The threat of this form of theory lies in its turning out to be another species of "flight from the ordinary." This essay represents the beginning of Cavell's argument with deconstruction, which he expanded in *A Pitch of Philosophy* (1994).[34]

Cavell envisioned *Here and There* as moving from longer essays to a section he called "Assignments." He characterized these pieces as "short responses to requests of various kinds from often unexpected quarters of a kind that retirement from teaching has given me more freedom to accept than I have been used to."[35] Cavell wrote the essays in question with an awareness that he might "never find time or occasion to pursue [any of the subjects] to an extent that matches the degree of my sense of its importance." His sense was that each, "even in its brief materialization, creates an effect that puts the whole of my efforts in a somewhat different light" (Appendix). *Here and There* includes nearly all of the shorter pieces Cavell intended for it as well as several additional essays. These writings reveal his ties to figures and topics important to his philosophical trajectory but for the most part only alluded to in his published works.

The second and third pieces in this section (Chapters 7 and 8) contain Cavell's most focused engagements with Walter Benjamin, a thinker he had long admired but rarely discussed in detail. One aim of this pair of texts is to respond to those who question whether Benjamin's critical sensibility qualifies as philosophical, a task Cavell approaches by aligning aspects of Benjamin's writing that produce philosophical resistance with controversial aspects of Wittgenstein's writing. Cavell focuses on Benjamin's "contesting of the philosophical with the literary," examining the idea that it is true of Benjamin, as, he believed, of Wittgenstein, that "pathos [is] indispensable to his writing."

Another cluster of shorter pieces constitutes Cavell's most concentrated discussion of psychoanalysis and its relation to philosophy, a topic in which he had a longstanding interest. He himself had been in psychoanalysis twice, once at the very beginning of his teaching career and once, approximately twenty years later, when he was completing *The Claim of Reason*—both times, considering the possibility of becoming an analyst himself.[36] From the time of his first book, *Must We Mean What We Say?* to his last, the autobiography *Little Did I Know*—both of whose titles have psychoanalytic overtones—Cavell paid close attention to psychoanalytic writings, debates, and institutions.[37] In the texts included here, he explores what he calls the "internal link" between psychoanalysis and ordinary language philosophy, both of which focus on recovering our authentic selves. If "the arrogance of philosophy is to show that I can speak universally, for everyone," the "confidence of psychoanalysis is to show that I do not so much as speak for myself" (Chapter 9). Psychoanalysis, like philosophy of a certain kind, is a mode of thinking where there is a life of the mind, and therefore a death.[38] If the mind were to lose the psychoanalytic intuition of itself as unconscious, it would lose, Cavell claims, the last proof of its existence. Cavell attaches importance to psychoanalysis because he takes it to be the site of a deliberate confrontation of our need for acknowledgment. By insisting on the intimate link of psychoanalysis and philosophy that is suggested in reflection on skepticism and on ordinary language, he presents himself as a true heir of Freud (Chapter 9).

Two short pieces recount portions of Cavell's side of an extended exchange with the anthropologist Veena Das. The exchange starts with Cavell's response to Das's essay "Language and Body: Transactions in the Construction of Pain," which was published in 1996 in an influential issue of the journal *Daedalus* devoted to the topic "Social Suffering." Das's writing expresses her sense of the urgent need to find scientific language adequate to expressing the extremity of the violence that had been perpetrated against women during and after the Partition of India in 1947. Her topic, Cavell tells us, is "pain, in a historical instance in which its 'enormity . . . is not in question.'" Das holds that, when faced with another's expression of pain, we are not, in Cavell's way of putting the point, "at liberty to believe or to disbelieve" but are "forced to respond, either to acknowledge it in return or to avoid it." Together, the two essays on Das included here—Cavell's initial response to her and his foreword to her 2007 book *Life and Words*—gave him a presence in anthropology, where his interpretation of the Wittgensteinian notion of form of life has gained purchase, and where he is sometimes represented as a founding contributor to a cross-cutting body of work called "ordinary ethics."[39]

The 1990s saw the appearance of the first translations of Cavell's work into other languages, including French, Italian, German, and Spanish. Cavell devoted great attention to these translations, as is made clear by several of the essays included here, such as "Silences Noises Voices" (Chapter 6), which was presented at the occasion of the publication of the French translation of *The Claim of Reason*. Translation offered Cavell "a further process of reassurance in the book's intelligibility."[40] International circulation and discussion of his work meant for him a different relationship to his words and new life for them. "It is only in being translated that a text, with a certain ambition to survive, perhaps surmising its own obscurity, achieves its existence. As if only then is it assured of its viability."[41]

In his draft preface, Cavell described the concluding section he planned for *Here and There,* which he entitled "Music," this way:

> The group whose emergence most surprised me I guess is that of the four pieces on music. Music is as old among my cultural practices as reading words or telling time, but except for a pair of forays in my first book, I have until quite recently avoided the issue.

Cavell had published on music only rarely, and even more rarely at length, since the time of the publication of *Must We Mean What We Say?* which includes the essay on "Music Discomposed." That he characterizes his stance toward music as one of avoidance is a function, he says, of its importance in his young life as a performer, as well as of the fact that his life's "formative intellectual or spiritual crisis," which had led him to dedicate himself to the study of philosophy, was discovering, when he began studying composition at the Juilliard School, that "music was no longer my life's work" (Chapter 23).[42]

As he recalls in *Little Did I Know,* he was, at the time, "confronting at Juilliard the disintegration of my ambition to compose music, replaced as it were by reading Freud ten to twelve hours a day, successively contracting the symptoms of hysteria and of obsession depicted in the *Introductory Lectures.*"[43] This experience may underlie Cavell's desire to collate in the present book his then-recent work on music: two pieces on opera, including one on Peter Kivy on Mozart's *Idomeneo,* an essay on Schoenberg, and an essay on Beethoven (Chapters 21–24). These pieces date from 1998 and were born of invitations to lectures, conferences, and eventually a regular spot on panels at the annual Bard Music Festival, which he had attended every year since its creation in 1990. The "Music" section of this book includes these pieces, as well as an essay on Mahler from 2003.

A consistent concern of Cavell's in the music essays is how, in his words, "the work I do in a certain manner of philosophy, and the work of studying the nature and cultures of music, might bear upon one another" (Chapter 21). Cavell is accounting for his awareness that part of what he has been demanding of philosophy is a grasp of what he had initially sought in music. He writes:

> I have known for most of [the past few decades] that something I have demanded from philosophy was an understanding precisely of what I had sought in music, and in the understanding of music, of what demanded that reclamation of experience, of the capacity for being moved, which called out for, and sustained, an accounting as lucid as the music I loved. (Chapter 23)

For Cavell, philosophical practice requires and develops the ability to detect the right pitch or tone—perhaps the harmony, or dissonance—in a conversation. If we grant that the sensitivities that are key to appreciating music are also internal to thinking, it makes sense to hold that, to quote a passage from Wittgenstein's *Philosophical Investigations* to which Cavell refers several times in these chapters, "understanding a sentence is much more akin to understanding a theme in music than one may think."[44] By the same token, it makes sense to hold that philosophy, and more exactly ordinary language philosophy, can be asked to supply the kind of reclamation of, or reconciliation with, sensibility that we may also seek in music. As Cavell recalls:

> Working in Austin's classes was the time for me in philosophy when the common rigors of exercise acquired the seriousness and playfulness—the continuous mutuality—that I had counted on in musical performance. . . . That Austin's practice had to do, in its own way, with the possession of an ear, was surely part of its authority for me. (Chapter 5)

Cavell's short pieces on music, which contain interwoven reflections not only on Mozart, Beethoven, Schoenberg, and Mahler but also on Freud, Kafka, Wittgenstein, Adorno, and Arendt, tie his philosophy to Austro-German thought. The excitement of these pieces lies not merely in Cavell's suggestion that in both philosophy and music we are thrown back on, and obliged to come to terms with, our experience, but also in his claim that we are thereby positioned to find the right pitch, which is to say our own voice. Cavell is speaking of both philosophy and music when he invokes the idea of "understanding without meaning," and declares, using imagery traceable to Plato's Cave, that "one might see the possibility of [such] understanding . . . as redemptive, like losing one's chains" (Chapter 21).

Cavell's writing about music coincided with the starting point of his concentrated autobiographical work. In the 1990s, when he wrote most of the pieces in *Here and There,* as well as his main works on Emerson, he also produced *A Pitch of Philosophy: Autobiographical Exercises,* in which he in effect links the human capacity for making and appreciating music with our caring about finding the right words, developing an ear for what is said when, why it is said, how, and in what context.

This book opens with a short piece, "A Site for Philosophy?" in which Cavell used the occasion of a 1994 invitation from the *Harvard Gazette*—an in-house university publication—to spotlight Harvard's distinct lack of interest in the profession of philosophy. It closes with an epilogue, "Bon Voyage," which we have added to this collection. Both essays reflect Cavell's dedication not only to thinking about education but also to professing. In the latter essay, written on the occasion of his retirement from teaching in 1997, Cavell reflects on Moral Reasoning 34, a core curriculum course that had been his most regular offering at Harvard and in which participants explored perfectionist themes through juxtapositions of Hollywood films and classic literary and philosophical texts.[45] He reports that "no comparable experience has had a greater effect on my quest for a sound of philosophical prose that I could place conviction in, nor has been more heartening to it." With these words, he congratulates the students who are graduating and heading out into a world that will place great demands on their capacities for thought, wishing them "bon voyage."

NOTE ON THE TEXT

The essays published here are in the form they were at the time of Stanley Cavell's death. For the purposes of this note, we refer to "final versions" as those closest to his own hand—either left as hard copies in his study, sometimes edited and with proposed changes scribbled in margins (which we kept), or in a few cases, as Word or PDF files on his computer.

The essays fall into three categories:

1. Six of the essays—Chapters 10, 11, 12, 18, 20, and 21—are either previously unpublished, or previously unpublished in English. They are presented here with only minor corrections for typos, style, and the like.

2. Eight of the essays—Chapters 3, 4, 7, 13, 14, 15, 16, and the Epilogue—have appeared in print in periodicals, books, or other publications. These are cases in which no other drafts prepared by Cavell were found, or the existing drafts are identical to the published version. The essays are reproduced here with only minor copyedits for grammar and style.

3. The remaining essays, including the Prologue, are cases of published work in which another draft prepared by Cavell exists. Printed here are the final versions, which differ in various ways from the published versions and have been edited as follows: we compared the final and published versions, sometimes appealing to the latter for references, quotations, or further information, including endnotes.

Our aim is to go as far as possible toward making Cavell's final versions available while also supplying information necessary for appreciating them.

Prologue

A Site for Philosophy?

This short piece is a version of remarks that Cavell gave in 1994 as part of a
public relations campaign on Harvard's part to "bring greater awareness about
the place of visual art in the educational mission of the University." It ran in
the university's public relations organ, the *Harvard Gazette*, along with seven
other perspectives on Harvard Yard from other staff and faculty members.
Cavell used the occasion to reflect on the place of philosophy, and of art, at
Harvard and in the university more generally.

I COME WITH TWO THOUGHTS and three quotations.

The first of the thoughts is that Harvard must somehow constitute a site
for thinking since arguably for the first half of the century-and-a-half in which
philosophy has been professionalized in this culture, Harvard was overwhelm-
ingly the major training ground of professional philosophers for the nation.
The date at which Harvard philosophy began its professional life has been
assigned (by Bruce Kuklick in his recent, influential *The Rise of American
Philosophy: Cambridge, Massachusetts, 1860–1930*) as follows: "When Transcendentalism attacked the foundation of accepted faith, Unitarian laymen looked
to philosophy [specifically to the philosophers at Harvard] to buttress the
established religion. The laity were not disappointed. . . . Adept and knowl-
edgeable in argument, the Harvard thinkers consistently outmaneuvered the

A version of this essay was published as "A Site for Philosophy?" *Harvard Gazette*, April 1, 1994.

Transcendentalists philosophically. Although Emerson and his well-known circle won over a band of converts, the philosophical bases of Unitarianism remained unshaken." This historian regards this event as a grander moment for American philosophy than I do, since for me it marks one decisive step in the early and continuing repression of Emerson as a serious thinker. But intellectual repression is hard to complete, as is emblematized by the fact that the building which came to house philosophy at Harvard is called Emerson Hall. Who can say what limits what here?

My second thought, or memory, is that there is an internal relation between philosophy and sites or spaces that is mostly unthematized in philosophy, but that makes its entrances from time to time when one recognizes philosophy's and architecture's yearning for one another. Perhaps one thinks of Kant congratulating himself for what he calls his conceptual architectonic, an aspiration that in our period is most intimately attacked by the idea of deconstruction; or perhaps thinks, as I have begun lately to do, prompted by our colleague Peter Galison's convincing demonstrations, how and why the great name of the Bauhaus movement is directly implicated in Rudolf Carnap's logical construction of the world (*Logische Aufbau der Welt*) to form a signal moment in the development of the concept of the modern; or perhaps one thinks of Socrates encountering the assertions of the young in the public spaces of Athens; or of Descartes making the world go away as he sits alone before his fire in his dressing gown; or of Hume, in what he calls his closet, discovering the terrible knowledge that we know nothing, and emerging from it in an effort both to put aside that knowledge and to protect his fellow citizens from its horror by playing backgammon in a public tavern.

Where does philosophy happen at Harvard? Supposing we imagine it happens indoors, a plausible answer is to say that Emerson Hall is its site, and Emerson Hall is part of Harvard Yard. What is philosophy's perspective from its doors, those that front the Yard?

Before answering, I should give the three quotations I promised. The first one is from Nietzsche (from *The Gay Science*): "Architecture for the search for knowledge.—One day, and probably soon, we need some recognition of what above all is lacking in our big cities: quiet and wide, expansive places for reflection. . . . The time is past when the church possessed a monopoly on reflection. The language spoken by these buildings is far too rhetorical and unfree. We who are godless could not think our thoughts in such surroundings." And now two quotations from a former Harvard student who made his name by writing a book about his building of a house, one of the great works of American thinking. I mean, of course, Thoreau's *Walden.* (When Jorge Silvetti earlier this morning read those wonderful excerpts from Robin Evans, I was chagrined not to have known of this writing. Evans in those excerpts was talking about something he called the courage of the ordinary, and of our failing it. The great American works of thought about precisely that courage I find in Emerson's *Essays* and in *Walden.* What measures the distance, or angle, between the School of Design and Emerson Hall?)

But here are the quotations from *Walden,* both of them from the opening chapter, entitled "Economy." First: "While civilization has been improving our houses it has not equally improved the men who are to inhabit them. It has created palaces, but it was not so easy to create noblemen and kings." (That citation, by the way, pretty much word for word, is quoted, and attributed to Thoreau, by Gary Cooper to Jean Arthur during a tender passage in *Mr. Deeds Goes to Town,* directed by Frank Capra in 1936. Was something then common to us that has since been enclosed?) Second: "Though we have many substantial houses of brick or stone, the prosperity of the farmer is still measured by the degree to which the barn overshadows the house. This town is said to have the largest houses for oxen, cows, and horses hereabouts and is not behindhand in its public buildings, but there are very few halls for free worship or free speech in this country."

Well, Thoreau is famous for having anticipated the idea of form following function. But he also distrusted building altogether that was unrelated to an idea of the kind of life to be lived in it. Can the life of philosophy be lived in Harvard Yard? When each day, if you work there, you leave Emerson Hall from the front you come out to Memorial Church on your right and Widener Library on your left and straight ahead you have the administration building, University Hall. Are we to think, therefore, that philosophy is to mediate between the church and the library and to face down the administration? I am reminded that while Emerson Hall opens in that direction, and opens also on its sides, it has no door at the back, which is the direction in which the visual arts live. You can, of course, get to them sideways, but what you mainly have to do is to cross the street. It sometimes seems to me that I spend most of my time as a teacher trying to get people to cross some street or other, including getting myself, naturally.

Two of the major philosophical voices of this century are Wittgenstein, whose *Philosophical Investigations* opens with builders putting stones together for some construction (one, I gather, whose identity is to remain unspecified until the identity of the human is specified—perhaps at the end of the constructions of Wittgenstein's text), and Heidegger, whose late essays "Building Dwelling Thinking" and "Poetically Man Dwells . . ." relate the idea of thinking to what he calls dwelling and building. Thoreau, a thinker who a century earlier attributed thinking to a way of dwelling and building, and makes that philosophy, had advanced beyond Heidegger's thoughts on these topics.

In that same first chapter in *Walden:* "When I first took up my abode in the woods [I assume this amounts to beginning to dwell there], that is, began to spend my nights as well as days there, . . . my house was not finished for winter." This meets Heidegger's thought that dwelling comes before building is done, and advances further in observing that you dwell somewhere when you go to sleep there, dream there, when you can awaken there. I ask myself what the iron fence is that outlines the Yard. That space has been a sanctuary, that is, it may fence something out. Then what does it fence in? What is fenced together there? Is there perhaps a community living there? In addition to the church, the libraries, the administration, the classroom buildings, there are the student houses, specifically allotted to the youngest students, who are accordingly the ones who sleep in the Yard, so awaken there. This vulnerability is a cause for trust, on both sides, something to measure our work by.

If, as it is said, Boston streets were laid out by cows, then I imagine the Yard paths were laid out by students, with their own particular and fruitful economy of hurry and procrastination. Since our students are our future, it is only just that we, part of the day, should walk the tracks that they have found themselves to need.

PART I | Departures

Time after Time

This essay was written and translated into French for a forum sponsored by *Le Monde* in 1994 in Le Mans, France. The forum was entitled "The Future Today," and participants were asked to envision a future for our polluted world. Cavell's contribution, which picks up the environmental thread running through a number of his writings, was published in the *London Review of Books* in 1995.

IN 1994, invitations to the Sixth *Le Monde* Forum held at Le Mans, with the title "The Future Today," posed to its participants an introductory statement for discussion that contained the following passage: "Everything is worn out: revolutions, profits, miracles. The planet itself shows signs of fatigue and breakdown, from the ozone layer to the temperature of the oceans." The disappointed or counter-romantic mood of this passage produced the following intervention from me, one that has distinctly affected my work since that time.

Keep in mind that I come from that part of the world for which the question of old and new—call it the question of a human future—is, or was, logically speaking, a matter of life and death: if the new world is not new then America does not exist, it is merely one more outpost of old oppressions. Americans like Thoreau (and if Thoreau then Emerson and Walt Whitman, to say no more) seem to have lived so intensely or intently within the thought

Versions of this essay were published as "Time after Time," *London Review of Books* 17, no. 1 (January 1995), and as "The Future of Possibility," in *Philosophical Romanticism,* ed. Nikolas Kompridis (Abingdon, UK: Routledge, 2006), 21–31.

of a possible, and possibly closed, future that a passage like the one I just cited would be bound to have struck them as setting, that is putting on view and enforcing, an old mood. Compare with that passage a sentence from the opening chapter of Thoreau's *Walden:* "Undoubtedly the very tedium and ennui which presume to have exhausted the variety and the joys of life are [themselves] as old as Adam." This is, I think we might say, a compounding or transcendentalizing of the sense of the worn out, showing that concept of our relation to the past to be itself nearly worn out. And this recognition provides Thoreau not with compounded tedium and ennui but with an outburst of indignant energy. He continues: "But man's capacities have never been measured; nor are we to judge of what he can do by any precedents, so little has been tried." This is why he can say, when he appeals to sacred writings and defends them against the sense that they are passé: "We might as well omit to study Nature because she is old." As if to say: Beware of the idea of The Future Today—that is, of Today's Future; it may be a function of Yesterday's Today, and you will discover that Today was always already Tomorrow, that there is no time for origination. Yet Thoreau's idea is that time has not touched the thoughts and texts he deals in. What chance is there for us to share his faith today, now? When is now?

An intricate intersection of old and new is also the burden of Emerson's great essay "Experience." Indeed it should not be surprising that America found its philosophical voice in thinking, and having to think, about the future—if you grant me the claim that Emerson and Thoreau represent the founding of the American difference in philosophy. Emerson writes in "Experience": "In liberated moments we know that a new picture of life and duty is already possible. . . . The new statement will comprise the skepticisms as well as the faiths of society, and out of unbeliefs a creed shall be found. . . . The new philosophy must take [these skepticisms] in and make affirmations outside of them, just as much as it must include the oldest beliefs." This demand for integration sounds like a beginning of that American optimism or Emersonian cheerfulness to which an old European sophistication knows so well how to condescend. But it has never been sure, even where I come from, that Emerson's tone of encouragement is tolerable to listen to for very long— as if it expresses a threat as much as it does a promise. I note that his words about finding a creed out of unbeliefs, unlike those of his familiar followers as well as detractors, contain no word of hope. What occurs to us in liberated moments is that we *know.* That "we" claims to speak for us, for me and for you, as philosophy in its unavoidable arrogance always claims to do; and moreover claims to speak of what we do not know we know, hence of some thought that we keep rejecting; hence claims to know us better than we know ourselves. I suppose Emerson is claiming to know this, as we do, only in liberated moments. Then presumably his writing the thought was one such moment—as if something about such writing tends to such moments. Does reading such writing provide us with further such moments? If—or when—it does not, how could we fail to find Emerson's claims intolerable?

Let us provisionally surmise just this much from Emerson's passage: if we are to think anew it must be from a new stance, one essentially unfamiliar to us; or, say, from a further perspective that is uncontrollable by us. If we formulate this by saying that to think the future one would have to be in the future, this sounds like a way also of summarizing Nietzsche's *Beyond Good and Evil,* whose subtitle is "Prelude to a Philosophy of the Future." This is as it should be since that text of Nietzsche's—like so many of Nietzsche's texts, early and, as in this case, late—is pervasively indebted to Emerson's *Essays,* "Experience" pivotally among them. But unlike his reiterated, implicit rebuke to Wagner's *Der Kunstwerk der Zukunft,* Nietzsche's continuous invocation of Emerson is something we will recognize and remember only intermittently, in liberated (vanishing) moments.

Beyond Good and Evil speaks, as Emerson does, of thinking through pessimism to affirmation. Nietzsche specifies pessimism as what is most world-denying; Emerson's name for this, in the passage I cited from "Experience," is skepticism; its opposite Nietzsche specifies as world affirmation, which is precisely what Emerson understands the new world to be awaiting. Nietzsche specifies the world-affirming human being as one who, reconceiving time, achieves the will to eternal recurrence; Emerson specifies this figure as one who finds the knack of liberation in moments. Since Nietzsche's thinking through pessimism in his articulation of nihilism, the philosophical stakes he puts in play are not alone the national existence of the so-called new world, but the continuation of old Western culture, of what it has so far told itself of the human.

Emerson and Nietzsche are variously explicit in saying that philosophy as such is thinking for the future—so that their sense of going beyond philosophy in what they say about the future is at the same time a claim to the stance of philosophy. In *Beyond Good and Evil:* "More and more it seems to me that the philosopher, being *of necessity* a man of tomorrow and the day after tomorrow, has always found himself, and *had* to find himself, in contradiction to today. . . . By applying the knife vivisectionally to the chest of the very *virtues of their time,* they betrayed what was their own secret: to know of a new greatness of man, of a new untrodden way to his enhancement." We might think here of Plato, who is explicit in his *Republic* in staging the moment of philosophy, specifically of philosophy's entrance into the public world, as in some future that is now datable only paradoxically, as when philosophers will become kings; in the meantime we (re)construct our city only with words, as with the text of the *Republic.* Or we may think of Kant, for whom moral sanity depends on a reasonable hope for future justice, and his necessary positing of the good city as a Realm of Ends—where each of us is legislated for in legislating for all. Unlike Plato's *Republic,* Kant's good city is essentially unrepresentable by philosophy: if we could represent it we could claim to know it, but that would leave room neither for genuine faith in our effectiveness toward a future nor for genuine knowledge of the present. (Among the choices we have for dating the modern, one may choose Freud's discovery that anything I think, except negation, I can dream, and anything I dream is a work of representation, hence a guide for myself to what I all but inescapably already know.)

Nietzsche's words about the philosopher as the man of tomorrow and the day after tomorrow, hence as necessarily having to find himself in contradiction to today, and his specifying this as his vivisecting the very virtues of his time, are virtual transcriptions (with a Nietzschean accent) of words of Emerson's. In Emerson's "Self-Reliance" there is a pair of sentences I have previously had occasion to variously cite and interpret: "The virtue in most request is conformity. Self-reliance is its aversion." I will merely assert here that Emerson uses his signature concept of self-reliance, in contradiction to the conforming usage of it in most request, to characterize his writing, hence his thinking; hence to place it, in every word, in aversion to, and as averse to, his conforming society. And assert further that Nietzsche's sense of the philosopher's words as in "contradiction to today" are not only rewriting of Emerson's "aversion to conformity" but that Emerson's citing of conformity as a virtue, and precisely as epitomizing the virtues of his today, from which in every word he writes his writing recoils ("Every word they say chagrins us" is another formulation in "Self-Reliance"), casts Emerson as the figure most directly captured in Nietzsche's terrible image of the philosopher as vivisectionist. (This is evidently a further shade of intervention than Socrates is colored with, as gadfly or midwife.) That Emerson is supplying words for Nietzsche's description of the philosopher—or himself, of course—comes out again later in the same paragraph, in his speaking of philosophical violence as the philosopher's betraying his own secret of a new greatness of man, which Nietzsche specifies as an untrodden way to man's enhancement.

The picture of philosophizing as taking steps on a path is an ancient one, but Emerson's "Experience" is remarkable for its concentration on the idea of thinking as a new succession, or success: "To finish the moment, to find the journey's end in every step of the road . . . is wisdom." This might strike one as giving up on the future; the possibility will come back. English translation of Nietzsche's passage rather loses another echo from "Experience" in rendering Nietzsche's philosophical secret of a new greatness of man by speaking of an untrodden way to man's "enhancement." "Enhancement" conceives greatness, which Nietzsche calls *eine Grösse,* as found on a path to his heightening, whereas Nietzsche's characterizing the newness as a *Vergrösserung,* enveloping and intensifying *Grösse,* leaves quite open what form the magnification is to take—"expansiveness" is one characteristic Emersonian term for productive human thinking.

The value of leaving open the proposed idea of human increase or expansiveness is that it is at the end of the section begun by Nietzsche's paragraph concerning the new greatness that he reformulates the question of the future by asking: "Today—is greatness *possible?*"; a question explicitly both about the human capacity to think and the capacity to will. Now Emerson's "Experience" can be taken as an essay on greatness, and greatness precisely as preparing a joyful future—if the human past of grief, with its endless cause for grievance, may be set aside, not so much survived as outlived. As Emerson here measures grief by his response to the death of his young namesake son, he repeatedly figures the possibility of expansiveness, in mood and in thought, as the greatness of pregnancy. (English used to speak about "being great with child.") This is how I read Emerson's call for the "soul [to attain] her due sphericity," and his account of "the great and crescive self," perhaps above all his report of insight from "the vicinity of a new . . . region of life," which he conveys as a region of new life giving a sign of itself "as it were in flashes of light." He reports: "And what a future it opens! I feel a new heart beating with the love of the new beauty. I am ready to die out of nature and be born again into this new yet unapproachable America I have found in the West." What's going on? What number of hearts does Emerson feel beating, one or two? If America opens a joyful future, why is it "unapproachable"—which seems to imply that it is forbidding, or hideous, or otherwise beyond clear grasp?

Put aside the arresting fact that Emerson identifies the writing of this essay with the growth of an embryo, and focus on the underlying Emersonian proposition (not without apparent contradiction elsewhere) that greatness is to be found only in little things. From Emerson's essay "Character": "Is there any religion but this, to know, that whenever in the wide desert of being, the holy sentiment we cherish has opened into a flower, it blooms for me? if none see it, I see it; I am aware, if I alone, of the greatness of the fact." This perhaps marks the point of Nietzsche's radical difference with Emerson. In *Beyond Good and Evil* we have heard: "The time for petty [*kleine*] politics is past: the very next century will bring the fight for the dominion of the earth—the *compulsion* to large-scale [*grossen*] politics." This prophecy made in the late eighties of the nineteenth century seems a fairish way of tracking the progress of the twentieth, including a certain prediction of an essential region of Heidegger's reflections on his century. Has the century ended? Was it in 1989? And in Berlin, or in Moscow?

Plotting the reticulation of differences implied in the audiences or possibilities of America and of Europe is still worth some patience; and I would like to sketch here two further encounters between Emerson's *Essays* and Nietzsche's *Beyond Good and Evil*—1. regarding the specific way time is reconceived and 2. regarding the appearance of the feminine in characterizing, or protecting, philosophy.

Take time first. In "Circles," perhaps Emerson's most concentrated pages on the concept of the new (pages from which Nietzsche cites explicitly and climatically near the end of his Untimely Meditation with the title *Schopenhauer as Educator*), the first paragraph contains these sentences: "Our life is an apprenticeship to the truth that around every circle another can be drawn." This is, whatever else, a formulation of what an Emersonian essay is, and does; each Emerson essay contains such self-formulations. Emerson goes on at once to gloss the image of the circle by saying that there is "no end in nature, but every end is a beginning," and that "under every deep a lower deep opens," and that "there is always another dawn risen on mid-noon." Thoreau—I suppose Nietzsche's only rival as an interpreter of Emerson—recasts the thought more famously in the concluding two brief sentences of *Walden:* "There is more day to dawn. The sun is but a morning star." The figuring of "more day" or of "another dawn risen on mid-noon" provides a hint for taking Nietzsche at his characteristic word when he says that the philosopher is "a man of tomorrow and the day after tomorrow."

English and French picture the leap over the day after today as its being "after" (*après*) that after. But German says *Übermorgen*, which plays uncannily into the attention Nietzsche gives to the prefix *über*. I take it we are to understand the relation of *Übermorgen* to *Morgen* on the model of the relation of *Übermensch* to *Mensch*—so that the *Übermensch* precisely is whatever the man of *Übermorgen* is, its discoverer or creator. This singles out the one who has learned (which must mean that he has taught himself) how to think of, and how to live in, a further day, which is to say, in the future—the thing Thoreau calls "more day" and that Emerson calls "another dawn," an after dawn. Such a day is not one assurable from the fact of the past risings of the sun (Hume was right enough about that), but one the course to which is plottable only through an ambitious philosophy, thinking it through, aversively, which is to say, by turning ourselves around, not presuming at once to *head* into the future. The future—call it America, or call it the world that may be— cannot be approached as in a picture of a boat approaching a shore, not even a magic boat called *Mayflower* (Emerson apparently, if momentarily, fantasizes otherwise in his first defining work, *Nature*); nor, as Nietzsche tried to explain in *Beyond Good and Evil,* can it be taken by the strength we picture as of blood and iron. (Heidegger, accursed, for a time neglected Nietzsche's warning not to take hope from this dangerous, self-prescribed healing.)

It seems that we have to learn to think after thinking has come to a dead end, or, say, has become exhausted. We may express this as philosophy's coming to conceive of itself as taking place in, or as, an aftermath, an aftermath of thought, sometimes now called a closure of philosophy or of history.

Here one should recollect philosophy's tendency to fantasize scenes of its own destruction, as if it becomes burdened with prophecy; I cite, for example, the knowledge Wittgenstein expresses in *Philosophical Investigations* that his thinking is repeatedly taken as merely destructive of everything important. Philosophy evidently has its melancholy side—why else would Emerson so insist, and so gratingly, on finding instants of joy, and Nietzsche on his tincture of laughter? Philosophy's knowledge was always painful, as when Emerson says, at the close of "Experience": "I know that the world I converse with in the city and in the farms, is not the world I *think*. I observe that difference, and shall observe it. One day I shall know the value and law of this discrepance." Take this as philosophy's ancient perception of the distance of the world from a reign of justice. (When philosophy refuses any longer to cede this reign to theology's afterlife, as Emerson and Nietzsche write to refuse it, the destruction entailed by justice becomes an event, and the approach of an event, within finitude, an approach the living may represent to themselves, without being able to decipher it.) This distance, or discrepance, is the world's public business, now on a global stage. I hope nothing will stop it from becoming the principal business of the twenty-first century. But it is, on my view, while a task that philosophy must join in together with every serious political and economic and, I would say, therapeutic theory, not now philosophy's peculiar task, as it was in Plato's *Republic*.

Philosophy's peculiar task now—that which will not be taken up if philosophy does not take it up—is, beyond or before that, to prepare us, one by one, for the business of justice; and to train itself for the task of preparation by confronting an obstacle, perhaps the modern obstacle, to that business: I mean a sense of the exhaustion of human possibility, following the exhaustion of divine possibility.

Nietzsche, after Emerson, links the sense of human exhaustion with the sense of the unresponsiveness of the future to human will (how different is that from the sense of the unresponsiveness of God?). As if the grief in witnessing the discrepance from the reign of justice has depended on, and been fixated by, a despair of change. Here we have to think of Emerson's description of the mass of men as in a state of secret melancholy; Thoreau will say "quiet desperation"; Nietzsche sometimes formulates the sense of exhaustion as "boredom"; I note in passing that it is as some intersection of boredom with melancholy that Wordsworth, at the beginning of a different romanticism, takes a general human withdrawal of interest in the world as the condition to which poetry is called to respond, or to teach response. It may be thought of as a state of tragedy not experienced as such—which is, I allow myself to add, a way of characterizing skepticism.

Secret melancholy, Emerson says. Naming a historical phenomenon, this names not an isolated matter of an individual sense of pointlessness in saying anything, but a more general sense of lacking, or failing, the language in which to express what has to be said, as if calling philosophical as well as political attention to a shared aphasia. Editing these remarks for publication to an English-speaking readership, I am moved to confess how swiftly, with how few steps, one can feel out of earshot of one's native company. It is my latecomer's view of Lacan that his emphasis on registers and textures of speech, and its failures (say, its wants), epitomized by his fascination with Roman Jakobson's ordering of the linguist's interest in aphasias, casts all psychoanalytic experience of discrepance as forms of what might be grasped as (a transfiguration of the concept of) aphasia. This reconstitutes, or re-enacts, Freud's early ("pre-psychoanalytic") interest in the phenomenon of aphasia; one might call the phenomenon of disexpressiveness.

So philosophy becomes a struggle against melancholy—or, to speak with due banality, against depression. It is here that I conceive the image of woman to enter into the thoughts of Emerson and of Nietzsche, in Emerson briefly and hopefully, in Nietzsche recurrently and scandalously. Those who find Nietzsche an essential voice in today's confusion of tongues will often wish that he had not spoken as he did about "the woman." Without a word of argument now, I simply state my sense that it is still today worth hearing his naming the struggle between the man and the woman as something that cannot without remainder be understood in political terms. (But then for Nietzsche neither can politics be so understood.) Nor does it seem to me that the struggle he names is simply an allegory of an individual condition, though that is no less true for his writing than it is for Plato's in the *Republic*. I would rather begin with the fairly open fact of Nietzsche's fear and need of the woman, seen as functions of his demand for a future, hence for a philosophy of the future. (How could his treatment of the thought of woman be exempt from the confession he makes about the way of his confessions, that they are crooked? The idea of the path to the future as crooked bears placing against Emerson's idea in "Experience" of the path to reality as indirect, or glancing.)

A sense of the image of the woman in *Beyond Good and Evil* could in practice begin by putting in conjunction its following ideas: that steps to the future are aversive, or put otherwise, that philosophy's way to the future is through destruction; that since this is the only source of genuine philosophy, the philosopher essentially risks suffering and melancholy, risks "suffocating from pity"; that woman is "clairvoyant in the realm of suffering," and her characteristic faith is that love, perhaps identified with pity, can achieve everything; and that "every profound thinker is more afraid of being understood than of being misunderstood." What I begin to draw from this conjunction is the sense of woman—I suppose leaving open where that turns out to exist—as Nietzsche's most essential audience, the best and the worst. She is the best, because she understands, through her power of love and of pity, his suffering and (as when he all but identifies his condition with that of Jesus) his insatiable, suicidal desire for love; so understands that in his words his body is on the line. But she is also his worst audience, because her faith cannot compass his terror of love, that it will crucify him, which means, in the terms of this book of his, that it will deny that he is "still unexhausted for [his] greatest possibilities," hence in those terms, since the future is what is new, she would deny him his future. Taking woman as his essential audience, he identifies with her while he differentiates from her—as when he characterizes man as "the sterile animal" and when he, too, perceives the philosopher as pregnant.

I think of philosophy's essential difficulty in representing its future in connection with its inability to establish the conditions of philosophy, the look and sound in which, in particular historical contexts, it can have its peculiar effect, take its aversive, unassertive steps. A group of half a dozen texts not usually associated with philosophy come to mind here—texts in which the future is presented as a course so puzzled as to call for philosophy. I first encountered these texts during the period of two or three years in which I was searching, not always hopefully, for a way to begin teaching and writing philosophy that I could believe in and make a living from.

I had begun reading Wittgenstein's *Investigations,* perhaps the first philosophical text which successfully for me staked its teaching on showing that we do not know, or make ourselves forget, what reading is. I found its attack on metaphysics—call it the history of philosophy as such—by, in Wittgenstein's formulation, "leading words back from their metaphysical to their everyday use," to be continuously and surprisingly surprising, discovering surprise where you least expect it, in the banal. So that philosophy came to begin for me with the question whether philosophy has a future, which means whether there is an event that has happened to end philosophy, or whether philosophy's ending is an event that happens within philosophy, hence precisely and essentially continues it.

This opening of philosophy for me, synchronized with the opening of philosophical and non-philosophical texts towards one another, was set in motion in the year or two leading into 1960, marked as the years in which three of the texts I name here, three films it happens, were released: Ingmar Bergman's *Smiles of a Summer Night,* Alain Resnais and Marguerite Duras's *Hiroshima, Mon Amour* and Antonioni's *L'Avventura*—each associated with the question about whether something new might happen (Samuel Beckett's *Godot* and *Endgame* were still new), shadowed by the question whether love is an exhausted possibility, a question incorporating some residue of a fantasy of marriage. In each case the answer is presented as in the hands of a woman— in Marguerite Duras's woman of Nevers it is one capable, in Duras's words, of giving herself body and soul, which she characterizes as discovering marriage; in Antonioni's Claudia (in the form of Monica Vitti) it is a woman capable of granting a man's terrible wish, as it were for her to change her love for him into pity; in Bergman's Desirée (Eva Dahlbeck) it is a woman who at the end sits smoking a cigar behind the head of a man who speaks to her with unaccustomed sincerity as he is lying on a couch, and who answers him by saying that she is putting his love into her big pocket, a man in whom she explicitly perceives the child—all a fair parody, in acceptance, of the image of Freud and what he called (around the period in which the film is set) his therapy of love. (One of Freud's debts to old philosophy.) These are works of cinematic art decisive in modifying concepts, as in America, of what were thought of as foreign films and as ordinary movies, hence in modifying concepts of high and low culture, and of what constitutes a medium of thought—ones which, in a word, served to alter the iconography of intellectual conversation.

Those presentations are oddly tied up in my mind with two works from Victorian England that one with my intellectual itinerary could hardly fail to know about but that it happens I had not read until the years in question; neither of them may be counted among the greatest accomplishments of their illustrious authors, but both took on the urgency of the doubts I was harboring then—a familiar story. One is Dickens's *Great Expectations,* an inspired title at once for all the ways human beings try to take the future by storm— by boat or by blood and iron—and, turned ironically, a title for the disappointment or depression that follows the deflation of that inflation. It is Pip who is explicitly said to be a young man "of great expectations," yet he can be said to have had no expectations great or small, but simply to have formed his character on a love quite independent of its fate in the world—on love, in short; a figure, therefore, with some hard things to learn, yet who survives the learning. Miss Havisham's expectation can be said to have been the greatest, measured by the power of her outrage and vengeance when she allowed it to be shattered—call it the expectation of being loved; it was a disappointment, a piece of learning she refused to survive, her body in its rotting bridal gown becoming a private monument of the institution of marriage. I recognize Miss Havisham as Cinderella, of course with a sublimed conclusion— *eternally* awaiting the glass slipper—a realistic conclusion, as it were, given the difficulty of locating and knowing her original away from the dance. I imagine it as Pip's princely understanding of her, from his hallucinating on a wall of her barn the shadow of a hanged woman who is missing one shoe. How far therefore is he imagining that the condition of women is more generally to be understood as laid down by fairy tales in the early transfiguring enchantments that never achieve their undoing; tales whose ending is not just unhappy but arbitrary, as though an ending is missing, possibilities not exhausted but cursed? But then what assures us that a given narrative is a fairy tale? Isn't

Great Expectations more or less a fairy tale? And while Dickens, significantly, wrote two endings for the novel—one in which Pip and Stella do not have a future together, and one in which they do—does either of them really untie the suffering we have come to know about?

Take Miss Havisham's story to be the projection of a woman's sense of the unapproachability of the future. The other book I adduce from that time and place is John Stuart Mill's *Autobiography*, which contains a man's companion sense of the event of the future, or of its non-event. He characterizes his early state of crisis exactly as a despair over the exhaustion of possibilities—a state in which he broods over the fact that Mozart and Weber had exhausted all the possible combinations of tones that will achieve beautiful melody. This is the form familiar to Nietzsche in assigning to philosophy the task of the future. Miss Havisham shows possibilities not to be everywhere exhausted but everywhere untried, which suggests that the step to the future is closed not through depletion but through fixation, through the withholding or the theft of love; it is the fate Nietzsche's fantasm threatens him with in the face of woman's fanaticism of love. The philosophers of possibility who see us not as sensing depletion or loss but as fixated through a lack of trial or experience are rather Emerson and Thoreau. The philosophers who later take fixation itself as the negation of philosophy, its most intimate opponent, are Heidegger and Wittgenstein. In the later work of both we are invited—or seduced?—to take steps, but without a path. And that is itself to acknowledge a future, the fact of futurity. Shall we say that this opens the future to the human will? It opens the will, like a hand.

The World as Things

Collecting Thoughts on Collecting

This essay was written for the 1998 catalogue of the exhibition *Rendezvous* at the Guggenheim Museum in New York. The Guggenheim was at the time hosting works from the Musée National d'Art Moderne at the Centre Georges Pompidou in Paris, which was closed for repairs. Cavell was invited to the opening of the exhibition to reflect on the philosophy of collecting.

> [Fleda] took the measure of the poor lady's strange, almost maniacal disposition to thrust in everywhere the question of "things," to read all behaviour in the light of some fancied relation to them. "Things" were of course the sum of the world; only, for Mrs. Gereth, the sum of the world was rare French furniture and oriental china. She could at a stretch imagine people's not "having," but she couldn't imagine their not wanting and not missing.
>
> —HENRY JAMES, *The Spoils of Poynton* (1897)

> The world is the totality of facts, not of things.
>
> —LUDWIG WITTGENSTEIN, *Tractatus Logico-Philosophicus* (1921)

Versions of this essay were published as "The World as Things: Collecting Thoughts on Collecting," in *Rendezvous: Masterpieces from the Centre Georges Pompidou and the Guggenheim Museums* (Paris: Centre Georges Pompidou; New York: Guggenheim Museum; distr. H. N. Abrams, 1998), and as "The World as Things," in Stanley Cavell, *Philosophy the Day after Tomorrow* (Cambridge, MA: Belknap Press of Harvard University Press, 2005), ch. 10.

I

Not this or that collection is my assignment here, but collecting as such, or, as it was also specified for me, the philosophy of collecting. And presumably not collecting as what dust does on shelves, or rain in pails, or as what is called a collector on certain roofs does (the one I saw is cylindrical, about the size of a stack of half a dozen coffee cans and made of aluminum, into which are fitted what look like coffee filters), collecting particulates to monitor air pollution; but as someone collects medals, coins, stamps, books, skeletons, jewels, jewel boxes, locks, clocks, armor, vases, sarcophagi, inscriptions, paintings, curiosities of unpredictable kinds. Krzysztof Pomian, in his remarkable study *Collectors and Curiosities,* declares that every human culture has collected and that every movable thing has been collected.[1] As if collecting for possession and display is as primitive as gathering food for survival.

But while we may sensibly speculate, or ask, why certain people collect stamps, jewels, skeletons, etc., and why different things seems favored for collection by different classes or ranks of society, or different genders or ages, in different historical periods, is it sure that it makes sense to ask (as it hardly makes sense to ask why people gather food), why people collect as such—any more than it makes obvious sense to ask what my relation to things is as such, or my relation to language, or what the point of thinking is?

Yet writers about collecting are characteristically moved precisely to advance some idea of what the point of collecting is as such, as a form of human life. For instance, Jean Baudrillard articulates collecting as an objectifying of oneself in a simulation of death which one symbolically survives within one's life; Pomian begins with the fact of collecting as removing objects from economic circulation and putting them on display, and speaks of a consequent establishment of connection between the visible and the invisible, the realm of religion, made possible (and inevitable?) by the advent of language; Susan Stewart as it were combines the withdrawal of objects from use with the establishment of a commerce between death and life (as if creating a realm of mock exchange [mock religion?]); Robert Opie is one of many who see in collecting an attempt to reproduce and hence preserve or recapture the world; Philip Fisher, concentrating on art museums since the Enlightenment, identifying stages of a history in which an object is removed from its original setting (of use, say, in battle or in prayer) becoming a thing of memory (a souvenir or a relic) and ending up as an object for aesthetic appreciation, arrives at a definition of the museum as a place of the making of art, an institution

THE WORLD AS THINGS | 35

of practices within which the function of art is operable; Foucault, in the paradigmatic onslaught of his *The Order of Things,* speaks of shifts in our ways of "taming the wild profusion of things."[2] I shall not refrain from certain similar speculations in what follows.

(Then I should note at the outset that an important issue about collections, one that makes news, plays almost no role here, that concerning the right to exhibit, or to own, objects improperly taken from, or identified with, another culture. My excuse for silence here is that such a conflict is apt to be poorly discussed apart from a patient account and interpretation of the forces in play in a concrete historical context, which is not how I have conceived the form of my contribution. James Clifford, in his deservedly admired *The Predicament of Culture,* provides such contexts for several cases, guided by the principle that living cultures worldwide are inherently appropriating the strange, the evidently predatory no more than the obviously victimized.)[3]

II

Speculation about the role of collections in human life has been explicit since at least the problem of the One and the Many, made philosophically inescapable in Plato's Theory of Forms, or Ideas, according to which the individual things present to our senses are knowable, are indeed what they are, by virtue of their "participation" in, or "imitation" of, the realm of Forms, which provide us with our armature of classification, to put it mildly. The Platonic hierarchy disparages the things, the life, of ordinary sensuous experience, this realm of the transient and the inexact, in contrast with the perfect, permanent realm of the Ideas. To know a thing in the lower realm is to know which Ideas it imitates in common with other things of its kind: there are many chairs, but just one Idea of (the perfect, hence perfectly knowable) chair; the Form of a chair is what is common to, the common aspiration of, the collection of the things that are, and are known as, chairs. Just how the relation between the many and the one (or as it came to be called in later philosophy, the universal and the particular) is to be conceived became at once a matter of controversy in the work of Aristotle, and the problem of the status of universals has not abandoned philosophy to this day.

But a perplexity other than the relation of universal and particular, or a more specialized version of the relation of a general term to a singular object, is more pressing for us in the attempt to bring the issue of the collection into view. We have in effect said that every collection requires an idea (or universal, or concept). (This seems to presage the fact, testified to by many writers on collecting, that collections carry narratives with them, ones presumably telling the point of the gathering, the source and adventure of it.) But can we say the reverse, that every idea requires (posits, names) a collection? This is a form of the question: How can signs refer to what is non-existent? What do expressions such as "Pegasus," "a round square," "the present King of France," refer to, and if to nothing, what do they mean, how can they mean anything, how can anything true be attributed to them? Bertrand Russell and Edmund Husserl were both caught by the importance of such a question; it was I suppose the last moment at which what has come to be called analytical philosophy and what (consequently?) came to be called Continental philosophy so clearly coincided in concern. It was Russell's solution to the question of the reference of such terms, by means of his theory of descriptions (which evaluates the terms by means of modern logic to demonstrate perspicuously that they do not assert reference to anything), that can be said to have established a preoccupation and determined the style of analytical philosophy, and the style appears to have outlasted that preoccupation. The preoccupation also outlasts the style. The first section of Wittgenstein's *Philosophical Investigations* announces its first interpretation of the passage from Augustine with which it opens, in which Augustine recalls his learning of language:

> [Augustine's] words give us a particular picture of the essence of human language. It is this: the individual words in language name objects—sentences are combinations of such names.—In this picture of language we find the roots of the following idea: Every word has a meaning. The meaning is correlated with the word. It is the object for which the word stands.[4]

It is a picture of language from which philosophers of both the Anglo-American analytical tradition and the German-French tradition continue to perform, in their different ways, hairbreadth escapes.

Of interest here is that the first example (the first "language-game" of a sort) that Wittgenstein develops in response to this picture materializes not around a single absent object but around a collection.

> I send someone shopping. I give him a slip on which stands the signs "five red apples"; he takes the slip to the shopkeeper, who opens the drawer on which stands the sign "apples"; then he looks up the word

"red" in a table and finds a color sample opposite it; then he says the
series of cardinal numbers.[5]

Reference—if this means linking a sign to an object—is hardly the chief of
the problems revealed in this curious, yet apparently comprehensible, scene.
How did the shopper know to whom to present the slip? Does the sign "apple"
on his slip refer to the sign "apple" on the shopkeeper's drawer? They may
not at all look alike. Would it have secured the linkage to have provided the
shopper with a photograph or sketch of the drawer and its sign? How would
the shopkeeper know what the point of the photograph or sign is supposed
to be? (Perhaps he will hang it on his wall.) Does the sign on the slip rather
refer (directly, as it were) to the items inside the closed drawer? But we are
free to imagine that when the shopkeeper opens the drawer it is empty. Did
the signs on the slip and on the drawer then become meaningless? And if there
were only four apples then would just the word "five" have become meaningless? Do you want an explanation of how it happens that signs retain their
meaning under untoward circumstances? Shouldn't you also want an explanation of the fact that the drawer was marked "apples" rather than, say, "red,"
whereupon the shopkeeper would be expected to look up the word "apple"
on a chart of fruits and vegetables (we won't ask how he knows which of his
charts to consult) . . . ?

Do we know why we classify as we do? In order to know, would we have to
memorize what Foucault says about changing conditions of possibility? Wittgenstein's primitive, and studiedly strange, opening example can be taken as
stirring such wisps of anxiety among the threads of our common lives that we
may wonder, from the outset of thinking, how it is that philosophy, in its
craving for explanation, seeks to explain so little, that is to say, how it conceives
that so little is mysterious among the untold threads between us that become
tangled or broken. Perhaps Wittgenstein may be taken as redressing philosophy's disparagement of the things of sense when late in the *Tractatus* he finds:
"It is not *how* things are in the world that is mystical, but *that* it exists."[6]

III

Baudrillard declares:

> [W]hile the appropriation of a "rare" or "unique" object is obvi-
> ously the perfect culmination of the impulse to possess, it has to be

recognized that one can never find absolute proof in the real world that a given object is indeed unique. . . . The singular object never impedes the process of narcissistic projection, which ranges over an indefinite number of objects: on the contrary, it encourages such multiplication whereby the image of the self is extended to the very limits of the collection. Here, indeed, lies the whole miracle of collecting. For it is invariably *oneself* that one collects.[7]

How well do we understand this final claim? Let us consider that one of the most celebrated plays of the middle of this century, Tennessee Williams's *The Glass Menagerie,* depends upon its audience's capacity for a rapt understanding of the daughter Laura's identification with her collection of fragile glass figures. And this understanding is not broken, but is deepened, when her Gentleman Caller accidentally steps on her favorite piece, a tiny unicorn, breaking off its horn, and Laura reveals an unexpected independence of spirit, refusing the suggestion of a clumsy castration and instead observing something like, "It makes him more like other creatures," a state she also has reason to desire. Another famous work of that period, Orson Welles's *Citizen Kane,* equally depends upon some identification of a person by his collection, but here some final interpretation of its meaning appears rather to be dictated to us by the closing revelation of the childhood snow sled. I like thinking that when Jay Gatsby is in the course of realizing his fantasy of showing Daisy his house, his showplace, and unfurls his fabulous collection of shirts before her, it is clear that the value he attaches to them, or to anything, is a function of their value to her. No other object contains him; he is great.

So let us not be hasty in arriving at very firm conclusions about what our relation to collections is, hence what relation they may propose concerning our relation to the world of things as such.

It may be worth remembering further here that two of a series of recent films breaking all attendance records are about the fatality of a quest for a unique object, *Raiders of the Lost Ark* and *Indiana Jones and the Last Crusade,* and that the closing shot of the former, the camera floating over an unclassifiably colossal collection of crated objects among which, some unpredictable where, the unique lost object of the quest is anonymously contained, seems some kind of homage to the closing roving shot of *Citizen Kane,* where now the integrity of civilization, not merely of a single unsatisfied millionaire, is at stake.

IV

Both Wittgenstein and Heidegger, in something like opposite directions, break with the ancient picture of the things of the world as intersections of universals and particulars. Wittgenstein's way is, characteristically, almost comically plain and casual.

> Instead of producing something common to all that we call language, I am saying that these phenomena have no one thing in common which makes us use the same word for all. . . . Consider for example the proceedings that we call "games." I mean board-games, card-games, Olympic games, and so on. What is common to them all? Don't say: "There *must* be something common, or they would not be called 'games'"—but *look and see* whether there is anything common to all. . . . [Y]ou will . . . see . . . similarities, relationships, and a whole series of them at that. . . . I can think of no better expression to characterize these similarities than "family resemblances."[8]

This idea has had the power of conversion for some of its readers—too precipitously to my way of thinking, since it does not account for Wittgenstein's signature play of casualness with profundity. He still wants to be able to articulate the essences of things.

Heidegger's way of breaking with universals is, characteristically, almost comically obscure and portentous. In a seminal essay "The Thing," he opens with the assertion, "All distances in time and space are shrinking," surely a banality we might expect to see in any newspaper.[9] Then he undertakes to show us that, as it were, we do not know the meaning of the banalities of our lives.

> Yet the frantic abolition of all distances brings no nearness; for nearness does not consist in shortness of distance. . . . How can we come to know [the nature of] nearness? . . . Near to us are what we usually call things. But what is a thing? Man has so far given no more thought to the thing as a thing than he has to nearness.[10]

Is Heidegger here constructing a parable of the museum, perhaps a rebuke to those who think art brings things near in the empirical manner of museums? He takes as his most elaborated example that of the jug, which holds water or wine, and he spells out a vision in which the water, retaining its source in the running spring, marries earth and sky, and in which the wine, which may be the gift of a libation, connects mortals and gods. Heidegger concentrates these and other properties of the jug in such words as these: "The thing things. Thinging gathers. Appropriating the fourfold [earth, sky, mortals, gods], it gathers the fourfold's stay, its while, into something that stays for a while: into this thing, that thing."[11] Without giving the German which has caused a diligent translator recourse to this near-English, I trust one can see the point of my saying that Heidegger, in this text (and it relates to many others variously) is a philosopher of collecting.

What I meant by speaking of the opposite directions taken in Wittgenstein's and Heidegger's perspectives I might express by saying that whereas Heidegger identifies things as implying the setting of the world in which they are and do what they surprisingly are and do, Wittgenstein identifies things as differing in their positions within the system of concepts in which their possibilities are what they surprisingly are. We cannot simply say that Heidegger is concerned with essence ("What, then, is the thing as thing, that its essential nature has never yet been able to appear?")[12] and that Wittgenstein is not so concerned (he in fact announces that grammar, which provides the medium of his philosophizing, expresses essence).[13] Nor can we say that Wittgenstein is concerned with language and Heidegger not, for while Wittgenstein says "Grammar tells what kind of object anything is"[14] (or more literally, "It is essence that is articulated in grammar"), Heidegger writes, "It is language that tells us about the nature of a thing, provided that we respect language's own nature."[15]

If Heidegger is a philosopher of collecting, Wittgenstein composes his *Investigations* in such a way as to suggest that philosophy is, or has become for him, a procedure of collecting. Only the first, and longest, of its two parts was prepared by him for publication and its 172 pages consist of 693 sections; in his preface he calls the book "really only an album." For some, me among them, this feature of Wittgenstein's presentation of his thoughts is essential to them and is part of their attraction. For others it is at best a distraction. Emerson's writing has also had a liberating effect on my hopes for philosophical writing, and I have taken the familiar experience of Emerson's writing as leaving the individual sentences to shuffle for themselves, to suggest that each sentence of a paragraph of his can be taken to be its topic sentence. I welcome the consequent suggestion that his essays are collections of equals rather than hierarchies of dependents.

V

I do not make the world which the thing gathers. I do not systematize the language in which the thing differs from all other things of the world. I testify to both, acknowledge my need of both.

The idea of a series, so essential to the late phase of modernist painting (epitomized in one major form in Michael Fried's *Three American Painters* catalogue of 1965, on the work of Kenneth Noland, Jules Olitzki, and Frank Stella)[16] captures this equipollence in the relation between individual and genus or genre. These manifestations of participation in an idea may seem excessively specialized, but the implication of their success (granted one is convinced by their success as art) seems justification enough for the existence of collections and for places in which to exhibit their members in association with one another, as if the conditions of the makeup of the world and of the knowing of the world are there put on display and find reassurance.

This is an odd point of arrival, this emphasis on knowledge as marking our relation to the world, after a bit of byplay between Heidegger and Wittgenstein, whose importance to some of us is tied to their throwing into question, in their radically different ways, philosophy's development of the question of knowledge as the assessment of claims along the axis of certainty, certainty taken as its preferred relation to objects. It is in modern philosophical skepticism, in Descartes and in Hume, that our relation to the things of the world came to be felt to hang by a thread of sensuous immediacy, hence to be snapped by a doubt. The wish to defeat skepticism, or to disparage it, has been close to philosophy's heart ever since. To defeat skepticism need not be a declared grounding motive of a philosophical edifice, as it is in Kant; it may simply be declared a bad dream, or bad intellectual manners, as in Quine, who finds skepticism vitiated by science, whose comprehensibility needs from experience only what Quine calls certain measured "check points."[17] Philosophers such as William James and John Dewey were appalled by what their fellow empiricists have been willing to settle for in the name of experience, they steadfastly refusing to give our birthright in return for, it may seem, so specialized a world. (Foucault calls it the world of black and white.)

When Walter Benjamin tracks the impoverishment of our (Western, late capitalist) experience, and relates it to a distance from objects that have become commodified, hence mystified in their measurement for exchange, he does not, so far as I know, relate this experience to philosophy's preoccupation with skepticism, to an enforced distance from the things of the world and others in it by the very means of closing that distance, by the work of my senses. But then Benjamin seems to harbor a fantasy of a future which promises a path—through collecting—to new life, a reformed practicality with, or use for, objects.

> The interior was the place of Art. The collector was the true inhabitant of the interior. He made the glorification of things his concern. To him fell the task of Sisyphus which consisted of stripping things of their commodity character by means of his possession of them. But he conferred on them only a fancier's value, rather than a use-value. The collector dreamed that he was in a world which was not only far-off in distance and time, but which was also a better one, in which to be sure people were just as poorly provided with what they needed as in the world of everyday, but in which things were freed from the bondage of being useful.
>
> The interior was not only the private citizen's universe, it was also his casing. Living means leaving traces. In the interior, these were stressed. . . . The detective story appeared, which investigated these traces.[18]

The collector knows that our relation to things should be better, but he does not see this materialized through their more equitable redistribution, or say recollecting. That the interior place of Art, and the collector as its true inhabitant, is registered as past may suggest that the place of Art is altered, or that the time of Art and its private collecting is over, or that interiority is closed, or that these proprieties of experience have vanished together.

Take the formulation, "living means leaving traces." In conjunction with the figure of the detective, the implication is that human life, as the privileged life of the interior and its "coverings and antimacassars, boxes and casings," is a crime scene, that (presumably in this period of exclusive comfort) human plans are plans contracted by the guilty. So presumably Benjamin's writing is at once confessing in its existence as traces the guilt of its privilege and at the same time declaring that its obscurity is necessary if it is not to subserve the conditions that insure our guilt toward one another. But the direct allusion to Marx ("[the collector] conferred on [things] only a fancier's value, rather than a use-value"), hence to Marx's derogation of exchange value as a realm of mystery, suggests a mystery in the living of the life of traces that cannot be solved by what are called detectives.

The idea that the evidence of life produced by each of us is of the order of traces, conveys a picture according to which no concatenation of these impressions ever reaches to the origin of these signs of life, call it a self. Then the thrill of the detective story is a function of its warding off the knowledge that we do not know the origins of human plans, why things are made to happen as they do. Traces relate the human body's dinting of the world back to this particular body, but how do we relate this body to what has dinted it? If it was something inside, how do we correlate the events (how compare the sorrow with its manifestation)? If it was something outside, why is *this* the effect (why sorrow instead of contempt or rage)? The discovery of the identity of the criminal is bound to be anticlimactic, something less than we wanted to know.

It does seem brilliant of Poe to have presented the traces of a crime, in "The Murders in the Rue Morgue," early in the genre, so that the solution depends upon realizing that they are not effects of a human action but of those of an ape, as though we no longer have a reliable, instinctive grasp of what the human being is capable of. Was the hand of man therefore not traced in this crime? What brings murder into the world? What detective responds to this evolutionary crossroads?

Beyond this, let's call it, skepticism of traces, I take Benjamin's portrait, or function, of the collector as the true inhabitant of the interior to suggest that the collector himself is without effective or distinctive interiority, without that individuality of the sort he prides himself on. So that when Benjamin goes on to identify the *flâneur's* search for novelty as engendered by "the collective unconscious" and its craving for fashion,[19] this can be taken to mean that what is interpreted by an individual as his uniqueness is merely an item of impulse in an unobserved collection of such impulses, hence anything but original; call it, after Emerson, the source of conformity, part of the crowd after all.

VI

How did it become fashionable for disparagers of skepticism to tell the story of Dr. Johnson, receiving Bishop Berkeley's "denial" of matter, kicking a stone and replying "Thus I refute you." People who know nothing of the motives of skepticism know a version of this story. How strange a scene it offers. Why, to begin with, is kicking a hard object more a "refutation" of immateriality than, say, sipping wine, or putting your hand on the arm of a friend, or just walking away on solid ground, or muddy for that matter? Why is a sensation in the toe taken to be closer to the things of the world than one in the throat or in the hand or on the sole of the foot? Does Samuel Johnson take himself to be closer to his foot than to his throat or his hand? Or is it the gesture that is important—the contempt in kicking? Emerson assigns to Johnson the saying that "You remember who last kicked you." Is Johnson's refutation accordingly to be understood as reminding the things of earth who is master, as an allegory of his contempt of philosophy left to its arrogance? Or is it—despite himself—a way of causing himself pain by the things of the world, implying that he knows they exist because he suffers from them? Then had he forgotten when he last kicked them, or brushed them by?

VII

Some I know, otherwise offended than Benjamin by claims to individuality, profess to understand the self—presumably of any period and locality—as some kind of collection of things, as though such a collection is less metaphysically driven on the face of it than the simple and continued self that Hume famously denies, or would deny to all save harmless metaphysicians. Leaving these self-isolating ones aside, Hume "[ventures] to affirm of the rest of mankind, that they are nothing but a bundle or collection of different perceptions."[20] This alternative picture, however, retains relations among the collection such as resemblance, causation, memory, and the incurable capacity of the whole to torment itself with "philosophical melancholy and delirium."[21] Then when Hume confesses here that "I find myself absolutely and necessarily determined to live, and talk, and act like other people, in the common affairs of life,"[22] how are we to take this assertion against his earlier, famous assurance in the section "Of personal identity," that "for my part, when I enter most intimately into what I call *myself,* I always stumble on some particular perception or other, of heat or cold, light or shade, love or hatred, pain or pleasure. I never can catch *myself* at any time without a perception . . ."[23] What idea (held or deplored) must we understand Hume to have of "entering most intimately into what I call myself"—what perception announces to him this entering? And what would count as a pertinent perception he has stumbled on when he declares his "absolute and necessary determination" to live like other people in the common affairs of life—what perception of absoluteness or determination? And is this determination meant to assure himself that he

is like other people? Do other people have such a determination to live . . .
like themselves? If they do, he is not like them (does not live like them); if
they do not, he is not like them (does not think like them).

Hume goes on to say, fascinatingly, that "The mind is a kind of theater,"
glossing this as emphasizing that "perceptions successively make their appearance, pass, re-pass, glide away, and mingle in an infinite variety of ways.
There is properly no *simplicity* in it at one time, nor *identity* in different . . ."[24]
But what isn't there? What is the metaphysical proposal that must be denied?
Setting aside whatever importance there is to be attached to our "natural pro-
pension" to seek some such simplicity or identity, the question Hume posed
was "From what impression could [our] idea [of the self] be deriv'd?"[25] I am,
for my part, prepared to say that, if we derive from the idea of the mind as a
theater the idea that what we witness there are scenes and characters—so impressions of a scene in which characters are in light and dark, expressing love
or hatred, manifesting pain or pleasure—these provide precisely impressions
or perceptions of myself, revelations of myself, of what I live and die for,
wherein I catch myself. They are not—I am happy to report—simple and identical the way impressions of simple, stable things are. They are ones I might
miss, as I might miss any other chance at self-discernment. I must discover a
narrative for the scene and an identity for the characters and see how to decipher my role in the events. No impression of a thing which failed to relate
that thing to itself as a witness or party to its own concerns (or to understand
how it fails in a given case in this role) would be an impression of a self, of a
thing to which to attribute personhood. Whether what I find is unity or division, simplicity or complicity, depends upon the individual case—both of the
one under narration, the collection, or the one doing the narration, call him
or her the collector, or adaptor, or ego.

VIII

In his Introduction to the *Treatise,* Hume remarks that "'Tis no astonishing
reflection to consider, that the application of experimental philosophy to
moral subjects should come after that to natural at the distance of above a
whole century"—he constructing his application of Newtonianism to human
encounter in the century after Newton's consolidation of the new (corpus-
cular) science, and considering how long it took Copernicus and the others
to arrive at the new science against the reign of Aristotelianism.[26] It took

another century and a half after Hume for the Freudian event to arrive with its methodical discoveries of what the "impressions" or "perceptions" are in conjunction with which we catch ourselves. Call the discoveries new laws, or new ideas of laws, of attraction and repulsion and of the distance over which they act. Whether this span is astonishingly long or short depends on where you start counting from—Sophocles, Shakespeare, Schopenhauer . . . More urgent than determining the time of the achievement is recognizing its fragility. This new knowledge of the self, as Freud explained, perpetually calls down repression upon itself. Since it is these days again under relatively heavy cultural attack (sometimes in conjunction with philosophy, sometimes in the name of philosophy), it is worth asking what would be lost if this knowledge is lost, what aspiration of reason would be abdicated.

That aside, the idea of a self as a collection requiring a narrative locates the idea that what holds a collection together, specifically perhaps in the aspect of its exhibition, is a narrative of some kind. We might think of this idea as the issue of the catalogue, where this refers not simply to the indispensable list of objects and provenances, but to the modern catalogue produced by curators who are as responsible for circulating ideas as for acquiring and preserving objects. Mieke Bal is explicit in positing a narrative among the objects of an exhibition; Susan Stewart more implicitly invokes narrative interaction in her perception of what she calls the animation of a collection; Philip Fisher presents his idea of the effacing and the making of art as a narrative of the stages an object undergoes as it makes its way to the status and stability of a place in a museum of art, a sort of counternarrative, even effecting a certain counteranimation, to that of a collection within itself.[27] The issue of the catalogue is, I think, a pertinent emphasis for Norton Batkin's proposal that an exhibition be informed by its objects' own preoccupations with their fatedness to display, for example, by their relation to the intervention of the theatrical, or to the pervasiveness of the photographic, or, perhaps, later, to what remains of the experience of collage, or of assemblage.[28]

IX

Batkin's concern, evidently, is that the current emphasis on the concept of collecting, on establishing a holding, not come to swamp the concept, and the practices, of the holding's exhibition(s). A shadow of my concern here, rather, has been that the concept of a collection not swamp the concept and perception of the particulars of which it is composed. Both are concerns, I think, that the worth of certain values in the concept of art not be misplaced, that is, lost—for example, that the demand to be seen, call it the demand of experience to be satisfied, however thwarted or deferred, not be settled apart from the responsiveness to the claims of individual objects upon experience.

This says very little, but that little is incompatible with, for example, the recently fashionable tendency among aestheticians in the philosophically analytical mode to let the question of conferring or withholding the status of art upon an object be settled by whether or not someone or some place or other puts it on display (with no Duchampian taste for naughtiness and scenes). If it comes to this, I should prefer to let the status be settled by the persuasiveness of the catalogue. But artists who work in series in effect declare that only art can determine which singularities can sustain, and be identified by, a collection of works of art.

The problem here is already there in Kant's founding of the modern philosophy of art, in his *Critique of Judgment*.[29] His characterization of the aesthetic judgment as placing a universal demand for agreement on the basis of one's own subjectivity in assessing pleasure and purposiveness perhaps draws its extraordinary convincingness from its transferring to the act of judgment what should be understood as the work of the work of art (of as it were the thing itself), namely, lodging the demand to watch. It is not news that we moderns cannot do or suffer without intellectualizing our experience. Then we should at least make sure that our intellectualizing is after our own hearts. Criticism, which (drawing out the implication of Kant's findings) articulates the grounds in a thing upon which the demand for agreement, after the fact of pleasure, bears a new responsibility for the resuscitation of the world, of our aliveness to it.

It remains tricky. When Thoreau one day at Walden moved all the furniture in his cabin outside in order to clean both the cabin and the furniture, he noticed that his possessions looked much better to him outdoors than they ever had in their proper places. This is an enviable experience, and valuable to hear. But it did not make his possessions works of art. Then recently I read of some new legislation proposed against schemes of price-fixing in certain prominent auction houses, about which a lawyer remarked that the movement of works of art is now being treated to legal constraints designed for deals in milk and cement. I reported this to M. Blistène, my host at the Pompidou Center, as we were about to enter a splendid exhibition there devoted to structures in cement and iron. He replied that he knew a German artist who works with milk.

But in what continues here I shall remain indiscriminate in collecting thoughts of collections in the world of things, leaving the differences in the realm of art mostly to shift for themselves, and perhaps, at times, toward us.

X

I saw the other week for the first time Chantal Akerman's breakthrough film, *Jeanne Dielman / 23 quai du commerce / 1080 Bruxelles,* known for the originality of its vision of film and of what film can be about, for its length (three and a half hours), for its director's age (twenty-four years when she made it), and for the performance of Delphine Seyrig. I adduce it here because it can be taken as a study, or materialization, of the self as a collection, in the particular form in which the one who is the subject of the collection is not free (or not moved?) to supply its narrative. I sketch from memory certain events, mostly of its first hour, already knowing that while little happens that in customary terms would be called interesting, the way it is presented, in its very uneventfulness, makes it almost unthinkable to describe what happens in sufficient detail to recount all it is that you notice.

It opens with a woman standing before a stove, putting on a large pot under which she lights a flame with a match. The camera is unmoving; it will prove never to move, but to be given different posts, always frontal and always taking in most of a person's figure and enough of the environment to locate them, once you know the complete list of their possible locations. It is hard to know whether everything, or whether nothing, is being judged. The camera holds long enough in its opening position that you know you are in a realm of time perhaps unlike any other you have experienced on film. A doorbell sounds, the woman takes off her apron, walks into the hallway to a door which she opens to a man whose face you do not see but whose hat and coat the woman takes and with whom she exchanges one-word greetings, and with whom she disappears into a room. The camera observes the closed door to the room, a change of light indicates the passage of an indefinite span of time, the door opens, the woman returns the coat and hat to the man who now appears in full length. The man takes money out of a wallet and hands it to the woman, says something like "Until next week," and departs. She deposits the money in a decorative vase on what proves to be the dining table, bathes herself, an evident ritual in which each part of her body is as if taken on separately, and then returns to the preparation at the stove. When she is again signaled by the doorbell she opens it to a young man, or schoolboy. Admitting him, she returns to the kitchen, dishes out the contents of the boiled pot into two bowls, one potato at a time, four potatoes into each bowl, and takes them to the dining room table, where the boy has already taken a seat, and we watch the two of them eat through each of their respective rations of potatoes. Near the beginning of the meal the woman says, "Don't read while you eat"; nothing more is said until the close of the meal when she reports that she has received a letter from her sister in Canada, which she reads, or rather recites, aloud: it is an invitation to visit the sister, saying she has sent a present to her and containing the suggestion that the sister wants to introduce her to a man, since it has been six years since her husband died. She asks the boy— we suppose by now he is her son—whether they should accept the invitation. After dinner she takes out knitting; it is a sweater for the young man; she puts it away after making a few additional knots. Her son meanwhile has been reading, she listens to him recite a poem from Baudelaire, evidently a preparation for school, remarks that his accent is deteriorating, that he doesn't sound like her, and they move to the stuffed chair on which the son had been reading and unfold it into a bed. As the woman stands at the door, the boy, now in bed, recites that a friend has told him about erections, orgasm, and conception, which he declares to be disgusting and asks how she can have brought herself to go through it in having him. She replies that that part is not important.

The first day, the screen announces, is over. About an hour of the film has passed. In the remaining two and a half hours the same activities are repeated, with different economies. The second day, for instance, we see the preparation of the potatoes for the soup, watching, of course, each potato being peeled. Kant says that every object which enters our world is given along with all the conditions of its appearance to us. I should like to say: Every action which we enter into our world must satisfy all the conditions of its completion. (Every human action is, as the German says, handled, performed by the creature with hands, the same action in different hands as different, and alike, as different hands.) With this knife with this blade, sitting in this garment at this table, with this heap of potatoes from this bowl, within these walls under this light at this instant . . . the woman knots herself into the world. Thoreau says the present is the meeting of two eternities, the past and the future. How does a blessing become a curse?

On this second day certain things, or conditions, are not in order—a button is missing from the son's jacket, a wisp of her hair is out of place after finishing with that day's client, she lets the potatoes burn, she cannot get her coffee to taste right, even after going through the process of beginning again, throwing out the old coffee grounds, grinding new beans, and so on. The film feels as if it is nearing its end when on the third day we are not kept outside but accompany her with that day's client into her bedroom. After an abstract scene of intercourse in which she is apparently brought to orgasm despite her air of indifference, she rises, moves about her room to her dressing table to freshen herself, picks up the pair of scissors which we had seen her find and take into her room in order to cut the wrapping of the present just arrived from her sister, walks with the scissors over to the man lying back on her bed, stabs him fatally in the throat, and slides the scissors onto her table as she walks out of the room. In the dining room, without turning on a light, she sits on a chair, still, eyes open, we do not know for how long.

I wish to convey in this selected table of events the sense of how little stands out until the concluding violence, and at the same time that there are so many events taking place that a wholly true account of them could never be completed, and if not in this case, in no case. As for a narrative that amounts to an explanation of the stabbing, it would make sense to say that it was caused by any of the differences between one day and the following— by burning the potatoes or failing to get the coffee to taste right or being unable to decide whether to go to Canada or receiving the gift of a nightgown from her sister or slipping against her will into orgasm. To this equalization of her occupations a narrative feature is brought that is as pervasive and difficult to notice as the camera which never moves of itself but is from time to time displaced. Each time that the woman moves from one room to another room of the apartment (kitchen, bathroom, the woman's bedroom, the dining-sitting-sewing-reading-sleeping room, all connected by a corridor) the woman opens a door and turns out a light and closes the door and opens another door and turns on another light and closes that door (except after the stabbing). The spaces are to be as separate as those in a cabinet of curiosities. (What would happen if they touched? A word for thought would be ignited.)

But if Akerman's film may be brought together with the cabinet of curiosities—an inevitable topic in any discussion of the history of collecting since the Renaissance—it suggests that from the beginning this phenomenon signified both an interest in the variances of the world and at the same time a fear of the loss of interest in the world, a fear of boredom, as though the world might run out of difference, exhaust its possibilities. A space I am trying to designate and leave here is for a consideration of Walter Benjamin's perception of the era of the Baroque as characterized by melancholy, marked by acedia, or depletion of spirit. As the era arguably of Shakespearean tragedy (*Hamlet* is the implicit centerpiece or touchstone of Benjamin's work on the twin of tragedy he calls "the mourning play"),[30] it is marked principally for me as the advent of skepticism. This is no time to try to make this clear; I mention it to go additionally with, for example, Pomian's suggestion that funerary display is at the origin of the idea of collecting, and with Nietzsche's suggestion that it is not God's death that caused churches to turn into mausoleums, but the other way around, that our behavior in these habitations unsuits them for divinity—precisely Emerson's point when he speaks, half a century earlier, of preachers' speaking as if God is dead.

The pivotal role claimed for Akerman's films as events in the unfolding of contemporary feminism would mean, on this account, that she has found women to bear undistractedly, however attractively, the marks of supposedly interesting social partitions or dissociations. Her pivotal role in the unfolding of filmmaking is then that she has constructed new means of presenting the world in which these marks perpetuate themselves, and has thereby made them newly visible and discussable. Call this a new discovery of the violence of the ordinary. In this she joins the likes of Beckett and Chekhov, but also Rousseau (in his revelation of mankind so far as free and chained—the easiest thing in the world not to notice), as well as Emerson and Nietzsche (in what the former called conformity and the latter philistinism). That Akerman's camera can as if discover suspense in what is not happening, as if we no longer know what is worth saying or showing, what is remarkable, shows a faith in the sheer existence of film that approaches the prophetic.

XI

That the occasion of the present reflections is the interaction of two great cities, Paris and New York, enacts the fact that major museums and their collections require the concentration of wealth that is to be found, in the modern world, in centers of population and power. I recall that it is in thinking of the connection between what Georg Simmel calls the metropolis and mental life ("Die Grosstadt und das Geistesleben") that he observes:

There is perhaps no psychic phenomenon which is so uncondition-
ally reserved to the city as the blasé outlook. . . . The essence of the
blasé attitude is an indifference toward the distinctions between things.
Not in the sense that they are not perceived, as in the case of mental
dullness, but rather that the meaning and the value of the distinction
between things, and therewith the things themselves, are experienced
as meaningless. . . . This psychic mood is the correct subjective reflection of a complete money economy to the extent that money takes
the place of all the manifoldness of things and expresses all qualita-
tive distinctions between them in the distinction of "how much." . . .
[T]he metropolis is the seat of commerce and it is in it that the pur-
chasability of things [this altered relation to objects; "this coloring,
or rather this de-coloring of things"] appears in quite a different aspect than in simpler economies. . . . We see that the self-preservation
of certain types of personalities is obtained at the cost of devaluing
the entire objective world, ending inevitably in dragging the person-
ality downward into a feeling of its own valuelessness.[31]

Simmel announces the topic of his essay by saying that "The deepest problems of modern life flow from the attempt of the individual to maintain the
independence and individuality of his existence against the sovereign powers
of the society, against the weight of the historical heritage and the external
culture and techniques of life."[32] Call the individual's antagonist here the collective and its heritage and techniques its collections, gathered, it may be, as
much like pollutants as like potsherds. Might there be some philosophical cun-
ning that permits us to learn from collections how to oppose their conforming weight?

Walter Benjamin evidently thinks not. From his "Eduard Fuchs, Collector
and Historian": "[Culture and history] may well increase the burden of the
treasures that are piled up on humanity's back. But it does not give mankind
the strength to shake them off, so as to get its hands on them."[33] For whom
is this said? It was such a perception that set the early Nietzsche writing against
a certain form of history, monumental history he called it; Emerson's first
essay in his first Series of Essays is "History," written against what he takes
us to imagine history to be. Quoting Emerson's essay: "I am ashamed to see
what a shallow village tale our so-called History is. How *many* times must
we say Rome, and Paris, and Constantinople! What does Rome know of rat
and lizard? What are Olympiads and Consulates to these neighboring systems

of being? Nay, what food or experience or succor have they for the Esquimaux seal-hunter, for the Kanaka in his canoe, for the fisherman, the stevedore, the porter?"[34] It is part of the concept of my telling another about an event, that I (take myself to) know something about the event that that other fails to know, and might be glad to know, or that I am interested in it in a way that other has not seen and might be interested to see. Emerson opposes a history of events that trades upon their having already received significance, so he demands a recounting of what has hitherto been taken to count. When Freud, in *Civilization and its Discontents,* introduces the issue of ethics—"the relations of human beings to one another"—into the problem he is bringing before us, "namely, the constitutional inclination of human beings to be aggressive toward one another," he goes on to say:

> The commandment, "Love thy neighbor as thyself," is the strongest defense against human aggressiveness and an excellent example of the unpsychological proceedings of the cultural super-ego. The commandment is impossible to fulfil. . . . What a potent obstacle to civilization aggressiveness must be, if the defense against it [the unslakable super-ego] can cause as much unhappiness as aggressiveness itself! . . . [S]o long as virtue is not rewarded here on earth, ethics will, I fancy, preach in vain. I too think it quite certain that a real change in the relations of human beings to possessions would be of more help in this direction than any ethical commands; but the recognition of this fact among socialists has been obscured and made useless for practical purposes by a fresh idealistic conception of human nature [namely, that the abolition of private property will eliminate difference that causes aggressiveness]."[35]

So you needn't be a socialist to recognize the necessity of a real change in our relation to things. (Lacan in effect develops this thought of Freud's, in the concluding chapters of Seminar VII, *The Ethics of Psychoanalysis,* in, for example, his assertion that the experience and goals of psychoanalysis demand a break with what he calls "the service of goods.")[36] What change in relation to objects might Freud have had in mind? The most prominent model of his own relation to possessions is figured in his well-known collection of some two thousand ancient Greek, Roman, and Asian objects, primarily statuettes. Putting aside psychoanalytically dependent explanations of Freud's tastes (that the statuettes of gods and heroes are father-substitutes, that archeological finds are emblematic of the finds excavated through the methods of psycho-analysis itself), we might consider certain facts of his reported behavior toward these possessions. Baudrillard, among the prominent theorists of collecting, uses Freudian concepts most explicitly, invoking relations to objects he characterizes in connection with oral introjection and anal retention; yet while he concludes "The System of Collecting" by observing that "he who . . . collect[s] can never entirely shake off an air of impoverishment and depleted humanity," he does not, so far as I am aware, express interest in Freud's own collecting.[37] John Forrester's essay "Collector, Naturalist, Surrealist" is indispensable on this topic, relating Freud's psychoanalytic practices throughout as modes of collecting (dreams, slips, symptoms) and emphasizing the life Freud maintained in his collections by adding to them and making gifts of them.[38] It is not easy, in the staid atmosphere of the so-called Freud Museum in London, formed from his residence in London, to imagine what it could be like alone with Freud in his apartment of study and treatment rooms, guarded or regarded by these figures. It is known that new figures, before taking their places within the collection, were initially introduced into the family setting, placed on the table at the communal meal. The suggestion has been that Freud used the collection to mark the separation of his working from his family life, but it seems more pointedly true (but then this should amount only to a redescription of the same fact) to say that it served to mark the separation of his patients' work with him from *their* everyday lives.

What could be more pertinent for a holding environment (to use an idea of British psychoanalyst D. W. Winnicott's)[39]—in which the claims of ordinary assertions are to be put in suspension (not to stop you, as in philosophical exercises, from saying more than you know, but to free you from stopping saying what you wish, expressing your desire)—than uncounted gods, who have seen and survived the worst and whose medium is revelation through concealment?

To imagine Freud's collecting anything else is like trying to imagine his having a different face (with apologies to Wittgenstein and his example of the ridiculous and embarrassing results in trying to imagine what Goethe would have looked like writing the Ninth Symphony).[40] Neither a series of objects that in themselves are more or less worthless (for example, the series of match boxes mounted in a curved line along a wall that Lacan cites as representing sheer thingness)[41] nor a collection each piece of which may suggest priceless-ness (perhaps like the objects in the Frick Museum) fits our idea of Freud. The random voracity of Charles Foster Kane's acquisitiveness, or (somewhat less?) of William Randolph Hearst's at San Simeon, California, on which Orson Welles's *Citizen Kane* was based, seems to fit (indeed to have helped construct) the personas of their acquirers, and to manifest, with touching vulgarity, the proposition—established clinically and theoretically by Melanie Klein,[42] and alluded to in such Romantic narratives as Coleridge's *Ancient Mariner*—that the loss of our first object is never fully compensated for.

XII

Is, then, the value we attach to things ineradicably compromised in its assumption of objectivity? The issue takes on various emphases in moral philosophy. It is essential to John Rawls's *A Theory of Justice* that "[A]s citizens we are to reject the standard of perfection as a political principle, and for the purposes of justice avoid any assessment of the relative value of one another's way of life. . . . This democracy in judging each other's aims is the foundation of self-respect in a well-ordered society."[43] How sure are we that we know what constitutes the aims of the ways of life depicted in *Jeanne Dielman* or in *The Glass Menagerie* or in *The Great Gatsby*? A fundamental implication of the avoidance of relative judgment—call it the rejection of snobbery, that sibling of envy—is that the bearing of another's life cannot be measured (beyond the requirements upon it of justice) without seeing it from that other's perspective. This is emphasized in Christine Korsgaard's Rawlsian / Kantian treatment of the question of the objectivity of value when she takes as an example of questionable value one in which a collection figures essentially.[44] In considering the question whether value is subjective or objective, a Kantian is bound to measure the question by the formulation of the aesthetic judgment in Kant's *Critique of Judgment,* in which the claim to beauty is both subjective and yet necessarily makes a comprehensibly universal claim—necessity and universality being the Kantian marks of the objective. So one can say the issue of conflict between the objective and the subjective (in aesthetic matters, as differently in moral) becomes a matter of how, as rational beings, we are to confront one another.

Korsgaard takes the case of someone who collects pieces of barbed wire—presumably a rarified taste—and asks in effect where the claim, if any, upon my respect for this activity is supposed to lie, in the sincerity of the passion for the wire, or in a property of the wire itself? No one else should be counted on to share the taste, and why be interested in someone who has it? A crucial point of moral order is involved for Korsgaard: our respect for other persons must not await our respect for their ends, but on the contrary, respecting their ends must be a function of respecting them as fellow persons. This must be right. But what does "respecting their ends" come to? Given that it cannot require sharing their ends, as the case of the barbed wire is designed to show, it evidently means something like finding the alien end comprehensible, seeing *how* it may be valued. A good society cannot depend upon our approval of each other's desires but it does depend upon our being able, and being willing, to make ourselves comprehensible to one another. Here is where the idea of a collection plays an essential role. What interest this piece of barbed wire has may only be communicable in associating it with other, competing pieces, to which a given piece may be taken to allude, comparing it with these others, perhaps, in its effectiveness, economy, simplicity, handling, or producibility. This may not succeed. It does seem that some minimum of the sharing of desire is required for reason to prevail. But then respect, or tolerance, should have a way to prevail in the absence of offerable reasons. It seems hard to imagine the members of a society flourishing in which their commitments to one another are based upon sheer indifference toward their differences.

It is to show that a commitment to democracy may have to imagine something like this, and to show the room there is for responsiveness to it, if not quite for offering reasons in it, that I can understand, and be grateful for, Dave Hickey's instruction, in his Overture to *Air Guitar,* in our "need [for] so many love songs"—there are so many things to learn, well within the range of justice, about satisfying desire.[45] You needn't share Hickey's taste for Las Vegas, but just a fragment of his love song to it, flying back another time from some respectable art panel—"coming home to the only indigenous visual culture on the North American continent, a town bereft of dead white walls, gray wool carpets, ficus plants, and Barcelona chairs—where there is everything to see and not a single pretentious object demanding to be scrutinized"—and you can rejoice that Las Vegas is, for him, part of the union.[46]

Early in my reading of Wittgenstein's *Investigations,* I summarized my sense of what I will come to call his vision of language, and what I might now call the stake of our mutual comprehensibility, in these words:

> We learn and teach words in certain contexts, and then we are expected, and expect others, to be able to project them into further contexts. Nothing insures that this projection will take place (in particular, not the grasping of universals or of books of rules), just as

nothing insures that we will make, and understand, the same projections. That on the whole we do is a matter of our sharing routes of interest and feeling, modes of response, senses of humor and of significance and of fulfillment, of what is outrageous, of what is similar to what else, what a rebuke, what forgiveness, of when an utterance is an assertion, when an appeal, when an explanation—all the whirl of organism Wittgenstein calls "forms of life." Human speech and activity, sanity and community, rest upon nothing more, but nothing less, than this. It is a vision as simple as it is difficult, and as difficult as it is (and because it is) terrifying.[47]

Terrifying because this seems to allow that my meaning anything, making sense, depends upon others finding me worth understanding, as if they might just *decide* that I am without sense. Childhood is lived under this threat. It is no wonder Melanie Klein describes the child's world as hedged with madness, negotiating melancholy for paranoia, reparation for destructiveness.[48]

XIII

In *Art and Money,* Marc Shell recounts through a thousand instances the millennial-long controversies in the West over the relation between the status of the representation of value by art and by money, and relates the controversies to life and death issues of the materialization and dematerialization of God (for example, over the status of the graven image, over the significance of reproducibility, over the definition of truth as "adequacy" between conception and thing), noting the issue to be alive in minimalist and conceptual art.[49] (Here Michael Fried's "Art and Objecthood" and Clement Greenberg's "Modernist Painting" and "After Abstract Expressionism" are pivotal texts.)[50] But the dematerialization of art and of reality are also at work from Andy Warhol's painted shoes to Martin Heidegger's creepy casualness about our relation to the atom bomb, or as he puts it, ". . . man's staring at what the explosion of the bomb could bring with it. He does not see that the atom bomb and its explosion are the mere final emission of what has long since taken place, has already happened."[51]

What has already happened to us is the loss of distance and ignorance of nearness—our thoughtlessness concerning the nature of the thing—that I glanced at in section IV. Even if, as I am, one is willing to go a considerable way with such signature Heideggerean soundings as "the thing things," there are junctures at the surface around which suspicion should form. What may be dismissed as, let us say, the poor taste of comparing the effects of the atom bomb with a metaphysical process, barely conceals a political claim marked by the careful distinction between the bomb and its explosion. Only one nation has exploded the atom bomb in war, showing "what it could bring with it." And the implication is that there is a metaphysical condition that makes the use of the bomb possible, or thinkable, and that Heidegger's thought has been alone in its efforts to outline and counter this condition on behalf of the globe.

And then there is that matter of Heidegger's exemplary jug, in "The Thing," which is suspiciously folkish—pre-technological, pre-capitalist, pre-democratic—in its extravagant aura.[52] I do not wish here to counter a healthy impulse toward disgust with philosophy. One finds oneself recovering the good of philosophy in one's own time, or not. Yet I will say that to miss Heidegger's narration in which the jug marries earth and sky and its contents form a gift of mortals to gods; and miss the unfolding in which a ring of celebration (alluding surely to Nietzsche's wedding ring of eternal recurrence) among the fourfold (earth, mortals, etc.) is the work of the thing thinging, but a work accessible to us only in stepping back from our millennia of constructions and representations within a heritage of philosophical concepts and leaping free to a form of thinking that is "called by the thing as the thing," and hence understand ourselves as "be-thinged" ("in the strict sense of the German word *bedingt*"), the conditioned ones (dictionary definitions of *bedingt* are "conditionally," "limited," "subject to"), a condition in which "we have left behind us the presumption of all unconditionedness" (unconditionedness for ourselves, as if we were the gods of creation)—to miss this narration of a new relation to things as such is to miss one of the most remarkable in the history of responses to Kant's derivation and puzzle of the thing-in-itself, and accordingly to risk slighting the distinct contribution Heidegger proposes for an understanding of gathering or collecting, namely one that affirms our finitude (the renunciation of our unconditionedness, of an identification with pure spirituality). This forms a counterweight to the impression, variously given in writing about collections, that collecting is a narcissistic, not to say imperialist, effort to incorporate the world. But would Heidegger consider an empirical collection to provide occasion for the event of entering on his new path toward a different gathering of the world? He himself evidently suggests no exercises for this change of heart.

In the sequence of proposals I have made, leading to Heidegger's, meant to account for our valuing of collecting—that we have an interest in learning nearness, in the stability of materiality, in achieving comprehensibility to others, and an interest in the endurance of interest itself—I am continuing a line of thought in earlier moments of my writing that I ask leave to name here: In "Finding as Founding," a reading of Emerson's "Experience," I cite Emerson's search for nearness in terms of his apparent distance from the consciousness of grief over the death of his young son Waldo, standing for all there is to be near to ("I cannot get it nearer to me"), and I observe his discovery that he must thereupon accept the world's nearing itself to him ("indirect" is his word for this direction), an acceptance of a certain revised form of life (philosophy may poorly call it animism) outside himself, outside any human power.[53] This reading goes back to my *World Viewed,* in which I relate the automatism of Jackson Pollock, and of post-Pollock abstraction (somewhat modifying the concept of automatism as introduced by William Rubin into the discussion of Pollock's work),[54] to the achieving of a candidness, or candor, or uncanniness and incandescence (all etymological developments of the idea of glowing or being white), from which I associate an unexpected, all but paradoxical, connection between these non-objective commitments and the power of photography and of nature's autonomy or self-sufficiency.[55] From here I derive the idea of this painting as facing us (an indebtedness to formative discussions with Michael Fried), as if to perceive them is to turn to them, all at once. This line of thought extends a step further back into my *Senses of Walden* and its discussion of Thoreau's concept of our "nextness" to the world, or our neighboring of it, as the condition of ecstasy.[56] I add here that the idea of automatism in painting leads, in the section that follows in *The World Viewed,* to the invoking of work that essentially exists in series, that is, in a collection.[57] (What I referred to a moment ago as philosophy's poor concept of animism, something that dogs, or should, a certain intensity in accounting for the work art does, can be taken, while not named, as a subtext of Heidegger's still formidable "The Origin of the Work of Art," as when he speaks of "let[ting] things encounter us," and claims that "All art is poetry," recalling—I take it—that, as we are forever told, poesis means making, but then goes on to ask what it is that art makes happen, and answers in such words as may translate this way: "Art breaks open an open place . . . in such a way that only now, in the midst of beings, the Open brings beings to shine and ring out."[58] It does seem sometimes that we are in our period destined to be told things unwelcome either because they are heard too often or because they are too unheard of.)

This line of thought was brought to mind in attending a fine presentation, at the recent meetings of the American Society for Aesthetics, by Stephen Melville, who in taking up the ideas of a painting's candidness and its facing of the beholder, cited among many other matters some of the material I have just alluded to, and startled me (I cannot in this speak for others) with the coup of projecting Andy Warhol's "portrait" of Marilyn Monroe in this context, which presents the image of her in ranks and files of differently tinted replications of the same frontal image.[59] It thus, I suppose, not alone declares the issue of a painting's facing us but posits that we may not see even a singular face in isolation, but only in its repetition, achieving its aura precisely because of its existence as a collective property, as if the mark of the objective now, even of existence, is celebrity.

XIV

What has happened to the idea of the capacity of knowing as our fundamental relation to the world—the capacity so treasured by modern philosophy, thus so exposing itself to its powers of skepticism? We have neglected, and will mostly here continue to neglect, the species of collection which may seem to have been made to inspire the response of, or motive to, knowledge, that of the natural history museum. If there is a decent justification for this neglect it is that such collections are no longer readable as the work of individuals (as in the case of the painting and collecting activities of Charles Willson Peale, given so excellent an account by Susan Stewart in "Death and Life, in That Order"), hence the interest in collecting is apt to shift from the desire of the collector to the quality of the collection, and from the matter of our relation to objects to our relation to that of a theory of the relation of objects to one another, so that classification becomes more fundamental in presenting the collection than juxtaposition.

In both arenas display is essential, but with the things dear to collectors, as is characteristically emphasized (most insistently, perhaps, by Pomian), the object is taken out of circulation (or, to respect Philip Fisher's alliance of the making and the effacing of art, say that the object is put into a different circulation), whereas one could say that in a natural history collection the object (or part or reconstruction) is put into circulation for the first time. Here the status, or life, of the work of art shifts again into view. If it is true, as said earlier, that objects of art are objects from their outset destined to be exhibited (unlike bones and stones), it might also be true that other objects share such a destiny without (quite, yet) being known as objects of art. Was it before or after cultures collected that they also decorated and selected among options, offering themselves grounds for a relation to an object of service not strictly required, or exhausted, by that service?

From that moment objects could exist within intersecting circles of circulation.

We should be cautious in saying that with natural objects we know where the next specimen or part fits, whereas with the artifact we have to find where it fits best—cautious because of what we learn from work made most famous in Foucault's texts, especially *The Order of Things,* that knowledge grounded in classification is not a discovery derived from a clear accumulation of facts but itself required a set of intellectual / historical conditions in which a new conception of knowledge (or episteme) was possible, in which a new counting, or order, of facts was made visible. This is an insight marked as belonging to the same intellectual era in which Thomas Kuhn startled philosophers and historians with the suggestion that physical science, knowledge at its most prestigious, goes through periods of crisis in which accumulation is not driving research, and reconceptualization appears to wish to remake rather than to refine the picture of the world.[60] And of course it was as if we had always known that.

And in both arenas of display death is invoked, even death as present in life, but in collections of art, or artifacts, it is my death that is in question as I enter into the stopped time of the objects (Pomian remarks that their display is as on an altar),[61] whereas the skeletons and parts of natural history speak of the death and the perpetuation of species, of their co-existence and succession, measured within the earth's time (one of Foucault's favorite expressions of the new episteme exemplified by the natural history museum is to say that it displays its items on, or in, a table).[62]

XV

But one event staged within a natural history museum is irresistibly pertinent for an American with a certain philosophical disposition asked to think about a collection being transported from France for a stay in the United States, I mean the declaration Emerson made to his journal at the time of his visit to Paris in 1833, that he has had something like a revelation in his experience of the great collections in the Jardin des Plantes. In a study that has recently appeared, *The Emerson Museum: Practical Romanticism and the Pursuit of the Whole,* Lee Rush Brown takes that experience, always remarked on by Emerson's biographers, as more decisively significant than has been recognized before.[63] He proposes that we understand what floored Emerson by the Paris exhibitions to be their presentation of an image of what he wanted his writing to be. I might formulate the image Brown constructs as one in which Emerson sees that his words may become specimens of a totality of significance arrived at otherwise than by a system (philosophical or scientific [or narrative?]), of which Emerson felt incapable. *The Emerson Museum* casts a wide net of social, philosophical, and historical reference and I do not imagine my formulation to do justice to it. The formulation leaves deliberately open, for example, whether Emerson's "words" refers to single words, to sentences, to paragraphs, or to essays; and to what the idea of system is to be credited if not to laws or argument. There should be another time for that. Here I wish simply to give credit for the insistence that Emerson's experience and vow in Paris ("I will be a naturalist") is some kind of revelation to him of his project and practice as a writer. I have myself been too long preoccupied with the sound of the Emersonian sentence not to welcome an addition to its understanding; but too long accustomed to asking how each of Emerson's essays characterizes its own writing not to be wary of a proposal of any fixed model for them.

This is too important a matter to me not to be a little more specific about it. Having indicated a connection between the concept of collecting and that of thinking (as in the history of disappointment with universals), and with the concept of the self (as in contemporary play with Humean ideas of the subject), I would not have satisfied my opening sense of my assignment to think publicly about the philosophical interest of collecting without including some speculation about its comparable connection with the concept of philosophical writing, particularly in the cases of Emerson and of Wittgenstein. An obvious cause for this inclusion at this moment is to recall Emerson's and Wittgenstein's relation, in their fashionings of discontinuity, to the medium of philosophy as aphorism, in counterpoise to its medium as system. Wittgenstein is explicit about this, but implicitly everything about Emerson's practice as a writer bespeaks this sense of aggregation and juxtaposition—from his culling from his journals for individual essays, to the sense of his sentences as desiring to stand apart from one another, each saying everything, each starting over.

XVI

The first impulse Emerson records, on 13 July, upon noting that he went "to the Cabinet of Natural History in the Garden of Plants," is "How much finer things are in composition than alone. 'Tis wise in man to make Cabinets." Here is some of what he took away with him that day.

> The fancy-colored vests of these elegant beings [in the Ornitholog-ical Chambers] make me as pensive as the hues & forms of a cabinet of shells, formerly. It is a beautiful collection & makes the visiter as calm & genial as a bridegroom. The limits of the possible are enlarged, & the real is stranger than the imaginary. . . .
>
> Ah said I this is philanthropy, wisdom, taste. . . . The Universe is a more amazing puzzle than ever as you glance along this bewildering series of animated forms . . . the hazy butterflies, the carved shells, the birds, beasts, fishes, insects, snakes,—& the upheaving principle of life everywhere incipient in the very rock aping organized forms. Not a form so grotesque, so sane, nor so beautiful but is an expres-sion of some property inherent in man the observer,—an occult re-lation between the very scorpions and man. I feel the centipede in me—cayman, carp, eagle, & fox. I am moved by strange sympathies, I say continually "I will be a naturalist." . . .
>
> Walk down the alleys of this flower garden & you come to the en-closures of the animals where almost all that Adam named or Noah preserved are represented. . . . It is very pleasant to walk in this garden.[64]

He does seem at the end of his visit to have well-recovered himself from signs of revelation. The scrupulous editor of this volume of Emerson's journals notes that beneath the ink entry "this is philanthropy, wisdom, taste—" is written in faint pencil: "Le moment ou je parle est deja loin de moi"—a learned quotation from Boileau presumably to mark that Emerson is unsure what he has learned.[65]

I think I can see that Emerson's sequence of descriptions of his state at the Jardin des Plantes—being pensive; calm and genial as a bridegroom; inspired as by a perception of philanthropy, wisdom, taste; moved by strange sympathies—produce an outburst of dedication to qualities he wants for his writing. But I am not so far able to see how Lee Rust Brown makes the transfer from, for example, Emerson's description of "a beautiful collection" (of elegant birds) to the way we are to see his sentences hang or perch together. An elegant bird, I should imagine, is, as Emerson says of a squirrel running over a lawn and up into trees, not made to go unobserved; linking his writing with a display of bright feathers or a casual virtuosity suggests that Emerson has his own uses for attractiveness. ("We are attracted to the standard of the true man," from the first printing of "Self-Reliance.")[66] And I think I can see, more specifically, Emerson's "Self-Reliance" as describing its own writing when it speaks of thinking as an aversion to conformity; and "The American Scholar" of its own when it speaks of thinking as a process of conversion going forward at every hour; and "Fate" similarly when it describes freedom as resistance or counter-stroke; and the so-called "Divinity School Address" when it speaks of communion; and "Circles" when it speaks of circular forms and seems to imply a circle as an intimate audience; and "Experience" when it speaks of "glancing blows" as opposed to direct grasps as the direction of knowing.[67] (Do we not have a kind of internal gag when "Experience" speaks of originating—as he says Sir Everard Home has discovered the embryo originates "coactively"—from three points, since three points define a circle, three gathered together in an arc.)[68] But I do not know that I have in any case made clear or concrete enough the transfer to Emerson's actual words, or made clear that the process is clear enough as it stands. Enough for what?

Perhaps I am too attached to Thoreau's more explicit interest in literal classification and listing as the basis for self-allegory, as when his series or tables of measurements or soundings in *Walden* (1854) show as emblems of the accuracy and systematicity he claims for his words.[69] As when his tabulation of his expenditures on food, in his first chapter, "Economy," shows as his "thus publishing his guilt," thus assigning to his writing the power to assess the guilt in acquiring, at who knows what expense to others, the sustenance of his existence; and the writing is the sustenance, declaring that its will is to make itself cost something to read.[70] The Emersonian sound seems different, otherwise, as in the passage cited earlier, in which Emerson expresses his shame of what we know and accept as History: "What does Rome know of rat or lizard?"—these neighboring systems of existence. There is an urgency here

THE WORLD AS THINGS | 65

of the incessant bearing of unseen processes, to be registered in each sentence, that Thoreau can allow to be suspended across sentences, or chapters, or years. The idea broached earlier of every Emersonian sentence as a self-standing topic sentence of the essay in which it appears, hence of his paragraphs as bundles or collections that may be moved, is linked, in my mind, with Friedrich Schlegel's remark that in good prose it is as if every word is stressed.

XVII

Emerson's visit to the Jardin des Plantes collects (or, more accurately, was itself collected earlier by) another pair of visits there by another translated American, Chris Marker, first as recorded in his film *La Jetée* (made 1962, released 1964) and then quoted in his film *Sans Soleil* (1982), that endlessly instructive autobiographical / anthropological meditation on art and technology, and culture and memory, and past and future, and space and time, and words and images, and desire and death, and nearness and distance. The scene from the Jardin des Plantes that Marker uses in the first and quotes in the second of these films is one in which two people are looking and gesturing at a cut from a giant sequoia tree, stood on its side almost to the vertical, inscribed with dates identifying the years for various of its rings, almost facing us, after which, in *Sans Soleil,* Marker continues by quoting the passage from Hitchcock's *Vertigo* on which the shot was based, in which James Stewart and Kim Novak, visiting the Muir Woods near San Francisco, are looking at its sequoia cut covered with historical dates and this woman, pointing, is saying, "There I was born, and there I died." The memory of a memory of a Hitchcock film about the fatality of memory is preserved in the collection of articulations on a tree whose birth preceded French and English and all they have had to forget.

Other collections to be mentioned are present in *Sans Soleil,* which assured that it had to find its place here.

Taking the Emerson / Marker / Hitchcock / California intersection with me to Paris last summer as I went to visit again, for instance, the Jardin des Plantes and the Pompidou Center after a lapse of some years (the Paris sequoia cut is still, or again, on display, but moved inside, into an entrance hall of one of the museum building), you may imagine my momentary vertigo on being informed that Chris Marker had accepted an invitation to make a piece to

mark the very event of the temporary transfer of its collection that is a cause
of these words. When returning to the Center I inquired of M. Blistène
whether there were documents recording the ideas with which Marker had
been approached for this commission, he replied, "There is something better.
Marker is downstairs shooting." What I found him shooting, or having just
ceased shooting, was a sequence in which a visitor to the museum is interac-
tively viewing a provisional CD-ROM that Marker had installed on a monitor, mounted on a stand with two chairs before it, in an otherwise empty
space. Marker held up the small camera he had been using and said, "I've
wanted this all my life. No more waiting for developing, adding tracks. . . .
Things like *Sans Soleil* are past. It is why I tore up the poster of *Sans Soleil* before putting it up." I had noticed the collage-like shape on the wall as I entered the installation space, and looking at it again I saw that it appeared to
have been torn twice, once lengthwise, then, halves together, once across,
then reassembled; the title was still quite legible, and the new form was no
doubt more attractive than the original rectangle of the poster would have
been. I felt encouraged that this master of his art, or arts, had found elation
both in breaking with an old practice (that of the movie camera) and in calling
upon an old practice (that of collage) in announcing the fact.

The CD-ROM turned out to be an elaboration of material pertaining to
Sans Soleil. On one of my routes interacting with it I came upon the reference to *Vertigo* where Marker's voice-over says that he has seen the Hitchcock
film—he calls it the best film ever made about time—nineteen times, and that
his remarks about the film are for others who also have seen it nineteen times.
And, I imagined, for those who will see *San Soleil* with that attention. (I think
here of Susan Howe's wonderful responses to Marker, and others, in her
"Sorting Facts; or, Nineteen Ways of Looking at Marker.")[71] This invitation
to obsession—must I decide whether it is fetishistic attachment, or honest
labor?—is something I have sometimes felt I must ward off. The temptation
is, I think, a reason I was struck early by Wittgenstein's self-reflection in the
Investigations:

> It is not our aim to refine or complete the system of rules for the use
> of our words in unheard-of ways. For the clarity that we are aiming
> at is indeed *complete* clarity. But this simply means that the philosoph-
> ical problems should *completely* disappear. The real discovery is the
> one that makes me capable of breaking off philosophizing when
> I want to.—The one that gives philosophy peace.[72]

The issue of completeness can haunt discussions of collecting, some writers (for example, Susan Stewart) taking it as essential to the desire in collecting, others (for example, John Forrester) taking it that a collection that is no longer growing is dead.[73] Regarding Wittgenstein's *Investigations* (Part I especially) as a collection, I have described the 693 sections of this work as showing the willingness to come to an end 693 times. Since I have understood the current over-insistence (so I judge it) on the idea of meaning as the deferral of significance, to be an expression of the fear of death, I find Wittgenstein's practice here to become a memorable realization of Montaigne's assignment of philosophy as learning how to die. Since Wittgenstein also describes his philosophical practice as "[leading] back words from their metaphysical to their everyday use" (§ 116), in which, or at which, philosophy brings itself to an end (momentarily?—but how can we know that there will be a further call upon it, a 694th call?) the ordinary, in Wittgenstein's philosophy of the ordinary, is the realm of death, of the life of mortality, subjection to the universal collector.[74]

Does the passion for collecting have something to say about such matters as coming to an end?

XVIII

A number of collections are depicted in the Tokyo sequences of *Sans Soleil*. One toward the beginning is of cat figurines lodged in a temple consecrated to cats; one around the middle is of dolls in a ceremony for the repose of the souls of broken dolls; one toward the end is of the debris collected together from the accessories and decorations of the communal New Year ceremonies.

The ceremony for the broken dolls and the one for the debris both conclude by burning the collections. The film does not make explicit the significance of the burnings, but the suggestion is that debris, whose burning seems fairly natural, has as much right to immortality as the souls of broken dolls do, but the burning of the dolls is shocking. Perhaps one thinks of Kurt Schwitters's collages incorporating debris, as it were tracing a fitful immortality of beauty upon what others have abandoned. There is also to ponder Robert Opie's self-described near-mania for collecting and displaying wrappings or packagings, enacting the mad wittiness of retaining and reorganizing precisely what is meant—is it not?—to be discarded.[75] Many collections convey the wish to make the world immortal by so to speak forming a reconstruction or impression or shadowy duplicate of it (what is new about film?); but Opie's idea, in description, projects a sort of defiance of the world's availability, or deliverability.

Thoreau, the philosopher of non-collection, of the way of responsible life as one of disencumbering oneself from false necessity (enacting and extending teachings from Plato and from Rousseau), is struck by a ceremony of burning what he regards as debris, late in the opening chapter of *Walden:*

> Not long since I was present at the auction of a deacon's effects, for his life had not been ineffectual: "The evil that men do lives after them." As usual, a great proportion was trumpery which had begun to accumulate in his father's day. Among the rest was a dried tapeworm. And now, after lying half a century in his garret and other dust holes, these things were not burned; instead of a *bonfire,* or purifying destruction of them, there was an *auction,* or increasing of them. The neighbors eagerly collected to view them, bought them all, and carefully transported them to their garrets and dust holes, to lie there till their estates are settled, when they will start again. When a man dies, he kicks the dust.[76]

Thoreau contrasts this ceremony, to its disfavor, with a certain celebration of a "busk" or "feast of first fruits," which Bartram describes as having been the custom of the Mucclasse Indians. Thoreau quotes Bartram: "When a town celebrates the busk, having previously provided themselves with new clothes, new pots, pans, and other household utensils and furniture, they collect all their worn-out clothes and other despicable things, sweep and cleanse their houses, squares, and the whole town of their filth, which with all the remaining grain and other old provisions they cast together into one common heap, and consume it with fire."[77]

After adding several further critical details, Thoreau concludes the section by remarking: "I have scarcely heard of a truer sacrament, that is, as the dictionary defines it, 'outward and visible sign of an inward and spiritual grace.'"[78]

This is not quite allowing the debris of life its own right to remembrance, or abandonment. That idea of right is announced by the film in connection with Sei Shōnagon's *Pillow Book* and her passion for lists, lists of elegant things, of distressing things, among them a list of things not worth doing, and one—an enviable mode of composition—of things "to quicken the heart." This passion has, in *Sans Soleil*, its own, to my taste, beautiful consequences, inspiring, for instance, ideas of visits to post office boxes without expecting letters but just to honor letters unsent or unwritten; and of pauses at an empty intersection to leave space for the spirits of cars broken there. And when the voice-over adds, to the list of things to be honored in farewell, "All that I'd cut to tidy up" (that is, in completing *Sans Soleil*), I found myself attaching a small prayer for thoughts that have never come, or never been given sufficient appreciation. Priceless uncollecteds.

Thoreau joins in recognizing the necessity to give abandonment, or farewell, to the character of what he calls an event of sacrament (as giving divorce to the character of marriage). But Thoreau's main emphasis falls still farther, to make his leaving even of Walden unceremonious, a step on a way. As if he has so burned himself into every event of Walden's days (the aroma of which is *Walden*) that he can trust both of their existences, entrust them to one another.

If collections can teach this, they may not exempt themselves from the knowledge they impart, that they are to be left. Some people need, or have, as luck would have it, a bequest to leave. Thoreau quite explicitly makes a bequest or deed of each form and depth and nameable object of Walden to whoever wants them properly. Thus he exhibits his obedience to St. Matthew's injunction, "Lay not up for yourself treasures upon earth where moth and rust doth corrupt." And he can say, evidently, in a worldly register, "A man is rich in proportion to the number of things he can afford to let alone,"[79] thus humoring the labor theory of possession running, in Locke's formulation: "Whatsoever [any man] removes out of the State that Nature hath provided, and left it in, he hath mixed his Labour with, and joyned to it something that is his own, and thereby makes it his Property."[80] Locke wants something of the kind metaphysically to define ownership, and Marx wants the denial of something of the kind to reveal itself to us in the phantasmagoria of the exchange of commodities; so it is bracing that Thoreau isolates and makes explicit the religious, or animated, bearing of the features of nature left to us, as when he characterizes a lake (in the "Ponds" chapter of *Walden*) as "earth's eye."[81]

But when Walter Benjamin declares, "There is no document of civilization which is not at the same time a document of barbarism," the very power of the perception disguises the fact that it is as much fantasm as insight, an illumination of things indiscriminately in their aspect as spoils or booty.[82] It can be done; in some moods it is irresistible. But in lashing together, say, the

Elgin marbles with, perhaps, a collection of old jazz records that preserve treasures of a harsh time, and these, perhaps, with a collection of silver objects
of observance which Jews carried from a disguised into an undisguised exile,
or with their steamer trunks desperately packed with evening gowns and
court slippers for which no future life will call—here is a frenzied invitation
to a madness of misanthropy as much as it is an enlightened liberation of conduct. For what is writing responsible? Not to hearten pointlessly; but not to
dishearten expansively.

I said earlier that we should encounter again the bearing of Wittgenstein's
and of Heidegger's work on the task of leaving or abandonment. In our relation to the things of the world, Heidegger proposes (as he translates a phrase
from Parmenides) "letting-lie-before-us" as the mode of thinking to be sought
in stepping back from our fantasies of thinking as grasping the world in fixed
concepts.[83] Wittgenstein explicitly mentions just once the pertinent idea of
leaving, as befits his discontinuous moments of philosophizing about philosophy: "[Philosophy] leaves everything as it is."[84] Perhaps he means to attract
the interpretation this has largely received, a confession of philosophy's con-
servatism. Then one is left with having to put this together with the radical
destruction of philosophical tradition that his writing undertakes. The immediate import of the claim is that modes of thought and practice other
than the philosophical—for example the political or the economic, as we
know them—do *not* leave things as they are, but subject them to violence,
the state in which they are given to us. "Our investigation must be turned
around the fixed point of our real need."[85] Our thinking is faithless to our
desire, oblivious to what it set out to express. Whatever instructs us here is
to the good.

"Don't take it as a matter of course, but as a remarkable fact, that pictures
and fictitious narratives give us pleasure, occupy our minds."[86] I know of no
better initial tip in matters of aesthetics. You are advised to consult yourself
as to whether a thing you have taken into your mind, have consented for that
time to bear upon your life, gives you pleasure, or perhaps otherwise disturbs
you, and if not, to demand of yourself the cause, whether the thing that so-
licits you is not remarkable or whether you are coarsened in what you can
remark, allow to matter to you. Why do we put things together as we do?
Why do we put ourselves together with just these things to make a world?
What choices have we said farewell to? To put things together differently, so
that they quicken the heart, would demand their recollecting.

Thanks are due to the following people for their contributions to this essay: Steven Affeldt, Norton Batkin, Gus Blaisdell, Arnold Davidson, Charles Warren, Bernard Blistène at the Centre Georges Pompidou, and the resourceful staff of the Publications Department at the Guggenheim Museum.

3

The Division of Talent

Cavell produced his own "author's note" for this essay, which was printed as a headnote to the published version. He wrote: "The following, here amplified in one or two places, was read to the Association of Departments of English at their conference held 21–23 July 1984 at Yale University. My title, obviously modeled on the notion of the division of labor, is meant to mark conflicts in current critical theory that express, and are expressed by, forces at once within individuals and between cultures. While I was, of course, asked for a title months before I knew what I would say on the proposed occasion, the outcome is, I believe, faithful to my intention in inventing it, however shallow the outcome's satisfaction of it. I hope it will be taken as a first installment, or invitation."

My letter of invitation to this seminar expresses the thought that "it will be very useful to have someone from outside the field help us see ourselves." Given my interests in what you might call the fact of literary study, I was naturally attracted by the invitation to look at literary study as a discipline or profession but also suspicious of the invitation. I thought: Do professionals really want to be helped to see themselves by outsiders? This is an invitation to get a group of people sore at me, and it will only result in the group's having an occasion *not* to see itself, since any member of it can easily dismiss anything I say as uninformed. But the invitation goes on to give the title for this session as "The Nature and Function of Literary

First published as "The Division of Talent," *Critical Inquiry* 11, no. 4 (1985): 519–538.

Study: As Others See Us." Reading that, I thought: That is different. That identifies me as an *other* to the "academic and professional concerns" of the field—hence, not just outside but intimately outside, as if my position were an *alternative* to yours. And how could I not be better informed about being *other* to you than you are?

But of course I know that there is no single and unified "you" to which I am other, that some of you, perhaps most, have *other* others than philosophy and see your practice not against philosophy but against history or criticism or literary theory. So I should perhaps say that I am not exactly single or unified myself, that I am also other to the Anglo-American profession of philosophy, to which at the same time I belong. A way of expressing my otherness to this profession of philosophy is simply to say that I take you as also among my others, that I recognize the study of literature to be an alternative to what I do—a path I might have taken, might still irregularly be taking—to occupy a relation to the way I think, that for most of the members of my profession would be occupied by a profession of logic or science. I will not try here to account theoretically for the intimate differences that may make philosophy and literature alternative studies, which means that I will not here systematically try taking the perspective of an other. But I will be bearing in mind its possibility as I spend my time now as an outsider, unsystematically reporting certain messages and rumors that have lately been coming my way from the field of literary studies. You have, for example, not kept it secret that you have been worrying, as a profession, about the nature and commitments of a profession, and sometimes in the form of conducting arguments about the obligation to literary theory as part of literary study, nor secret that these arguments sometimes take on the color or texture of strong statements of, or against, something called deconstruction. I will try to say something about these poorly kept secrets.

By bearing in mind the possibility of the perspective of the other, I mean primarily that I will just assume that it is internal to what philosophy is and to what literature is that students of one periodically regard students of the other as blind and deaf to the significance of one another's defining texts, as evasive of the seriousness of one another's issues. It is my impression that the idea or practice of deconstruction feeds, and feeds upon, this opposition, on the intimacy of this sense of mutual evasion. This might help explain why some take up deconstruction as, let me say, an ideology (in which literature is to overcome philosophy), while others avoid it as a nemesis (in which the very impulse to overcome philosophy signifies that literary study has itself already been overcome by philosophy), and still others embrace it as what I think of as one particular mode of the continuation of Romanticism, specifically a Romanticism represented for me by William Wordsworth, Samuel Taylor Coleridge, Ralph Waldo Emerson, and Henry David Thoreau, whose defining mission I have sketched as the redemption of philosophy and poetry by one another. I am coming to think of what I do as seeking my relation to some such mission, which means that I see in some of what I know of deconstruction an affinity with what I do, something to which I also bear an intimate outsideness. It expresses my otherness to that "approach" (so Jacques Derrida seems to name it in an address of his I will discuss later) to repeat that I continue to take the Anglo-American constitution of philosophy also as my other, something to which deconstruction is, I think I can say, merely outside, making itself strange (to which it is at best a pseudo- philosophical representative of the continental philosophizing that the best Anglo-American analytical philosophy has always shunned).

Gifted and sensitive students increasingly ask my advice about how they should plan their further educations and acquire credentials, to help them negotiate this web of allegiances that seems to them perhaps rich but perhaps hopelessly tangled. I find the advice I have for them to be increasingly thin and repetitive. We go over again the pluses and minuses of places of graduate study that have strong departments in *both* philosophy *and* literature, or places that have two universities near one another, and we discuss again the pluses and minuses of individual scrambling for this double education, as against the better-known interdisciplinary programs. As I write this, I am alarmed afresh at the implication of these increasingly frequent conversations, the implication that our graduate students, the future of our subjects, are increasingly finding their educations inefficient, insufficiently helpful. Then what future are we to hope for?

(If I were to arrive at some curricular proposal directed to the sense of literary studies and philosophy as alternative paths, each the other's untaken path, it would have to respond to my companion perception of Romanticism as naming a time from which thinkers and writers no longer know what they need to know in order to say what they have it at heart to say. The sense of not knowing what you need to know, which is describable as not knowing where or how to begin on knowing, is how I have understood the fact that characteristic masterworks of Romanticism take the form of studies in education—for example, *Biographia Literaria, The Prelude,* and *Walden.* My insistence on emphasizing that Ludwig Wittgenstein's *Philosophical Investigations* is a work of education is an effect *and* a cause of my seeing in Wittgenstein's later philosophy a continuation of what I called Romanticism's mission; and I would say roughly the same, for the same reason, about Martin Heidegger's *What Is Called Thinking?* So my idea of a curriculum is of a program that would have to make sense of the fact that there may no longer, or for the foreseeable future, *be* a *course* of study—a uniform, runnable direction—to the goal of a study that seems to me the most urgent.)

In now going on to cite four or five instances in which the antagonism of literary and philosophical studies has recently come to my attention, I take note first, in passing, of the notorious magazine article, "The Crisis in English Studies," published just about two years ago by my colleague at Harvard, Walter Jackson Bate.[1] I have no wish to contribute either to the public answers it has received, composed in the spirit of contempt that it exemplifies, nor to the private fervor of praise it has inspired, exemplified by the behavior described to me of a university trustee who had the article copied and distributed to every member of his faculty. All this is lamentable and predictable. I mention the article because I seemed to find an odd acting out of it one day last spring when I visited the Shakespeare Association meetings. A senior scholar in a plenary gathering of the association voiced the opinion that the educational reforms of what he called "the sixties" had gone too far and that teachers of Shakespeare now had an obligation to reassert to their students the values of the English Renaissance. An hour or so later, in a panel discussion entitled "Post-Structuralism," one young professional referred derisively to the address we had heard earlier, and he submitted the view, uncontested explicitly by any of his dozen or so fellow participants—perhaps out of agreement, perhaps out of speechless disagreement—that what he thought it was important to teach was independent of any particular texts, that it would make no difference to him whether his teaching assignment was to consider Shakespeare or, say, John Marston. Now here is a field of study, I thought to myself, some of whose members believe that the values of the Renaissance have gone without serious challenge over the past 350 years and can simply be reasserted, while others feel that Shakespeare's particular writings are inessential to how we characterize what our values were and to how we understand what has happened to them. Such a field, I said to myself, seems to have a crisis on its hands. (The willingness for crisis may be to its credit or for its promise. It is definitive of the humanistic professions, as opposed to the scientific, to be at any time subject to the charge, or confession, that they are in crisis—and also to be always capable of denying that charge—as if a *question* of crisis is itself normal to the humanities, when they differentiate from the sciences. [I am of course thinking here of Thomas Kuhn's picture of scientific crises, or "revolutions," as *breaking in upon* a science's normal periods of progress.] This wants understanding. For example, Stanley Fish's reply to Bate's article takes every development Bate reads as a sign of death to be [where recognizable] a sign of life.)[2]

I felt the air of crisis also in reading through the spate of responses that the editors of *Critical Inquiry* reported receiving in record-breaking numbers to "Against Theory," an article in their pages by Steven Knapp and Walter Benn Michaels.[3] But here I felt more specifically that someone with my intellectual tastes seems to have no way of contributing to such discussions. The article refers to Wittgenstein and, indirectly, to the philosophical practice of J. L. Austin, but in a context and in a way that are foreign to me. I take those philosophers, especially Wittgenstein, along with Heidegger, as major representatives of the impulse to philosophy in this century, and the thing they most notably share as philosophers is the understanding of philosophy as the continuous struggle to end philosophy—as Wittgenstein puts it, to bring philosophy peace; you may call it a struggle to turn aside philosophical theory, as if philosophy has become the most intimate enemy of genuine thinking. It follows that the last gesture to expect help from in these struggles against philosophy is one that simply recommends the abandoning of theory, particularly on the apparently sensible ground that it is empty, as if the will to philosophy were less fundamental an aspiration in human life than the will to science or to art. Indeed, Wittgenstein and Heidegger seem to have discovered in philosophy something I have called a "will to emptiness" (it is one of the characterizations I have given of skepticism), which they have dedicated their teaching to turning us from. So essential does this seem to me in their teaching that to invoke their names apart from this aspect of their work, in a discussion of the emptiness of theory, is bound to strike me as not invoking them philosophically at all.

(The editors at *Critical Inquiry* found a note of something like stuffiness in my tone toward Knapp and Michaels' paper, and they have asked me whether I, as I think I may put it, really meant that. I agree that there is something off about my tone there, and I think I see some causes.

The background would be a pair of essays I wrote about twenty years ago ["Music Discomposed" and "A Matter of Meaning It"] whose preoccupations resemble those of Knapp and Michaels on various counts: my essays were written in suspicion of theory [while at the same time they imply that being "against" theory's new historical role in artistic practice would make roughly the same sense as being against a particular historical development of artistic practice], and they trace intimacies between meaning and intention that a work like W. K. Wimsatt and Monroe Beardsley's "Intentional Fallacy" serves to deny.[4] My diagnosis of Wimsatt and Beardsley was that they work with a concept of intention that is empty or illusory, a concept of intention that seems to bear no relation to the concept as it is so prominently appealed to, say, in legal and in moral argument. This left open *why* they are pushed to work with a constricted concept, but the suggestion was that it is part of a more general philosophical constriction [as my essays left open how one might then account for the historical success of the Wimsatt and Beardsley paper]. Knapp and Michaels' diagnosis of "The Intentional Fallacy" is that its theory of meaning or language requires "subtracting intention," in contrast to other theories which require "adding intention"; whereas it is the thesis of their paper that "intention cannot be added to or subtracted from meaning because meanings are always intentional" ["AT," p. 736]. Issue should be joined here, I felt, because correct diagnosis in such a matter is the heart of it. Knapp and Michaels' words seemed to me to foreclose the issue, since there is not much interest in understanding why people persist in something that "cannot" be done, none beyond asking why people persist in any folly. Compare: mortality cannot be added to or subtracted from humankind, because all men are mortal. Does this settle the question of immortality?

The foreground of my doubtful tone was, I think, a response to an odd combination I felt in Knapp and Michaels' proposal of evident intelligence together with philosophical impatience. I wondered [perhaps too impatiently, so I tried to avoid expressing it] whether they meant, or intended, the extremity of claim in an assertion like: "In *all* speech what is intended and what is meant are identical" ["AT," p. 729]. For consider: if I glance at you meaningfully, that is between us, but if I glance at you intentionally, I am including a third. I may give up a pawn unintentionally in poorly carrying out a strategy, but if I give it up meaninglessly, the strategy itself was poor. I know how to give the meaning of a word but not how to give the intention of a word, though I might tell you what someone intended in using a certain word in a certain place. If Hamlet had asked, "Do you think I intended country matters?" Ophelia might well have been even more alarmed than she was.

One way Knapp and Michaels apply their view is as follows: "If meaning and intended meaning are already the same, it's hard to see how looking for one provides an objective method—or any sort of method—for looking for the other; looking for one just *is* looking for the other" ["AT," p. 725]. Here compare: if the woman who dropped the slipper is the same as the woman who ran from the ball, you can say truly that looking for the one [the one the slipper fits] just *is* looking for the other [the runaway love]. But is it [therefore] *hard* to see how looking for one provides an objective method for looking for the other? It seems, on the contrary, that in this case it is *because* the woman in question is the same under two [or three] descriptions that a method for looking is established. Knapp and Michaels may wish to claim that my Cinderella identity is merely empirical [hence may variously fail] whereas the identity they speak of is stronger, say, an identity of meaning [or intention]. But my little budget of suggested examples ending with Hamlet's revised question shows that "meaning" and "intention" are not, on one clear test of identity, identical in meaning.[5] So the relation between the concepts remains to be worked out.)

The next instance I have to report of antagonism between literary and philosophical studies carries less the air of crisis than of chronic dissatisfaction. I refer to a piece published in *Critical Inquiry* last year by the late Paul de Man, one of the explicit targets of the Knapp and Michaels proposal and an implicit target of the Bate article (de Man's reply to which is singled out for praise in the address by Derrida that I will get to): The essay of de Man's to which I refer here is a reply to criticisms leveled against his earlier essay on Hegel's *Aesthetics* by a professional American philosopher, Raymond Geuss of Princeton.[6] Geuss had ended his remarks with the following paragraph:

> Hegel's views may be unintelligible, unenlightening, implausible, or just plain wrong, but I don't see that de Man has made the case that in his aesthetics Hegel unknowingly vacillates between two incompatible positions.[7]

(Geuss' suggested list of what I call "terms of criticism" invites a discussion, which I cannot follow now, concerning the terms by which intellectual positions habitually position themselves against competitors and, more specifically, concerning the way intellectual innovation will issue in new terms of criticism which cannot be understood apart from understanding the innovation as such.) De Man's reply to Geuss is immensely refined, ending by confessing and questioning (certainly without seeming to excuse) his compulsion to have repeated himself "with worse intolerance" and appearing to praise Geuss' relentless professionalism in philosophy as "in the best sense, 'literary'"

("RRG," p. 390). The beginning three paragraphs of de Man's eleven-paragraph reply treat what he describes as "the tenuous relationships between the disciplines of philosophy and literary theory" (and hence imply that the relationships between philosophy and literary theory themselves are something other than tenuous). This beginning and ending—especially in light of de Man's opposing what he calls his "manner of reading" with Geuss' way—suggest that de Man's entire reply, brief, somewhat informal, but full, is to be taken as a demonstration that these opposed ways of reading allegorize the antagonistic character of the relations between the literary and the philosophical as such ("RRG," pp. 383, 384).

Because I find this very congenial, it troubles me that, from de Man's writing which I have studied thus far, I have not been able to derive sufficient help in understanding what causes and what permits not merely multiple readings but these antagonistic readings of a text. This may be, it goes without saying, simply my fault. Yet I am about as certain as I am about anything I know in criticism that, for example, contrary to de Man's sense of the matter, the antagonism has exactly nothing to do with what Austin means by the distinction between constative and performative utterances, which in turn has nothing to do—and is motivated philosophically exactly to *show* that it has nothing to do—with the difference between the referentiality and the non-referentiality of language.[8]

I focus here on just one piece of advice de Man offers in replying to Geuss:

> Geuss' stance . . . is to shelter the canonical reading of what Hegel actually thought and proclaimed from readings which allow themselves . . . to tamper with the canon. Such an attitude, I hasten to add, is not only legitimate but admirable. . . . The commentator should persist as long as possible in the canonical reading and should begin to swerve away from it only when he encounters difficulties which the methodological and substantial assertions of the system are no longer able to master. ["RRG," p. 384]

This sounds very sensible and reassuring—the sort of advice one might give to a class of interested but somewhat restive students some weeks into their first course in the practice and theory of deconstruction. And it interests me that this advice seems constructed in answer to one particular term of criticism, or accusation, out of the many more or less anxiously random accusations brought against the practice of deconstruction, namely, that it is "willful"—a charge de Man explicitly denies near the end of his reply ("RRG," p. 390). That he cares particularly about this charge seems to me philosophically alert of him, as does his effort to answer the charge, however briefly and abstractly, by indicating how his work begins, as if to show what necessitates it. I think it is this commitment to account philosophically for one's intellectual origination that primarily accounts for the feeling I have of kinship, however strained, with such writing as de Man's and Derrida's. (And I daresay it is the commitment that causes most bafflement about my writing and most offense taken from it among my colleagues in the profession of philosophy.)

I said de Man's advice that one "should persist as long as possible in the canonical reading" sounded sensible and reassuring, but I have to say that I am not at all clear that I know how to apply the advice. I think over a number of texts I have written about with some consecutiveness, each of which follows lines pretty well opposed to what I felt was currently or typically said of them (and hence, it seemed to me, worth my saying). There may be good reason for calling the various current or typical readings of the texts I took up "canonical" readings of them, but in no case do I feel that my opposed readings make sense of the advice to "persist as long as possible in the canonical reading."

In the case of Wittgenstein's *Philosophical Investigations,* the canonical reading is, let me say, that it is meant as a refutation of skepticism, a reading that I find to render Wittgenstein's words helpless against this ineradicable possibility of human nature, to make his words seem to deny what is undeniable in skepticism. To say, therefore, that this reading should be persisted in would seem to me more or less senseless, whereas to show (which my reading is at pains to do) how it *can* be persisted in, why it is so tempting to drift with its persistence, seems to me philosophically essential. Again, say that Thoreau is read canonically as a writer in praise of nature. It is true that I found, in writing about the writer of *Walden* as a thinker—in the line of Kant and something like the equal of Heidegger—I had to turn many, I guess most, of *Walden*'s sentences apparently against themselves. This process typically eclipses *Walden*'s praise of nature, but it does not show the praise to be misplaced or unwarranted. Now I could not advise the reader to persist in *Walden*'s nature description *as long as possible,* because my view is that it must never be given up (altogether). Or again, if the canonical reading of Samuel Beckett's *Endgame* is that it perceives the breakdown of language in a meaningless universe, my reading shows this perception as itself in service of an effort to escape our complicity in the totality—what I called the totalitarianism—of its meaning. Similarly, with respect to *King Lear*, I claim that certain traditional readings (for example, of Lear's opacity or Edgar's purity) repeat the avoidance which the play uncovers as the cause of tragedy. The moral is not that we should persist in such canonizations but that it is tragically, or comically, or ironically, difficult not to. And then, with respect to Emerson's "Fate," against the going view that Emerson is there tempering his optimism with a rueful recognition of the limits of our nature, I claim that he is in effect deepening his optimism by successfully antagonizing (sometimes he calls this "mastering," sometimes "obeying") the limits, or conditions, of language, freeing us to see what I call our "fatedness to language." I might well call this text "duplicitous" or "vacillating," but then I would mean not that it comes to difficulties it cannot master but that it permits or invites obedience to itself in more than one direction, indeed, that it is part of its instruction to leave itself, in this particular way, unguarded.

Nothing yet follows about the seriousness of difference between de Man's claims for reading and mine. It may be that de Man and I are speaking at different levels, of differing realms of texts, holding ourselves answerable to simply different intellectual professions or cultures. I do not imagine that he, any more than I, would be happy to conclude so. And this means to me that one who shares this unhappiness might take as a measure of our philosophical-literary culture, or lack of one, that we cannot at present survey such matters with genuine intellectual satisfaction.

I will cite one further instance of this present incommensurability before I conclude with a proposal or fantasy concerning what ought to be done about it. The instance comes from "The Principle of Reason: The University in the Eyes of Its Pupils," Derrida's inaugural address on the occasion of his accepting a special professorship at Cornell University.[9] His address takes up the grounding or establishing of the university, initially and recurrently in the form of an interpretation of the grounds or landscape of the Cornell campus, and situates itself as interpreting, perhaps I may say as depositing, Heidegger's portrait of reason as representative thinking. Derrida cites passages from, among other of Heidegger's works, *Der Satz vom Grund*, in which "Heidegger asserts that the modern university is 'grounded' (*gegrundet*), 'built' (*gebaut*) on the principle of reason, it 'rests' (*ruht*) on this principle." Then Derrida continues: "But . . . nowhere do we encounter within [the university as such] the principle of reason itself, nowhere is this principle thought through, scrutinized, interrogated as to its origin" ("PR," p. 10). There is, and I suppose there is meant to be, at this stage, ambiguity concerning this "nowhere," an ambiguity as to whether the university is the place, is a somewhere, in which the principle of reason *can* be thought through and an ambiguity as to whether the principle is always to be thought through (and perhaps is being thought through) only in a nowhere, a region that can or will not be grounded. Yet Derrida also says: "The principle of reason installs its empire only to the extent that the abyssal question of the being that is hiding within it remains hidden, and with it the question of the grounding of the ground itself" ("PR," p. 10).

Someone with my bucklings of background will have a crowd of responses to such claims. One response will be to question, and perhaps defend, what the positivists were calling, in the first years in which I was in graduate school, the "meaningfulness" of such propositions, here the proposition that speaks of, or takes off from, the ground's ground. The phrase sounds like Heidegger's saying of the nothing that it "nothings," a proposition that Rudolf Carnap bounded from in his early manifesto of logical positivism as the very type of metaphysical meaninglessness. We are all somewhat more sophisticated now, and even those with an itch to speak of the meaningless would now hesitate to scratch this way in public. Such a one might instead recognize that Derrida's question concerning grounds has something to do with the problematic, in Anglo-American circles, of "foundationalism" in epistemology, and perhaps in ethics; and since "antifoundationalism" is fashionable, one might encourage Derrida to give up his unnecessary search for grounding. Some such may even suggest that his search is the product of a (bad) picture of grounding. But suppose that he were to reply that this criticism rests on (or is grounded in?) the same picture and that, while in a sense his search for grounds is *unnecessary,* in a sense it is also more immediately and more significantly *under prohibition,* say, off-limits. Is this conceivably the beginning of a meaningful exchange?

Another background of my responses begins from finding Emerson and Thoreau meaningful beyond argument, and intellectually rigorous, and moreover to bring to American ground an indefinite measure of Heidegger's preoccupations, most particularly, as I have urged elsewhere, the Heidegger of *What Is Called Thinking?,* very much the Heidegger who provides a critique of representational thinking. (The obvious bridge from Emerson to Heidegger is Friedrich Nietzsche, who loved Emerson's mind and without whom there is no later Heidegger. Whether the bridge is reparable for and by us and whether the idea of a bridge is in place here are other stories.) Now Emerson's first Emersonian essay, *Nature,* provides in its way a grounding, or surveying, for a certain way of placing Derrida's thinking in his inaugural address at Cornell; I mean especially in Derrida's thinking through terms of the Cornell landscape of height, views, bridges, barriers, and the gorge, as when he says of Heidegger's passing praise of the university that it is all "elaborated above an abyss, suspended over a 'gorge'—by which we mean on grounds whose own grounding remains invisible and unthought" ("PR," pp. 10–11). The grounding or surveying in Emerson's *Nature* is expressed in its idea that "it is not words only that are emblematic; it is things which are emblematic."[10] (Though some may feel that this is less to ground thoughts than it is to sky them.)

It was from such an idea that I developed my meditations on *Walden*, taking off, for example, by remarking that while "we seem to be shown [its] writer doing everything under the sun but, except very infrequently, writing . . . [,] each of his actions is [to be understood as] the act of a writer, that every word in which he identifies himself or describes his work and his world is the identification and description of what he understands his literary enterprise to require."[11] What this turns out to mean is that events such as the writer-hero's borrowing an ax; buying a shanty for its wood and nails; hammering; humming; moving his belongings in the sight of others; leaving; carving a stick; marking with it in the ground; wearing a track; standing on tiptoe; sitting quietly in some attractive spot in the woods; trailing and listening for a lost hound, bay horse, and turtledove; reading footprints in the snow; reading a page of Homer; finding himself in his shadow; hoeing his field and knowing his beans; and (speaking of foundations) calculating and mapping the bottom of the pond—events such as these—are all to be taken literally *and* as acts (or, you may say, allegories) of writing. Yet just last week I read a discussion, by a professor of English and American literature, of my book on *Walden* that, while not exactly unfriendly, declares somewhat impatiently, it seems to me, that I am not original in taking on what he calls the "theme" of "Thoreau the writer" (even though the acts I have noted as acts or figures of writing are mostly *not* thematized as such by Thoreau nor, as far as I know, by the literature on Thoreau) and praises me for "generally [avoiding] the lifeless jargon of philosophy" (quite as if I had by that avoidance managed to escape philosophizing altogether).[12] These descriptions, while not quite untrue, do not afford me the sense of being well understood. For example, I implicitly account for the, as it were, lack or absence of literal human writing as much of a theme or image in *Walden* on various grounds: the human act of writing (in contrast with the constant publications of nature) is in a sense no more or less interesting or important a human occupation (the writer of *Walden* can say it is no more or less poetic) in *Walden,* in human life at its Walden, than buying, borrowing, reading, sitting, standing, walking, listening, tracking. More particularly, if less concretely, writing is the human action that figures, as it is figured by, human action at its active best, its most finished, action that alters existence closer to the heart's desire (having encouraged the heart's capacity to desire); and, most generally, these relations must not (cannot truly) be related, I mean they are not (yet) to be said—I mean voiced—but only, at Walden (wherever that turns out to be), written, that is, shown—they are, I am taking it, what the writer of *Walden* calls secrets of his trade. Then the question was, for me, inevitable: What did I think I was doing in writing about this writing? And then there was no turning back from that work as a work of philosophy. And from where does a professor of literature, an expert on Thoreau, get the urge, and feel sufficient safety, to denounce philosophical jargon? In *Walden* you find the sentence: "The universe constantly and obediently answers to our conceptions," which I have said summarizes accurately the *Critique of Pure Reason,* in part by accurately assessing Kant's jargon of the concept.[13]

Emerson's statement of the emblematic casts its light on a passage from the earliest paper in which I ever studied Wittgenstein, a passage that I learn has been adduced in recent controversies over Wittgenstein's account of what you may call the normativeness, or rule-governedness, of meaning, or what you may think of as the matter of its grounding against skepticism. My passage speaks against the position which contends that Wittgenstein takes rules as providing a ground or explanation of language.

For what has to be "explained" is, put flatly and bleakly, this:

> We learn and teach words in certain contexts, and then we are expected, and expect others, to be able to project them into further contexts. Nothing insures that this projection will take place . . . , just as nothing insures that we will make, and understand, the same projections. That on the whole we do is a matter of our sharing routes of interest and feeling, modes of response, senses of humor and of significance and of fulfillment, of what is outrageous, of what is similar to what else, what a rebuke, what forgiveness, of when an utterance is an assertion, when an appeal, when an explanation—all the whirl of organism Wittgenstein calls "forms of life." Human speech and activity, sanity and community, rest upon nothing more, but

nothing less, than this. It is a vision as simple as it is difficult, and as difficult as it is (and because it is) terrifying.[14]

In *The Claim of Reason* I develop this sense of shared interests, and judgments, and so forth, through a concept of what I note as our agreement or attunement in language.[15] Looking at that earlier passage now, I notice at once the image of human life as sharing certain "routes" of response, and as "rest[ing] upon" something—or is it resting upon nothing, as over an abyss, as the idea of the vision's being "terrifying" suggests? Am I saying there that human reason has, or that it has not, a foundation? And is my apparent wish to maintain the tension in this question (that is, to deny that it has, as it stands, one answer) the same as the tension Derrida apparently wishes to maintain on what seems the same issue? Is it the same issue? Or is there this decisive difference, that, following Wittgenstein, I am saying that explanations come to an end somewhere, each in its time and place, to be discovered philosophically, let us say, time after time, place by place. Whereas Derrida is following the path this opposes, or reverses, suggesting that there is a somewhere, as if some metaphysical space, at which all explanations come to an end, or else there is nowhere they end. Say he follows this path only to undermine it. Is this different? (If I make it explicit that in using phrases such as "bounded from" and "takes off from" I am experimenting a little with the title *Der Satz vom Grund*—I mean with the fact that *Satz* can mean "leap"—then I can put my recent question this way: Is the issue one of a leap [not of faith but, let us say, of reason] from a ground that is itself implied or defined by the leap? Or is the leap from grounds as such, to escape the wish for such definition [as if reason itself were a kind of faith]?)

And now the way is open for other questions of alignment. Is what Derrida means by the "space" in which a university is located the same in European as in American locations? He expects his space to be filled or spanned by a discourse on reason that invokes the names of Leibniz, Kant, Schelling, and Heidegger. Where I come from, I would not expect such a discourse to reach past the walls of one of our university departments, and it would mostly require spanning the distance between two such departments—carefully selected philosophy departments—hence, at least two places we call universities, in order to get its elements under very interested philosophical consideration. Does *this* span suggest *a* space? And if I were to emblematize the universities I have lived in, I would speak, for example, of Berkeley (and I would guess that more than one commencement speaker at Berkeley has taken the example) in terms of the geological fault that runs under its campus. This ties the campus to the fate of the remaining California coast, but is it not at the same time a feature continuous with the Cornell gorge? If I lived from a culture, call it France, the chief city of which had for some five centuries been producing world-historical literature, and which knew it, and fed the same samples of it to all the young who will occupy public positions, I would doubtless also be thinking of space as room and of some excavation or deconstruction in which to have my own thoughts. But here in North America room comes first, and it is always doubtful—apart from connections to the international world of science—whether our voices, without echo, can make it to one another across the smallest fields.

I have said or implied that the question—whether my question (about the resting of human reason and communication on nothing more, nor less, than shared attunement in the human voice) is or is not the same as Derrida's question concerning the foundation and the abyss of reason—is unanswerable in our philosophical-literary culture as it stands. And I have implied that I do not know whether many of you will recognize in this unanswerability a comparable puzzle of your own, amounting even, as for me it is seeming to do, to an intellectual crisis. But if you do find this in yourself, your thoughts or fantasies must turn, as mine have, to curricular matters, to educationally reparative possibilities. It is, as we say, no accident that Derrida's thoughts about universities also turn at a certain moment to institutional innovation, when he reports that at the request of the French government he is helping to set up an international college of philosophy in which, he adds at once, philosophy would not only be taught but questioned (see "PR," p. 16). And it is no accident that my thoughts are something like the reverse of his. For what is the point of questioning the subject of some profession, that of philosophy or that of literary studies (what subject is not in need of questioning?), when philosophy or literary studies, in my culture, are not common possessions but objects or subjects of fear and contempt for those who do not practice them? (Unless the idea is that what you teach is not philosophy unless it is—philosophically—questioned.)

My fantasy is of finding a way to repair the education of those of us who sense the need of reparation, a way of going back to the path not taken, not in order to change our direction or field for some other but to take the measure of our own, to see where, or how, maybe how often, the path not taken may have crossed our own—*is,* over long stretches, our own but so obscured by false or blocked perspectives as to be unusable to us. I do not know how this can be done, but I know it is not to happen by academic leaves to do what we have it at hand to do, painfully as we need them; nor by residence in some place alongside other residents, pleasant as that can be; nor by teaching across disciplines for the benefit of others, laudable as that is. I am talking about going back to school to one another, yielding for a moment, or a couple of months of moments, our professional autonomies. I want to know what you think it essential to know in order to do what you do; I mean I want you to show me, not just lecture me (as they almost say in show business), which means allow or trust me to know how to learn something new from watching honest work. And I want you to know something of what I think essential to what I do—for example, to spend the two dozen hours it would take to go sensibly over the opening half-dozen pages of the *Philosophical Investigations* and come to an end somewhere.

You may be pained, or pleased, by the so-called flight from theory; I am pained by what I might call the flight from the ordinary, which I think far scarier than theory. And if I find shameful your or your (literary) colleagues' readiness to undervalue (while you may abstractly overpraise) philosophy, I find it exactly as shameful that my (philosophical) colleagues are ready abstractly to overpraise (while they certainly undervalue) the experience of literature. There is a fear of experience that fully matches the fear of intellect, and professional students of literature and professional philosophers are each subject to both. My name for our lack of common ground in our otherness is the repression of Emerson and Thoreau as thinkers. For this repression students of philosophy and students of literature are jointly responsible. If we are unwilling to do something to mend our ways, make reparation of our bridges, I at least will remain without advice for students and young teachers who ask for places to study in which the philosophical and the literary paths are not unnaturally closed to one another.

POSTSCRIPT

In the discussion period after my talk, J. Hillis Miller joined issue with me in terms and in a spirit that I found amiable and useful, doubtless most useful where we had to leave matters most unresolved. Among other issues, he asked, if I understood him well, why I was so unmoving in my insistence on de Man's particular words of self-explanation to Geuss concerning a faithfulness to or a protectiveness of "canonical" reading. Since de Man was obviously being conciliatory, why did I persist in remaining unreconciled? Mightn't he just have meant what Miller himself sometimes feels like saying to critics of his criticism—that they should just read what he has written and not simply assume they know what he is going to say? My response was twofold.

1. Miller's appeal, real or imagined, to his readers is an understandable reaction to certain of one's less responsible, or especially distrustful, critics; and de Man, elsewhere in his reply to Geuss, does indeed enter an appeal against Geuss' implied charge that de Man is such a reader. Here, I was remembering the sense of such a passage as this: "The necessity to revise the canon arises from resistances encountered in the text itself (extensively conceived) and not from preconceptions imported from elsewhere" ("RRG," p. 384). But this hardly justifies de Man's advice to persist in the canonical as long as possible, especially not if I am right in taking his reply to Geuss as a whole to be exhibiting allegorically the exchange of philosophy and literary study—something that I said I found very congenial. In that light, de Man's self-description as, in effect, threatening the canonical (as from the elements—he speaks of Geuss' stance as "sheltering" the canonical ["RRG," p. 384]) must bear up as a philosophical claim within his literary practice, within its allegory of the struggle with, and for, philosophy.

2. A more specific claim to, or mark of, the philosophical—apart from accuracy in one's self-descriptions; I mean apart from a commitment to such descriptions as internal to the practice under description (a commitment I sometimes describe as necessitated by the realization that there is no metaphilosophy)—concerns what I spoke of as a "commitment to account philosophically for one's intellectual origination," indicating that this is another point in my feeling of kinship with the writing of de Man and of Derrida. It is in view of this concern that I imagined de Man's advice as constructed in answer to the specific criticism of willfulness and as the sort one might give to restive students beginning, and presumably puzzled in the face or gaze of, the study of deconstruction. My consequent trouble over the bit of advice is partly over its role in pedagogy, over how necessary such a statement may be in maintaining orderly discussion. No doubt the teaching of (certain) disciplines must begin with statements whose significance cannot be assessed by those submitting themselves to the discipline. But I have rather suggested that the statement of de Man's to which I took exception seems to resist any effort to clarify it sufficiently. Of course, it may be objected that, should that prove to be the case, this specific statement is not indis-

pensable, that others would serve as well. Naturally I do not deny this, but it is hardly for me to propose an alternative formula. I am assuming here only that we will all be prepared to worry over just which moments that seem essential to the teaching of our teaching we can afford to leave insufficiently clear or, say, unteachable.

It may be that my harping on de Man's remark about persistence simply exhibits the ticklish or overly suspicious disposition caused by my experiences, both as a student and as a teacher, in dealing with philosophical skepticism. In classes in epistemology during my student years, the presentation of the role of the senses (of seeing, this mostly came to) in establishing certainty in our judgments of the world was inevitably met—not in my mind alone—with a restive awareness of arbitrariness and abstractness, as if matters were forced upon our acceptance that for all the world are open to assessment by each of us: the power and revelation of skepticism, what Descartes calls our "astonishment" by it, depends upon its being producible without expertise or esotericism. Teachers would have to have at their command, accordingly, some gesture of philosophical conciliation in order to get on with the material. There were in those days something like four habitual such gestures: (1) to say that we are being asked to do something special, something more precise or advanced than the ordinary person ordinarily does, something therefore philosophical or even prescientific; or (2) to say that there are two senses of words like "see" not ordinarily noticed, in one of which senses we do not, contrary to our ordinary beliefs, see material objects; or (3) that we are not talking about real doubt but some fiction or philosophical facsimile of doubt; or (4) that we should keep our peace and see what comes. In the presence of the boredom and the bullying this philosophical diet entailed, Austin's question about the ordinary use of words could cause—I saw as well as felt this—the elation of liberation. The awful suspicion may or may not have supervened, two weeks or two decades later, that something important underlay those conciliatory gestures, and that Austin, in devoting himself to preventing this cause of boredom and (self-) bullying from running its course, in order to prevent its bad things from getting started, was mostly distracting us from the region of boredom, not clearing it up, hence not only keeping it in place but keeping us from sufficient philosophy.

Here enters what I suggested might be an oversuspiciousness on my part toward the conciliatory gesture I cited from de Man. In my classes, in broaching the subject of skepticism, it is the heart of the matter to have to say, to have always to come back to saying, something that sounds like "Persist in the canonical." In dissociating myself, or wishing to, from the academic teaching of skepticism that had caused the restiveness I speak of, I wish to say something like, "Be serious. Don't trade your interest in being born on earth for a messy theory. Persist in your birthright." But suppose what I manage to say on a given occasion takes the form, or the sound, of a further turn of conciliation (it would not seem a particular gesture; it seems fully undistinctive, anonymous) that any traditional epistemologist will have to make, to the effect that of course we all begin our lives, or anyway mostly continue them, in the belief that, for example, the world exists. Now to portray my relation to the world as one of *belief* is already to put my birthright up for exchange. It is something Wittgenstein and Austin might have called the first move in the metaphysical conjuring trick, the one that seems always already to have taken place. Which means, I may always already have fallen for it. (To know whether I have is not the beginning of philosophy but is a standing goal of philosophizing.) Something like this trouble over "belief" seems to me to go with the idea of the "canonical" in de Man's use of it to describe what he threatens. In thus naming the relation to the world (of reading) before he enters it critically, is de Man (are we to take it) marking the beginning of his investigative, antagonistic, reading or revealing part of its philosophical conclusion? That I do not find it a good conclusion is implied in my saying that I do not find that it applies to cases I recognize. That it is not a good beginning is implied in my speaking of a philosophical portrait that puts my birthright up for exchange—for the sense of "canonical" may itself be produced by the sense of oneself as threatening (a sense left undiagnosed), not the other way around, not by the canonical leaving itself vulnerable to what it excludes.[16]

I should like just to cite, before leaving the issue of philosophical defense, one of the earliest of my explicitly philosophical dissatisfactions with a self-definition used as a gesture of conciliation or compromise. (Since such things, in fact and in theory, go with, that is, are the opposites of, what I call "terms of criticism," I will call them "terms or modes of defense.") Because this dissatisfaction came in response to a move of Austin's, its coming was critical for me, even parabolic. The defense I have in mind here concerns a reply Austin gave to a member of the seminar on excuses he conducted at Harvard during the spring of 1955, while he was the William James Lecturer (presenting as his obligatory public lectures *How to Do Things with Words*). The seminar member had asked, in effect, why Austin's attention to the minutiae of words was important. (As if Austin carried the air of one examining the parasites living within the eyes of insects, while in fact he had failed to prove that he had so much as a sizable bug before him.) Austin replied, as I have recalled it: "I am often asked about importance. I generally like to say that importance is not important but that truth is." (Versions of this reply may be found in his "Ifs and Cans" and in "Pretending." Both occur at the end of their respective texts, as if taking up the question of importance were part of Austin's getaway.[17] At the close of his William James Lectures, he would cast this kind of glance back at the analogous question whether, and where, his lectures had touched on anything interesting.)

A couple of days later, in one of the private discussions Austin seemed then always to have time for as continuations of his classes or lectures, I took exception to that moment in the seminar, launching something of a tirade. I reconstruct it as follows: "Why did you dismiss that question, as if it could only be understood as hostile? You certainly do think that importance is important, you merely do not take what most of going philosophy considers to be important to be in human fact important. What you think is that genuine philosophy now must require a shift in what academic philosophers (or most traditional ones) permit to interest them, that is, to strike them as important. What's more, a habitual address of yours to language, forever asking for the reason (or context in which) a given question may be asked, or an assertion made, and so forth, is exactly an address to the *worth* of asking the question, making the assertion, and so forth, and this is exactly a way of asking for the importance of uttering things, taking importance as internal to the import of words, or their significance, hence as part of the coherence and meaning of using them when and as they are used." My reconstruction pretty clearly suggests that I was showing off (along with other matters, I assume); and in my immediate enthusiasm for Austin's work, I would have been wishing to distinguish myself from, even if also to protect, the outsider who had posed the question of importance and, reposing it myself, to declare myself already an insider to Austin's teaching.

It seems to me that an indefinitely large set of my commitments and turns in philosophy are condensed in the dissatisfactions (and satisfactions) of that moment—not just, for example, concerning terms of criticism, and the role of esotericism in (modern?) philosophy, and the nature of philosophical importance but concerning the necessity of, or willingness for, philosophical vulnerability or unguardedness, put it as the limits in saying why what you say is interesting (like explaining why what you have said is credible, or funny). Unguardedness here, accordingly, means that there is no defense of a philosophical teaching apart from continuing with it.

Some of the instruction I see in the moment I am recounting is contained in what I remember Austin's response to have been to my little tirade, perhaps in the very fact that I am uncertain of his response. I remember him saying: "They are already afraid the floodgates are opening." I know that he used these words to me more than once. The time I remember most clearly was after an hours-long discussion throughout which a very accomplished colleague (educated when *Principia Mathematica* was the last word, or the last of words, but about to give way to faster logic) had refused to concede that any word in a natural language was sufficiently clear to forward any philosophical thought. In application to the case in question now, from the excuses seminar, the motivation of Austin's words to me would have been less apparent. A reasonable gloss would take him to have wanted to leave room for the content of my tirade while at the same time indicating that it was not the sort of thing he was prepared to offer as an answer to the question of why what he did was important; that the question of importance was not philosophically to be answered, but, with a certain sympathy, rebuked; and that if its rebuke served to produce a tirade productive for me, it may be expected to prove equally productive for others.

I call this a reasonable gloss, but I do not think it would have been how I took Austin's reply at the time. The gloss depends on regarding him as having known all about the spirit of my tirade and taken it kindly; whereas I remember being alarmed that I had gone too far, and feared his disapproval. Why my imagination of his being generous toward me suffered deferral is, to my mind, a good question. Part of its goodness is to demonstrate the sense in which it is unimportant whether he used the familiar words about floodgates on the occasion of my tirade or whether I have transported them and made this conjunction on my own. If I have, that itself shows a certain faithfulness to what I learned from him. It shows, or confirms, that I thought of the exchanges we had at Harvard in 1955, together with those when he visited Berkeley for a semester four years later, as episodes of one conversation—one, I am always happy to discover again, that, from those times to the present, while not continual, continues.

4

To Place Wittgenstein

After publishing *The Claim of Reason* in 1979, Cavell wrote or taught on Wittgenstein—he here reports—"only on isolated occasions." This essay, written in 2001 for a special issue of the journal *Philosophical Investigations* commemorating the fiftieth anniversary of Wittgenstein's death, reflects on his first encounter with Wittgenstein's *Philosophical Investigations* and the reasons why "his words and example, such as I conceive them, are never far from my thinking."

WHILE MY PHILOSOPHICAL LIFE suffered a kink, to say the least, in encountering *Philosophical Investigations,* I at first, and repeatedly, shunned or resisted it. Having studied no philosophy as an undergraduate at Berkeley in the mid-1940s, except for a course in aesthetics, my first glimpses of the name Wittgenstein came, a couple of years later, after I had speculatively enrolled at UCLA (at that time, residence in California and thirty-four dollars per semester were the only requirements) perhaps to do graduate work in psychology. Finding Freud to be something of a figure of fun among the psychologists there, who were primarily experimentalists, I followed rumors of intellectual excitement over to the philosophy department, where the rumors seemed to me well founded, and began seeing Wittgenstein's name attached in footnotes to the *Tractatus,* always as a general influence, never, as I recall, to cite and interpret a passage. But upon finding a copy of that text I recognized rapidly, having had some experience of what a systematic education in

First published as a contribution to "On Wittgenstein" in *Philosophical Investigations* 24, no. 2 (2001): 89–96.

other fields might be, specifically in music and in literature, that philosophical illiteracy was not apt to be the best preparation for getting the most out of it. I don't remember ever hearing the name Wittgenstein in those years (perhaps it was mentioned in connection with truth-tables), but I did see it in another context, on the cover of a typescript in the UCLA departmental office called The Blue Book. (It was in the bottom drawer of a filing cabinet, where blank paper was stored.) Upon opening it and reading, "What is the meaning of a word?" and arriving at the answer, "Roughly: 'let's ask what the explanation of meaning is, for whatever that explains will be the meaning,'" I closed it abruptly. Obviously a question was being evaded: How can what we *say* have any bearing on, let alone constitute the clue to, what something *is*? I know distinguished philosophers who seem to me to have had a similar experience but never been moved to question it. Since the better part of a decade passed before I came to question it, I hope I have never underestimated the power of the experience. A cause of my thinking of my reaction as a resistance was its disproportionate violence—it was not simply a case of being unconvinced. And then the memory of opening the typescript of Wittgenstein's text would occasionally recur in my experience over the years, as if to nag my sense of its obvious irrelevance: something in it must have inspired the air of illicitness or inspiration in the wish to prepare a copy of it.

The overcoming of the particular sense or picture of language and world, whatever it had been, that made Wittgenstein's question seem obviously irrelevant, came not in reading Wittgenstein but in the seminar Austin gave on Excuses during the term he spent at Harvard, in the spring of 1955, to deliver that year's William James Lectures (on the performative utterance). That knowing the difference between doing something by mistake and by accident and the difference between a sheer or mere or pure or simple mistake or accident, or between doing something heedlessly and thoughtlessly and foolishly, was a matter of language, of what we called a mistake and an accident and what we mean when we say an act was heedless or thoughtless, *and* at the same time a matter of what mistakes and accidents *are,* now in turn became violently obvious—together with a sense of revelation that such examples, and a few score of others not unlike them, were nothing special, but representative of what we have to say everyday. My relation to my language—and my world—as such had been thrown into question. How to proceed in philosophy would never for me be the same. I had heard of conversion experiences, but I think I had never before had anything I would be willing to call such a thing, at least no shock that led to so sustained a period of work.

No part of that work, for some years, was concerned with trying to see the connection between my two fits of seeing opposite causes of the obvious—that language is not, and that it is, the thread to the real. That connection awaited my return to the *Blue Book* some three years later, beginning to teach at Berkeley, accepting the assignment to review it, together with the *Brown Book,* on their joint publication in 1958. I have elsewhere recounted beginning to read *Philosophical Investigations* when its translation appeared in 1953, in a discussion group at Harvard organized and led by Paul Ziff. I was impressed by what Ziff was saying, but the book itself seemed to me flat, and arbitrary in its progress. (This is another experience whose significance I hope I have not underestimated.) It's hard not to see this as resistance, given the sustained pressure that text will soon enough bring to bear upon my sense of philosophy; but initially it seemed something, as I have also reported, that I had already heard too many times in the writing of John Dewey, with its emphasis on context and use and the denial of privacy. While Dewey's pages no longer seemed to me images of what I wanted philosophy to be, Wittgenstein as yet offered no alternative.

This time the opening direction of the *Blue Book*'s questioning of the question of meaning no longer seemed dismissible, and the notes I was taking in response, or association, to reading Wittgenstein's texts were becoming so extended that much of a summer went by without my arriving at the end of an initial reading through of those two sets of dictated notes, together making up a volume so modest in bulk. What philosophy should and could be was reforming in my mind, but progress in seeing what had caused my change of perspective was halting. Things came to a head when Thompson Clarke and I offered a seminar jointly on the *Investigations* in the spring of 1960 and I began a course of lectures on the work the following fall. Clarke's use of something like Austin's sense of ordinary language rather in support than in denial of the force of skeptical questions seemed to me compelling and to shatter Austin's implied claim to have shown philosophy culpable of "having cast us out of the garden of the world we live in" ("Other Minds"). To deny, for example, when, after a bit of philosophical softening up, I am asked whether I see *all* of an apple, that I am at best puzzled and at worse have to answer No—to deny this (as Austin must) seemed to me dishonest, anyway uncandid. It is true that the question and the answer are forced, but to say how they are forced, and forced to a particular conclusion, and what language is that it can be forced in these ways, were long and necessary roads ahead. The *Investigations* was the work of philosophy I knew, within touch of the tradition of analytical philosophy, to which my education was committed, that did not deny my experience of such matters, that indeed encouraged, or liberated one for, an interest in one's experience more generally that so much of the work of philosophy, as I was exposed to it, seemed to discount or deplore.

The roads in exploration of skeptical questions would prove, over the next decade, to lead to my claim of the *Investigations* as a work written not to refute skepticism, but to uncover its possibility, and allure, which incurred the necessity of reconceiving skepticism's self-interpretation as a thesis announcing, let's say, the discovery of the uncertainty or groundlessness of empirical knowledge. In a sense the *Investigations* accepts the experience of groundlessness (while it questions the need for a generalized ground or stratum in experience or in language—this much can be found in Austin) and it goes on, one could say, to reassign our being cast out from the garden of the world not to the folly of philosophers but to the possession of language, not to our lack of certainty but to our disappointment with certainty itself, our unappeasable discomfort (Hegel, I believe, calls this restlessness) with finitude. It is we who cast ourselves adrift from the world. (Language's temptation to its own defeat is not something Austin interested himself in. He would doubtless have disapproved of the formulation.)

Working this out, for me, circled around attempts to reconceive the nature of what Wittgenstein appeals to in the idea of a criterion, as the pivot on which the possibility of skepticism, in its repudiation of the ordinary, rests; hence as precisely powerless to defeat skepticism, the role to which other philosophers had wished to assign it. I had arrived at a fairly stable conception of such matters by the early 1970s, represented in the first three parts of my *Claim of Reason*.

What became part 4 of that book was a further story, still fully within my attempt to inherit, or receive, the event of the *Investigations* in Western philosophical culture. While I moved in that part concentratedly to further topics, especially that of privacy and of other minds, I was evidently determined, having been so fundamentally affected by Wittgenstein's text, to explore not merely the topics it proposed, and transfigured, but the mode in which it presented them, the fact of its remarkable writing. While it was clear enough that the writing was essential to what was convincing, not to say transforming, about the thinking of the *Investigations,* it was not only a difficult matter to describe and assess, but it was pedagogically forbidden territory. I mean, in part, literally that I refused to allow students to submit papers for my courses on Wittgenstein that concentrated on what could conveniently be called its metaphilosophical remarks (as for example those from sections 90–133). I knew from experience that such concentration led to what seemed an evasion of the work in the *Investigations,* but I never felt satisfied to say just that in justification of my prohibition since clearly those passages are not evasions within Wittgenstein's text.

On several occasions, given my background, I cited Schoenberg's pedagogy, which concentrated on training in classical fundamentals, not in his atonal and twelve-tone compositional departures. This went along with my having, from the first of the lectures I started in 1960, described the *Investigations* as a modernist work, on a par with Wittgenstein's contemporaries among European novelists, painters, and composers, one whose relation to the past is problematic and internal to its procedures, and somehow causes a perpetual self-preoccupation. But this was of limited usefulness, even as an aside, as modernism gave way to other cultural preoccupations (among them postmodernism) and as I began to relate the work of the *Investigations* to other writers exploring the everyday—Emerson, Thoreau, Wordsworth, Beckett, Chehkov—and among Wittgenstein's contemporary anti-metaphysicians, to Heidegger.

My solution, in the concluding part of *The Claim of Reason,* was in practice to let Wittgenstein's writing inspire a sequence of experiments in allowing my experience to collect more freely in parables and to associate more unpredictably in examples and in literary reference than I had allowed myself previously. For precisely the freedom to consult my own experience, to register whatever intimation of intellectual duress I felt in philosophical argumentation, to counter whatever degree of falsification I felt in the formulation of a philosophical problem, in a word to speak philosophically about what mattered to me even when it was something my education had trained me to think of as irrelevant, trivial, or transient, was essential to what I was grateful for in Wittgenstein's writing. If, for example, in that writing I find it significant that the work begins not with its own but with an other's voice (Augustine's); or find that Augustine's childhood memories of learning language give the impression of the child as invisible to his elders and in effect as stealing language from them; or that the primitive language of section 2 strikes me as a language of primitives, of early man, and that I imagine them intoning their four words as sluggishly as I imagine them to move; or that the image of the spade that is turned after justifications have come to an end is an image both of a tool of cultivation and of a writer's pen; then I will say so, even when I am not in the moment able to say how or why these impressions may be significant. And that means that I will have to voice these reactions as sufficiently remarkable to demand returning to.

After publishing the material that went into *The Claim of Reason,* in 1979, I have written directly and concentratedly about Wittgenstein only on isolated occasions (to publish my early lecture notes on the opening of the *Investigations;* to suggest what might be called an aesthetics of the writing in that work; to respond to the idea of the work as that of a criticism of culture), and taught the *Investigations* (the only text of Wittgenstein's that I have lectured on systematically) more rarely still. But his words and example, such as I conceive them, are never far from my thinking. How could they fail to be, given that they represent for me not merely an agenda of topics or problems—though I keep being astonished at the topics to be discovered there—but an attestation that convincing philosophy, something that is neither one of the sciences nor one of the arts, is still urgently called for, so far as I feel I have a contribution to make to that urgency?

Since what I called Wittgenstein's encouragement to consult and register my own experience (as though philosophy threatened to deny it to me, a charge that Dewey roughly leveled at the classical empiricists) expanded for me into an encouragement to follow my experience of film, of Shakespearean tragedy, of American transcendentalism, etc., but in each case to follow them as part of what I had to say philosophically. I should say that when fragments of Wittgenstein's thought continue to appear in my texts, they are not meant to authorize my methods or conclusions but often to serve as periodic checks that I am continuing to grasp the thread of philosophy, leading to some form that my contemporaries might approve. That the claim to philosophy has become inherently questionable is part of my conviction about philosophy. So it will, as recently, fall to me to be asked, for example, whether Walter Benjamin is to be considered a philosopher. To get past the "in a sense yes and in a sense no" response, I note that Benjamin is alive to the question of whether I am in possession of my own experience, or instead follow dictations laid down by profession or by fashion or by some more private identification; and I add that when he speaks of the characteristic melancholy of German baroque tragedy, he associates it with the classical iconography of Melancholy, which includes the dog, the stone, and the sphere, I note that these images figure in the *Investigations,* all in contexts bearing on skepticism. May this be seen to have some bearing on the characteristic tones of the *Investigations,* its moments of strangeness, disappointment, madness, perverseness, and so on? I feel I am being confirmed in an old claim of mine about an internal connection between tragedy and skepticism, now not in the direction of Shakespearean tragedy as a tale of the consequences of doubt or jealousy, but of the quest for knowledge as an enactment of tragedy.

So what? Am I prepared to conclude that Benjamin is a philosopher if Wittgenstein is one? I am much more interested in whether the way I have arrived at the conjunction has created philosophy in me. And in the fact that it was in reading Benjamin that I asked myself what, if anything, is interesting about the fact of the number of animals in the *Investigations*—beyond the dog, there is the lion, and a goose, and a couple of cows, not to mention the beetle and the fly and the duck / rabbit. This should seem quite in order in a philosopher one of whose fundamental appeals is to what he calls life forms, and one of whose philosophical aims is to unfold the life form of what he calls talkers—that is, us—but it might make us wonder why animals figure so limitedly in other philosophers, at most, if memory serves, in some abstract contrast with the human.

I hope these reflections have gone far enough to raise again the question, or difficulty, I have in thinking of teaching the *Investigations.* It is, as I have insisted from my first remarks about the book decades ago, clear that it is, whatever else, a book of instruction; but how it is itself to be taught is anything but clear. To approach it from the *Tractatus* is one method. To move through it section by section is another. Following, perhaps adjudicating, arguments among interpreters of the text is another. But these familiar protocols are not what I mean. How it is to be taught is a matter of where and when it is to be taught. I know of philosophy departments in which it goes untaught, and others in which it is a shared atmosphere. Neither seems to me a fully reasonable pedagogical solution. To what? To the fact that the work can remain an uninteresting mystery even to diligent students, and to others can become a weapon, or inoculation, against all other philosophy. This suggests that my early experiences of resistance and conversion remain issues in entering the text. But that only redescribes the question, which is whether such a text (as I see it) fits comfortably into an academic philosophical curriculum.

I have no answer to the question, beyond the sage advice to have students begin its study only in conjunction with canonical figures in the history of philosophy, whose works have their own powers of attraction. (Another tip:

Have the good fortune I have had in finding friends with whom discussions about Wittgenstein, among other matters, remain inspiring.) But not to avoid the question, I ask that it raise the further question of the role of philosophy in the modern research university, an institution that serves so perfectly the cooperativeness (or competitiveness) and progressiveness of science and of social or humanistic research, and where the arts are, let's say, necessary luxuries. Philosophy as such is apt there to find itself in a state of discomfort, however much it would be missed, unless it claims for itself the status of a chapter of science. But this is perhaps the last status Wittgenstein would have desired, and though compelled, as philosophers seem almost inescapably to be, to teach or exchange their thoughts, the role of professor was one he evidently could not endure.

5

Notes after Austin

This brief memoir about Cavell's relationship with J. L. Austin was first published in the *Yale Review*, in an issue that brought together what, in his autobiographical *Little Did I Know*, Cavell described as "a collection of memoirs of various figures from various hands in 1987, calling them Encounters." Each memoir in the issue, which was subsequently published as a book, is a combined portrait of the author and his or her subject. Cavell went on to integrate a portion of this text, his first sustained autobiographical effort, into *Little Did I Know.*

WHEN IN THE EARLY 1950S I came from California to Harvard for graduate study in philosophy, the grip of logical positivism was loosening a little with age and success. The new thing in question—this was before the translation into English of Wittgenstein's *Investigations,* and while Heidegger and Continental philosophy in general were still largely rumor to American philosophers—was the so-called philosophy of ordinary language, represented by a seemingly endless supply of papers from a seemingly endless supply of talented philosophers at Oxford. Many young teachers of philosophy here, and, it seemed, most of the really promising graduate students I was meeting, were finding ways to spend at least a year working at Oxford. I had not wanted to. I was too unsettled in my relation to the profession of philosophy to know whether time at Oxford or rather in France and Germany was more to the point for me.

Versions of this essay were published as "Notes after Austin" in *Yale Review* 76, no. 3 (1987): 313–322, and in *Encounters,* ed. Kai Erikson (New Haven: Yale University Press, 1989), 116–123.

Then after J. L. Austin came to Harvard as the William James Lecturer in the spring of 1955, I felt I already had a life's work ahead of me—at least so far as the claim of the ordinary, that mode of thinking of which he was the purest representative, would enter it. The purity was clear enough from his essay "Other Minds," a miniature encyclopedia of ordinary language concerns; and it was testified to by tales from those returning each year from Oxford about the weekly discussions Austin held for the young teachers of philosophy there, one of which he reportedly gave over entirely to the distinction between signing "Yours sincerely" and "Yours truly." But it took his presence for me to come to experience his inexhaustible interest in what he called the jump of words—an interest arising (I of course supposed) from an inexhaustible faith in the philosophical yield of the details of the language we share and that shares us, and yet a faith that also turned in a direction somewhat opposite, to face the concerns of linguists and of poets. Like linguistics and poetry, Austin's philosophizing, I felt, allowed me—demanded of me—the use of myself as the source of its evidence and as an instance of its conclusions. Whatever philosophy's pertinence to me, I felt for the first time my pertinence to philosophy; I stopped looking for ways to leave the subject.

The year after Austin's semester at Harvard I returned to California to begin teaching, so it happened that I was present with Austin also during the other semester he spent in America, at Berkeley in 1959, the year before he died, not yet fifty. My memories of him are accordingly solely and fully American.

I have had other teachers, as well as friends and students, with wider learning, or greater creative sweep, or smarter powers of reasoning, but I have encountered no one with a clearer and more constant fastidiousness of mind, joined with a respect for the vicissitudes of daily life—call it moral imagination. The thinkers I admire most have this joint power. Sometimes, I know, I prefer thinking that allows more of the darkness of its findings to appear than Austin's does. But I suppose darkness is nothing, or useless, without something of the lightness, the freedom of mind, that Austin demanded of himself and expected of his students. I had after college "given up" (so I called it) music for philosophy. Working in Austin's classes was the time for me in philosophy when the common rigors of exercise acquired the seriousness and playfulness—the continuous mutuality—that I had counted on in musical performance. This may have meant to me that what was happening in Austin's classes was not, as it lay, quite philosophy; but I was at the moment too happy with whatever it was to have cared. That Austin's practice had to do, in its own way, with the possession of an ear, was surely part of its authority for me. (Here I have to think through the fact that my mother was a professional pianist, with perfect pitch, while my father was musically illiterate.)

———————————

Others found Austin cold. Of the legends that formed around him a number had to do with a quality that might strike you as coldness, but perhaps rather as reserve or even strictness. Some concerned a certain awe he inspired by his work in army intelligence during the Second World War. Then there was the story about Austin as eccentrically pure teacher, told by a colleague with whom he gave one of his classes. Attendance had fallen with each week's session until at the final meeting, before Christmas break, it fell to zero. The colleague made as if to leave, but Austin insisted—stated rather, or perhaps simply reminded them both—that they had contracted themselves to do philosophy for this period, and that he intended to do it. So the two of them talked philosophy together for the assigned time. I experienced Austin's relentlessness over the course of falling attendance at his William James Lectures, the primary obligation of his invitation to Harvard. The lectures were entitled "How to Do Things with Words." How, I felt, could it have dawned on so few a number—not more at the end than one in twenty of the several hundred who had begun the course, or anyway who came to the initial lecture—that something of world-historical significance was happening here? But there are worse forms and causes of reception. And some people knew. Enough.

I also experienced a version of the strictness. Already full of admiration for Austin, and already feeling some credit with him for my knack at producing examples he found pertinent, I responded impatiently, during a discussion at lunch in Adams House with a circle of students, to a question concerning whether something must be common to things sharing a common name, saying, in effect, "If people want to say there are universals, let them. It doesn't matter as long as they know the facts." I was sitting next to Austin, and he turned toward me as if startled, and said hard, straight between the eyes, "It matters." I felt an utter, quite impersonal, shame—shame, and a kind of terror, as if before the sacred task of philosophy, for having been faithless to its calling. Whatever the values to be assessed in this exchange, whatever the chances of illusion or romance, personal coldness is hardly the issue. How could mere coldness have lasted, have profited me, to this moment?

Rarely in a lifetime can one know intellectual gratitude of the kind I felt toward Austin after his first seminar meeting on the subject of excuses. I left elated, as if I had been shown a route out of the realm of arbitrary, massive demands for consent, as if I were tasting intellectual liberty, my own intelligence, for the first time. No doubt it was not the first; and it will not be the last. But it remains astounding that it happened with respect to such seemingly trivial matters. Those matters remain as hard to convey as ever, but (to my mind) it is no less necessary to continue to try to do so.

The matter of ordinary language philosophy—its content, so to speak—is trivial, is nothing, without its method(s). In practice the gratitude for the seminar was for the continuous pleasure of discovery and agreement, for the community of purpose Austin's work suggested as he laid out a geography of concepts ranging from the tyrants of philosophical thought—intention, will, consequence, reality—to the all but unnoticeable workers and operatives of everyday thinking life, such as heedlessness, thoughtlessness, inadvertence, and the mistaken and the accidental. He was going over matters he had gone into more thoroughly than anyone else; he was a master of something. This was no longer the provision of a great result or paradigm of philosophical thought such as Russell's Theory of Descriptions, building on Frege's invention of the quantifier, which we were then to apply with endless unoriginality to a thousand identical situations. The questions raised, on Austin's sphere, are to be decided by us, here and now. No one knows more about what mistakes and accidents are, or heedlessness or lack of thought, than we do, whatever we think we do or do not know. It is a frightening, exhilarating prospect.

Sometimes I disliked Austin's handling of contention. Not even he could always get beyond the note of the personal, of fear produced from outside, as from mere force, and not from my sense that I am bound to know, that somehow one already knew. But to my mind there were moments in Austin's seminar of perfect spiritual tact, as on the day, after his stories to distinguish among excuses such as doing something mistakenly, accidentally, heedlessly, and so forth, when he distinguished among modifiers such as something's being just or simply or purely an accident (one, say, in which nothing further, or nothing more complex, is in play, or mixed in) and a mere or sheer accident (one to which you could be assigning undue significance, or one whose accidental quality is transparent). A student interjected that *sheer* could not mean *transparent* because there is such a thing as sheer wool. Austin was taken by surprise, lifted his pipe from his mouth, and asked intently, "Is there? What is it?" The answer began immediately, but continued with a distinct ritardando: "Well, it's a weave you can see through." It was the sort of shocking moment, here in the hilarity of its sheer contradiction, that might cause conversion. Indeed it is my view that the power of the philosophical appeal to ordinary language is always only to be appreciated by an overcoming of resistance, which is to say by conversion—an appreciation, I mean, at once of the apparent triviality of the appeal and of the radical revelation of its successes. Without now seeking to comprehend the state of the student who as it were did not know that *sheer* continued to go with *transparent* even when applied to wool (as if the very meaning of wool contains the idea of opacity and as if mere ordinary words, such as *mere* or *sheer,* could not possibly be so controlled as for example to transfer their figure and everyday energy intact, without our realizing it, from silk or cotton to wool); and without now seeking to formulate the state of the student's understanding that the transfer had after all happened (as if the prior state of conviction that it could not happen is part of our agreement that what happens to us is inherently trivial, that we live as if our daily experience were not ours, or just because ours, of no general significance): I recall here the moment of Austin's response to the explanation, "Well, you can see through it," a moment I described as of spiritual perfection. The eyes that had been fixed wide with attention were now almost closed, and wrinkled at the corners, with satisfaction; the lips were pursed as if to keep from letting forth laughter; and the pipe came back up, the tip not quite to the mouth but to be punched lightly and repeatedly against the chin. Here was serious mirth in progress, and what I read as perfection was the projection of my utter faith, then and now, that the mirth was impersonal, that here a class had witnessed not the private defeat of an individual's experience but the public victory of sweet and shared words—mirth over the happy fact that the world is working out and that we are made for it. I suppose I again romanticize a moment. Then a form my gratitude to Austin takes is for the power of such moments, and successors of them, to bear this romance.

My daughter Rachel was two years old the fall Austin was in Berkeley. He once came to our house carrying a box of colored pencils and a drawing tablet, neither of them wrapped, and after saying hello went at once to the coffee table, knelt on the floor before it, and began to draw. Rachel joined him and received some pencils and paper in case she too wanted to draw. By the time they finished comparing sketches it was somehow clear whose pencils and papers these had become.

Seeing this and knowing that Austin had four children (his devotion to his family and to his farm were also the subjects of legend) I was moved to mention something to him that I felt pressed by and which I was not able to talk to others productively about. I said in effect that I found myself full of philosophical confusion and ambition that I would gladly give all my time to, and found myself at the same time glad to be committed for a lifetime to caring for a child. A banal anxiety, no doubt itself as confused as my feelings about philosophy. What Austin said was: "They keep one young." Was that a wise or a banal (call it merely an ordinary) thing to say? I found it better than either, because responsive. It responded to my evident wish to know how he handled the issue, or rather whether it was an issue for him. I took his response to signify that it was of course an issue, that I was not silly to feel pressed by it, but that since, like him, I was a father, I had better accept that fact into my normal day—into (if it comes to that) my philosophical confusion and ambition. And I took him further to be offering some such piece of advice as this: Do not expect or need to say or to hear something interesting about what is not out of the ordinary; the struggle you speak of is common, and the struggle is worthwhile. But that is exactly, so I felt and feel, what I wanted to hear from him.

Someone may take it that I draw too much Zen out of this plainness. Then still once more that is a form my gratitude bears toward Austin, a form it is for me to know he would bear.

Something of the gratitude can arise fresh at any time I feel the pretension and emptiness of the din of claims to advanced theories (say, in the field of literature, among others) that seem to me at once to know nothing of the difficulties of plainness and to function as defenses against them. And then there is another level of gratitude for Austin's plainness—his philosophical willingness to be ignorant. If sometimes this meant he did not wish to muse upon the darker side of the world, it also showed his healthy terror of it—he whose expertise in army intelligence concerned German matters—along with his contempt for those who toy with it, as perhaps he felt Wittgenstein too much did, or encouraged.

I write this on the flight back from a week's glimpse of Japan. During the obligatory twenty-four hours in Kyoto I learn, after a fragmentary Bunraku puppet performance, that a conference on Zen Buddhism is in progress there.

It is for me to know the un-Zen-like spirit in which the thought crossed my mind that Austin's work would probably not have been cited at this conference. (I have some sense of why business gets big, and why big physics is called for; but what good are big theology and big philosophy?)

The Bunraku puppet that was presented for us—a female figure named Oshichi in a gorgeous robe—was carried centrally by one man, with her robes and props managed by two additional men whose bodies were completely clothed and whose heads completely wrapped in black cloth (were they men?). The moment of crisis is brought on by Oshichi's reading a letter. Who reads the letter? Reading here is an intentional act. Whose intention is it? I believe Austin would have accepted an answer that I believe Wittgenstein would have accepted: "*She* reads it, of course," meaning Oshichi. But Austin's reserve must be imagined in play. He is on record as urging such thoughts as this: You can say a cloud looks exactly like a camel (he may even have allowed that a cloud can *be* a camel) exactly because you know that a cloud is not (and looks nothing like) a camel. Here you glimpse something of what the concept of looking like depends on: an unquestioned sense of the practical systems of contrasts between realities and appearances, not on one general contrast between appearances and nonappearances. And I imagine he might have been willing to urge this: You can say Oshichi reads the letter exactly because you know that the puppet—the thing in gorgeous cloth worked by three men—is not a thing that reads. Here you glimpse something of what the concept of intention depends on: an unquestioned sense of who owns the intentions of one's actions, which seems to suppose that one owns one's actions, or at least some of them. Suppose I say that in the case of the puppet you do not know—are meant not to know—whether the puppet obeys the men or, since every movement of the men serves the demands of the puppet, whether the men obey the puppet. If life were this way ordinarily, our concept of intention would in a sense be empty, hollowed out. That Austin would perhaps not affirm this possibility is to my mind less important than that his writing, in the very goodness of its humor, is at every moment obedient to it.

I would like to assume that anyone interested in such matters will see, or come to see, in the response I have imagined, its bearing on the communications Derrida and Searle traded some years ago concerning Austin's disturbed footnote that remembers—as if suddenly—some hollowness in performative utterances on, among other places, the stage. From that date Austin seems to have come under the protection rather of the literary than of the philosophical profession. Whatever the justice here, the cost of this protection—so far—has been, from my angle, exorbitant, because the literary profession takes it—so far—that ordinary language is contrasted in Austin with *literary* language, whereas its contrast and contest is with words as they appear in *philosophy* (if you can spot that). Austin for the literary profession is to that extent not real but toy or stuffed or a decoy.

The time of Austin's departure from Harvard came within a few days of the Society of Fellows annual picnic and softball game. I thought Austin might enjoy ending on this note among others, and he accepted my invitation with interest. When we arrived the softball game was already in progress and it was somehow understood that if we wished to play, we should join the team batting and take our at bats at once. Austin could have seen enough from the play as we approached the field to recognize roughly what the batter was meant to do, if not fully why; if he had not seen enough he would decline. In response to my hesitating glance and gesture toward home plate, Austin walked to it, took off his suit jacket and laid it neatly aside on the grass, leaving his tie in place and his French cuffs closed. His stance seemed stiff, the knees were too straight and the bend from the waist crowded the plate. I felt certain he was going to swing at the first pitch if he could possibly react to it— there was no umpire and he was informed that he could look at pitches without cost to himself. He hit the pitch sharply over the second baseman's head and as he rounded first he touched the base smartly with his hand. I thought he should have stopped there but he made it to second standing up. I was of all things most surprised by how fast he was, and as I write this I still seem to see him standing on second with a trace of a smile, as if with an appropriate pride at a moment exactly realized, the world working out and we made for it.

That was thirty-two years ago, outside Boston. Half a century before that, in Poland, outside Bialystok, there had evidently been no call for my father, about fourteen the year his family sailed for America, to learn to hit to the opposite field. But I have known for a while now that my affinity for ordinary language philosophy and Austin's practice of it was prepared by my father's reaching, say, the point of my birth with no language ordinary or natural to him (the old gone or frozen, the new broken from the beginning); and by his nevertheless being famous in our small circle as I was growing up for his ability to tell stories full of leavening pleasure in a life on the move, and of argumentative pertinence. So he was part of the conditions of felicity in my invitation to Austin to that picnic, part of why I was in the position to extend it. Then, reciprocally, Austin's happy double entered into and has eased the long journey of forgiving my father his suffering.

PART II | Assignments

| 6

Silences Noises Voices

This lecture was delivered in October 1996 at a celebration at the Maison des Écrivains, in Paris, on the occasion of the publication of *Les Voix de la Raison* (1996), the French translation of *The Claim of Reason*. This translation, by Sandra Laugier and Nicole Balso, was followed by translations into Italian, German, and Spanish. The French translation provided *The Claim of Reason* with what Cavell called "a new life" and gave him the opportunity to reflect on its origins.

WHAT COULD I HAVE BEEN THINKING, those months ago when I was asked for a title for my remarks tonight, in proposing the words "Silences Noises Voices"? Imagining the occasion on which I would see *The Claim of Reason* appear in French, I surely would have wanted to commemorate the painful elaboration of detail in that text marking the dangerous geography in which human urgency has to find its intelligibility. Moreover, my gratitude for having this occasion of remembering would have magnified my sense of danger, because the presence of my teacher J. L. Austin and of the later Wittgenstein in my text extends their desire, almost to obsessiveness, to depose philosophy's chronic efforts to neutralize the contexts of human utterance, as if neutralization would make our utterances pure. Extends their efforts, for are not nations, or do they not remain, contexts, and

A version of this essay was published as "Silences Noises Voices," in *Future Pasts: The Analytic Tradition in Twentieth-Century Philosophy,* ed. Juliet Floyd and Sanford Shieh (Oxford: Oxford University Press, 2001), 351–358.

is not the occasion of translation one in which the difference of context is limitlessly at stake?—every passage to communication becoming a barrier to it. A text in translation has the chance of a new life. A speech of gratitude for that chance has only its present moment in which to give thanks for that new life. The odds of doing the moment justice are vanishing.

Considering those title words at this distance, as I set down my thoughts for this occasion—Silences Noises Voices—they seem to me to name the perceptual preoccupations of a child in a haunted house. Perhaps I wanted this resonance all along, since it is a fair way of describing a register of Thoreau's experience at Walden, not a fear of his surroundings but a sense of the strangeness and morbidity in the way his fellow townsmen inhabit their town; and also a way of capturing Emerson's experience of what he calls our "chagrin" in response to "every word they [his neighbors] say." Emerson claims indeed that in their fear of their own words they miss the discovery of their existence and hence can be said to haunt the world. (So, at any rate, I claimed for Emerson's words when he dawned on me as a philosopher; it was the year *The Claim of Reason* was published.)

No doubt I was also recalling specific occurrences of noises in my book, as when it justifies the traditional epistemologist's fastidiousness (however much it seeks to avoid the animus of skepticism) by remarking, "There are not *just* noises in the air," in which I am commenting on the human being's responsibility for making sense of every particle or corpuscle of his or her experience. And I would have recalled the passage in Wittgenstein's *Philosophical Investigations*[1] in which he dramatizes this moral by inviting the image or memory of a noise we might produce:

> What reason have we for calling "S" the sign for a *sensation*? For "sensation" is a word of our common language, not of one intelligible to me alone. So the use of this word stands in need of a justification which everybody understands.—And it would not help either to say that it need not be a *sensation*; that when he writes "S", he has *something*—and that is all that can be said. "Has" and "something" also belong to our common language.—So in the end when one is philosophizing one gets to the point where one would like just to emit an inarticulate sound.—But such a sound is an expression only as it occurs in a particular language-game, which should now be described. (§ 261)

There could hardly be a stronger indication from Wittgenstein of his recognition of the dominance of the signifier. Even the expression of philosophical inarticulateness, my reduction to making a noise, is subject to its law.

And I know other noises that would have been on my mind—for example, the noises in the attic that the woman in Cukor's film *Gaslight* refuses to name, which are therefore cause and consequence of her maddening loss of all words and desires of her own; and the noises the wife in another of Cukor's films, *Adam's Rib,* hears her husband make in the night, whose interpretation she is willing to name and which leads her to take him to court.

But certainly I would have wanted my title words to evoke the earliest essay of mine in which I describe the experience of encountering Wittgenstein's *Philosophical Investigations* and characterize its all but incessant dialogues as occurring between two voices (at least) which I characterize as the voice of temptation and the voice of correctness and which I take to have two insistent implications: that since both voices are Wittgenstein's, neither is his (exclusively); and that there is a beyond of these voices, a before and an after, occupied in Wittgenstein's prose by parables, paradoxes, fantasies, aphorisms, and so on, which do not and did not strike me as expressing identifiable voices exactly but which I did not know then how to characterize further. That essay of mine formed the introduction to my doctoral thesis, large parts of which, sixteen years after it was submitted for my degree, were reconfigured, and much of the remainder of it hammered apart for certain irreplaceable elements, to become about half of what appears as *The Claim of Reason.*

The original introduction was dropped and was to be replaced by an account precisely of that beyond of the voices, the place, as it were, out of which they arise. In the lectures I had begun offering on Wittgenstein at the time I was writing my thesis, I characterized that sense of origin as expressed in a recognition that philosophy does not speak first, that it maintains silence, that its essential virtue is not assertiveness (since it has no information of its own to impart) but responsiveness, awake after all the others have fallen asleep. The *Investigations,* for example, begins with the words of someone else, St. Augustine's description of, in effect, the silence of infancy, wandering among the elders whose powers of expression it is fated, and seeks blindly, to adopt. When a few years ago I got around to publishing my notes on those lectures,[2] mostly those concerning the beginning moments of the *Investigations,* I accounted for not having included them, as planned, as a new introduction to *The Claim of Reason* on the ground that the book was already too long. I might have said it was because I had not yet arrived at an understanding of the other silence (if it is other) at the other pole of the beyond of voice in the *Investigations,* the silence not out of which philosophy arises but the silence in which philosophical problems, according to Wittgenstein, end—he calls it peace.

Wittgenstein refers to this end of philosophy as the achievement, or construction, of perspicuous presentation, something that he claims captures the sense of the form in which he casts his philosophizing. The arrival at perspicuous presentation is applied by Wittgenstein characteristically to the work of mathematical proof; only once does he apply it to the work of the *Investigations* as a whole. And it is only within the past year or two that I have been able to articulate to my satisfaction how the concept of perspicuousness applies no more precisely to Wittgenstein's interpretation of the mathematical than to his use of the aphoristic—which is to say, to the most obviously literary passages of the *Investigations*—as when its work describes itself as showing the fly the way out of the fly-bottle, or speaks of the human body as the best picture of the human soul.

But my inability to relate satisfactorily the silences that surround philosophy can hardly be what prevented my broaching the subject at the time I was trying to let go of my *Claim of Reason.* A truer account seems to have awaited the context of my speaking in France. I wonder if I can say briefly how I see this.

The silence in which philosophy begins is the recognition of my lostness to myself, something Wittgenstein's text figures as the emptiness of my words, my craving or insistence upon their emptiness, upon wanting them to do what human words cannot do. I read this disappointment with words as a function of the human wish to deny responsibility for speech.

The silence in which philosophy ends is the acceptance of the human life of words, that I am revealed and concealed in every word I utter, that when I have found the word I had lost, that is, displaced from myself, it is up to me to acknowledge my reorientation (Wittgenstein describes the work of philosophy as having to turn our search around, as if reality is behind us), that I have said what there is for me to say, that this ground gained from discontent is all the ground I have, that I am exposed in my finitude, without justification. ("Justifications come to an end," is a way Wittgenstein says it.) That the end of philosophy here occurs as a punctuation within philosophy, that it is dictated neither by the conclusion of a proof nor of a system, that philosophy is brought so inconsequential a form of peace (to bring which to philosophy Wittgenstein pronounces with pride) is the hardest news for

Wittgenstein's readers to accept. The news is expressed by his announcing that philosophy has no place to advance theses. What is hard in this news is that being at the end of my words strikes me as my being at the end of my life, exposed to death. It was just this past summer in Paris that I noted, in response to a request to describe my interest in *Philosophical Investigations,* that taking as a rough measure the 693 sections of the first and longest part of the *Investigations,* philosophy there comes to an end 693 times. I had noted that fact on other occasions, for various purposes. But this time I found myself going on to say that its endings are so many deaths to so many issues whose fervor has come to nothing, a nothing that Wittgenstein calls the ordinary; it is a field that we have never occupied. If—I went on then—one can say that this is Wittgenstein discovering philosophy as learning how to die, learning my separateness (I do not know whether Wittgenstein had read Montaigne), then one can say that arriving at the ordinary is its companion teaching of the commonness of our humanity. Putting these thoughts together, it seemed right to say that in ordinary language philosophy the ordinary is the scene of recognition of one's own death. Saying such a thing for the first time seems to be a condition for knowing it.

Why was it, as it seems, necessary for me to leave home in order to say and know that? What presents itself as unsayable at home, as if there what urges silence is not alone the fear of illogicality but of indecorousness? Have I, in finding the immeasurable relief of translation, found another or a truer home?

I learn from the review of *Les Voix de la Raison* in *Le Monde* that I am spoken of by some of my American colleagues as a continental philosopher. Part of what I mean by the relief of translation is that in Europe I am taken as an American philosopher. The relief lies not in the correctness of either description but in the fact of their conflict, confirming my conviction of my role as insisting where I can on the split within the philosophical mind. It is something I have known about myself since at least the moment I recognized that Heidegger's characterization of the human task as one of dwelling, finding home, is intimately contradicted in Thoreau's dramatizing of its task as leaving home, the thing Emerson names abandonment, meaning both a yielding and a departure.

In a recent book of mine, *A Pitch of Philosophy,*[3] I characterize this split by claiming that for Wittgenstein—unlike the case of Heidegger and his aftermath, and for that matter unlike the case of John Dewey—there is no standing dispensation of philosophy that philosophy now, or what has replaced philosophy, is to overcome. It is as if Wittgenstein felt that in the modern academization of philosophy, what in it is illusory will fall of its own weight. The issue for philosophy remains what it was from the beginning, the threat of human thinking to lead itself astray, to exempt itself from the need for human intelligibility, to torment itself with shadows of its language, to deny the world rather than to recognize its strangeness in the world, to deny its hand in its works, its interest in its concepts, to bore itself to distraction.

I suppose my favorite way of epitomizing the splitting of philosophy has been to invoke what I call the two myths of philosophical reading, that is, of the intellectual preparation for writing philosophy. On the one myth the philosopher proceeds from having read, and knowing, everything; in the other from having read, and knowing, nothing. Perhaps this duality is prefigured in the division between Plato's writing and Socrates' talking, but it is purely enough illustrated in this century by contrasting Heidegger's work, which assumes the march of the great names in the history of Western philosophy, with that of Wittgenstein's, who may get around to mentioning half-a-dozen names, but then only to identify a remark he happens to have come across and which seems to get its philosophical importance solely from the fact that he is thinking about it then. Common to the two myths is an idea that philosophy begins only when there are no further texts to read, when the truth you seek has already been missed, escaped. In the myth of totality philosophy has still not found itself—until at least it has found you; in the myth of blankness philosophy has lost itself in its first utterance.

Where does this leave us, who know the truth that we have read neither nothing nor everything? Or may we question this? We might consider how it looks to the Emerson of "Self-Reliance" and to the Thoreau of the chapter entitled "Reading" in *Walden,* who apparently judge that we have mostly not begun to read, and that there is nothing in print necessary to read.

But I was saying, or asking why, in the dominant philosophical dispensation in the English-speaking world of philosophy, it would be indecorous to speak in unguarded terms, say untheoretical words, of the presence of death in speech. If philosophy must preoccupy itself with questions of what can and cannot be said, it must not shrink from utterances whose saying is merely indecorous.

It will help articulate this matter if we distinguish the indecorous from the improper. The improper has on both sides of the Atlantic received its share of attention, in questioning and in asserting philosophy's quest for, its authorization by, the pure, say the self-possessed. The indecorous, we might say, speaks rather of the outside of that quest, of the communal requirement for rules, for the avoidance of the unseemly. (The improper risks nonsense, or emptiness, say estrangement; the indecorous courts excess, or outlandishness, say exile.) My writing has from its beginning been subject to both charges. That is, at all events, how I understand the most common charge brought against my writing by philosophers in my neighborhood of philosophy who disapprove of it, namely the charge that it is self-indulgent, some may have said instead self-absorbed. It would only have increased the sense of the indecorousness or impurity of my manner had I suggested a diagnosis of those charges. I have not in any case been moved to do so. But here, in the confidence that translation, in its overcoming of its impossibilities, brings to the sense of being understood, I register my sense of the philosophical stakes in this double charge.

The perception of impurity, or impropriety, I take as a displacement onto my writing of the sense that the appeal to the ordinariness of words—which is to say, the demonstration of our investment in words—is as such philosophically improper. Since this is a cause of the recurrent dismissals to which both Wittgenstein's late work and most of Austin's are open, I will add nothing here to what I have said elsewhere about *this* impropriety, nor any more about its bearing on philosophy's chronic flight from the ordinary. The twin perception of indecorousness remains to be located. That is what shows itself, I believe, in the repeated attention in negative reviews of *The Claim of Reason* to its opening sentence, where each time that sentence has been stated to run longer than 200 words. Imagine the reviewers in each case taking the trouble to count those words and verify the magnitude of their transgression. Why is so plain a thing the cause of distress? I can think of a number of reasons that I might have wanted to begin my book with a sentence about beginnings that fairly obviously dramatizes a problem about philosophical beginnings, hence about philosophical endings. And I can imagine that that itself is something which may strike a different philosophical sensibility as unnecessary, or impertinent, or ostentatious. But why as something bordering on the outrageous?

Consider that Wittgenstein's response to the passage from Augustine with which he opens the *Investigations* confesses, with a tentativeness and openness unusual for him, that "it seems to me" that "these words [of Augustine's] give us a picture of the essence of human language. It is this: the individual words in language name objects—sentences are combinations of such names."

But that picture is given by the very first of Augustine's three cited sentences: "When they (my elders) named some object, and accordingly moved toward something, I saw this and I grasped that the thing was called by the sound they uttered when they meant to point it out." The last of Augustine's sentences goes on to give a companion picture, one equally under discussion throughout the *Investigations:* "Thus, as I heard words repeatedly used in their proper places in various sentences, I gradually learnt to understand what objects they signified; and after I had trained my mouth to form these signs, I used them to express my own desires." The companion picture I point to—concerning the expression of my own desires—is blurred, or rather ambiguous: it might suggest that to express my own desires is to indicate which objects I desire (which may or may not be the ones my elders desired); or it might suggest that my coming into possession of language means that my every proper utterance bespeaks my desire, as sign or as signal; that my language, like the mind and body from which it originates, or which originate in it, becomes as a whole a field of expression. As Freud says of us, "No mortal can keep a secret. If his lips are silent, he chatters with his finger-tips; betrayal oozes out of him at every pore."[4] Emerson voices a comparable revelation by casting us as victims of expression. This avowal of radical subjection of the human to language is placed at odds in the text of the *Investigations* with philosophy's wish to escape what appears to it as the radical arbitrariness of our given language, as if it stands in need of logical repair.

Now I might say that my way of impressing upon myself, perhaps upon my reader, the human subjection to words as well as the human disappointment in words, is to get my writing to recognize, in every word if I can, that it does not know all that it knows. This may seem a terrible confession for a philosopher to make, and it is here that I understand the charge of the indecorous to fit what I do. But what it fits is not so much, I think, my own relatively mild tone of indecorousness as it does my sharp sense of, even my call for, an understanding with the indecorous. I suppose there can be no philosophical understanding in this field without philosophy's acknowledging the existence of psychoanalysis, not as posing something like a problem for the philosophy of science, but as an intellectual competitor in the placement of reason. In philosophy I have to recognize the arrogance with which I arrogate the right to speak universally, for all other possessors of language; in psychoanalysis I have to recognize the disgrace that I do not so much as speak for myself.

I conclude, accordingly, with a pair of passages, the first from a psychoanalyst, Lacan, the second from Wittgenstein's *Philosophical Investigations.*

In "The Freudian Thing,"[5] from 1955—it was the year Austin came to Harvard to give as the William James Lectures *How to Do Things with Words,* along with two graduate and faculty seminars, the result of which was that I put aside plans for a Ph.D. thesis that I did not believe in, and other plans to leave the field of philosophy—Lacan devotes a section to a disquisition on the subject of speech that he attributes (the disquisition) to the speaking of a desk. I draw from the example at least the following moral: Even psychoanalysts (most egregiously perhaps the ego-psychologists among them) do not know what it means that certain things speak, that there are subjects; their treatment (and theory) of what is said to them fantasizes a source of speech that has about the consistency of a piece of furniture. Wittgenstein begins a section toward the middle of the *Investigations,* § 361, with the fantasied claim: "The chair is thinking to itself," followed by indications of a long silence, and then the outburst, "WHERE? In one of its parts? Or outside its body? Or not *anywhere* at all? But then what is the difference between this chair's saying something to itself and another one's doing so, next to it?—But then how is it with man; where does *he* say things to himself? How does it come about that this question seems senseless . . . ?" I draw a companion moral: In our desperation for closure or order or sublimity in our concepts—in our disappointment with our criteria for their application—we ask criteria to do something or to go somewhere that they are not fit to do or to go, and so we repudiate, as it were, their intelligence. We can arrive at a philosophical position from which it seems that to ground the application of the concept of another's thinking to herself you have to be able to locate the *place* of that thinking. Then imagine applying the concept to a chair and you may transform disguised nonsense into patent nonsense.

There is evidently more than one form of human self-defeat, or temptation to emptiness in our aspirations, or distortions or neglect of our experience of things. Until it is shown that there is some general form that all human folly takes, it is not safe for us to do without any of the fields that have some perspective upon it.

In the course of writing these remarks, I asked myself why I had come to thoughts of the tragic character of human experience, of philosophy's requirement, hence I suppose that of any serious writing, to incorporate death (you might, more decorously, say finitude) into its reflections. I seem to have answered on this occasion, stirring memories that span the decades in which I have been writing publicly, that the appearance of *The Claim of Reason* as *Les Voix de la Raison* is a sign of life for me as reassuring as catching my breath.

Benjamin and Wittgenstein

Signals and Affinities

This essay, originally delivered as a lecture at Yale University, was written for and published in a 1999 issue of *Critical Inquiry* entitled *"Angelus Novus:* Perspectives on Walter Benjamin." This and the piece in Chapter 8 of this book are two of Cavell's few sustained discussions of Benjamin, motivated by what he calls "a sense of affinity between Benjamin and Wittgenstein" resting on two radically different versions of an "anti- or counterphilosophy."

THE INVITATION TO participate in a small conference on Walter Benjamin at Yale's humanities center meant to assess the appearance of the first volume of Harvard's *Selected Writings* of Benjamin as a measure from which, as the letter of invitation frames things, nonspecialists in Benjamin studies are asked to "evaluate Benjamin's contribution to their respective fields," was irresistible, allowing one to speak from, without quite parading, an ignorance it is otherwise hard to overcome. Whatever the exact perimeter and surface of my field, let us say, of philosophy, judged by the work from which I have made a living for most of a lifetime, it is, and, while partially and restlessly, has wanted to be, territory shared with those who, however different otherwise, acknowledge some affinity with the later Wittgenstein and with J. L. Austin, if just so far as those thinkers are recognizable as

First published as "Benjamin and Wittgenstein: Signals and Affinities," *Critical Inquiry* 25, no. 2 (1999): 235–246.

inheritors, hence no doubt betrayers, of a tradition of philosophy that definitively includes Frege, Russell, Carnap, and Quine. Seen from that shared territory, an honest answer to the question of Benjamin's actual contribution to
the field is that it is roughly nil. But if that were my sole space for an answer,
I would not have accepted the prompting to respond to the question.

Two helpful anthologies of writing about Benjamin—one from two or
three years ago edited by Andrew Benjamin and Peter Osborne and one from
ten years earlier edited by Gary Smith—are explicit in their wish to present
Benjamin in his aspect, or should one say semblance, as a philosopher; both
are explicit in wishing to counter the dominating semblance of Benjamin as
a great critic, as lent to him in the English-speaking world by Hannah Arendt's
portrait and collection under the title *Illuminations,* as they are explicit in recognizing that Benjamin at best created, and aspired to, as Adorno put the
matter, "a philosophy directed against philosophy," which they are also prepared to recognize as something that a creative canonical modern philosopher, since I suppose Descartes and Bacon, is rather bound to do.[1] This gesture of a disciplinary or counterdisciplinary appropriation of Benjamin focuses
two points of interest for me (I do not suppose them incompatible with those
editors' intentions): (1) Benjamin's anti- or counterphilosophy may be seen
specifically as immeasurably distant from and close to Wittgenstein's anti- or
counterphilosophy in *Philosophical Investigations;* (2) there is an economy of
inspiration and opacity in Benjamin's prose—sometimes it is, as Emerson puts
things, a play of intuition and tuition—that suggests a reason that the idea of
philosophy should not simply replace or succeed that of criticism in coming
to terms with his achievement. Benjamin enacts, more or less blatantly, a con-
testing of the philosophical with the literary, or of what remains of each,
that seems internal at once to the exceptional prestige of his work and to an
effect of intimacy or concern it elicits from its readers.

A sense of affinity between Benjamin and Wittgenstein helped produce the
signals in my subtitle, when, with the memory in my head of Benjamin's frequently cited letter to Scholem (17 April 1931) in which he expresses a phan-
tasm of his writing as a call or signal for rescue from the top of the crum-
bling mast of a sinking ship,[2] I came upon a piece of his with the title "Program
for a Proletarian Children's Theater" containing these sentences: "Almost
every child's gesture is command and signal," and "it is the task of the director
to rescue the children's signals out of the dangerous magic realm of mere
fantasy and to bring them to bear on the material."[3] One hardly knows
whether Benjamin is there identifying more with the director than with the

child, whose world Benjamin of course enters elsewhere as well (apart from his interest in the history of children's books, I cite Jeffrey Mehlman's fascinating *Walter Benjamin for Children: An Essay on His Radio Years*).[4] And I know of no other major philosophical sensibility of this century who attaches comparable importance to the figure of the child with the exception of Wittgenstein in the *Investigations,* which opens with Augustine's portrait of himself as a child stealing language from his elders, an autobiographical image that haunts every move in Wittgenstein's drive to wrest language back from what he calls metaphysics, and what we might perhaps still call the absolute.[5]

To the extent that opening a path for Benjamin's contribution to my field will be furthered by opening certain passages between his writing and Wittgenstein's *Investigations*—which is the object of these remarks—I have to give an idea of how I have wished to see the *Investigations* received.

My interpretation of that work is as a continuous response to the threat of skepticism, a response that does not deny the truth of skepticism—that we cannot coherently claim with certainty that the world exists and I and others in it—but recasts skepticism's significance in order to throw light upon, let's say, human finitude, above all, representing all, the human achievement of words. I go on to relate the resulting understanding of skepticism to the problematic of knowledge worked out in Shakespearean tragedy, whether in Othello's tortured doubts about Desdemona's faithfulness, or in Macbeth's anxiety about his wife's humanity, or in Lear's presentations of his worthiness for love, or in Hamlet's desire never to have succeeded, or acceded, to existence. Reading tragedy back into philosophical skepticism I would variously, in various connections, characterize the skeptic as craving the emptiness of language, as ridding himself of the responsibilities of meaning, and as being drawn to annihilate externality or otherness, projects I occasionally summarize as seeking to escape the conditions of humanity, which I call the chronic human desire to achieve the inhuman, the monstrous, from above or from below. (I wonder what might, or should, have happened to these ideas had I read earlier than mere months ago Benjamin's frightening portrait of Karl Kraus as a misanthrope and satirist. This is I trust for another time.)[6] Pursuing the "I" or "we" of the *Investigations* as the modern skeptical subject, I find specific, quite explicit, sketches there of this figure as characterized by fixation, strangeness, torment, sickness, self-destructiveness, perversity, disappointment, and boredom. It was in a seminar I offered three or four years ago on Heidegger and Thoreau, to a group of advanced students with whom I could more or less assume my reading of Wittgenstein, upon my saying of

Walden that it is an exercise in replacing the melancholia of skepticism by a mourning for the world, letting it go, that a student—not of philosophy but of literary studies—blurted out that I must read Benjamin's *Trauerspiel* book (*The Origin of German Tragic Drama*).

I had years earlier read just the "Epistemo-Critical Prologue" to the book profitlessly, unprepared to divine its motivations by what I had then read of Benjamin (essentially no more than, to say the banal truth, the essays collected in *Illuminations*), and I put the thing aside, vaguely planning to seek reliable advice and then go back. It is always an issue to determine whose advice or warning you will accept in such matters, and for some reason I allowed myself, after a while, to accept this student's unguarded appeal, with its registering of an unknown affinity. As an example of the results, I shall specify here something of the perspective from which I follow Benjamin's identification of saturnine melancholy as a feature of the mourning play, especially in its theological conception, as *acedia*, "dullness of the heart, or sloth," which Benjamin counts as the fourth or fifth of the deadly sins, and of which he nominates Hamlet as the greatest modern portrait.[7]

The conjunction of melancholy with, let me call it, ennui or boredom, speaks to one of the guiding forces of Wittgenstein's thoughts in the *Investigations,* the recognition that his mode of philosophizing seems to "destroy everything interesting (all that is great and important)" (*PI,* § 118). Wittgenstein voices this recognition explicitly just once (and once more can be taken to imply it [see *PI,* § 570]), but it is invoked each time he follows the method of language-games, that is to say, punctually through the bulk of the *Investigations.* That this destruction, as Wittgenstein notes, leaves behind as it were no scene of devastation, no place that has become "only bits of stone and rubble" (*PI,* § 118)—everything is left as it is, your world is merely as a whole displaced, transfigured by withdrawing your words from their frozen investments, putting them back into real circulation—suggests that the imaginary destruction of what we called great and important reveals our investments to have been imaginary, with the terribly real implication that so far as philosophy was and is our life (and there is no surveying the extent) our life has been trained as a rescue from boredom, delivered to an anxious twilight of interest.

That Benjamin's *Trauerspiel* book can be thus entered as a study of a peculiar preoccupation with Shakespeare and skepticism is of pressing interest for me. (The baroque date of Benjamin's genre seems roughly to fit, but Benjamin's concept of the baroque, which he ties to the Counter-Reformation, is so far as I know unsettled in its application to the English-speaking dispensation. This discrepancy may prove fateful.) Continuing for a moment the theme of melancholy, one may well be struck by the fact that Benjamin's report of the emblems of melancholy, which features the dog, the stone, and the sphere (following Panofsky and Saxl's celebrated work on Dürer), turns out to list figures that all appear in *Philosophical Investigations*.

The dog, possessed classically of a melancholic look and a downward gaze, as toward the center of gravity, appears in the *Investigations* at a moment in which Wittgenstein, in one of his images of human finitude (distinguishing that from animal limitation), remarks, "One can imagine an animal angry, frightened, unhappy, happy, startled. But hopeful? And why not?" The text continues by instancing this nondespairing hopelessness, as it were, of animals as follows: "A dog believes his master is at the door. But can he also believe his master will come the day after tomorrow?—And *what* can he not do here?—How do I do it?" Wittgenstein's answer here is to reflect that "the phenomena of hope are modes of [the] complicated form of life [of humans]," a life form he here identifies as of those who can talk, which for him seems essentially to mean, those who can fall into philosophical perplexity (*PI*, p. 174).

The stone appears in an equally fateful path of the *Investigations'* territory, that of our knowledge of pain, of our basis (under the threat of skepticism) of sympathy with the suffering of others. "What gives us *so much as the idea* that living beings, things, can feel anything?" (*PI*, § 283). Countering the theory that I transfer the idea from feelings in myself to objects outside, Wittgenstein observes: "I do not transfer my idea to stones, plants, etc. / Couldn't I imagine having frightful pains and turning to stone while they lasted? Well, how do I know, if I shut my eyes, whether I have not turned into a stone? And if that has happened, in what sense will *the stone* have the pains?" The further working out of metamorphosis here is briefly Kafkaesque, and the association of pain with stone has a precedent in the poem of Trakl's ("A Winter's Evening") that Heidegger interprets in his essay entitled "Language."[8] (Is Wittgenstein's move against a narcissistic diagnosis of our knowledge of suffering not pertinent to a political imagination?)

Of course such considerations would, at best, be responded to as curiosities by more representative members of my field, and at worst, not without proper impatience, as an avoidance or betrayal of philosophy (as if I perversely emphasize the aspect of the *Investigations* that is itself a betrayal of philosophy). And I am not even mentioning Wittgenstein's place for the fly, the beetle, the lion, and the cow. Benjamin's recurrence to animals (as well as to stone and to angels) is a principal theme of Beatrice Hanssen's recent book, *Walter Benjamin's Other History,* which opposes Benjamin's new conception of natural history to, importantly, Heidegger's articulation of Dasein's historicity.[9] So I might note that I am also not mentioning in connection with Benjamin's new conception of natural history that the concept of natural history occurs significantly also in the *Investigations,* in accounting for our species' ability to attribute concepts to others that imply membership in our species, such as commanding, recounting, chatting, walking, drinking, playing (*PI,* § 118) (and, of course, accounting for an inability to exercise this ability in particular cases).

Nor will impatience be stilled as I now list the sphere—understood as the earth, the third of the emblems of melancholy—as appearing among the countless paths along which Wittgenstein tracks the philosophical pressure on words that forces them from their orbits of meaningfulness: "[An] example [is] that of the application of 'above' and 'below' to the earth . . . I see well enough that I am on top; the earth is surely beneath me! (And don't smile at this example. We are indeed all taught at school that it is stupid to talk like that. But it is much easier to bury a problem than to solve it)" (*PI,* § 351). (Preoccupied with Benjamin, we should perhaps recall that Brecht, in his *Galileo,* found it of politically revolutionary importance to provide the right explanation for the error of supposing people at the antipodes to be "below" our part of the earth. It is worth considering whether Brecht was in his way a bit burying the problem, I mean the intellectual resources of the Counter-Reformation Church.) Perhaps a more pertinent invocation of the sphere, or its surface—pertinent now to Benjamin's struggle with German idealism—is the following instance of Wittgenstein's unearthing our untiring requirement of the ideal:

> Thought is surrounded by a halo.—Its essence, logic, presents an order, in fact the a priori order of the world. . . . We are under the illusion that . . . [this] order is a *super*-order between—so to speak— *super-concepts.* [*PI,* § 97]
>
> The conflict [between actual, everyday language and our requirement of the crystalline purity of logic] becomes intolerable; the requirement now threatens to become empty—We have got on to slippery ice where there is no friction and so in a certain sense the conditions are ideal, but also, just because of that, we are unable to

walk. We want to walk; so we need *friction*. Back to the rough ground!
[*PI*, § 107]

Where other theorists of melancholy emphasize the relation of the human
to earth's gravity, working out the fact of finding ourselves bound or sunk
upon earth, Wittgenstein, the engineer, works out the fate of our capacity
to move ourselves upon it, to go on—a different insistence upon the Benjaminian theme of our existence in materiality, our new relation to objects.

Something is right in the exasperation or amusement such considerations
may cause those within the tradition of Anglo-American analytical philosophy.
One who insisted on such matters as the melancholy or disappointment in
the *Investigations,* in the absence of, unresponsive to, the matters it instances
in its preface—matters concerning "the concepts of meaning, of understanding, of a proposition, of logic, mathematics, states of consciousness,"
along with attention to Wittgenstein's insistence on the procedures he calls
his "methods"—would not be, I would be prepared to join in saying, talking
about Wittgenstein's *Philosophical Investigations* (*PI,* p. iv). (Though I am not
prepared to identify ahead of time every way responsiveness to such matters
can look.) But then why not be content to say that? Why the exasperation?
Why *does* Wittgenstein write that way? Couldn't the occasional animals and
the odd flarings of pathos, perverseness, suffocation, lostness, be dropped or
ignored and a doctrine survive? Many, most serious scholars of the *Investigations* have felt so, and behaved so.

Benjamin may provide a further fresh start here, from an odd but characteristic place, in his decisive interpretation or illumination of the animals in
Kafka's stories—help specifically in grasping how it is that matters that can
readily seem negligible, and which after all occupy so small a fraction of the
actual sentences and paragraphs of the text of the *Investigations,* can nevertheless seem to others (who do not deny the presence of the other shore) to
contain, as it were, its moral, the heart of the counsel it offers. Kafka's parables, Benjamin suggests—the old friend of Gershom Scholem's—"have . . . a
similar relation to doctrine as the Aggadah [the nonlegal part of the talmudic
and later rabbinic literature] does to the Halakah [the law or doctrine in that
literature]." And Benjamin asks:

> But do we have the doctrine which Kafka's parables interpret and
> which Kafka's postures and the gestures of his animals clarify? It does
> not exist; all we can say is that here and there we have an allusion

to it. Kafka might have said that these are relics transmitting the doctrine, although we could regard them just as well as precursors preparing the doctrine. In every case it is a question of how life and work are organized in human society.[10]

The application to the *Investigations* must be rather topsy-turvy. It is a work that quite explicitly claims not to advance *theses* (see *PI,* § 128), a claim few of its admirers, I believe, believe. The closest thing to a doctrine I discern in the *Investigations* seems to occur in three short sentences that end its opening paragraph, in which Wittgenstein announces what he calls the roots of the idea of language that he sees in the picture conveyed by the paragraph from Augustine's *Confessions* referred to earlier. The idea Wittgenstein formulates is as follows: "Every word has a meaning. This meaning is correlated with the word. It is the object for which the word stands." The 693 ensuing sections of the *Investigations* can be said to discover relics transmitting this doctrine, or precursors preparing the doctrine, ones that show the doctrine—which seems so obvious as to be undeniable, if even noticeable—to come not merely to very little, but to come to nothing, to be empty. Yet it announces in its roots—in every one of the words Augustine employs to express his memory of receiving language—the theory of language as a means of referring to the world and as expressing our desires that every advanced philosophy since Frege and Husserl and the early Russell, up to Heidegger and Benjamin and Lacan and Derrida have in one way or another contended with. Wittgenstein's originality, to my mind, is to show that the doctrine, as reflected in its countless relics, is nothing we believe, that it is its very promise of emptiness that we crave, as if that would be not less than redemption.

Students of Wittgenstein have heard something from me over the years not unlike this skeptical news, or rather this news about skepticism, and have taken it to attribute to Wittgenstein a vision of the end of philosophy, an attribution some deplore and others embrace. It will hardly be of interest to either of these receptions of Wittgenstein to hear that the dismantling of a false redemption is work enough for an ambitious philosophy. But that is in any case not the direction of issue for me at the moment, which is to suggest that if readers of Wittgenstein should be interested in Benjamin that is because readers of Benjamin might find they have an interest in Wittgenstein. And any specific news I have from this direction, as a beginning reader of Benjamin, can only come from testifying to specific interests that I am finding in it, its bearing on the work I do, obvious and devious.

I cite one or two sentences of Benjamin's taken from each of the two most elaborated essays in the first volume of *Selected Writings:* from "The Concept of Criticism in German Romanticism," Benjamin's doctoral dissertation and most extended, I believe, investigation of the concept of criticism; and from the essay "Goethe's Elective Affinities," containing stretches of Benjamin's most concentrated, I believe, work of concrete, or what used in my circles to be called practical, criticism. (Some, I know, find Benjamin's later work to surpass the earlier. But can it be true, any more than in Wittgenstein's case, that the later *obviates* the earlier?)

Start with the essay on criticism: "The entire art-philosophical project of the early Romantics can . . . be summarized by saying that they sought to demonstrate in principle the criticizability of the work of art."[11] Part of what this summarizes is the idea of criticism as a sober "continuation" or "consummation" of the work of art; together with the idea that "every critical understanding of an artistic entity is, as reflection in the entity, nothing other than a higher, self-actively originated degree of this entity's consciousness," and the corollary idea or "principle of the uncriticizability of inferior work."[12] That movies—the best even of Hollywood talkies—are as responsive to the pressure of something like the degree of critical unfolding as, say, the texts of Shakespeare, is the explicit basis of my treatment of Hollywood comedies in *Pursuits of Happiness.* It is the thing that book has often and variously had charged against it, often put as my taking these films too seriously. In part the charge is a reflection of the unexplained yet decisive fact of aesthetics in the Anglo-American dispensation of philosophy, that the questions it characteristically addresses to artistic entities neither arise from nor are answered by passages of interpretation of those entities, say as represented in Benjamin's Goethe essay, as in the following sentences from it:

> Is Goethe . . . really closer than Kant or Mozart to the material content of marriage? One would have to deny this roundly if, in the wake of all the literary scholarship on Goethe, one were seriously determined to take Mittler's words on this subject as the writer's own. . . . After all, [Goethe] did not want, like [his character] Mittler, to establish a foundation for marriage but wished, rather, to show the forces that arise from its decay. . . . [In] truth, marriage is never justified in law (that is, as an institution) but is justified solely as an expression of continuance in love, which by nature seeks this expression sooner in death than in life.[13]

This view of the justification of marriage unnervingly resembles the view taken in my articulation of Hollywood remarriage comedies in *Pursuits of Happiness,* namely, that marriage is justified not by law (secular or religious, nor in particular, to cite a more lurid connection with *Elective Affinities,* by the presence of a child) but alone by the will to remarriage. That articulation, however, denies Benjamin's rider, which proposes that continuance in love seeks its expression sooner in death than in life (perhaps Benjamin means this as a smack at a romantic suggestion that it is easier to love eternally than diurnally). This is to say that the remarriage narratives I isolate as among the best classical Hollywood talkies (the ones best able to bear up under what I call philosophical criticism) locate the idea in a comic form, one to define which I find to require, for example, a concept of repetition grounded in Kierkegaard's and in Nietzsche's ideas of repetition and of recurrence; a concept of the relation of appearances to things-in-themselves that challenges Kant's curtaining between them; a concept of attraction or magnetism that does not depend upon beauty; and a theory of morality that requires a working out of Emersonian perfectionism in its differences with the reigning academic forms of moral theory, deontological or Kantian, and teleological or Utilitarian. I would like to claim that this represents on my part a struggle, in Benjamin's perception, "to ascertain the place of a work or a form in terms of the history of philosophy," something Benjamin implies is his project in the *Trauerspiel* book (*OG,* p. 105).

I hope to get further into a discussion of this claim with Benjamin's writing more than with any other, but I anticipate trouble from the outset. For his inescapable essay of a few years later, "The Work of Art in the Age of Mechanical Reproduction," in its sense of the invention of photography and of film as perhaps having "transformed the entire nature of art," does not seek confirmation for this sense of film by means of the criticism of individual films, nor does it suggest that film (some films) can be read as containing the idea that philosophical criticism is to consummate. (Of course not, if the consequence of this transformation is that we no longer possess a developing concept of art, that [in Wittgensteinian terms] nothing any longer plays this role in our form of life.) It would be worth knowing more surely (I seem to persist in counting on some reasonably positive answer) whether film, for example, within the trauma of its role in transforming our ideas of the authorship and the audience and the work of the work of art, has mysteriously maintained, in something like the proportion of instances one would expect in any of the arts in the modern period, the definitive power of art to suffer philosophical criticism; and if film, then perhaps postfilm.

Supposing for the moment that an interest in Wittgenstein's work taken from the perspective of Benjamin's would lead to contributions of Benjamin to something like my field, or to modifying the field, I ask in drawing to a close, more specifically, what the profit or amplification might be for Benjamin's projects. I cite moments from two projects that seem to me to cry out for consideration within and against a Wittgensteinian development, that is, for subjection to the exposure of mutual translation.

First from "On Language as Such and on the Language of Man": "The enslavement of language in prattle is joined by the enslavement of things in folly almost as its inevitable consequence."[14] This is an early reflection of Benjamin's insight into the language of the bourgeois for which Scholem (in the letter I alluded to earlier) praises him as he rebukes him for disfiguring his metaphysics of language by claiming its relation to dialectical materialism. Benjamin responds by recognizing a necessary intellectual risk here, but what were his options in theorizing the Kierkegaardian / Heideggerean theme of prattle? Evidently he does not wish to endorse either Kierkegaard's Christianity or Heidegger's own mode of explicating Dasein's thrownness and falling, which would mean in effect accepting his articulation of life in the crowded everyday. Has he an account of what language is such that it *can* corrupt itself?

Here is a great theme of Wittgenstein's *Investigations,* an essential feature of which (in which Austin's work adjoins Wittgenstein's) is the investigation of thinking's internal relation to nonsense, an investigation of course related to logical positivism's obsession with meaninglessness, but radically and specifically opposed to its mode of accounting for it. (I do not know how far one may go in taking the interest in nonsense to be definitive of what came to be called analytical philosophy, an interest that fruitfully differentiates it from its estranged sibling, called Continental metaphysics.) Naturally a philosophical attention to the essential possibility of nonsense in human speech can be taken to avoid Benjamin's concern with a historically specific source of human violation, say that of late capitalism. But what is the theory (of history? of philosophy? of nature?) according to which it must be so taken? And what of the possibility that an attention to history is used to avoid the glare of philosophy?[15]

The second, related project is announced in "Theses on the Philosophy of History":

> The themes which monastic discipline assigned to friars for meditation were designed to turn them from the world and its affairs. The thoughts we are developing here originate from similar considerations. . . . Our consideration . . . seeks to convey an idea of the high

price our accustomed thinking will have to pay for a conception of history that avoids any complicity with the thinking to which these politicians [traitors to the cause of anti-Fascism] continue to adhere [or, as he goes on to say, to conform].[16]

Here I appeal to my various efforts to show Wittgenstein's and Austin's differently cast attentions to the ordinary as underwritten in the work of Emerson and of Thoreau, and I note the presence of the concept of conformity, an Emersonian master-tone, in aversion to which, as aversion to which, he defines thinking. The language of conformity in his society presents itself to Emerson's ears as sounds from which he finds himself continually shrinking ("Every word they say chagrins us")[17] and which he interprets as an expression of depression—Thoreau famously characterizes (early in *Walden*) the lives of the mass of people as ones of quiet desperation; Emerson had explicitly said "secret melancholy" (in "New England Reformers").[18] Thoreau's invention and demonstration of civil disobedience registers the knowledge that massive depression has, whatever else, a political basis. Specifically, it interprets the emergence of consent as a political phenomenon to signal the recognition that I must acknowledge my voice as lent to, hence as in complicity with, the injustice in my society, hence recognize that I become inexpressive, stifled, in the face of it. Pathos is one response to this knowledge, and who is capable, from time to time, of grander semblances of pathos than Benjamin (as at the close of the Goethe essay)?: "Only for the sake of the hopeless ones have we been given hope."[19] Here is the point at which to assess Emerson's violent efforts at cheerfulness, at raising up the hearts of his neighbors, which so grates on intellectual ears.

I suppose that this Emersonian note is a sound of hope in democracy, a kind of cost of participation in it. Emerson's formidable essay "Experience" enacts a relentless demand for attaining, or for mourning the passing of, one's own experience—adjoining signature themes of Benjamin's—an enactment through a process of judging the world that Emerson names thinking, something he also calls patience, by which he says we shall "win at the last."[20] One might take that formula in Emerson's dialect to suggest, "ween at the last," *ween* meaning to think something possible, as though realization is a function of active expectation now. (As in Shakespeare's *Henry VIII:* "Ween you of better luck . . . than your Master, / Whose minister you are?")[21] And is it sure that Emerson's affirmation is too American a proposition, asking too much of that old part of us so fascinated by the necessity and the freedom of being uncomprehended? Except of course by children.

8

Remains to Be Seen

Initial Responses to *The Arcades Project*

This is a review of Walter Benjamin's unfinished book *The Arcades Project*, which was translated by Howard Eiland and Kevin McLaughlin and published in 1999. In his review, published in *Artforum*, Cavell brings together *Arcades*, which presents Paris as a center not only of cultural production but of modernity, with Wittgenstein's *Philosophical Investigations*, as well as with works of Freud and Emerson.

So IT WAS FOR THIS THAT Walter Benjamin summoned voices to blend and to contend with his, and with each other's, ones that he found to flow along his dreams (e.g., p. 467)—his and (he claims, as a philosopher must) ours (e.g., pp. 212, 391)—from which the work of this work now scrupulously translated and generously presented is variously to join in awakening us (e.g., pp. 388, 458), rescuing (e.g., pp. 473, 476) or say redeeming (e.g., pp. 332, 462) the phenomena of our world, processes that require blasting phenomena from their historical successions (p. 475), suggesting thought as a volcano (p. 698), forming new constellations (e.g., p. 463), allegorizing (e.g., pp. 211, 330, 367) the dialectical in every genuine image (e.g., 462, 473), where the place one encounters such an image is language (p. 462), in which the past and future are polarized by means of anticipating as it were the present (p. 470) (a thought

A version of this essay was published as "Remains to Be Seen," review of Walter Benjamin, *The Arcades Project*, trans. Howard Eiland and Kevin McLaughlin, *Artforum* 38, no. 8 (2000): 31–35.

Benjamin compliments Turgot for formulating [p. 478]; for us it is quite pure Thoreau), and where, further, "the present" is not a fixed point but a scene of ruins (p. 474), illuminated by flashes of lightning (e.g., pp. 91, 226, 456) (a melodramatic but recognizable vision of Wittgenstein's Investigations), each of which marks a now, a dawn, of recognition (e.g., pp. 463, 473), allowing thought to be drawn, as by the magnetic North Pole (which others correct for, which Benjamin claims to correct by) an American, analogously associating the North Pole with the direction of freedom, allegorizes somewhat otherwise, as in Walden, toward the end of chapter 1: "The sailor [on the sea of his being alone] or the fugitive slave keeps the polestar in his eye," not toward purported permanencies and their petrified (p. 366) understandings (supporting our familiar forms of social cohesion) but to the debris or detritus of a culture (pp. 460, 543), occasions for reading, for rebuking the idea of decline as much as the idea of progress in history (e.g., 460).

For those of us frightened away from this most rumored of unfinished or unpublished or unwritten modern works by how much we must miss in Benjamin's deployment of German, the labors of love manifested in this English presentation expose us—I speak for myself—to a preliminary question: How much do I understand of my present state, as registered in the skipping recording I just improvised for that opening paragraph, in reading this work? I am not so much asking what it would be to understand the linking of Benjaminian concepts as they come to me, but what it would be to see how such instigations are manifested in the work of *The Arcades Project*. This is only my way of registering what anyone obliged to give even, or especially, a brief account of the text is apt to express, that its form or texture—with its citations, often multiple, lasting from a sentence to a long paragraph, from more than 800 texts, mostly French, otherwise German, bearing on the life and works of Paris through the nineteenth century, interspersed at varying intervals with one or more similarly sized comments of Benjamin's own, all collected into thirty-six as it were dossiers—is as urgent an issue to respond to as any citation, or any juxtaposition (Benjamin says montage) of citations within the structure; indeed that its form, the visibility of its existence as discontinuity and accretion, is its pervasive and inescapable issue. It is this condition of process rather than the question of the work's evident sense of unfinishedness (or uncompletability) that strikes me as constituting its aura of modernity, together I mean with its mode of incessant self-mirroring.

Whether—both have been done—one takes the work as incomplete or as complete in its controlled fragmentation, prior facts are that it exists as a collection, and that the concept of a collection is one of its master tones, surrealist in its reach. Again, if you find that montage is what determines its endlessness, then you must note the pertinence of the concepts of constellation and of dispersion in the text, distinguishing allegorizing from collecting. My emphatic perception at the moment is of this text as work, as production without a product (a way to think about its claim to philosophy, or rather, to philosophizing). It is how I respond to the German title *Passagen-Werk* (I believe Benjamin's working title was as his *Passagenarbeit*). This might be some protection against a tendency to conceive too simply of Benjamin's volume, or package, as itself arcades, breaking passages through established constructions and putting commodified sayings on display: after all the figure of the flâneur, made for arcades, is a figure Benjamin proposes for his reader: "In the flâneur, one might say, is reborn the sort of idler that Socrates picked out from the Athenian marketplace to be his interlocutor. Only, there is no longer a Socrates. And the slave labor that guaranteed him his leisure has likewise ceased to exist" (p. 334). If Benjamin is here staking his claim to a certain afterlife of philosophizing, his *Arcades Project* may be taken as establishing the conditions (of memory as thinking, of thinking as explosion, of perception as allegory, of the chances of concurrence in Poe's crowd) under which philosophy is now, after all, and keeping itself useless to a reign of oppression, still possible.

Then if I think how the concept of work (or labor) occurs within his work, I think of Benjamin's handsome compliment to Fourier: "To have instituted play as the canon of a labor no longer rooted in exploitation is one of the great merits of Fourier. . . . The Fourierist utopia furnishes a model, of a sort to be found realized in the games of children" (p. 361). Can we say that Benjamin responds to Fourier as allegorizing children's games so as to rescue the missed opportunities of industrialized human work? How is it that Benjamin (together perhaps with Wittgenstein, who also remarkably invokes children and games) is one who, among the dominating presences of modern thought, is unafraid of pathos; or rather, why does he find pathos indispensable to his writing? Clearly not out of nostalgia for the past of which we are the dream and the dreamers. But out of something like the reverse: Kant said that in human knowledge objects are given to us along with the endless conditions of their appearing. Benjamin wishes us to bear the knowledge—that is, demands of his words that each bears the pain of perceiving—that each thing given to us appears not only through the work of endless others but through a contortion in what should count as work.

Is this reading Benjamin? About reading he says, for example: "The image that is read—which is to say, the image in the now of its recognizability—bears to the highest degree the imprint of the perilous critical moment on which all reading is founded" (p. 463); and "The historical index of the images not only says that they belong to a particular time; it says, above all, that they attain to legibility only at a particular time" (p. 462); and "Image is that wherein, by dint of lightning, what has been enters into a constellation with the now" (ibid). In which now of recognizability is Benjamin legible—for example, this bulk of pages compiled in a labor begun in 1927, read and reported on over the years to friends destined for fame (Adorno, Scholem, Brecht), who were variously inspired and dismayed, introduced to strangers in abbreviated forms, left hurriedly in 1940 to be buried somewhere Georges Bataille would know about in the Bibliothèque Nationale in Paris, surviving the war to be edited and published in Germany in 1982? May I make a constellation of Benjamin's repeated idea of a flash of lightning with Emerson's remark near the opening of "Self-Reliance" (no more famous than it is unknown, to Benjamin for example), also about reading: "A man should learn to detect and watch that gleam of light which flashes across his mind from within, more than the lustre of the firmament of bards and sages"? Doesn't Emerson confirm this in his essay "Experience," when the idea of "persisting to read or to think" is associated with "flashes of light," marking sudden arrivals (nows) as after perilous journeys?

But then, recursively, how is it that Emerson constitutes a now of recognition for me? (Herman Melville's image of a "shock of recognition" would have interested Benjamin.) I might say it is because of the way I read Wittgenstein's *Philosophical Investigations,* the only part completed for publication signed in 1945, after various rumors and dictations to pupils over more than a decade, published with editorial addenda in English in 1953, followed by a stream of *Nachlass.* It was not until 1960 that I had found the (or a) now of legibility for Wittgenstein's work. And how shall I know that my conviction was or is sound? It might help to say that it is confirmed in noting that Benjamin's redemptive reading invokes the idea of rescuing phenomena. This is a way of indicating how I put together Wittgenstein's remarking "What we do is to lead words back from their metaphysical to their everyday use" with his observing "We feel as if we had to *penetrate* phenomena: our investigation, however, is directed not towards phenomena, but, as one might say, towards the '*possibilities*' of phenomena." This last observation, as I argued a lifetime ago, virtually quotes Kant's idea of critique, but unlike Kant, for whom our possibilities of phenomena are fixed, Wittgenstein's vision is rather of human existence as perpetually missing its possibilities; put otherwise, as captivated by false necessities. One of Benjamin's definitions of "basic historical concepts" is: "Catastrophe—to have missed the opportunity" (p. 474). Thoreau sometimes puts the perception comically, once when depicting his being interrupted in his kind of reading: "There never is but one opportunity of a kind" (*Walden,* chapter 12). I note that Benjamin declares that his comments are saturated with theology, if necessarily inexplicitly (p. 471), and that Wittgenstein advised a student to read *Philosophical Investigations* from a religious point of view.

Then I should not forbear seeking, or questioning, another of my nows in the anti-theological Freud (not unrelated to a certain rescuing of Freud in the philo-theological Lacan), when early in the *Introductory Lectures* Freud confesses: "The material for [the] observations [of psychoanalysis] is usually provided by the inconsiderable events which have been put aside by the other sciences as being too unimportant—the dregs of the world of phenomena." This picks up Benjamin: "Method of this project: . . . I shall purloin no valuables. . . . But the rags, the refuse—these I will . . . allow, in the only way possible, to come into their own: by making use of them" (p. 460). (Freud's dregs and Benjamin's refuse are each interpretable with Wittgenstein's ordinary; the differences are where I come in.) But ours does not seem to be a time in which for many people Freud is legible, or usable. Nor is it propitious for the later Wittgenstein, nor for the other philosophers of missed possibility I have cited. None has the intensity of prestige that Benjamin's work seems here and there to have acquired. If this is true, is it because Benjamin now brings something seriously new, unheard of, which would have to mean, for him, some other access to the archaic? Is it somehow his old capacity for having to be cared for taking hold on a large scale? Does it express our drive to reparation for having missed him? Is it that his isolation, expressed in his unforgettable suicide, is now to become legible?

Sometimes, in *The Arcades Project,* passing to a new entry, one reads what is a citation as something from Benjamin's own pen, neglecting to have noted that the entry began with a signal of citation, most obviously with an initial opening quotation mark, and then finds that an interesting stretch of prose is identified as the work of some monster of fame, such as Baudelaire or Hugo or Zola or Balzac or Proust, or alternatively of someone quite unknown.

(There is ample reason for this: Benjamin declares it essential to his work "to develop to the highest degree the art of citing without quotation marks" [p. 458]. I assume this does not mean learning to plagiarize unseen but rather managing to make one's contributions irresistibly appropriable, which may mean, in a world of, say, performance, learning to keep them all but invisible.) Is this to be allegorized as the impenetrability of the ways of fame, or say of the needs of a culture, or of a culture's interpretation of its needs; or a reminder of the insufferable, seemingly unsurmountable taste and talent of the French for literary discussion? The perpetual assault of expressiveness, of the sheer clamor of articulateness, becomes an oppressive demand for response, for the reader, for the writer. In the Baudelaire dossier—much the longest, mined variously by Benjamin for separate publications, real and imagined, to reveal something of the ungovernable *Project* beyond the circle of friends who found it sane—there comes eventually a stretch of some ten pages of entries from Benjamin alone. The intensity becomes so cruel that one finds oneself longing for a citation which could relieve this obligation to perform with incessant, simultaneous brilliance, surprise, and philosophy. A measure of the size of the Baudelaire material: The following two entries (I mean the flash of illumination which may arc between them) span more than 100 pages: "His [Baudelaire's] utterances, Gautier thought, were fully [full?] of 'capital letters and italics.' . . . I do not even criticize his jerky gait . . . which made people compare him to a spider. It was the beginning of that angular gesticulation which, little by little, would displace the rounded graces of the old world" (p. 248); "The 'jerky gait' of the ragpicker is not necessarily due to the effect of alcohol. Every few moments, he must stop to gather refuse, which he throws into his wicker basket" (p. 364).

Why (according to what allegories) make a work that cannot be read through? Perhaps to remind the reader that his and her work must perpetually find its own end. Why make a work that cannot be written to an end? Perhaps to remind the writer of a reason to suffer awakening without end. It is work that is capable of recognizing, in a response to Nietzsche, "suicide as signature of modernity" (p. 369). Then *The Arcades Project,* constructive, modernist, and unending, is not so much an argument against suicide as it is an attestation, so long as the work can continue, that deprives suicide of its point.

9

Finding Words

Adam Phillips's Ordinary Language Psychoanalysis

This essay is a review of *Terrors and Experts* by Adam Phillips, which Cavell wrote for the *London Review of Books* in 1997. Phillips, a prominent psychoanalyst, child psychotherapist, essayist, and writer, is the author of numerous books, including *On Kissing, Tickling, and Being Bored* (1993)—quoted by Cavell here—and *Becoming Freud* (2014). His writings have been strongly influenced by Cavell.

EARLY IN HIS LOVELY AND USEFUL BOOK on D. W. Winnicott, published in 1988, Adam Phillips gives a sketch of certain aims and fates of that increasingly treasured figure of British psychoanalysis which maps certain of his own directions in his recent collection of psychoanalytic essays called *Terrors and Experts*:

> [Winnicott] would also enjoy playing off a language of common-sense against a language of professional expertise. In 1970, in a talk he gave to Anglican priests, he was asked how he would tell whether a person needed psychiatric help. "If a person comes and talks to you," he said, "and, listening to him, you feel he is boring you, then he is sick and needs psychiatric treatment. But if he sustains your interest,

A version of this essay was published as "Finding Words," review of *Terrors and Experts* by Adam Phillips, *London Review of Books* 19, no. 4 (February 1997).

no matter how grave his distress or conflict, then you can help him all right." There is a commitment here, unheard of in psychoanalysis, to affinity between people rather than to a technique of professional help. Winnicott's almost religious commitment to an idea of simple and personal truth, to an ordinary-language psychoanalysis, was inevitably to make his institutional loyalties problematic.

The self-portraiture in narrative portraiture is hardly uncommon, but Adam Phillips is uncommonly fortunate in this choice among his precursors since independence from, or playfulness with, precursors—refusing to comply with them is a way Winnicott liked to put it—is part of the surface and of the depth of what Winnicott stands for. Two ways catch my attention in which Adam Phillips's writing departs creatively from his sketch of Winnicott's "playing off a language of common-sense against a language of professional expertise": first, Phillips's specification of the play of language as entering into "an ordinary-language psychoanalysis," in alluding to so-called ordinary language philosophy, is an invitation to think of psychoanalysis in connection with philosophy, specifically with the work of J. L. Austin and of the later Wittgenstein; second, Phillips's own manner of writing is openly literary, suggesting a wish to play off not alone the ordinary against the technical but to keep in view the competition, as it were, insisted upon by Freud, between psychoanalysis and literature. I find this invitation to philosophy congenial and find this way of writing attractive, and I shall accordingly let these departures in Phillips's *Terrors and Experts* guide my responses to those essays here.

I would understand if someone felt right off that I take too solemnly the allusion to ordinary language philosophy. It seems clear enough that Phillips repeatedly invokes such ideas as Wittgenstein's of language games and as Austin's of how to do things with words. But, it may be felt, Phillips's use, for example, of the idea of words "doing something," as in the second essay ("Symptoms") of *Terrors and Experts,* is not Austin's, as when we find there: "It is always worth wondering, as a prelude to a case-presentation such as this [of a young boy with eczema], what picture we have of what words can do to someone's body, of how they work inside him." This is not the sort of thing Austin would be likely to say, or to find philosophically palatable, yet it is interestingly seen as a call for a development of, hence a response to, Austin's sense of words: Austin wanted an account of the ways in which to say something is to do something, an account that turned out, in *How to Do Things with Words,* to require an un-heard of study of what Austin called the performative utterance; this was in turn one path "in the long-term project of classifying and clarifying all possible ways and varieties of *not exactly doing things*" (from "Pretending"). (This project is pushed aside in the recent development of Austin's work in what is called Performance Theory.) But an unhappy performative utterance—e.g., saying "I bet" when no one within earshot is eligible to take up the bet—is describable both as not exactly doing something (placing a bet) and not exactly saying something (placing words into the world). Austin was apparently wary of speaking of ways of *not exactly saying things* (philosophers might call them speaking nonsense). One reason for this is that he, unhappily, felt he already knew why philosophers did not exactly (or could readily be shown not exactly to) say things, namely that they are lazy, impatient, drunk with pretention, heavy with conformity, etc. Another reason is that to have used the description ("not exactly or really saying") would have risked blurring the very motive of Austin's theory of the performative, namely to counter the philosophical assumption that fully meaningful sayings are statements, i.e., are always (and essentially only) coherently assessable as true or false. But the motive, judging by Austin's reception, seems to have become blurred anyway.

A further reason, I conjecture, is that failing exactly to say something (where it is not artful or obtuse) is understandable as suffering from words, a matter Austin may have felt philosophy could help prevent (as well as cause) but not treat (unlike Wittgenstein). And suffering from words is a way of describing something Adam Phillips takes as the subject of his work (but still unlike Wittgenstein's)—a particular work of listening. ("The patient who comes into the analyst's consulting room, always comes because he cannot speak" [p. 11].) It was evidently to devote himself to this work that he went through the training to become a psychoanalyst.

But Phillips is not devoted to the way psychoanalysis tends to think of itself as a science or as a field of expertise. It is importantly to counter this tendency that he writes his psychoanalytic essays, which accordingly do not sound like most psychoanalytic writing. It is heartening to go through his struggle with psychoanalysis, within psychoanalysis, on this ground, particularly in a time when further depressing attacks and defenses on and of psychoanalysis as such, leading intellectually nowhere, are rather to be expected. (Like, and unlike, attacks on philosophy or religion or science as such.) But what Phillips has against psychoanalysis's picture of itself is not always clear to me.

"In so far as the psychoanalyst becomes an expert on how people should live—becomes, that is to say, any kind of guru, any kind of official or unofficial expert—he has complied" (p. xv). "Complied" is Winnicott's term for a person's having given up on finding their spontaneity, or True Self. (For good reason Phillips cites Emerson on his first page of epigraphs. It is, however, worth saying that Emerson rather denies the idea of a True Self.) Yet Phillips allows himself to remark: "The psychoanalyst is an expert on the ways in which the patient pretends to be an expert on himself; the ways, that is, in which he gravitates toward consensus" (p. 12). Why the air of paradox? Why say more than that "The psychoanalyst uncovers, or helps the patient see, the ways in which . . ."? Because, presumably, neither analyst nor patient are willing to let it go at that: the patient persists in craving belief and authority, and the analyst is always drawn to play to it—not necessarily, I suppose, because the analyst takes himself or herself to be authoritative, but because he takes psychoanalysis to be.

In the concluding paragraph of Phillips's preceding collection of essays, *On Kissing, Tickling, and Being Bored,* he had said: "With the discovery of transference Freud evolved what could be called a cure by idolatry; in fact, potentially, a cure of idolatry, through idolatry." We have heard—have we not?—or said to ourselves, roughly similar things, both about psychoanalysis and about philosophy: they are the overcoming of seduction through seduction; the defeat of mastery by mastery. Isn't this the ancient paradox of teaching? Socrates in the *Protagoras* complains against his disciples that they want to shed their own voices, and at the same time he awaits their agreement. Nietzsche promises to return to his disciples only when they have denied him. And the paradox is enacted on every page of Wittgenstein's *Investigations,* in its sometimes maddening oscillation between arrogance and innocence.

Has psychoanalysis taken no further step of its own? Well but didn't Phillips just point it out? Freud's discovery of transference. And is Phillips claiming that transference is never really resolved? Or claiming that it is not resolved if the patient becomes an analyst—in which case mightn't idolatry be overcome by finding true belief in the one God? But I seem to have met analysts who are so fearful of fetishizing the Freudian text that they no longer study it. And ones who refer to Freud's contributions to psychoanalysis as pre-scientific. You might as well smash the idol and then worship the rubble.

Sometimes there are rather neutral, or somewhat deflationary formulations that affect to lower the rhetorical heat: "From my point of view a psychoanalyst is anyone who uses what were originally Freud's concepts of transference, the unconscious, and the dream-work in paid conversations with people about how they want to live" (p. xiv). There is nothing here about the requirement of having been on the receiving end of those conversations, that is, having your own analysis, as a way of acquiring Freud's concepts. And nothing about what entitles you not so much to the money but to the interventions. Why toy with formulations that preempt the words that people who have no love for psychoanalysis might be amused to say?

But this deflationary mood passes when a patient enters the picture. It is when he is about to present the case of a seven-year-old boy that Phillips gives his most straightforward answer to his recurrent question of the analyst's entitlement:

> But what kind of expert, then, is the psychoanalyst? What, if anything, does he know that the patient or his family don't know? . . . If a family brings their child to see me, I can make available to them my knowledge of child development, my clinical experience of child and family therapy (informed by an array of theory), my willingness to listen, and my moral sense of how children and families should live. I might think of myself as something of an expert on children, or even on life. Or I might think of myself—mindful, in so far as I can be, of the potential for mystification, for covert seductions—as someone enabling the family to learn their own language. (p. 34)

That he does not know more than the family knows about its own language is, in a sense, so true and so important that, if you like, you can insist on it by saying that the analyst is not an expert. But who fails, in such a case, to know this? The other's dream is the other's, and its meaning is the other's to deliver. And what if someone replies to Phillips's distinction between making available certain knowledge he has and enabling the family to learn more than he knows (an instance of the distinction Phillips marks by speaking of the Enlightenment Freud and the post-Freudian Freud), that what Phillips calls "enabling" here is indeed all that expertise can mean, or should, in this science?

Then Phillips will, I can imagine, wish to say that this pictures his relation to his patients as, if effective, one of knowledge, and pictures, what is more, the relation he attempts to enable them to achieve toward themselves as, if healthy, one of knowledge, and these pictures he deplores. But does this opposition require denying expertise? It requires telling the difference between knowing someone and acknowledging that they matter to you (and you to them—though they may get the wrong idea of the subjects in play, or call them "objects"). Sometimes Phillips sounds to me as if he wishes to correct the idea that acknowledgment is a function of expertise, on the ground that you have in each case to find out what is to be said, what is responsive to whatever demand/summons/call you discern. And sometimes sounds as if he wishes to correct the idea that knowledge of another is such a function, on what I might call a double ground—that no set of facts about another (any more than about yourself) is exhaustive of subjectivity, and that the way they are not "exhaustive" is not the way facts about an object are not exhaustive. The more you know about an object the less likely that what you know will be completely overthrown, that what you have grounds to claim is a hawk will turn out on further examination to be a handsaw; but about a subject, likely or not, perhaps never more unlikely than not, overthrow remains in question, redescription may at any time be called for, the duck turns out as in a dawning to be a swan. Horror movies anxiously toy with this realization; melodramas act it out; comedies revel in it.

Perhaps the difference between these occasions for, or temptations to, false claims of expertise can be measured, for further study, by adducing two sites of philosophy, one in an Anglo-American mood, one in a German.

In speaking of listening for a cue of response (often called supplying an interpretation), Phillips warns that psychoanalysts "are always tempted to become the experts on the canon of plausible interpretations, of what should be said when" (p. xvi). This echoes a rare passage from Austin in which he is giving reasons (even somewhat theoretical ones) why with certain topics it is attractive "to proceed from 'ordinary language,' that is, by examining *what we should say when* [Austin's emphasis], and so why and what we should mean by it" ("A Plea for Excuses"). A very good reason for Phillips to echo, or allude to, this passage is this: it is fundamental to Austin's practices with language (and, with due differences, to Wittgenstein's)—ways of getting us to imagine what we should say under various circumstances—that our responses to his invitations to speak require no more than the (native) mastery of a language; linguistic expertise, in a word, is not only unnecessary, but stands to be corrected by listening to us. (It of course takes more than mastery of a language to produce Austin's examples on which we are to exercise our mastery. If this something more were expertise, there would be more people producing Austinian examples. It is obvious that it takes a knack, call it talent. But since it is sometimes awkward to recognize that a practice proposed for university study demands talent, you may try thinking of it as expertise.)

But there is an equally good reason to be wary of the application of Austin's formula for ordinary language procedure to the psychoanalytical procedure of interpretation, or intervention. The reason is given, or implied, in the continuation of Austin's sentence: "and so why and what we should mean by it." In the philosophical case, we can (each of us) say, speaking for "us," arrogating this power, why and what we mean by what we say when. If someone finds me to be wrong in a given case, he or she may correct me. But in the psychoanalytical intervention the analyst speaks exactly neither for an us nor for himself / herself. Sometimes, even characteristically, one could say, he means nothing and has no reason for what he says; or better, what he means and whether he means anything depends entirely upon what the patient had in mind when the analyst's words were prompted, and upon what, if anything, the patient does with that response.

This comes out in the brief but deeply engaging glimpses Phillips gives of his therapeutic exchanges.

> Mother told me that Tom's eczema was much better but that they were all concerned with their poor housing conditions . . . above all the starlings "kept banging at the window like they want to get in." . . . Tom started frantically scratching his arms for the first time. . . . He was, she told me, terrified of the starlings. I asked Tom if the starlings felt left out. He stopped scratching as though the question had concentrated him, and said, "No . . . they're pretending . . . they like being outside really." I said, "Perhaps they are worried you'll forget about them?" And he agreed and started furiously scratching. I asked him if it was the question or his answer that made him scratch. He shrugged his shoulders despondently and said, "The answer," and I suddenly felt a great pull of sadness. I said, "Sometimes boys are worried that their mums will forget them and sometimes they wish their mums would forget them." He giggled, as though I had told him a rude joke. . . .
>
> I suggested that they might both be in a muddle; they weren't sure whether they wanted to be together all the time or apart all the time. . . . I suggested that the eczema made her look at him, but made her unable to do anything for him. . . . She interrupted with a kind of relish of disgust, "But it's revolting!" Prompted by something, I immediately asked how Tom's dad fitted into the picture. . . . I wondered whether Tom was holding on to his father by making himself revolting. Tom, coming to life, stopped scratching and shouted "No!" and told me his dad was a pig and he never thought about him and

never would. . . . There was a great deal of anxiety in the room and
quite quickly we found ourselves talking about their housing problem.
(pp. 38–39)

In philosophical exchange, as I have had occasion to put a founding experience of ordinary language procedure, we are all in the same boat, I know no
more than you, nor you than I, about what we say. In psychoanalytic intervention, it seems, the analyst hears cries, jumps in the water and tries to get
taken aboard, asks after the crew, and sees if he can get those implicated to
wonder what their bearing is and who they imagine he is that he has a right
to hear.

The arrogance of philosophy is to show that I can speak universally, for
everyone. The confidence of psychoanalysis is to show that I do not so much
as speak for myself. To claim expertise for either of these demonstrations is
empty. There is no knowledge of what and when to say something beyond
the capacity to say it then. The claim of expertise in the matter (not of knowledge but) of what is to be acknowledged, is evasive. Not to acknowledge
what is said may be a refusal of its appeal to a relationship, or a refusal of
compliance with its bearing; to be instructive, you have to understand who
you are taken for. The other may know himself as an ugly duckling, not seeing
the possibility of a redescription; it is worth refusing to cooperate with such
knowledge.

The opposing site of philosophy I had in mind in connection with false expertise is Heidegger's claim that the understanding of the human life form
takes the form of attributing to it not predicates of identity but existentials
of possibility. To come into terms with Tom is not to know that he is a child
and has eczema but to follow how he conceives being the child he is, the needs
and demands of this needy, judging mother and that judged and flighty father,
and what solution his eczema expresses. He has, and there is reason to suppose he wishes for, other possibilities. Heidegger's idea is a systematizing of
the German Romantic notion, announced and pervasive in Emerson, of becoming who you are, the perspective of moral perfectionism. It is a perspective on the human. As is Freud's idea that he once expresses (in the Dora case)
in these terms: "He that has eyes to see and ears to hear may convince himself that no mortal can keep a secret. If his lips are silent, he chatters with his
finger-tips; betrayal oozes out of him at every pore." (Compare Phillips, in
the opening sentence of the essay that presents Tom: "People come for psychoanalysis . . . when they find that they can no longer keep a secret.") How

to "convince oneself" of this? By what expertise? By what evidence? (Freud introduces it with the biblical threat "He that has eyes to see . . . ," implying that the failure to find this perspective is not a competing perspective but a damning failure to witness the human.) In the citation I gave from Phillips in which he is prepared to offer his patients his "moral sense" of what a family should be, I take him to mean that he is prepared first and last to convert the register of description from actuality into possibility. (It is on a small scale the sort of thing Emerson calls "experimenting," or "unsettling things," as when he announces "A man is a golden impossibility." That is: It is for the human to transmute what is called an impossibility into what is called an opportunity, proverbially recognized as, at its best, golden.) It is ground on which I could wish to see philosophy and psychoanalysis meet.

Experimentally is rather how Phillips welcomes psychoanalysis itself, in his unflagging redescriptions of it, and thus offers it his moral sense—as something that fails to see its own further possibilities, as more creative than it knows. (That its discovery was what makes such a discovery possible is one more opportunity for evading it.) The truth of the offer is that psychoanalysis exists only in its (re)discovery.

I believe Winnicott testifies that this is true of the analyst (I cannot find a citation for this at the moment); I can testify, I hope without undue illusion, that it is true of the analysand. The process can seem all words; sometimes it is; then sometimes you find you have arrived elsewhere. Over the years I have named an analogous condition of the existence of philosophy, sometimes saying that it demands its own mood, sometimes that it has to be turned to, as by conversion. It is not everyone's idea of (even one condition of) philosophy. For me it is another way of locating ground on which philosophy and psychoanalysis might meet, if to begin with just to articulate their ample grounds, or opportunities, as they stand, for mutual antagonism.

Philosophy and psychoanalysis can both be said to be about the mix-ups between necessities and contingencies, or, say, ordinariness and extraordinariness. Philosophy will characteristically portray the strangeness of our ordinary lives—Plato of our cave of compliance, Thoreau of our cage of woods (even after putting a certain distance between ourselves and the phantasmic self-mortifications of neighbors), Wittgenstein of our resemblance to a trapped fly, or to one stranded on a field of ice, or to a builder building, so far as we know, nothing. Psychoanalysis will characteristically trace the unstrangeness of our extraordinary expressions of desire (in our eruptions of words, or giggles, or skin). Some writing does both.

I pick two of Phillips's redescriptions to suggest certain further lines in which philosophy as I care about it most might do well to encounter his work, one of which I find most promising, the other mostly not.

The unpromising line is Phillips's repetitive insistence that psychoanalysis tells itself, as we tell ourselves, stories. Fashionably, someone says that we tell ourselves stories in response to someone else's claim that we must tell ourselves the Truth, accompanied by an offer to provide us with some portion of it to Believe (that language mirrors the world? that language does not mirror the world?). Even in this role of response (which hardly prepares us for the powers of fable) the idea of theories as stories has its creative use in keeping the mind open—to further judgment, to redescription. But it becomes useless as it becomes indifferent, with everything and nothing becoming a story—Darwinism is a story, the inheritance of acquired characteristics is another; Divine Right is a story, consent is another; patriarchy is a story, the equality of women is another.

One good use of the idea of a story is to prompt us to ask who is telling something to whom in service of what. It is a version of the question why or how I find something worth saying. (This is a question of guiding significance for Austin and Wittgenstein and Heidegger, in their different ways. But no more than for Kierkegaard and Marx and Nietzsche and Freud.) This is not what I get out of the following passage:

> Psychoanalysts are well placed to take a strong stand against the enemies of ambiguity. But when psychoanalysts spend too much time with each other, they start believing in psychoanalysis. They begin to talk knowingly, like members of a religious cult. It is as if they have understood something. They forget, in other words, that they are only telling stories about stories and that all stories are subject to an unknowable multiplicity of interpretations. (p. xvi)

In response to the phrase "stories about stories," I wish to say that psychoanalysts are also well placed to take a strong stand against ambiguity. The concept of story is different in the two occurrences and in a way that seems to me to falsify (or lessen the value of) what Phillips goes on to reveal of his practice. When Tom's mother recounts her and her son's early times together Phillips reports: "It sounded as though Mother had brought Tom home, given him to her mother—by whom he had been very well loved—and in considerable confusion and distress resumed her 'wild' adolescence. It was a palpably desolate story." Phillips makes a judgment about the grand-mother and registers the pain in the mother's words. Is this his story about her story? Is anything here to be called his story? And when, as he records, he responds in the words, "So you and Tom have had to find a way of getting to know each other?" can't we say that he is showing a way to understand what has been said? Psychoanalysts are well placed not to give in to an overly phil-osophical picture of what understanding must be, something always like de-riving something from some more general something, but to take seriously the picture of understanding as the word seems to picture it, as bearing up under something, as if sharing a burden.

The promising line of redescription is well articulated in a passage that comes to hand from *Kissing, Tickling, and Being Bored:* "The art of psychoanal-ysis, for both participants, is to produce interesting redescriptions; redescrip-tions that the patient is free—can bear—to be interested in" (p. 26). *Terror and Experts* suggests a further step: "Psychoanalysis, as theory or practice, should not pretend to be important instead of keeping itself interesting (importance is a cure for nothing)" (p. xv). The linking of interest with an idea of distrusting or destroying representations of importance, as prelude or consequence of reconceiving philosophy, is given in one of Wittgenstein's characterizations of his later work: "Where does our investigation get its importance from, since it seems only to destroy everything interesting, that is, all that is great and important?" (*Philosophical Investigations,* § 118). Austin, in the paper I cited a moment ago, in effect chimes in: "I owe it to the subject [of Excuses] to say, that it has long afforded me what philosophy is so often thought, and made, barren of—the fun of discovery, the pleasures of co-operation, and the satis-faction of reaching agreement." But for Austin the pain in reaching what both he and Wittgenstein conceive as freedom (Austin speaks of unfreezing, Witt-genstein of our being held captive) seems to require less passage through the pain and confusion of renouncing old certainties (or uncertainties).

Now Phillips, in his apparently casual, humorously catty observation about psychoanalysis keeping itself interesting (as if with age the enterprise had rather let its appearance slide), invokes the implied concept of boredom, a concept I believe neither Wittgenstein nor Austin ever makes explicit. (Even though nothing is of greater concern to Wittgenstein in the *Investigations* than to determine wherein the interest of philosophy lies: "Philosophy simply puts everything before us. . . . For what is hidden, for example, is of no interest to us" [§ 126].) Philosophers, who do not shrink from using terms of criticism about one another's work such as that it is crazy, or nonsensical, seem to shrink from going so far as to call one another's work boring. But Phillips treats the mood of boredom, following Winnicott on the topic, with great and telling respect.

The essay entitled "On Being Bored" (in *On Kissing, Tickling, and Being Bored*) discovers convincingly the creative drive in the capacity for boredom, for both patient and analyst, that is, for anyone.

> Is it not, indeed, revealing, what the child's boredom evokes in the adults? Heard as a demand, sometimes as an accusation of failure or disappointment, it is rarely agreed to, simply acknowledged. How often, in fact, the child's boredom is met by that most perplexing fear of disapproval, the adult's wish to distract him—as though the adults have decided that the child's life must be, or be seen to be, endlessly interesting. It is one of the most oppressive demands of adults that the child should be interested, rather than take time to find what interests him. Boredom is integral to the process of taking one's time. (p. 69)

It is indeed, I find, revealing; and I might recommend this essay to someone looking for a place to begin with Phillips. I might also recommend, to someone with unusual amounts of time for the taking, taking a look at the massive bearing on this material of Heidegger's study of boredom in *The Fundamental Concepts of Metaphysics* (English translation, 1995), hence of course considering, at the same time, the pointed bearing of the Phillips-Winnicott material on Heidegger's study. (That Heidegger's is the most detailed study of the topic known to me is not much of a recommendation for many philosophers, I realize, either of philosophical reading or of the topic. Then it will not help to say about this lately published text that if you never finished *Being and Time*, and have some inclination to try again, start this one instead.)

But is Phillips's essay on boredom a piece of psychoanalysis, or does it at least require an interest in psychoanalysis? It, to my ear, almost ostentatiously neglects to raise the question whether boredom may be a cover not only for discovering an interest but for denying a forbidden interest. It is true, as noted, that Phillips speaks here of the analyst as well as the patient: "So the paradox of the waiting that goes on in boredom is that the individual does not know what he was waiting for until he finds it, and that often he does not know he is waiting. One could, in this sense speak of the 'analytic attitude' as an attentive boredom" (p. 78). But while the rest of us are not in a position to assess this proposal, neither is it necessary to do so to assess what this essay says about us adults. And it is true that Phillips quotes Freud from "Mourning and Melancholia" and makes a superb connection: "What, we might ask, following Freud's approach in this extraordinary paper, is the work which boredom performs for the child?" (p. 72) But I do not see that the answer Phillips gives, about the child's giving himself time to find what interests him (which Phillips once words as "waiting for himself"), is one that a differently trained reader of Freud's might not, with very good luck, have found for him / herself. And when Phillips notes Freud's remark about mourning that "It is really only because we know so well how to explain it that this attitude does not seem to us pathological," we might well ask of Freud, Is this psychoanalysis? Shouldn't anyone with an exploratory command of a language and an interest in his or her own experience in principle be capable of such an observation?

What is psychoanalysis? Taking this is as the question of Phillips's essays whose answer is never assumed, but is always in question, I have suggested that his recurrent redescriptions of his profession are meant to keep the question alive, and I shall conclude by suggesting that this aim is also served by the manner of the writing, its tendency—as I suppose everyone notices who cares about such things—to, let's say, the epigrammatic or aphoristic. More or less at random from the opening section of "Symptoms," from which I quoted earlier: "Suffering, like desire, is the secret we may not be able to keep"; "Because desire is always, in part, constituted by the forbidden, every wish is ambivalent, its own best enemy. In this psychoanalytic picture we can't help but communicate, and we can't help but be baffled by each other"; "People are only ever as mad (unintelligible) as other people are deaf"; "The analyst can be useful as someone who can say something at once odd and pertinent (which is what the patient does all the time without noticing)."

I can see that one might take these recurring moments as signs of an overconfident assertiveness, claims well in excess of any evidence in evidence. I take them otherwise, according to the theme of finding and refinding interest, as instances of themselves. Each is, or would be, a little baffling, and a small confession of madness linked with the insinuation of the reader's deafness, and a brief instance of saying something at once odd and pertinent. All are intriguing—miniature intrigues—baiting allure with a passing promise of conspiracy. In short they are offers of moments of analysis, in a form to be made good so far as (this) writing can, can create its audience. To the extent that Phillips's audience is to include other analysts, he is offering his psychoanalysis to psychoanalysis. Which is to say, he is claiming that what he does is part of the history of psychoanalysis, as he is claiming that the Freudian event is not just an event within psychoanalysis. (The necessity and difficulty of finding a cultural location from which to enter this double claim seems reason enough for his citing in his Acknowledgments the journals *Raritan* and the *London Review of Books* for having "made the kind of things I write possible.")

This is on the way to saying how I take his remark, "A good-enough environment [another concept of Winnicott's] can only be constituted by putting it at risk (like a good-enough theory)" (p. 44). If putting at risk is subjecting to test, then Phillips is in effect claiming that what tests psychoanalytic theory is not exactly what tests other theory, and this is something that the repeated denial of the requirement of expertise is, I suppose, meant to cover. Does the seriousness of Phillips's denial to the analyst of expertise not demand the provision of an alternative, positive account of the analyst's powers, and impotencies? And would this not amount to the demand for an alternative account of analytical training? But then can Phillips not insist that this is exactly, though not concretely, what he has given measures for, along such lines as these: Analytical training is what leads to a practice, and to the understanding of the effects of the practice, of what Phillips once (re)describes as "attentive boredom"; it puts one in a position, intellectually, practically, and emotionally, to test the environment of psychoanalytic thinking, to put it at risk, which is to say, to determine what it is that "holds" (Winnicott again) this thinking (in its exchanges with other texts and practices, psychoanalytic and nonpsychoanalytic) and rewards it well enough with pertinent responses to its responsiveness (to demands placed by its readers, its subjects, analysts and others).

Disparagers will like contending that what can present itself as the lack of expertise betokens the lack of intellectual grounding altogether, hence that psychoanalysis deserves no further holding environment. It may be that the cause of disparagement now, after a hundred years, is less a function of intellectual threat and resistance than of intellectual weariness and projection. What is true, I believe, is that the inheritance of the psychoanalytic experience, like inheritance elsewhere in the life of the mind, becomes increasingly hard to secure. And it is hard for me not to see as one reason for this, or redescription of it—in our era of the increasing academization of intellectual life, which in turn contributes to the transfiguring of what the academy is—the persistent inability of psychoanalytic institutes (with exceptions) to conceive the training they require in conjunction, if necessarily in tension, with the differently inheritable, differently chancy, work of universities.

Reports of Adam Phillips's celebrity suggest that his redescriptions are being rewarded. What I have noted here, in considering the relation of certain of Phillips's texts and practices with certain philosophical others, are various cues for finding, so far as my present competence and time have served, that this cause for raising a glass is well placed.

10

Welcoming Jean Laplanche

These are introductory remarks, previously unpublished, that Cavell delivered in 1994 at Boston University, at an annual event called the Boston Colloquium for Philosophy of Science, where the French psychoanalyst Jean Laplanche was lecturing on "Theory—Its Levels and Functions—in Man and Psychoanalysis." Laplanche was the editor, with Jean-Baptiste Pontalis, of *Le Vocabulaire de la Psychanalyse* (1967), a reference work in the field, and also the editor of *Freud's Complete Works* in French (1989). Cavell was interested in Laplanche's book *Life and Death in Psychoanalysis* (1974), which he discussed in a number of his graduate seminars.

THIS YEAR MARKS THE ninety-ninth anniversary of the publication of Freud and Breuer's *Studies on Hysteria,* and we all know people who believe that the program of practice and research this publication announces will not—its enemies are persuaded that it ought not—last ninety-nine more, or nine. It is internal to the knowledge that psychoanalysis develops that it knows it will be opposed, and Freud accordingly, as is familiar, attempted to make provision for its future in the formation of special institutes of training and accreditation. There are those among the friends of psychoanalysis—I count myself among their number—who are persuaded that our late generation of such institutes will not be in a position to provide a further sufficient intellectual future for psychoanalysis apart from their willingness and ability to open and to move their work systematically toward the interest and participation of the academic community, and especially, I believe, toward the discipline of philosophy and its associated disciplines. In this effort, the work of Jean Laplanche, in both its pedagogical and its intellectual accomplishments, is the most significant known to me.

To have an occasion to say this publicly is reason enough to feel happy and honored to be invited to join in welcoming Jean Laplanche to Boston. But that does not sufficiently express my personal sense of gratitude to his work as a companion encouraging my own sense of the calling of psychoanalysis and philosophy for one another. To give a glimpse of this cause I will pick up a moment from a characteristically rich and subtle essay, or lecture, of his translated as "The Wall and the Arcade," published in a handsome dossier by the Psychoanalytic Forum of the Institute of Contemporary Arts in London, along with translations of three other of his recent papers and transcripts of an interview and of three seminars held with him, and altogether serving to introduce a substantial, fascinating weave of his recent work to the English-speaking world.[1] In each panel of it you learn of new intellectual paths opened by recurring attention to the concepts, and the interaction of the concepts, of seduction, of its enigmatic signifiers, of the drive to translation, of consequent issues in the directions and possessions of time. If some will wish to trace this sequence back to the discussion in Laplanche's celebrated *Life and Death in Psychoanalysis* of "the essentially traumatic nature of human sexuality," hence I suppose of human experience as such, who could have predicted this later flowering of conceptualization and reconceptualization? We are bound to witness it further tonight.

"The Wall and the Arcade" is inspired in the number and range of its juxtapositions of ideas and texts, nowhere more, to my mind, than in its two brief, deceptively casual, opening paragraphs. The first names the philosophical as a perspective Laplanche habitually takes up and expects to be recognized as taking up; the second reports that the working title he privately gave his text was one that incited him, adding "and three-quarters of the exercise lies in incitement." From which I gather that what then follows is meant as a meditation on incitement and as expressing an incitement to meditation, an occasion, accordingly, for creative thoughts. And we are not disappointed.

I will give as a miniature instance of something I regard as an incitement, that this text of Laplanche has afforded me, the moment at which he stops, as it were, to announce that he is "[shifting his] direction to talk about something apparently different"—in a text in which shifts and breaks are characteristic gestures, variously opposing in its practice, as Laplanche does in his theorizing, the inevitable psychic tendency toward fixed constructions. In the present instance he moves from André Chouraqui's translation of the Old

Testament and the New Testament and his beginning to translate the Koran, to something Laplanche calls the "proof of the unconscious," which, he adds, "of course relates to the 'proof of the existence of God,' and invokes Descartes with his non-syllogistic demonstrations as his precursor here—the Descartes who had said, 'The whole force of the argument I have here used to prove the existence of God consists in the fact that I recognize that it would not be possible for my nature to be what it is, possessing the idea of a God, unless God really existed'"—a citation, hence, implying that apart from what Laplanche names the "[arrival] of conviction in the necessity of the unconscious," what you might call the human being does not recognize its own nature, hence for all it knows is not intact. This implication is not the claim of a thinker who doubts the ultimacy of the stakes for which he is playing.

Laplanche gives four proofs, of which I mention two. One is the almost sheer fact of "the analytic experience," the fact that, in his words, "one can't get away from postulating that some of our words and acts don't place their reason, cause, or motivation at our disposal"; together with the consequent, somewhat less sheer sense of our words and acts as compromises between desire and acceptability. A second proof suggests what he calls a "dialectic of repatriation," by which Laplanche refers to "what Freud articulated in saying that metaphysics ought to be reconverted into metapsychology,"[2] an articulation that seeks to bring us back, or forward, to the reality of the psychic, unconscious origins of our concepts of a world.

The beauty of these considerations can be seen in their at once pointing back to one of Freud's earliest and least complex texts, *The Psychopathology of Everyday Life* (about which Freud insisted in a late note, "This book is of an entirely popular character; it merely aims, by an accumulation of examples, at paving the way for the necessary assumption of *unconscious yet operative* mental processes, and it avoids all theoretical considerations on the nature of this unconscious"), but a text that at the same time contains the specific features which show the potentiality of comic vulgarity (unconscious I suppose) in a certain revelation, forever renewed, that the scientific claims of psychoanalysis are "unproven." (The revelation becomes no less comic when certain forms of denials of this denial are equally comic. The interaction may yet prove tragic.) The revelation can be said to consist of a deadly combination of two fixations: first (and here I merely report my reading and conversation, not my expertise), on a philosophy of science that takes proof to require verifiability, or falsifiablity, by predicted experiences rather than a unifying and explanatory power over a field of phenomena; second, on a conception of psychoanalysis as based upon something else than experiences that demand explanation, that indeed have always received explanation. Freud's call for the "[transformation] of metaphysics into metapsychology" (*Psychopathology of Everyday Life*) is precisely a call to replace supernatural explanation with science, a science which is in its initial stages, that program of research which, should it become recognized as one among the sciences, will help to alter the concept of science. (This is a place to see the importance of Laplanche's insistence that psychoanalytic theory maintain a studied independence from psychoanalytic practice.)

So when Freud, as he characteristically does, imagines someone questioning him as to, for example, whether or not his proposed elucidations might purport to explain things that may be explained another way, he replies, with a carefully straight face, "In answering this question my experiences leave me in the lurch." That is, I propose intellectual nourishment to replace intellectual poverty, and you offer me instead precisely nothing.

I should, I think, note that Freud fantasizes this line of questioning as beginning with a character he describes as "a colleague with a philosophical education" who had replied to some examples Freud had given of the forgetting of names, hastening to say that in his case the forgetting happens differently—whereas, Freud goes on, there was no reason to believe that the "colleague had ever before thought of analyzing the forgetting of a name, nor could he say how it happened differently in his case." It seems to me that I have quite frequently encountered this very colleague.

The idea of psychoanalysis as lacking proof may be seen as an exact blindness to the process of psychoanalysis as, in each instance of its undertaking, setting the task of recovering one's own proof of its reality, call it psychic reality—as it were an overcoming of skepticism with respect to the existence of mind. If I can formulate this by saying that the first task of psychoanalysis is the rediscovery of itself, I would take this as attesting to the internal link of psychoanalysis and philosophy, which latter I understand as the perpetual rediscovery or transformation, of itself. So I note—before a final word of welcome—that when Freud claims that the construction of the supernatural realms of superstition, myth, religion, and metaphysics are "destined to be changed back once more by science into the 'psychology of the unconscious'" (metaphysics into metapsychology) I find myself thinking of Wittgenstein's claim for his later philosophy that in it "we lead words back from their metaphysical to their everyday use." (Wittgenstein speaks of this as a return to their

Heimat: recall that Laplanche entitles a comparable dialectic "repatriation.") Wittgenstein's everyday is fascinatingly like and unlike Freud's; but both are projects that require returns to something that never was—like the discoveries Laplanche finds in inspired translation.

I requested to be allowed to speak before Laplanche because in a thoughtful letter to me a week or two ago he said that he likes to lecture not from a finished text (so that he would not be sending one ahead) but rather from careful notes. This strikes me as fitting for a creative thinker who demands of himself a contribution to "[his] present speculative journeying," and I would not have chanced coming between his current incitements and those he will provide for all of us.

On a Psychoanalytical Response
to Faulkner's Form

This is a comment Cavell gave at the Boston Psychoanalytic Institute in 2001, in response to a presentation by Gilbert J. Rose, who was lecturing on "The Music of Time in Faulkner's *Light in August*." Cavell's comment, hitherto unpublished, is his only known discussion of Faulkner.

I DO NOT THINK I DISAGREE with anything Gilbert Rose has to say about the significance of aesthetic form in general or about style in Faulkner's *Light in August* in particular. Naturally there are points he makes about which I wish I felt clearer than I do. I propose to take my few minutes here to put a little pressure on three main points at which I feel basic agreement and so especially feel the need for more clarity; to put the points—if I can—in a somewhat different perspective, so that Dr. Rose's way of stating them may be assessed.

1. The first point concerns his assumption of the obligation of psychoanalysis to respond to and to interpret the form as well as the content of works of art; its obligation, if it interests itself in objects of art, to respond to them, one might say, *as* art.

2. His way of understanding the centrality of time in the structure of Faulkner's novel.

3. (and this is perhaps the point I like best, and therefore most urgently want to get clearer about) His recognition that our connection with the

art object, its value to us, is a function of its standing for the working of the mind.

One word about each of these matters in turn.

Dr. Rose criticizes the psychoanalytic tendency—no doubt instigated by Freud—to force an object of art to yield up its contents apart from a sufficient respect for its form, you might say, apart from a respect for its autonomy. This is something that might be meant in speaking of certain psychoanalytic interpretations as reductive. Each mode of interpretation will have its own temptation in this regard. Doubtless Dr. Rose's criticism is in service of Freud's own declaration (apparently opposed to his practice with art) that psychoanalysis has been anticipated in its discoveries by significant literature and art, which suggests that psychoanalysis still stands to learn something substantive from significant art. But while Dr. Rose's insistence on form, his respect for the autonomy of the work of the artist—his effort to shun the reductive—is one of the most attractive features to my mind of the way he thinks about art, I find that he does not let Faulkner's specific work of art do all it can to help guide and formulate what it is he says about it. This may be put as not letting the content of the novel help to determine what its form is—which it ought to be able to do if form and content are "inseparable." But I would rather say that it is not letting the specific novel do all it can to determine what constitutes a matter of form for itself. For example, Dr. Rose lists as one among what he calls stylistic devices that of the alternating of active and passive grammatical modes, and he takes this device to parallel the issue of bisexuality. But bisexuality is part of this novel's more general understanding of the human being as a struggle between two natures, call them the soul and the body, or the eternal and the temporal, or the female and the male, or the black and the white. Should each of these dimensions be expected to have its own stylistic device to express it? Or does the alternating of active and passive modes somehow express all of them? And indeed how would we know whether it expresses any of them specifically?

What I mean by not letting the book help all it can may become a little clearer in turning to the second of the points I said I wanted to be clearer about. It has to do with the central topic of time. Dr. Rose's thesis or hypothesis about *Light in August* takes it as "orchestrations of time and timelessness" in such a way as to reflect "the task of the mind in accommodating, not necessarily reconciling, two intrinsically discordant streams of mental activity—an accurate registration of objective events and subjective needs" (p. 275).[1]

Kant's registration of "two successions" constitutes the world, the distinction between subjective and objective. But I find Rose calls so many things modes or kinds of time that I lose a firm grip on what he takes to support his hypothesis. He speaks of various circles of time "embodied in the lives and thought processes of the principal characters." Here he lists "dead, detached time; instinctual, appositive time; a dawning time of cause, consequence, and personal accountability; and natural, amoral, cyclical time"; then a little later of "moralistic, vindictive time," of "wishful time," and of "human-relational time." These do not seem to me to be equally useful rubrics. Does saying that Mr. McEachern and Doc Hines "live in moralistic, vindictive time" (p. 255) say more or less than that they are at every moment moralistic, vindictive? And is that true? And is to say—truly—that "Mrs. Hines wished that just for one day it could be as though the murder had not been committed" the same as to say that Mrs. Hines "represents wishful time"? This idea seems to me to cause, or to be caused by, some unhappy descriptions of the situation. Dr. Rose writes: "When Lena's newborn son cried it was as if thirty years had been obliterated by wishful thinking, and she imagined Lena to be her dead daughter brought back to her and the baby the grandson she had not seen since birth" (p. 255). But Faulkner takes some pains to deny that things happen this way, in particular to deny that time can be obliterated by *wishing* it away—or, in this novel's work of such a thing, by *hoping* it will go away. Take this fragment from the Faulkner passage Dr. Rose is, I believe, alluding to:

> She [Mrs. Hines] made no attempt to see Christmas. . . . I don't think that the hoping machine had got started then, either. [I imagine that after thirty years the machinery for hoping requires more than twenty-four hours to get started, to get into motion again.] I don't think that it ever did start until that baby was born out there this morning, born right in her face, you might say; a boy too. And she had never seen the mother before, and the father as all, and that grandson whom she had never seen as a man; so to her those thirty years just were not. Obliterated when that child cried. No longer existed.[2] (p. 422)

So rather than time lapsing in response to hope, hope, on the contrary, begins again in response to the lapsing of time. What Mrs. Hines then goes on to hope for may be desperate, but the logic of her emotions is not desperate. In case this is a novel about the conceiving and the refusing of hope, it would be essential not only to get this logic straight but to ask whether there may be other hopes that a lapse of time may make possible (as in Byron Bunch's life), and other ways of time's lapsing that make hope impossible (say as in Reverend Hightower's case and differently as in Percy Grimm's case).

My impression is that the word "time" is one of the two most frequently and most variously used words in *Light in August,* where we hear repeatedly of someone's having time, having plenty of time or no time, of doing something at one time or next time or the other time, of there being a good time for something, of something happening in time, or on time, or on someone's else's time, of the time for something being now, or soon, or the time's having come for something or being lost. My guess is that no thesis or hypothesis of the sort Dr. Rose offers about the orchestration of the time and timelessness stands much of a chance of doing justice to the range of these occurrences. This is of course not something that can be proven, but it may help relevantly complicate the situation if I propose a different hypothesis about the understanding of time in this novel, not to show Dr. Rose's hypothesis false, but perhaps partial.

Before doing this I turn for a moment to the third of the points I wish to take up, the point I said I liked best in Dr. Rose's discussion, in which he accounts for the psychological value of objects of art by speaking (as he puts it in the prelude to the book from which his Faulkner paper is taken) of our "partial fusion with an idealized object standing for the self," an object "standing for the harmonized working of the mind" (p. 13). My problem here is to understand why or how the novel's "harmonizing of its issues" seems something I should be encouraged to model myself on. It seems to achieve its perfection in ways either not open to live human beings (say by being finished, final) or by a combination of means unacceptably costly to normal human beings (for example, by mayhem, murder, abandonment, insanity).

What I think we have need of in accounting for our recognition of another mind, perhaps an idealized mind, in an art object, is a way of understanding such an object as doing what minds most intimately do, namely reflect upon themselves, interpret themselves, understand themselves. This is the role that the idea of the artist's intention ought to play in thinking about art; and it is something we mean, I think, when we speak of an object's autonomy, that it is the only authoritative guide to itself. *Light in August* has a particularly direct way of declaring its understanding of itself; I think of it as assuming responsibility for itself, for its existence as a novel.

This is in its use of the other of its two most frequent, or characteristic, words, one it harps on even more obsessively than it does on the word "time,"

I mean the word "tell." On a thousand occasions someone wants to or cannot or asks or forces someone to, or finds it is the time, or not the time, to tell something, to tell themselves something or tell someone else something. I take this as Faulkner's acknowledgment of the task of writing a novel, understood as the knowing of when it is time to tell something, and by whom, and to whom, and in what circumstances and in what mood. The task of telling goes with the necessity of concealment, of secrecy, and both with the need to be listened to. It is in his work of telling and concealment and listening that the novelist's success or failure is to be judged. Understand this novel's acknowledgment of its task as every bit as much a matter of form as of content. Its encouragement for us would then lie in the originality of the ways in which it discharges its task of telling.

Now I can give my alternative hypothesis about time in *Light in August*. It is a novel about telling and failing to tell when the time for something has come, sometimes the time for telling something and sometimes for doing something. Above all about the possibility of knowing when it is *your* time for something, which means having the luck or taking the freedom to take your time, not forever to have to take another's word for it, to be dictated to, victimized, by others, by the past, or by your revenge against others, or the past, by your despair of yourself. The dominating image of one's time coming upon oneself is that of pregnancy; an image of beginning, which occurs at the beginning of the book and presides over it, as it were an image of the book's own commitment to creation. There are many images of the failure of time ever to be one's own, which in this book are various images of sterility, or of being, as the novel puts it, impregnable, whether that of Janna Burden and her autumn; or that of Miss Bobbie Allen, the waitress, to whom time comes once a month as a curse; or of Reverend Hightower with his fixation in another time, in another's life; or of Percy Grimm and his sense of belatedness in the world. I suppose the summary of the failure to know and to take one's time is laid out by Joe Christmas's horrifying parody of the figure of Christ. The figure whose victimization by his father and by the world was to redeem the human; whose incarnation, or double nature, was to bring eternity (or timelessness) into time and thus establish the center, hence predict the end, of history; this figure is now figured in a universal victim (recognized by neither white nor black) whose life exemplifies merely that victims are created by victims and themselves create victims, a life which is not the source but the negation of hope, that is to say, the embodiment of despair. How, then can we not despair? Where, if the human task remains to hope, do we learn hope?

We are to learn that time is neither a circle nor a line, though we may interpret it, tell it, one way or the other, to learn that to hope is just to begin, and that to make a beginning you need not get behind or above time and enter it again; you need rather to adopt or to understand your time as upon you, wherever you are, whatever road, in the opening image of the book, you happen to be sitting beside. Byron Bunch is the closest thing in the book to an imitation of Christ, and he is more obviously a Joseph figure, on the road with a woman who has just borne to him a child not his own, a woman in whom he places his hope, and one about whose virginity he has had a crisis of belief. I take it that we are to understand that to be Joseph is to be the only Christ there is.

12

Notes Mostly about Empathy

These "notes" are remarks on Bennett Simon's book *Tragic Drama and the Family* (1993), which Cavell delivered at a celebration of the book in 2009. In his book, Simon analyzes a number of literary tragedies—Aeschylus's *Oresteia*, Euripides's *Medea*, Shakespeare's *King Lear* and *Macbeth*, and Beckett's *Endgame*—that involve family and the killing of children. In his blurb for the book, Cavell describes Simon as continuing "the conversation begun in Freud between the genre of tragedy and the modern generations of psychoanalysts," and in this essay he raises concerns about Simon's reliance on the concept of empathy.

IN ACADEMIC PHILOSOPHY—in the form I was taught the field, largely the form in which it still exists in the English-speaking world, the form called analytical philosophy—the topic I have chosen to say something about here is known as the Problem of Other Minds. In psychoanalysis the problem is known—or I think might well be known—as psychoanalysis (more easily if the problematic is pluralized). My professional life, since composing my Ph.D. dissertation some five years after beginning to teach philosophy full time in 1956, has for this past half century periodically been haunted by what, so far as I knew, or know, has been a widespread, of course not universal, reluctance of practitioners within the fields of philosophy and psychoanalysis as I have primarily encountered them, to feel periodically inclined, let alone sense a fundamental need and commitment, to converse with each other with persistence and seriousness. When I had my first say about the subject of other minds, in an essay of mine called "Knowing and Acknowledging," my sense of dissatisfaction with what I had been able to say led me to follow that longish essay with an essay three times longer studying tragedy, specifically staying with Shakespeare's inexhaustible *King Lear*. I must assume that this is a particular cause of the pleasure and honor of being invited to today's celebration of the work of Bennett Simon.

In refreshing my memory of Simon's book *Tragic Drama and the Family* I paused and returned to a sentence which particularly struck a chord of enlightenment for me, which runs as follows: "In brief, the space I ascribe to the audience [of tragedy] is one in which empathy can grow. That growth— or construction—of empathy mirrors processes taking place within the play and among the characters. I use the terms empathy . . . as well as sympathy rather loosely here, in large part because the terms themselves, particularly empathy, have acquired such a range of connotations that it would take a book-length work to begin to order them. *Empathy* is the English version of a nineteenth-century German term *Einfühlung* referring to the aesthetic act of 'feeling one's way into' a work of art. The terms pity, sorry for, weep for within *King Lear* cover some of the semantic range of *empathy*." Yet the very attractiveness and immediacy of the idea that the audience of a great play is in a position, or space, that allows the capacity for empathy to grow somehow made me uneasy with the idea of empathy as a task of feeling into something or to someone. Lear's madness, Cordelia's helplessness, Edmund's villainy, appear rather to leap out at us, as though marking the task such matters present as one of working one's way *out* of something. Is this merely a quibble?

I felt that there might be a way from here to see why or how the concept of empathy creates a sense of looseness or disorderliness, namely that what is required may not alone be a book-length treatise to clarify the concept but some perspective from which to see conflicting forces as so to speak symptoms of the concept itself, that is, in our need of it. It presented itself to me as itself incoherent, suggesting why I have studiously avoided appealing to the concept, as if it pictures knowledge in a mode that precisely blocks the knowledge it claims. What follows is an attempt to throw light on this intuition. (An implied eventual question for me, is whether too hasty and continuous a confrontation of philosophy and psychoanalysis may serve to do harm as well, potentially, as good. For example, is the idea or fact of philosophical skepticism, dominating Western philosophy from its rebeginnings in Descartes and Hume and Kant and continuing in the motivation of

Wittgenstein's *Philosophical Investigations,* really a philosophical problem, uncovering a fundamental issue of establishing the validity of human knowledge, or instead a psychoanalytical problem, revealing symptomatically a fear of, let's say a shrinking from, the human responsibility for claims to know?)

My dissatisfaction with my early essay was something that writing the essay itself taught me, namely that I had not been able to open far enough to view my sense that what philosophy regards as ignorance of the other, and pictures as the absence of something, is rather the presence of something, namely the refusal of knowledge, or said more plainly, an avoidance or rejection of the other. It was then perhaps a smaller step to recognize that the history of the great tragedies explores fields of such rejections, warranted or unwarranted, hence provides a rich and detailed conceptual arena concerning matters in which philosophy, as I inherited it, for some reason remains relatively unversed. The history of great tragedy was, we know, immortally fruitful for Freud, however long it took me to begin to make philosophical sense of that discovery. (Hegel and Nietzsche, for example, as well as Freud, were routinely absent from, indeed had been largely banished from, the Anglo-American dispensation of philosophy.) My teacher J. L. Austin wrote a brilliant and substantial, in many ways permanently valuable, essay entitled "Other Minds," the first two thirds of which he devotes to studying, in his ways, phrases and words such as "I know," or "real" and "really," or "sureness" and "certainty," as specific preparation for the task of getting clear about the particular case of knowing with sureness or certainty whether others really feel what they claim or seem to feel, for example, anger. Austin remarkably but truly felt that philosophers needed to be cautioned and instructed that the existence of other minds presents philosophical questions of its own that go beyond, or transfigure, questions concerning the existence and recognition of things. It was, for me, even shockingly original and fruitful that Austin used among his examples of material things not simply the traditional philosopher's tables and chairs and paper and pencil (which repetitively produced the discovery that we do not strictly speaking know their existence since we are limited to sensing at any time only a part of their surfaces) but went beyond such things to include the recognition of birds, which brought some breeze of realism to the epistemological project. But Austin was not able in the final third of his paper to establish the subject of the other as a case of its own in his version or vision of philosophy.

Austin ends his paper, helpfully and revealingly, by appending what he calls a Final Note, running as follows:

> One speaker [at the symposium for which Austin's paper was pre-pared] said roundly that the real crux of the matter remains still that "I ought not to say that I know Tom is angry, because I don't intro-spect his feelings"; and this no doubt is just what many people do boggle at. The gist of what I have been trying to bring out is simply: One: *Of course* I *don't* introspect Tom's feelings (we should be in a pretty predicament if I did). Two: *Of course* I *do* sometimes know Tom is angry. Hence Three: to suppose that the question "How do I know that Tom is angry?" is meant to mean "How do I introspect Tom's feelings?" (because, as we know, that's the sort of thing that knowing is or ought to be), is simply barking our way up the wrong gum tree.

This "gist" epitomizes it seems to me Austin's philosophical virtues along with his vices. At his philosophical best he will not stand silently and conde-scendingly by while philosophers content themselves with moralistic asser-tions which he shows to be empty, even somewhat mad. At his philosophical worst he displays a bewildering lack of curiosity about how intelligent people can be led to preposterous assertiveness, even when he is himself thereby led to advance dogmatic, complacent assertions of his own. In the sense in which "of course" we sometimes are uncontested in claiming to know that another is angry (or was it actually perhaps rather a case of alarm, or anxiety, or an-guish, or argumentativeness, or acting, or an attack of asthma?), there is no *of course* about whether any one of us knows—in the words Orson Welles thrillingly intoned half a century ago every week in his radio portrayal of the Shadow—or ever will know, what evil lurks in the heart of man.

Austin's failure to impress the philosophically inclined sufficiently in these matters (as he did successfully with respect, say, to the establishing of the idea and importance of the performative utterance) may be a function of his failure to take the estranged impulse to penetrate to the life of the other—said other-wise, the mad impulse to *be* the other—with more sustained seriousness. His observation that if miraculously we were, as it were, literally to *have* Tom's feelings this would not yield knowledge of this other but merely produce a chaos of consciousness, is something I find to be an interesting and instruc-tive insight on Austin's part. But Austin treats it simply as a joke—and, most surprisingly to me from other striking moments in his work, he does not treat this joke with due respect. For all Austin's efforts to "unfreeze" philosophy he succumbs to the philosophical rigidity of treating the problem of knowing others in the way philosophy has characteristically treated knowledge, namely as a matter of achieving certainty, in this case certainty over the existence of feelings in others. Here Austin fails to follow the welcome complexity and subtlety motivated out of his healthy, playful, disruptive proposal of identifying birds as an additional epistemological issue—disruptive (and so for some dismissive) of philosophy's inevitable litany of tables and chairs and pieces of chalk and tomatoes repeatedly invoked to reveal the eternal limitations of human perceiving and knowing.

Austin's failure results not, to be sure, from *accepting* the idea of metaphysical limits, but by the way in which he attempts to oppose it argumentatively in responding to the other presenter in the symposium for which his text "Other Minds" was prepared, namely the philosopher John Wisdom, one of Wittgenstein's most interesting and faithful disciples after the end of World War II (the other is also his translator Elizabeth Anscombe). Austin takes up toward the end of his study a question with which Wisdom begins his series of articles on other minds, the most impressive and sustained examination of the topic in the English-speaking tradition, I believe, before Austin's. Wisdom had asked whether someone "might not exhibit all the symptoms (and display everything else) of anger, even *ad infinitum,* and yet not (really) be angry?" Austin proposes what he names "three distinguishable doubts which may arise," as follows: "One: When to all appearances angry, might he not be laboring under some other emotion [one we should expect in these circumstances] but in this particular case he is acting abnormally? Two: When to all appearances angry, might he not be laboring under some other emotion . . . which we, if we experienced it, should distinguish from anger? Three: When to all appearances angry, might he be feeling no emotion at all?" These considerations are designed to suggest that such doubts are highly special and in no instance a formidable threat to our knowledge of others.

Austin's drummed-in phrase "When to all appearances angry" suggests that one or another blatant displays of this common and blatant state may be feigned or otherwise misunderstood by us or express some other way of being stricken (say in suddenly remembering an appointment you are pained to have forgotten). Now such cases are most obviously ones in which conversation would swiftly clarify what is happening, but I recall no instance in these texts of a suggestion that conversation might even be essential in becoming clear about one's feelings, hence none about the importance of failing to appreciate what another, or oneself, is going through, the importance to the other or the importance to you, no suggestion, one might say, concerning why or how humans matter to one another. This suggests to me another range of questions about the reality of another's emotion, a suggestion concerning whether you are in a position to know how it is with me. What do you, with your protected life, know of despair or shame or failure or ecstasy? The question is evidently not about certainty but about—perhaps we might say—empathy.

But I am ahead of myself here, probably ahead of anywhere we can get briefly in a reasonable time, since the issue is about a matter that comes up virtually anywhere in philosophizing as I care about it most, namely the issue of having the right to speak, as it were to ask that some of the world's time be spent with my thoughts. Wittgenstein, for example, is raising this issue in criticizing philosophers as misusing the word "know" in asserting, for example, "I know that the world exists." Wittgenstein's objection to the claim is that "my life *shows* that I know." (Why, one may well ask, might this prevent me from asserting it? A possible answer is that my position here is not different from that of all others. All our lives show this, if mine does.) This is a juncture of Wittgenstein's thought that is bound to cause ugly disagreement and no doubt misunderstanding. So I should perhaps just say now that I will want to say something like this about empathy, namely that it is not coherently asserted, as philosophy attempts to justify its assertion, but only to be shown. This must come back.

Much as I admire Austin's impatience with philosophy's sometimes loud-mouthed superficiality, I have had occasion to deplore his apparently taking this to suggest that there is no such thing as a profound observation, as opposed to a useful or fruitful one. My distress at Austin's stance came eventually from his clear indications that the figure whose air of profundity most rubbed him the wrong way was Wittgenstein, another whom I recognize as my philosophical master. (In a sense this is not surprising in Austin, since Wittgenstein's later work, especially his essential and characteristic criticisms of past philosophy drawn from his perspective of ordinary or everyday concepts, persistently crossed Austin's paths.)

An essential part of my gratitude, reasonably early and unending, to Wittgenstein's writing came from his describing the work of his *Philosophical Investigations* in connection with the concept of therapy. In the *Investigations* we find the following declaration: "There is not *a* philosophical method, though there are indeed methods, like different therapies" (§133). Is there a reason Wittgenstein uses the idea specifically of different therapies here, rather than, for example, different games or techniques of gardening or modes of government? Later (§254) Wittgenstein writes: "The philosopher's treatment of a question is like the treatment of an illness." So it must be right to take his choice of the idea of "therapy" as considered and deliberate; yet he is also careful to add the qualification, in both of these cases, that philosophical methods, or treatments, are "like" therapies. How then are they *unlike* treating an illness?

The clearest case of similarity would seem to be with what used to be called "the talking cure." Here if a patient is puzzled, say, by his chronic tendency to being late, or distressed by her repeatedly finding herself involved in terminating fights with her intimates, or by recalling the number of injuries she has sustained to one or other of her hands, the therapist will want to hear about the circumstances of these incidents and is unlikely to take the patient's explanations to amount, so to speak, to credible or rational explanations, but themselves to be symptomatic, signs of a hidden condition. The critical dissimilarity between such cases and issues over which Wittgenstein produces his grammatical (as he calls them) therapies is that what he means by grammatical treatments is not something personal, or not strictly so. They are not directed, Wittgenstein emphasizes, to something hidden, not (I take it) to matters on which the patient, and only the patient, can throw definitive light through his or her private associations. Rather, they are collections of such human, conceptual conditions as that an episode of anger has an object and a cause and perhaps a long preparation and these may be obscure or obvious, private or public; and what we call anger can grow or it may mount suddenly (sorrow may deepen but not mount), and that it may express itself explosively or silently and be shaped differently in different cultures, and that the confession "I was angry" can be an explanation, or an apology, and will naturally produce the desire for a further explanation, and that a response to a passion has to judge the appropriateness of the passion to its causes—those defining it and those in which it is expressed. Such conditions, and countless more, are parts, or Wittgenstein says are criteria, of what he means by a concept's grammar, and as such are necessary to what we understand, for example, anger to be.

I would accordingly like to say that grammar is Wittgenstein's version of what Kant proposes his twelve categories of the understanding to accomplish, namely to assure us *a priori,* as it were from our human beginnings, before all assertion, that there is a comprehensible, communicable world. For Wittgenstein, however, it would make no sense to limit the number of our fundamental concepts, partly because there must be as many concepts as there are words and their combinations, and partly because in any case of puzzlement we will have work to do to articulate what these are. Austin is particularly good at this work, exemplified by his unforced display of the difference between doing something by accident and doing it by mistake, or inadvertently, or automatically, or impulsively, and his sense of how such matters bear on what our concept is, more generally, of human action.

But the idea of what Wittgenstein calls *different* therapies should not be lost, since for example the treatment of one who has come philosophically to the conviction that the world is unknowable presents a different issue, or different stage of an issue, from one who has discovered that he or she sees the world only indirectly. And of course there is the prior, always haunting, question: Who is to say, remembering an earlier point, that such convictions are not real discoveries, hence to be believed, or contested rationally, and only insultingly, insufferably, to be regarded as requiring therapy? From what I hear, Wittgenstein is now, as a generally reduced philosophical presence, sometimes described as exhibiting some vein of pop therapy, hence repetitive and boring, hence best to be left aside.

Certainly I left his writing aside for some years. It seemed impossible for me to interest myself in the paragraph from Saint Augustine with which the *Investigations* opens by quoting. Something that prompted my returning and eventually staying with this text is my having for some reason become impressed by the sheer fact of Wittgenstein's book opening with the words of someone else, and my taking this as a tip to think about whether this is meant to raise a question about how philosophy begins, and most immediately to suggest that philosophy does not speak first. But then I had trouble understanding why Wittgenstein found something interestingly amiss, or controversial, in Augustine's description or memory of learning language, granted that it was obviously sketchy; and even greater trouble in seeing the justification of Wittgenstein's attaching importance to his tentative proposal that this very general, unargumentative description of a memory embodied a particular and prejudicial idea of how language functioned. I quote Augustine's paragraph:

> When they (my elders) named some object, and accordingly moved towards something, I saw this and I grasped that the thing was called

by the sound they uttered when they meant to point it out. Their intention was shown by their bodily movements, as it were the natural language of all peoples: the expression of the face, the play of the eyes, the movement of other parts of the body, and the tone of voice which expressed our state of mind in seeking, having, rejecting, or avoiding something. Thus, as I heard words repeatedly used in their proper places in various sentences, I gradually learnt to understand what objects they signified and after I had trained my mouth to form these signs, I used them to express my own desires.

I dare say countless philosophical readers of Augustine's *Confessions* over the centuries have passed by this passage without feeling puzzled by it, not by the strangeness of the description of "training my mouth to form these signs" (which if anything seems an activity familiar from learning a foreign language, not from learning meaningful utterance), nor by the assumption that at the time the child was learning the connection between sound and thing it was already able to distinguish intentions from bodily movements, an assumption Wittgenstein directly undercuts when he asks "What gives us *so much as the idea* that living beings, things, can feel?" (§283).

Eventually I became puzzled as I took seriously the dreamy or trance-like quality of Augustine's paragraph—with its implied figure of the invisible child wandering undirectedly, laboriously stealing words from the surrounding big people—and I came slowly to perceive connections between Augustine's approaching language through individual words, specifically proper nouns, and how Wittgenstein's ensuing portrait of a group whose language consists only of a few nouns constitutes what turns out to be a portrait of a fantastic culture of subhuman enforced laborers whom Wittgenstein presents as "[possessing] a language for which the description given by Augustine is right." Indeed, at some point the entire 693 fragments of part 1 of *Philosophical Investigations* began to seem at various angles of register and departure to be responses to Augustine's modestly but distinctly elaborated fantasy.

And I am by now prepared to go back to that paragraph and see in it something still further, a transcription and revelation of a further philosophical prejudice, or unexamined, trance-like habit of investigation, that has in recent years repeatedly come to trouble my thoughts. I mean the description of understanding another's mind as a matter of "interpreting their bodily movements" and the implication that expressing my desires was something I was able to do only after I was able to use language. If that were so my elders would not have known that I was, for example, cold or lonely or hungry until I was better than a year old, and since my case would be typical, the human race would perhaps never have raised a second generation. Well, Augustine does speak of extra-verbal behavior as "the natural language of all people," so he can be taken to mean in saying *"after* I had trained my mouth to form these signs, I used them to express my own desires" simply that at *that* stage I could, in addition to this language of nature *also* express, and further specify, my desire by the language of culture and convention. But if Augustine had tarried longer with the idea of the natural language of all peoples, he might have considered longer and become more impressed with the natural fact that the child itself possesses some such mode of communication essentially at birth, and perhaps been moved then to stress the ability to understand, or say to *respond* to that language, as an essential part of that that possession, hence that the connection between one's sounds and bodily babble, and the satisfaction of one's desires or needs, begins not even with the ability to imitate, however significant that ability will soon prove to be, but with the recognition that the sounds and motions one produces without—indeed distinctly before—anything to be called training one's mouth in imitation, are always already significant to others who are therefore of transcendent importance to my life. It is worth saying that one is understood before one understands.

Yet no philosopher I think of takes the problem of other minds to be marked by the issue of making or allowing myself *to be* understood, to be an other—the position of *being* known—as the fundamental or essential direction of the problem of the knowledge of others. It is in adopting, or skipping to, the opposite direction, namely from me to the other (I habitually call this the active rather than the passive or receptive direction) that forces the realm of issues that concern how I get past the other's body to the living other, and that on one familiar line of inquiry (popular in my graduate school days) poses the necessity to discover the other by means of analogy between him or her and me, since I know that I have a body that goes with something "more," and on another line requires the capacity to introspect the other's feelings. So why did this, for so long, become the established route in explaining the knowledge of the presence of other minds?

My general answer, however it becomes specified, will always, so far as I can see, be guided by the realization that the origin and shape of the modern study of epistemology, the theory of knowledge, as in Descartes's *Meditations,* associates knowledge with overcoming skepticism, and associates the possibility and shape of knowledge with the coeval, traumatically successful rise of modern science in Bacon and Galileo and Newton. This rise struck the Western philosophical mind as finally to have shown what it is to know the world, exemplified in this piece of wax, in this falling or rolling ball, in this star, this animal, this human. I am not here interested in such sidelight consequences as the perception of the animal as a machine, but rather in the prior and undoubted sense that to know whatever it is must proceed the way knowing any material thing has been revealed to proceed. Descartes exempted God and oneself and one's other others from yielding essentially to this purely sensory process, which omits the essential power of reason in acquiring knowledge. Of course. Descartes was the first of the great Rationalists, together with Leibniz and Spinoza, at the opening of modern philosophy. And the interjection at Austin's symposium concerning the failure to introspect Tom's feelings had the distinct virtue of honesty in expressing and keeping alive intellectual disappointment over philosophical solutions to the problem of knowing the mind of another. Philosophy's mode of investigation (what I am calling its active or outward direction in proposing knowledge of the other) has worked to determine that it leave out, or close out, the heart of the matter. Well, better the pain of skepticism than a shrug of mystery.

Now I can perhaps indicate my interest in, and I guess my suspicion concerning, the concept of empathy, namely my sense that it remains drawn to the philosophical tropism in which we come to sense the need for a passage past a standing barrier to knowledge of the other, call this the human body, a sense that strikes me as a desire to overcome our separateness from each other. The desire seems to be produced, or controlled, by the same route that produces the demand for taking on the other's introspection. Freud's intervention in Western culture may be regarded, however else, as having shown what is right in this idea—call it knowledge as intimacy—but also what is missing from it, namely the necessity, in understanding another, of *my knowing and understanding my response* to the other.

Austin treats ordinary language as having this power of philosophical necessity: "We may be deceived by the appearance of an oasis, or misinterpret the signs of the weather, but the oasis cannot lie to us, and we cannot misunderstand the storm in the way we misunderstand the man."[1] The necessity expressed in saying, for example, "the oasis cannot lie" might equally be expressed in Austin's announcing a thought in the form "We cannot straightforwardly *say* that the oasis lied to us, or normally or straightforwardly say that we misunderstood the storm." But Austin shies from attempting to treat such necessities with more than brief, charming but telling, remarks. He once asks in passing: "Do we focus the telescope or the battleship?" Wittgenstein's lack of modesty in this region (claiming in effect that what he describes as grammar lays out the region of a priori necessity) leaves him exposed to the demand to produce a pedagogy that leads, when not to conviction, rather to rage, or contempt, or utter rejection, expressed by silence, explosion, or studied ignorance.

How can I be confident that the philosophical avoidance of the human condition, with its unsure experience of separateness, will not again find ways to cast doubt on my feeling for the feelings of others, in short to become subject to the surmise, or picture (as Wittgenstein invokes the idea) that manifestations or expressions or symptoms or appearances, or whatever they are supposed to be, are not the essence of the matter, indeed quite miss the point, the point namely that my anger is mine; it is a feeling and therefore something that some individual must have (or perhaps it is an emotion or passion or state—might such differences matter here?). And of course another's feelings, or whatever they are, are his or hers; she and I cannot swap them or exchange them any more than we can sell them or choose them or package and store them. Or can we? Wittgenstein's identifying of such considerations as contributions to the grammar of our concepts means that on his view to neglect such matters is to condemn and accustom ourselves to living metaphysically in the dark. But as Wittgenstein also pointedly, and to my mind frighteningly, asks: Only who needs to be *informed* of such things? Who, in what circumstances, could fail to know such matters, and their importance?

But this time, led philosophically to the brink of perpetual isolation from the minds of others (while accordingly supposing ourselves to remain firmly and transparently lucid and connected with our own), we may actually stop to ask what our own feelings are imagined to be *in response to* another's anger or pain. Encountering a person to all appearances in a rage or in pain, when might we (perhaps out of fear or embarrassment) hurry past him or her; or when, or how, would we offer assistance to the one writhing on the ground (it might matter whether it was a child or some species of foreigner or a soldier in uniform), or when might we attempt to intervene in a quarrel approaching the boiling point; or when, eventually, might it occur to us to speculate whether the feeling is genuine? And by what routes can the speculation proceed and become settled?

What is essential is that the discovery that you were wrong about another is as important, as well as painful, as the pleasant conviction that you were right. If for example you were wrong in giving the name of the composer of

Der Freischütz or in naming the best route from upper Manhattan to Brooklyn, your natural embarrassment may naturally warrant a brief apology, varying with the depth of your pride, private or public, in knowing opera or with the degree of wasted time in getting on to the better road; but it would likely be boring, and prolong exasperation, to hear from you how it happened that you were, or seemed, so insistent with your information. But if I mistook your embarrassment for anger, or your silence for acquiescence, either of us or both of us might have a stake in coming to an understanding of what misled me, for example a lingering guilt over your behavior to me last week, which I had forgotten about, or your own effort to cover the superficiality of spirit revealed in your state of embarrassment. If conversation is the golden path to—and from—the other, the only process that seems to allow of an idea of order in this realm naturally subject to hurried imprecise or simplified description, conversation may also, briefly or permanently, close or disguise its paths. And people vary in their willingness or ability to traverse again and explore such paths. Depth of perceptiveness and interest are not granted freely along with the possession of depth perception and of the desire for information. Relatedly, acquiring knowledge of the grammar of one's concepts is an unending, endlessly interrupted, study.

Perhaps the idea of conversation is the background against which to suggest what I meant by speaking of the concept of empathy as perverse, inherently inviting disorder. The reciprocity, the necessary responsiveness, in continuing conversation throws light on the denial of reciprocity produced by the philosopher's sense of the solution to the problem of knowing the other as requiring "introspecting the other's feeling." Reciprocity does not have to be *denied* in cases of knowing of the existence of tables or tomatoes, nor even generally in the case of identifying birds. Acknowledgment of my claim to knowledge is in such cases not in the picture. The intellectually empty harm expressed in the forced picture of introspecting the feelings of another, so irritating to Austin, can I think be seen to display symptomatically something still essential in what was troubling Austin, yet could not get himself beyond, namely that the philosophical problem of knowledge (what I am calling its "direction of knowledge") presents itself as requiring the active direction, say a matter of our getting from ourselves over to the other. (Eventually we have to ask what causes this choice, or tropism, and take up how the concept of knowledge requires arriving at certainty, conceived a certain way, and consequently seems to require knowing *all* of something, and all at once—the presently invisible back and inside of the apple as well as its present front, and its perhaps rotten insides.) This problem arises in producing the helpless attempts to determine whether what I aim to do, or need to get to, or get to first, in knowing the other, is the other's insides or outsides. It is the direction that inevitably produces and confirms a skeptical impasse, with a long history of unstable solutions or refutations. What goes into this idea of "getting over," or getting across, as if spanning an immeasurable distance?

An alternative to the hopeless demand to span an immeasurable abyss between myself and the other would be to understand how it is that I am always already on the other side of a distance, or say separation, from the other, always already responsive, or defensive against response, to that other. If one insists that this simply begs the question whether my responsiveness *is* to another's consciousness, to the innerness of what shows, its invisibility, I might speak of this as my occupying the space of trust. But how, among many questions, do I, or am I to, conceive of coming to occupy such a space? I have said that it has helped me to reverse the direction or mode of knowledge and consider what others know of me, how it is that I become, and sense, my exposure to others. I have noted that it is not a direction I know other philosophers out of my tradition to have contemplated toward things, that is, toward persons. Pertinent philosophers from what has been taken as an opposed tradition, in reaction to the wake of Kant, are Hegel and eventually Heidegger. But to adopt or adapt such thinking for my present purposes here would feel to me like abandoning my own thinking by merely quoting words whose serious content would have to be derived by me in order to bear the weight they have to serve.

Not surprisingly here I would like to invoke Freud's recognition of the fact of transference as spanning the abyss, the mechanism of my getting over to the other. But then the cost, and the resultant indispensable therapeutic value, of the mechanism lies in my understanding that it is not *you* whom I thereby reach. How can philosophers persist, so far as I know, in not being interested to understand the extent to which this mechanism of spanning plays an irreducible role in everyday encounters? That would help in understanding that the knowledge of others, as of myself, is not an act, but an adventure; if one is lucky it is an interesting and unending one.

Harking back here to my early essay "Knowing and Acknowledging," I felt I had to remind philosophers that saying "I know I am in pain," like saying "I am in pain," is an expression of, exposure of, pain, not a mere description of pain. Both are, intended or not, *demands* upon us for response, which may range from the empathic to the educative to rejection, in each instance justified or not. —Here again I feel particularly moved to rehearse Wittgenstein's question "Only who needs to be informed of this?" I might, in answer now, recommend to any who missed the turning point of the modern history of philosophy with the advent of logical positivism in the 1930s and 1940s—a group which includes by now most people alive—a couple of hours spent with A. J. Ayer's *Language, Truth, and Logic* from 1936, a semi-popularization of logical positivism which became the most widely read work at that period of professional philosophy, selling ultimately something like a million copies. It is a work containing a hundred versions of the claim that aesthetic and moral and religious claims are mere expressions of emotion and therefore are literally or cognitively or strictly meaningless; being neither true nor false they strictly say nothing. Exasperation with philosophy is born with philosophy, but the modern version of exasperation I allude to was widely held and fervently advocated by professional philosophers dominating many departments of the subject (including both of the departments in which I did graduate work). The positivists were an essential segment of Wittgenstein's audience (one he had earlier and decisively helped to create); and they in turn helped create an environment in the United States in which an aspiring student, such as myself, looking for a foothold with himself, was as it were invited to depression. Today it may be that moral and religious and aesthetic dogmatism or fundamentalism are replacing something like cynicism's dominance. A world in which cynicism and fundamentalism become humanity's exhaustive choices is a world in which philosophy and psychoanalysis will have no home.

In thinking of the mode of being known by the other as the passive, exposed, direction in the knowledge of others, I have to ask myself how it is that I *make* myself known, or fail to, to the other. And while here I do not at once come upon the veil or obstacle of the other's body, I am faced with my own consciousness as the aim of my questioning, my response to the other's response to me. Doesn't this simply mean, philosophically, that I am in that case merely assuming that there is a proper other in question, a not-me? Here I can only confess that I am exploring the passive direction, the making of oneself known, as the fundamental case. I am above all, I think, impressed by its coming first in the development, or say continuing evolution, of the human infant, who must make its existence, hence what it depends upon for existence, known, by its restlessness and by its restfulness. Here, so I would like to say, this new presence, preparing for awareness of a further presence, is as yet at no measurable distance from the source of existence; or say there is as yet no discernible abyss. This state of, as it were, pre-existence, is how I place the origin of empathy, the compassion in passion. The fundamental problem accordingly is not to get over to the other, and work our way in, but to learn separateness. This becomes what is fundamental. (The failure to learn the acceptance of separateness seems accordingly something expressed in fantastic tales of being torn to pieces by monsters. The question whether human life is tragic perhaps then becomes the question whether the metaphysical condition of separateness is as such tragic or whether the tragic lies in our efforts to deny this condition.)

If it follows that the knowledge of others therefore requires a phase of infantilization of myself, I am not entirely surprised; it goes with the fact that an expansion of knowledge of myself requires irreducibly a certain willingness for, or submission to, destruction.

This is a way I understand Bennett Simon's perception of the role of the family in tragedy. The space in which one learns to love, say to trust love, is the space in which, as Rilke framed the matter, one forever says farewell, not once and for all, but repeatedly. As if human experience, and a human education, can be said to be matters of undergoing many births. William James, bless him, in speaking of the once-born and the twice-born rather makes them, for my taste, at once too stable and too opposed, human light and human darkness too opposed to one another.

This reminds me to acknowledge that while philosophy, as I care about it most, seeks to free us from self-imposed metaphysical darkness, it does not in that process protect us from empirical darkness to ourselves. I have only wished to suggest that the metaphysical and the empirical are not everywhere reliably independent of one another.

Having confessed my wariness of the term empathy, or empathize, or empathetic, I report my experience the other night in the course of watching an interview aired on the evening national news of a distinctly self-possessed and charming woman of a certain age who had just been released after serving seven years of imprisonment for a crime she had not committed, and who in the course of her responses to questions at one juncture memorably replied, "People have been quite empathetic toward me." My immediate response to this perfect use of the concept was to form the thought: Who would dare to say to her, in the active mode, "I empathize with you," even if one felt in the moment stricken in facing her? Her former use, in the third person, expressed her appreciation and acknowledgement of whatever variety of expressions of concern and gestures of solace have come her way, in the passive mode. People vary greatly in their talent for such expressions, call them confessions.

It requires experience to judge the appropriateness of passion, ranging from responses to grief and to joy, and the possession of a temperament that allows one to risk ineptitude and embarrassment. As the young W. H. Auden put the fact, if I recall, "Intellectual disgrace stares out from every human face." The cause of disgrace or embarrassment that I have been trying to locate is a function of attempting to ascertain by divination or telepathy of the other what can only be revealed by owning one's own experience and one's responses, and failures of response.

Before closing I must suggest a relation between that asymmetry between first and other persons' announcements of empathy and Wittgenstein's claim I cited near the opening of my remarks, that philosophers misuse the expression "I know" in the claim "I know the world exists." In my hearing Wittgenstein's claim is taken to suggest that this claim is radically too strong, as if to say: The world goes beyond all we know of it. But this is precisely captured, and illuminated, in Wittgenstein's point, which, as I take it, suggests that the claim to know the existence of the world is radically too weak. Wittgenstein goes on to say that everything in our lives *shows* that we are in touch with the things of the world, our ease in asking that tables be moved or cleared or trees be pruned or snow be shoveled or persons be alerted and helped. Why then we cannot *say* what can (only) be shown is not, however, something I find that Wittgenstein makes notably clear. It may help to consider here that what I have been urging about the concept of empathy, taken as our route to knowing the existence of the world of others, namely those things that acknowledge our own existence, may provide a more directly intuitive case. It suggests that what philosophy does not consider in pondering our claims to know the existence of the world is that they are neither weak nor strong, but disgraceful.

When I said a moment ago that the cure for this condition lies in owning one's own experience and responses, what I was hoping we could achieve in that circumstance is no longer a mere shrug of mystery in knowing others but a human gesture of acknowledgment before the depth of the mystery of human separateness.

13

Comments on Veena Das, "Language and Body"

This piece is a commentary on Veena Das's essay "Language and Body: Transactions in the Construction of Pain," which was published in a landmark 1996 issue of *Daedalus* entitled "Social Suffering." Cavell wrote his remarks in response to a request from the editors after two anonymous reviewers of Das's essay reported that they weren't competent to evaluate her remarks about Wittgenstein's thought. Having gotten Cavell to offer a third opinion, the editors then asked to publish his response as a commentary alongside Das's essay. This is Cavell's first engagement with anthropology as a discipline.

THIS ESSAY LEAVES ME WITH A SENSE not only of achieved depth but of inexhaustible tact, of simplicity and attention in the face of unencompassable devastations of spirit. With no thought of doing it justice, I will trace a line or two of Veena Das's more elusive thoughts, which readers of her essay may be having some difficulty with.

The first sentence of her essay ends by confessing that she finds that the languages of pain "often elude me." In what follows I will be guided by the thought that to understand her perplexity is the surest route to understanding her readers' perplexity.

Veena Das's topic is pain, in a historical instance in which its "enormity . . . is not in question." Her problem presents itself to her as the lack of "languages

First published as "Comments on Veena Das's Essay 'Language and Body: Transactions in the Construction of Pain,'" *Daedalus* 125, no. 1 (1996): 93–98.

of pain through which social sciences could gaze at, touch or become textual bodies on which this pain is written." This opening sentence fairly obviously enacts, in its open tolerance of obscurity, the absence of such standing or given languages for such pain. If the scientific intellect is silent on the issue, she who speaks scientifically—committed to making herself intelligible to others similarly committed—is going to have to beg, borrow, steal, and invent words and tones of words with which to break this silence.

Her entire essay can be taken, thereafter, as providing an understanding of why this is a reasonable, sometimes necessary, way for an investigation of pain to begin, since, evidently, agreement about this is no more to be taken for granted than is agreement upon a language of pain. Das is exactly, I believe, in this beginning, being faithful to the concept of pain. She epitomizes this concept, in effect, in the last paragraphs of the essay in remarking that "denial of the other's pain is not about the failings of the intellect but the failings of the spirit." She accounts for this quality of failure early, in response to the passage she quotes from Wittgenstein (from *The Blue and Brown Books*), by noting that the utterance "I am in pain" is one that "makes a claim asking for acknowledgement which may be given or denied. In either case it is not a referential statement that is simply pointing to an inner object." In a text of mine to which Veena Das calls attention, I note that the utterance "I am in pain" is not simply a statement of fact (a point the logical positivists had their reasons for emphasizing) but is (as well) an expression of the fact it states; it is at the same time an utterance whose expression by me constitutes my acknowledgment of the fact it expresses (a point the positivists had no use for emphasizing, and that even J. L. Austin, in his critique of positivism's theory of expressive language, missed). One might even say that my acknowledgment is my presentation, or handling, of pain. You are accordingly not at liberty to believe or to disbelieve what it says—that is, the one who says it—at your leisure. You are forced to respond, either to acknowledge it in return or to avoid it; the future between us is at stake. Two implications follow: 1) Not to respond to such a claim, when it is you to whom it is addressed, is to deny its existence, and hence is an act of violence (however momentary, mostly unnoticeable); as it were, the lack of response is a silence that perpetuates the violence of pain itself. 2) If the study of a society requires a study of its pain, then so far as there is an absence of languages of pain in the social sciences—which is, after Veena Das's text, to say, languages in which pain is acknowledged, in which its existence is known ("witnessed" is the term she offers us, correctly and threateningly)—social science participates in the silence, and so it extends the violence it studies.

This is not exactly a "fault" of science. It happens, given what pain is, that its demand for acknowledgment is bound to be questionable in the everyday life of a society—with respect both to the justice of the demand for acknowledgment and to the degree to which that demand has been answered. (This may be taken to be what Rawls's "conversation of justice," as I have named it, is meant to take up; unsuccessfully in my view.) So, I understand Veena Das's more or less implicit claim to be a double one, namely that the study of social suffering must contain a study of a society's silence toward it (or, say, the degree of its incapacity to acknowledge it), and that the study of that suffering and that silence must contain an awareness of its own dangers in mimicking the social silence that perpetuates the suffering. (Why "dangers"? One might say that a society must be allowed some degree of unconsciousness of itself, to disguise itself from itself. But a science can make no allowance for itself of such a kind. To recognize what it does not know is part of its mission of knowledge.)

But does not such a claim as I am making on Veena Das's part make a drastic, unwarranted general assumption about the relation of social science to its object of study? The assumption, as I have put it, is that the social suffering it may have to study is in fact "addressed" to the practitioner of the science, that science owes its subject a response of acknowledgment. The wish to speak of what science "owes" its subject is, I think, quite similar to the way Veena Das's writing elicits the question that dominated the thoughts of contemporaries of mine in graduate school who were engaged in social scientific fieldwork, namely whether the claim to objectivity in the description of a culture must come from a stance inside or outside the culture.

I understand her writing to seek to put such a distinction into question. It is here that the point of her citation of Wittgenstein on pain is most precise. *Philosophical Investigations* is the great work of philosophy of this century whose central topic may be said to be pain, and one of its principal discoveries is that we will never become clear about the relation of attributions of the concept of pain, nor any of the concepts of consciousness, nor, hence, of unconsciousness—neither of my attribution of pain to myself nor of my attribution of pain to others—without bringing into question the apparently endless pictures we have in store that prejudicially distinguish what is internal or private to creatures (especially ones with language, humans) from what is external or public for them.

And I take it that no escape from Veena Das's prose will be provided by hurrying to suppose that she feels addressed by her subject because it is hers by birth, that she is an Indian woman, so naturally she is concerned about the fate of Indian women. As Austin used to ask about hurried assertions, "How many things are wrong with that statement?" One thing that is wrong with that statement is that her being an Indian woman seems to have more to do with her dissatisfaction with what she has said than with her motivation to say it. Something else that is wrong is the neglect of her claim that Indian women and Indian men have said plenty about the suffering she is trying to name, but that they have spoken out of frozen positions (from different idolatries, of women, of men, of nation, of God), not freely, not humanly. Something that is further wrong is the neglect of her claim (again in her final paragraph) that she has herself failed to say something specific, perhaps essential: "I have been unable to name that which died when autonomous citizens of India were simultaneously born as monsters." She goes on to remind us that one who tried to name it, whom she quotes, himself touched madness. The overarching neglect in that imagined attribution of her desire for speech and her doubts of speech about her scene of suffering is of her identifying herself, as well as being an Indian woman, as being a social scientist. It is for science that she (also) speaks, and on behalf of which she is disappointed. She does not give up on the idea that the unknown language of mourning and of healing that she seeks to name might take the form of a tone we may recognize as knowledge, as science.

But what she says, or implies, of that tone as it stands is that neither a standing idea of participation nor of observation will suffice to achieve reason in the present case. Participation is doubtful (does a society have available in every case the means to participate in its suffering, and when it does might not any given member or group of members decline to participate?), and observation is complicitous (the official response to the women's suffering precisely avoids the experience of it). I put this point earlier by suggesting that science as it stands in this case mimics its topic. This is one way in which Veena Das's idea of pain entering the body of a text realizes itself (but negatively, uncreatively): not to experience the death of these women, alive or dead, is to avoid the experience, deny it, refuse its acknowledgment; and that is either to incorporate a woman's private, unshareable, unspeakable knowledge of her death, and of the monstrousness that caused it, or to incorporate the men's public, civilized ignorance of that death and of that cause.

Let me offer a speculation in conclusion. The difference between natural and social science is not that one is interpretative and the other is not, but that in the one case conviction in its objectivity is continuous (except in intellectual crises), and that in the other conviction may have to be won afresh in each project (as if there are nothing but crises). But is there not something else? Has not Veena Das begged the question, proving only what she already assumes—that pain is a spiritual as well as an intellectual problem, that to fail to know the pain of others is to deny it, to annihilate the existence of the one who suffers? If there is a circle here, it means that something is ungrounded, at least in a sense in which we had expected grounding. But perhaps the ground is already under our feet.

This seems to me a place Veena Das finds company in work of mine, especially that on Wittgenstein. So, I will testify to my conviction in two moments in which she finds her ground: first, in her appeal to her own experience (e.g., "In my own experience the question of how good death and bad death is to be defined by the act of witnessing is a more complicated one"), an appeal in her writing that I unfailingly place confidence in and am grateful for; second, in her use of Wittgenstein's example of "feeling pain in the body of another," a passage that no one, to my knowledge, has put to more creative, nor sounder, use. I take Wittgenstein's fantasy in that passage as a working out of Descartes's sense that my soul and my body, while necessarily distinct, are not merely contingently connected. I am necessarily the owner of my pain, yet the fact that it is always located in my body is not necessary. This is what Wittgenstein wishes to show—that it is conceivable that I locate it in another's body. That this does not in fact, or literally, happen in our lives means that the fact of our separateness is something that I have to conceive, a task of imagination—that for me to know your pain, I cannot locate it as I locate mine, but I must let it happen to me. My knowledge of you marks me; it is something that I experience, yet I am not present to it, as in the experience (as Veena Das cites from Julia Kristeva) of giving birth. (I think in this connection of a remark of Catherine Clément's near the end of her book on opera: "The uterus . . . is an organ where the thought of beings is conceived." If such a thought marks an essential route toward overcoming skepticism with respect to the existence of oneself and others, and if skepticism with respect to others is one tacit, if blurred, model for skepticism with respect to the so-called external world, then it is perhaps no wonder that philosophers have characteristically failed either to defeat skepticism or to ignore it.) Wittgenstein had asked, "What gives us *so much as the idea* that living beings, things, can feel?" (*Philosophical Investigations* § 283). This idea of the knowledge of the existence of others more or less reverses Kant's insistence that knowing is an active process, and that sensing is a passive one. My knowledge of myself is something I find, as on a successful quest; my knowledge of others, of their separateness from me, is something that finds me. I might say that I must let it make an impression upon me, as the empiricists almost used to say. (Whether that is sufficient empiricism to establish some part of a scientific discourse is perhaps a question worth trying to articulate.) And it seems reasonable to me, and illuminating, to speak of that reception of impression as my lending my body to the other's experience. The plainest manifestation of this responsiveness may be taken to be its effect on a body of writing. Whether this is ever true of one's own writing one is oneself not in a position to say. But I am sure it is true of the work of Veena Das now before us.

Foreword to Veena Das,
Life and Words

Cavell here continues the conversation with the anthropologist Veena Das that began with his commentary, included as Chapter 13 of this book, on her essay "Language and the Body: Transactions in the Construction of Pain." This further piece is his foreword to Das's influential *Life and Words: Violence and the Descent into the Ordinary* (2007), in which Das weaves together anthropological and philosophical reflections on the ordinary in a book that defines contemporary thinking about violence and how it affects everyday life. This essay is notable for Cavell's reflections on the relationship between what Wittgenstein called "forms of life" and "life forms."

VEENA DAS SPEAKS OF HER "repeated (and even compulsive) reliance on Wittgenstein" as playing a role in the philosophical friendship that has developed between us. Beyond the clear evidence for this observation, the truth of it, from my side of things, is further confirmed, if perhaps less clearly, in an early and in a late thought of mine, each expressing my sense of an anthropological register in Wittgenstein's sensibility, thoughts not reflected in Wittgenstein's well-known recurrence, in his later (or as the French put it, his second) philosophy, to imaginary "tribes" different from "us." I would like to mark my pleasure in contributing prefatory words for Das's

First published as the foreword to Veena Das, *Life and Words: Violence and the Descent into the Ordinary* (Berkeley: University of California Press, 2007).

wonderful book *Life and Words* by putting those easily lost thoughts into words, into the world.

My early thought was directed to a passage in *Philosophical Investigations* that roughly sounds to me like a reflection on a primitive allegory of incipient anthropological work: "Suppose you came as an explorer into an unknown country with a language quite strange to you. In what circumstances would you say that the people there gave orders, understood them, obeyed them, rebelled against them, and so on? The common behaviour of mankind is the system of reference by means of which we interpret an unknown language" (§ 206).

This may, as other moments in Wittgenstein's text may, seem either too doubtful or too tame to be of much intellectual service. "Common behavior" seems quite unargumentative in referring to the behavior of salmon and mallards and anthropoid apes, not quite in referring to that of human beings. But let's turn the card over. Take it that the allegorical air comes rather from the fact that to ask a question of the form "In what circumstances would you say . . . ?" is precisely Wittgenstein's most obvious (ordinary language) procedure directed to and *about us,* about us as philosophers when we are, as we inevitably are, variously tempted to force our ordinary words to do what they, as they stand, will not do, disappointed by finitude. It is *our* language that is, or that we perpetually render, foreign to us. The point of the allegory would then be that the explorer coming into an unknown country with a strange language is a figure of the philosopher moved to philosophical wonder by the strangeness of the humans among whom he lives, their strangeness to themselves, therefore of himself to himself, at home perhaps nowhere, perhaps anywhere. (I have spoken of the *Investigations* as a portrait more specifically of the modern subject.)

Asking us either to find our behavior strange (*seltsam*), or not strange, is a familiar gesture in the *Investigations,* anticipated, for example, in Plato's image of the everyday as a cave, and in Rousseau's fantasm of the first word (the first naming of the human other) as a giant, and in Thoreau's perception in the opening pages of *Walden* of his fellow townsmen as self-tormenting "Bramins" (Thoreau's spelling). The intersection of the familiar and the strange is an experience of the uncanny, an intersection therefore shared by the anthropologist, the psychoanalyst, and the Wittgensteinian (Socratic, Rousseau-like, Thoreau-like, etc.) philosopher. (Here an anthropological perspective is the counter to what is sometimes called, and disapproved of as, a humanist perspective, satisfied in its knowledge of what humanity should be. What I call Wittgenstein's anthropological perspective is one puzzled in principle by anything human beings say and do, hence perhaps, at a moment, by nothing.)

This brings me to the second, later thought prompting the sense of Wittgenstein's seeking perspective on his unknown culture. I once shared a podium to discuss, perhaps debate, Wittgenstein's later views with a friend who is fully recognized as one of the most accomplished philosophers of our generation. In his introductory remarks he asked, in effect: Why is Wittgenstein content to accord the status of a culture or an imaginary tribe to virtually any group of strange creatures with apparently the sole exception of philosophers? When my turn to speak came I replied that for Wittgenstein philosophy is not a culture, not one among others. It is without (no matter how persistently it craves to have) a persistently accepted and evolving language of its own, retaining only some local terms that will be disputed and repudiated by other philosophers; "houses of cards" Wittgenstein will call its parade of discourses. The locale of its originating form of life is the singular human being dissatisfied with itself, a fate inherent, or say natural, within any civilized human society. We (moderns, philosophers) are likely often to accede to the idea that philosophy has become a profession like others, say, since its incorporation into the Western university curriculum over the past two and a half centuries. But that is something Wittgenstein fairly clearly finds as strange as it is familiar.

It seems clear to me that Das's sense of compulsive turning to a companionship with Wittgenstein's later work is her recognition that his address to the human other is, like her own, one that can be said to revolve characteristically around the study of pain. I have heard this tropism of Wittgenstein's criticized as in effect making things too easy for himself, since the criteria of pain are epistemologically so well defined, the feeling so well known. This strikes me merely as one of numberless ways of defending oneself against Wittgenstein's uncovering of philosophy's defenses, say, against the everyday, against finitude. But the question of the sense of pain's pressure in Wittgenstein's text is a good one. Since I have for a long time been following out my sense of Wittgenstein's work as directed to an understanding of skepticism, I am likely to regard pain as especially suited to be a philosophical example for him precisely because of its commonness and its recognizability, something knowable about the other if anything is. And I would emphasize two other facts of the phenomenon, first that over a large range of its occurrences its manifestation is more or less repressible or disguisable (paradoxically more easily than the manifestation of joy or mild surprise or a prompting of laughter), so that one may be said in such cases to have to care whether to understand what is happening; second, that unlike joy or surprise or laughter, with pain there is a moral demand to respond to its expression. (A killjoy is obnoxious but not immoral.) I find that one appropriate use of Das's work is as a companion to Wittgenstein's preoccupation with the other.

What kind of task is it to study social suffering? To follow Das into events in which social convulsion lays bare the question of a society's will and its right to exist, to name and honor itself, is to arrive repeatedly at the feeling that to know a society is to know its capacity to inflict suffering upon itself. In her perception of the cases she principally studies, the extended total event of the Partition and the comparatively confined event of the aftermath of the assassination of Indira Gandhi, states of chaos are as if called upon to hold the mirror up to what society has called its order. Here the philosophical image or myth of pervasive but hidden chains or iron bars keeping us in place—yet variously perceptible in Plato (where in the Cave we are each chained) and in Rousseau (where we are free and everywhere in chains) and in Thoreau (where we are caged in the woods) and in Marx (where most of us have nothing to lose but our chains)—can seem to come to a terrible enactment in the moment at which these bonds bewilderingly are broken. In the instances Das places before us, a reality of pain is released for which she finds that there are no standing words.

She nevertheless discovers a path of articulation into this chaos by confronting the tradition of philosophy and transforming or reinhabiting—and, what is more, showing the resultant relation of—two of its familiar sites of perspective on our common lives, that of the social contract establishing consent to the political order, and that of our common language appearing as inherently unreliable. She takes on the perception that the social contract has been sexualized, that the roles of men and women are systematically contrasted in the events of partitioning, where consent is declared and forced (hence horribly parodied) by symbolizing it in the abduction of women, and where this violation simultaneously produces silence in women and, in men, a volubility that fails to express what they see and do. Das characterizes the men's speech as taking on the register of rumor, as if the events they describe were caused otherwise than by themselves, as if they have made themselves into creatures lacking both desire and responsibility. This psychic catastrophe is a kind of living parody of something philosophy has meant to capture in its portraits of skepticism, where one is invited to feel that it is language itself that causes the human being's ignorance of itself and of its role in the world, and not a self-distancing and self-blinding relation to one's words.

Something that has kept drawing me back to the topic of skepticism, from the time of completing my doctoral dissertation, so largely concerned with understanding Wittgenstein's *Philosophical Investigations* as an original response to the threat of skepticism, was my sense that skepticism with respect to other minds was, whenever I heard it discussed in classes and conferences, made derivative from, or made to imitate, skepticism's modern inception in Descartes and its continuation in Hume and its opposition in Kant, each of whom had treated skepticism essentially with respect to material objects, or, say, to the system of objects philosophers have called the external world. Hence the philosophical problem of others was shaped as one of assessing whether, or how, we know about others what we claim to know. A decisive turn in my own studies in skepticism came from the realization that a skeptical process toward other human beings (others like myself, Descartes says) results not in a realization of my ignorance of the existence of the other, but in my denial of that existence, my refusal to acknowledge it, my psychic annihilation of the other. That there is a violence that is not directed to the defense of the self's integrity or to a rightful demand for equality or for freedom, but expresses this wish for the other's nonexistence, strikes me as a further way to take up Das's insight of "healing [the consequences of violence] as a kind of relationship with death."

I was prompted to ask myself whether her cases of extreme manifestation of a society's internal, one could say, intimate and absolute violence are comprehensible as extreme states, or suddenly invited enactments, of a pervasive fact of the social fabric that may hide itself, or one might also say, may express itself, in everyday encounters. The background of my question is double, one part coming from a further perception of Das's, and one part coming from my having in recent years begun to register unacknowledged yet inevitable manifestations of what Wittgenstein pictures as the pervasive, irreducible recurrence of human nervousness or restlessness, as it were the human incapacity for and refusal of peace (which Wittgenstein specifically pictures as features of the modern subject, ones he portrays as torment, perverseness, disappointment, devastation, suffocation, and so on), a kind of perpetual preparation for violence that has led me to speak of our dealing among ourselves "the little deaths of everyday life," the slights, the grudges, the clumsiness, the impatience, the bitterness, the narcissism, the boredom, and so on (variously fed and magnified and inflamed by standing sources of social enmity, say, racism, sexism, elitism, and so on). No wonder a philosopher (I am thinking at the moment of Thoreau) will from time to time allow himself to be overcome with the feeling that human life, as it stands, stands in need of, and is without, justification, as when, adding up the amount he has spent on food in a year, that is, on supplies to keep himself alive, he announces, "I thus unblushingly publish my guilt."

The further insight of Das's that I refer to is her recognition that in the gender-determined division of the work of mourning the results of violence, the role of women is to attend, in a torn world, to the details of everyday life that allow a household to function, collecting supplies, cooking, washing and straightening up, seeing to children, and so on, that allow life to knit itself back into some viable rhythm, pair by pair. Part of her task is to make us ponder how it is that such evidently small things (whose bravery within tumultuous circumstances is, however, not small) are a match for the consequences of unspeakable horror, for which other necessaries are not substitutes. (Here the pity and terror that Aristotle finds in the catharsis provided for the witnesses of tragedy seem in everyday time to yield healing for the healers of catastrophe.)

In the background of my sense of these matters a remark from Wittgenstein's *Journals*, collected in a volume entitled *Culture and Value*, plays a role that I know I still imperfectly, or only intermittently, understand but that I feel sure is illuminated by this nearly inconceivable mismatch of harm and healing: "The whole planet can suffer no greater torment than a single soul." We are touching here on matters that will seem to take moral philosophy, with its assessment of goods and its exhortations to duty and to contracts, quite beyond its accustomed paths.

A parting word. I spoke just now of evidently small things in response to tumultuous things, and I spoke earlier of Das's work as reciprocating Wittgenstein's preoccupation with the everyday life of the other, where the modification "everyday" asks attention to the specificity (however perhaps normally missed) of a current locus of interest and desire and need. The bridge for me here between these representatives of philosophical and anthropological work is my perpetual harboring for philosophy an idea or image—I guess in unpropitious times—of the first virtue of philosophy as responsiveness. I have sometimes put this thought by saying that philosophy does not speak first. It is a recurrent cause of wonder to me that in philosophy's modern rebeginning, where philosophy finds the power to wipe clean the intellectual slate and ask for proof that we know anything exists—most poignantly expressed as wanting to know whether I am alone in the world—Descartes passes by, I have to say denies, the answer provided in the existence of the finite neighbor. My heartfelt gratitude to Veena Das for her *Life and Words*.

15

Foreword to Northrop Frye,
A Natural Perspective

In 1963, the famous literary critic and theorist Northrop Frye delivered a series of Bampton Lectures at Columbia University, which were published in
1965 under the title *A Natural Perspective*. Thirty years later, in 1995, Columbia
University Press asked Cavell to write the foreword to a reissue of Frye's book.
The topic of Frye's lectures—Shakespearean comedy and romance—was one
with which Cavell was intimately familiar, having himself written critical essays on a range of Shakespeare's plays, many instances of which are published
in the collection *Disowning Knowledge* (1987).

> SEARCHING, IN THE LATE 1950S, if you can imagine, for a way
to begin teaching and writing philosophy that I could believe in and make a
living from—having had one fruitless encounter with Wittgenstein's fairly recently translated *Philosophical Investigations,* but somehow again moved to
fight my way through it—I came to recognize something that for better or
worse guides my desire for philosophy, that it has essentially (not, of course,
exclusively) to include texts whose task of writing comes to be for me as
important as its inventory of topics. That the systematically fruitful or the
logically exact have their beauties is not exactly news; but the damnable beauties of *Philosophical Investigations,* together with its apparent lack of system
or even, mostly, of argument, seemed actually to get in the way of conclusions.

First published as the foreword to Northrop Frye, *A Natural Perspective: The Development of Shakespearean Comedy and Romance* (New York: Columbia University Press, 1995).

Of course I tried thinking to myself that this must be the point—systematicity without system, conclusiveness without conclusion, the fervor of morality and of art, even of piety, without ethics or aesthetics or religion. But how does it all actually happen, sentence by sentence? And what is philosophy if it can look and sound this way?

It was within the crisis produced for me by the incidence of such questions that Northrop Frye's *Anatomy of Criticism* appeared, with its proposals to redraw the chart of what might be called literary studies. Its evident fearlessness, and its tirelessly intelligent responsiveness, in the face of virtually anything that might count as writing, struck me as apt to have some unanticipated perspective on those presentations of writing held to do the work of philosophy.

This proved to be true, but not at once. The reigning second and third generations of logical positivism in philosophy and of New Criticism in departments of English (because of their own original achievements) had prepared an environment mostly impatient, to say the least, with the idea that philosophy and literature were close enough to be in a crisis of mutual denial. Those colleagues in literary study who admired Frye's work had understandably picked it up by different handles from mine. It was not uncommon to hear Frye praised for having demonstrated that works of literature were essentially sets of conventions; and I remember a distinguished professor of literature, responding to my early expressions of fascination with Frye's work, saying in effect, "Of course we know the *Anatomy* is a remarkable book. But it is of no serious use to us in its claim that judgments of literary value have no place in the serious teaching of literature." Coming from the *Investigations,* where ideas of conventions or practices or rules are of phenomena formed in response to the insistence of something to be called natural reactions, and where in philosophy rules undermine themselves just as they are to be of the surest help, this praise of convention, or structure, seemed to me, well, simple. As for the wish to authorize judgments of value, what I just called the fervor of the *Investigations* alerted me to the possibility that the importance of what you might call the literary, as of what you might call the philosophical, is too pervasive to be captured in studied passes of approval and disapproval. Decades later it will occur to me to wonder why Frye's challenge to academic judgment seemed not to have pertinence to, say, theorists of literature suspicious of their discipline's habits of unexamined valorization. Perhaps the answer is that the later theoretical suspicion runs, not without cause, right up to the category of the masterpiece, and Frye's testimony concerning literary judgment took the form, awkwardly, of a masterpiece.

In the prefatory statements to *Anatomy of Criticism,* Frye measures his accomplishment this way: "What is here offered is pure critical theory, and the omission of all specific criticism, even, in three of the four essays, of quotation, is deliberate. The present book seems to me . . . to need a complementary volume concerned with practical criticism." Among the various candidates for this supplementary role which Frye may be taken to have offered in the range of work he made, none that I know strikes me as handsomer than *A Natural Perspective.* For this reason alone, among other expectations of good from truly good work, it is heartening to know that it will be in circulation again.

Written for delivery as lectures in 1963, signed for publication the next year, this text does not know the particular causes opened in the ensuing decades for political and philosophical aspiration and exhaustion, for mad uncertainties and madder certainties, so that its joining of extreme learning and good spirits, or, say, of pedagogical generosity and intellectual sociability, may for a while, on picking it up now, seem signals from an irretrievable past. How it will in fact be taken, or re-taken, is a function of how we will understand, for example, this remark from the opening quarter of chapter 2: "In every poet there is a craftsman who is trying to put words together into a structure solid enough to communicate with audiences remote in time and space and cultural assumptions." We will of course be suspicious of claims for a poet's immortality and communicability based on some picture of architectural accomplishment. But how about the modesty attributed in shading "solid" by "enough"? What if, even, Frye is there proposing a kind of definition of the poetry in any enterprise, for example in his. If his work mattered in its time and place, helped tell what its time and place were, then it existed for that time and place; I suppose we do not know what brings such existence to an end. Whether it will be, or again be, taken on by us, matter to us, whether we let it help tell us what our time and place are, or may be, is with this reprinting about to become knowable. If it proves to matter, we will have, as usual, some explaining to do about how such things get waylaid or mistaken.

Take for a moment the sentence succeeding the one I just quoted: "There is also in every poet, as in every man, an ego that wants to harangue and buttonhole, to sound off and impress, to impose opinions and project fantasies, to make enemies squirm and friends glorious by association." Without stopping to give thanks that people of learning used to talk so, I gloss this quick fingering of the "ego" with the concluding sentence of that paragraph: "It is an offense against [Shakespeare's] privacy much deeper than any digging up of his bones to reduce him from a poet writing plays to an ego with something to 'say.'" You might take this as a genteel appeal to the primacy of the savorable (poetic writing) over the rational (the message or moral) in the poet's dish. But you might take it, as I do, as an independent (I assume), workable intuition of a Lacanian understanding of the ego as the field of misrecognition; so that a mistaking of Frye here would suggest that we do not know, or do not care, where speech that matters to us comes from, which would mean that we have forgotten how to listen.

I get to this point—from a context in which I am asking myself, in effect, whether we believe that either the good or the evil that men do survives them—by reading Frye's reference to Shakespeare's bones as an allusion to Mark Antony's crack that "The evil that men do lives after them, / The good is oft interred with their bones," thus remarking on our ingratitude as well as our tendency toward magic thinking, identifying what is good for us or bad for us with relics. But whom do we appoint to teach us differences?

In the brief preface to *A Natural Perspective*, Frye announces genially that "the perspective taken in these lectures is . . . , I hope, uncommon enough to be of some value," and goes on to specify its uncommonness, within the tradition of Shakespeare criticism, as its "[retreat] from commentary [on individual plays] into a middle distance, considering the comedies as a single group unified by recurring images and structural devices." Are we to wonder over some relation being struck between the banal idea of taking a perspective and the title idea of a natural perspective, a title that may strike one either as banal or as unheard of, or if heard of, mysterious, when Frye identifies it as from near the end of *Twelfth Night:* "A natural perspective, that is and is not." I take this as an instance of Frye's knack for putting frozen investments back into circulation. (I have in mind this signature touch from *Philosophical Investigations* [§116]: "What we do is lead words from their metaphysical to their everyday use." I assume that Frye's counter-Wittgensteinian taste—for example, for system—needs no emphasis.) The reader is already, before knowing it, given a glimpse of Frye's way of facing theory and practice with each other, letting a work under theoretical questioning provide the terms of its questioning, as if confessing from the beginning that the theory or science of the literary that he wants—which turns out to be as inclusive as a science of whatever may be called writing as such—must be made of the same words, and the same ways of extending words, as any other work in words; which is to say that his theory or science, his goal of ordering a knowledge of writing, is a further work within the world of writing, a contribution that may modify the gravitational field it occupies, but which claims no perspective on that world that depends on a fantasy of freedom from its force.

I wish my use of the term *perspective* in that last clause to be unobtrusive but therewith to sound the moral of my claim about Frye's practice of theorizing—that you do not know a priori which terms are to do theoretical work in his prose, as if nothing short of the powers of each word in the language is sufficient to understand the powers of language. Suppose something that waylaid the full effect of Frye's work (I am not well placed to assert that this is generally true of it; it seems quite true in my corner of things) is the advent, a few years after the appearance of *A Natural Perspective*, of, let's agree to call it, poststructuralism. Then this development had taken, not wrongly, Frye's use of *structural* as a theoretical term. It is, however, no more theoretical in force than, in the text to follow here, the term *perspective;* put otherwise, Frye is as much (or as partial) a perspectivist thinker as he is a structuralist. This contains a double emphasis about Frye's practice and thinking: First, there is no fixed structure that a given work obeys, that as it were determines its significance (unless in a particular case, or in a particular field of writing, say double-entry bookkeeping, the work works to have it so, and fails, if it fails, in that particular cause); on the contrary, the extent to which certain structures are determinative sets the drive of an argument, not necessarily conclusive, between a work and, say, its genre. Second, no extent of obedience to a structure (unless, in a particular case, a work works to have it so) determines the tone in which the work is taken, is in this sense understood; in a word, structure does not determine perspective (there is to be expected, for example, a character within a comedy—or without—who fails to find its events comic).

Such a distinction, between structure and perspective, would take some place along Frye's endless play, in *A Natural Perspective*, with chains of what he calls the "device"—in particular, the beginning device—of the dichotomy. Its all but beginning third sentence reads: "We are told, by Coleridge, that all philosophers are either Platonists or Aristotelians; by Gilbert, that all girls and boys are either liberals or conservatives, and, by popular rumor, that all human beings are either girls or boys." The next sentence characterizes these pleasant statements as rhetorical rather than factual, providing perspective rather than truth, and goes on to say that all literary critics are either *Iliad* critics or *Odyssey* critics. The following paragraph begins with the distinction between literature's function as delight and as instruction and continues: "On the most naive level of literary study there is the contrast between the person who reads to improve his mind or his command of the language and the person who reads detective stories in bed." (Leaving open whether what is naive is reading detective stories, reading them in bed, or doing that in bed.) "Naive" turns out to be contrasted, implicitly, as the paragraph goes on, with "more highly developed" and with "best and wisest." Not until the concluding dichotomy of the final paragraph of the chapter does the naive find its flat contrast with the sophisticated. After a distinction between the moral critic and the, let us say, aesthetic critic, we move to that between the spectator and the participator, and then between construct and experience, and then we have: "The kernel of the Jonsonian tradition is something abstract and sophisticated; the kernel of the Shakespearean tradition is something childlike and concrete"— so that the initial distinction into which the naive (or childlike) entered, and seemed to be somewhat disvalued, is overturned by its role in the Shakespearean as distinguished from the Jonsonian, a distinction in which the childlike is at least as highly valued as its opposite.

Reexperiencing the lighthearted, improvisatory air of these tracks of pairs, I remember the pleasure they afforded of liberation from the fixed disfavor into which the habit of dichotomizing had fallen in my days of graduate studies, as if some power of ultimate unification were known to be the natural destiny of the human intellect. A famous academic text of the 1930s, preceding my years, Arthur Lovejoy's *The Revolt Against Dualism,* had complained of this disfavor, revolted against this revolt. Let us say it echoed an old complaint, here in the name of realism, against German Idealism and its drive for absolute unification, call it monism. In another culture it would take Kierkegaard's *Either / Or* to provide a serious motivation for the complaint against monism, say against Idealism's removal of human aspiration from its entrapment within human decision, of infinite concern amid finite concerns. I associate the early disfavor of dualism particularly with John Dewey's incessant structural device—a derivative of his formative study of German Idealism—of mounting an argument by pitting obviously unattractive alternatives against each other (e.g., repetitive behavior against random attempts at the solution of a problem) and then offering as a middle way the solution he already knew (e.g., unification through intelligent conduct). The move against intellectual fixation is admirable; but the value of the particular move is no higher than the accuracy of the description and diagnosis of the paired fixations.

Our more recent experience of a disfavor with dichotomizing, also associated with a move from Idealism and its purely resolving dialectic, is with assaults on binary oppositions. Here the motive is rather the sense that the sides of a duality split into victor and victim—natural versus historical, natural versus artificial, human versus natural, sophisticated versus naive, native versus foreign, serious versus parasitic, writing versus voice, voice versus writing, rational versus intuitive, mind versus body, justice versus mercy, men versus women. But whereas the earlier revolt against monism took the form of a defense of dualism, the new, continuing revolt against monism takes the form (paradoxically, it may seem) of another revolt against dualism. It may help grasp the difference to say that formerly the intellect was charged with denying real differences (say, between men and women or between earth and heaven); latterly the intellect is being charged with affirming false differences (say, between women and men or between earth and heaven).

It does not seem unreasonable to me to feel torn between these perspectives, and to seek a way through. In Frye's practice, where every distinction releases another, the moral is that fixation or absolutism of mutually negating concepts is humorous, fit for comedy, a case of speaking in solemn stupidity. I suppose this is a reason, following his suggestion that all literary critics are either *Iliad* critics or *Odyssey* critics—having glossed this as the sense that "interest in literature tends to center either in the area of tragedy, realism and irony, or in the area of comedy and romance"—that Frye locates his perspective or tone by confessing, "I have always been temperamentally an Odyssean critic, attached to comedy and romance." He conceives of the opposite attraction—to tragedy and irony—as epitomized by "what Freud calls the reality principle." I think that is right about Freud. And it fits the claim of philosophy, to be awake when the fixations of our culture have moved beyond the capacity for ridicule or parody. Or must we take it that reality now altogether outstrips surrealism?

I have been musing here, glad of the occasion to express gratitude for Northrop Frye's achievements. Since this is what should justify my being given the moment, perhaps I may be allowed, before ending it, to specify certain more private causes for my gratitude. They began early, in the second essay I published that I still use, "The Availability of Wittgenstein's Later Philosophy," in which I attribute to my reading of *Anatomy of Criticism* a year or two earlier my capacity to say that philosophy as a genre of writing is subject to conditions—call them literary, call them structures—that it cannot in its moment survey. The causes continued, emphatically with *A Natural Perspective* (but even before that, and in preparation for it, having caught up with Frye's "The Argument of Comedy" from the late 1940s). It specified for me my sense that certain Hollywood films form an unnamed genre of comedy that

I felt sure must be some unpredictable consequence of Shakespearean romance, and therewith went into making the writing of *Pursuits of Happiness*, with its gradual articulation of the genre of the comedy of remarriage, more continuous fun than I had thought my writing would afford me.

And then there are the further, dispersed moments of ratification or education throughout the conversation Frye lavishes on his topics. I pluck two instances from late pages of *Anatomy of Criticism*, just before its conclusion. "What distinguishes, not simply the epigram, but profundity itself from platitude is very frequently rhetorical wit." This is good to hear—if threatening to remember—for someone like me for whom the material of philosophy is so frequently our banalities. That it is itself epigrammatic, witty, and profound makes it hard (as hard as it can) not to remember. Again, "Nothing built out of words can transcend the nature and conditions of words." The thought that every working word circles the language that encircles it is one, permitting differences, that attracts the attention of Wittgenstein, Austin, Quine, Derrida, and Lacan. If I may, considering that this is a moment of North American respect, I will include Emerson, here from "Power," allegorizing the idea of human life as a weaving, say a text, hence as on the loom of language:

> The world-mill is more complex than the calico-mill, and the architect stooped less. In the gingham-mill, a broken thread or a shred spoils the web through a piece of a hundred yards, and is traced back to the girl that wove it. . . . A day is a more magnificent cloth than any muslin, the mechanism that makes it is infinitely cunninger, and you shall not conceal the sleazy, fraudulent, rotten hours you have slipped into the piece; nor fear that any honest thread, or straighter steel, or more inflexible shaft, will not testify in the web.

The tone is not one Frye precisely permits himself, but his example enables the connection. The conditions of our weaving are more than we know and the power of our text to judge us is appalling. Yet the condition of its testimony is that throughout the making of days, say of time, the fabric's uncountable crossings all move to our touch. As with intention, touch is far from everything, and far from nothing.[1]

16

In the Meantime

Cavell was invited to contribute this short piece to a 1992 issue of the *Yale Journal of Criticism* on the topic "Authority, Tradition, and the Future of the Disciplines." At the time, Yale was the epicenter of the deconstructionist movement in criticism inherited from the French philosopher Jacques Derrida. For Cavell, Derrida's way of approaching philosophical problems represented an alarming capitulation to what for human beings, he thought, is a standing temptation to avoid our humanity and the humanity of others.

I AM GOING TO CONTRIBUTE some anecdotal material to our proceedings, along certain marginal or interstitial lines; and in characterizing the work I do I will stick pretty much to thoughts collected in my first book, *Must We Mean What We Say?*, written between 1957 and 1967. Those years represent for me the challenge within analytical philosophy posed by ordinary language philosophy (as developed in England just after the war) to the radically successful revolution in American academic life of logical positivism (brought from Austria and Germany just before World War II). This challenge is emblematized within Wittgenstein's work by the relation of his *Philosophical Investigations* (1953) to his *Tractatus* (1929). I suppose the more recent intellectual revolution caused by French thought in the past two decades is, however oddly, related to those earlier ones in its struggle to overcome metaphysics, as well as in its distrust both of literature and of ordinary language.

First published as "In the Meantime," *Yale Journal of Criticism* 5 no. 2 (1992): 229–237.

The rhythm of my private history, living as I have through the two later revolutions, is that in the ordinary language challenge I felt released, cleared to do work that seemed mine to do, whereas still, in these late days of the French onslaught, I can feel the contrary—no doubt in part because this time I feel akin to the currents that I am also countered by. In my twenty minutes today I will not look for explanations of my somewhat torn condition, but give a few instances of what it is, in my part of the forest, to live within that condition, as this bears on the titular concepts of this session: authority, tradition, and discipline.

Let's say that tradition is a name for handing something on—call it knowledge, in the sense either of knowing that something is so, or of knowing how to make something happen—and grant that tradition bears an internal relation to treason, hearing this as a name for handing something over; and say that discipline, and its disciples, is a name for taking something, on or over. Then if we can say further that authority is the right to speak for something—a person, an institution—(where speaking is the mode in which this handing and taking happens); then philosophy may be viewed as born of the question: Who has the right to speak, and first the right to speak for philosophy, to turn aside from whatever is happening, in assertion and in action, and to wonder out loud about it?

I weave the concepts of this session in this way as a kind of summary of the topics of the foreword and of the earliest and title essay of *Must We Mean What We Say?*, in which the question of ordinary language, of who has the right to say what we say, to speak for "us," is taken in effect to allegorize the question of philosophy, especially the feature of its question that brings itself into question. In that feature, philosophy's claims to authority over itself and over other disciplines or discourses inevitably takes a form of challenging authority, so that its faithfulness to itself will show itself in its bringing itself to an end, or in its questioning, at each step, whether it exists.

Ordinary language procedure presses philosophy to ask, as J. L. Austin casually put it, "what we say when"; or, as Wittgenstein argued more portentously, it requires philosophy to bring words back from their metaphysical to their everyday use. Since the only first person I am systematically bound to satisfy or disappoint in responding to this philosophical work is myself, ordinary language philosophy proceeds as a kind of abstract autobiography. The freedom or permission this seemed to grant to the way I started writing philosophy (if that is what I do) was bound up with my sense of saying no more than I knew—which seemed a proper philosophical modesty—or saying no more than I could follow by continuing with the same unfolding work of saying. Others (including, in a way, myself) were bound to find this program intellectually arrogant, since these autobiographical results, however abstract, were evidently also meant to hold true for others; and by what right? The main form the charge against this procedure took thirty-five years ago, in my institutional setup, was that claims about "what we say when" are empirical, hence require evidence, which if not lacking altogether in these first-person accounts, was irremediably inadequate to the magnitude of the claims addressed. Hence, the charge was explicitly that philosophy as I care for it most is unscientific, and implicitly (since philosophy was then, and there, unchallengeably linked with science), the charge was that this philosophy is unphilosophical.

I was not then and there prepared to insist that philosophy is inherently autobiographical, even confessional, and always arrogant, that is, that its authority is always arrogated. And what conceivable good would it have done? If I had adduced as examples the figures of Emerson or Nietzsche or Heidegger or Wittgenstein, they would have been returned to me as proving that those predicates are precisely not of philosophy. (Whatever part of Wittgenstein's thought analytical philosophy may have wished to preserve could be dissociated from his arrogance if arrogance was understood as merely stylistic or temperamental.)

Always in the background of such memories there is the question: Why did it matter so much to me whether such figures, in their textuality (as opposed to certain of their isolable topics or puzzles) are accepted as philosophers by the academic discipline of philosophy? These figures are what they are; I could teach them if I wished, from within my favored positions. I would from time to time so concentrate on the satisfaction offered by their comparatively private company that their failure to command the kind of institutional standing I felt they deserved stopped mattering; one can take pleasure in marginality. But I would always once again lose satisfaction in that economy of renunciation. The issue was not merely one of the canon or curriculum of philosophical study. It was over the question whether—or how far, and at what cost to itself—philosophy belongs in an academic institution, as one among other (let us say humanistic) disciplines. Science is at home in a university; the arts are guests; philosophy is in both conditions, hence in neither.

Emphasizing what I just called the abstract autobiography in that first essay of mine—in content and in method—I look in amazement now at certain of its apparently involuntary confessions, as for example in two of its footnotes. One contains the passage: "[Ordinary language philosophers] are continuing— while at the same time their results are undermining—the tradition of British Empiricism; being gifted pupils, they seem to accept and to assassinate with the same gesture."[1] In another: "Wittgenstein's . . . combatting of the idea of privacy . . . and emphasizing the functions and contexts of language" are "teachings fundamental to American pragmatism; but . . . keep in mind how different their arguments sound, and admit that in philosophy it is the sound which makes all the difference."[2] Since I am in that essay claiming an inheritance of Austin's teaching and practice, am I proposing my intentions—and those of inheritance generally—as ones of ambivalence and violence? And if so, did I think of these as aimed more at Austin's work than at the work Austin's own proper violence was aimed at?—namely, at most of the work that I had been dutifully if restively learning? And if I could then have offered some theory of intellectual violence—perhaps through Freud's account of the transmission of tradition by way of the monotonous din of the super-ego—would that have alleviated or would it have exacerbated the violence with which that early essay of mine was greeted by analytical philosophers? And who, then and there, could I have been imagining might be in the least interested in the proposal that the tone of philosophy is as important to its acceptance—to what it teaches—as its argumentation is? This proposal is surely no part of a critique of reason, but merely a sign of its surrender.

Yet what could I say? As long as the concept of, the request for, empirical evidence that my words speak for "us" seemed in place, the subject of the authority to speak—of the authority of philosophy—was, according to my lights, unbroachable. What I *wanted* to say, and more or less mumbled, was that the seeming necessity of the request for evidence was itself forced by unassessed—perhaps unnecessary—conditions; that it was like asking for evidence that the world exists, after the world has irretrievably withdrawn under a skeptical surmise. Our language was not ours to prove in general any more than it is ours to dispose of or dispense with in general: it precedes us, whatever "us" there is. But this must seem, to those to whom it needs saying, that—so far as it is meaningful at all—it begs the question of the power of ordinary language.

Proceeding without justification, with a sense of something unsayable as a burden, is not for me a thing of the past. I said that in the present struggles, unlike the past ones, I feel akin to the currents that I am countered by. For instance, I am, for about the third time, and not just out of shame at my ignorance, trying to read Derrida in a reasonably consecutive way. Where I expect help seems to be where I feel most helpless. (That of course might be a function of some kinship.) Against the passages I have cited from *Must We Mean What We Say?* on the theme of the right to say "we," of the arrogation in saying it, I read this passage in Derrida's "The Ends of Man," from 1968: "What about this *we* in [Heidegger's] text [,] which better than any other has given us to read the essential, historical complicity of metaphysics and humanism in all their forms?"[3] Where Derrida invokes "complicity," my use of "we" invokes antagonism, arrogation. These are not necessarily incompatible pictures, but how is the difference to be assessed? As Emerson more or less says, philosophy characteristically finds itself more or less reversed in the text of another. For Emerson, this authorizes one to speak for oneself, as it were striking down prisons of tradition. But can I believe, in view of the patience I ask in reading, for example, Emerson—patience which seems not unrelated to Derrida's nearly obsessive calls for textual precision and patience in reading him—that the tradition in which Derrida writes, following Heidegger, or stalking him, can be struck in this way? Then what was the matter with positivism's way? And I have, I recall, argued elsewhere that Emerson, through Nietzsche, is at work in that tradition that Heidegger and Derrida seek, by continuing, to discontinue. But I let this go for the moment.

In 1968, in the foreword to *Must We Mean What We Say?*, a formula concerning philosophical authority looks this way: "When . . . I feel pressed by the question of my right to speak for philosophy, I sometimes suggest that I am merely speaking for *myself,* and sometimes . . . that philosophy is not *mine* at all." This state of philosophy I go on to characterize as its esotericism. A student of mine finds something like this divided cause described as, and worked out as, esotericism in the introduction (1801), written mostly by Hegel, to *The Critical Journal of Philosophy* he and Schelling were beginning to publish. The same idea of esotericism comes up early in Hegel's preface to *The Phenomenology of Spirit;* but if to understand that occurrence I must have an understanding of the *Phenomenology,* then I would not dream of claiming to understand it. And yet, yet again, Hegel's preface places esotericism in an historical time, "our time," which he speaks of as a "birth-time" and as descrying a "new world" in its entirety. These ideas are so pervasive and definitive in Emerson's essay "Experience," as I have read it, that I can almost believe that Emerson knew, and cared, that the original title of the *Phenomenology,* as Heidegger remarks in the opening sentence of his *Hegel's Concept of Experience,* was "Science of the *Experience* of Consciousness," and that Emerson's essay is recasting or reclaiming Hegel's preface. Should that authorize me to read Hegel? Why hasn't it? Is this neurosis about reading merely mine, or is it possibly philosophy's?

I have sometimes characterized the opposition between German-French philosophizing and English-American philosophizing by speaking of opposite myths of reading, remarking that the former thinks of itself as beginning by having read everything essential (Heidegger seems a clear case here) while the latter thinks of itself as beginning by having essentially read nothing (Wittgenstein seems a case here). And since I believe that Western philosophy really is split between these traditions, that each bespeaks a certain present of philosophy, and since I feel that a signal task of philosophy is to voice or reflect that split, it follows that I find the inheritance of philosophy now to propose its inheritance as split.

I conceive no intellectual place, no intertraditional place, from which this abrogation can proceed in predictable or stable ways. Here is where my reading of Thoreau and of Emerson comes into the work I set for myself— as opening a space that I think of as reachable before the split (measured in American intellectual time) produced two mutually shunning traditions or presents of philosophy. The lack of what I called an intertraditional place may accordingly be mapped practically as a lack of interdisciplinary place, since no present Western discipline is prepared to attend to Emerson and Thoreau as philosophers. (I mean to register that I attach great value to the attempts by both Thoreau and Emerson to align moments of their thought, in however inexpert a way, to moments of Eastern philosophy.)

There is a widely surmised but as yet, to my mind, unsurveyable affinity between the Heidegger of *Being and Time* and the Wittgenstein of *Philosophical Investigations.* Suppose I try positioning, against Derrida's taking up of Heidegger's interpretation of the history of Western metaphysics as a determination of presence, the interpretation I have proposed of Wittgenstein's notation of metaphysics as a denial of the ordinary, hence as essentially bound with, the other face of, skepticism.

I find that the tracing and dismantling of the consequences of presence taken as "the major determination of the meaning of Being"[4] does not strike me as describing the work I do. In my work, the concept of presence—on a par with that of acknowledgment or avoidance or intention or conversation or pleasure or language or metaphor or reference or necessity or perfection—may follow or strike paths within ordinary language, or else may fatefully be (or may inescapably work within the threat of temptation of being) impressed, fixated, by metaphysical service. The detailing of the possibility and the necessity of this impressing or fixation is a way of saying what my reading of Wittgenstein is for. (I was just recasting moments from the essay on *King Lear,* also collected in *Must We Mean What We Say?,* which recasts the issues of skepticism from the earlier essays as issues of lost presentness—this is, I surmise, a principal reason I have been asked over the years to say how my work relates to Derrida's.)

It is to be expected, given the spaces for which I have thought to find thought, in and out of the traditions, that what I do has sometimes been denied the title of philosophy, or deplored under that title. But as I went on doing it anyway, other terms of criticism have characteristically been levelled at it—that it is literary, or is some kind of psychology, or, as philosophy, is soft. My private response to such terms, whose justness I do not exactly wish to deny, was to say that the institution of philosophy, as known to me, is reactively male, as if silencing some doubt about itself, or about reason itself. This perception was, for lots of reasons, unsayable where I came from. I now think of it as having occurred too soon. And now that it is no longer too soon to say, it seems to have become too late for me to say—still untimely; but now less because of masculinist than of feminist authority. And I think now that my dodging with time is marked out in what I have written whenever I identify the skeptical problematic as a working out of the intellect's disappointment with itself, shaded toward melancholy. But one may well form an impression of this state as still suspiciously male.

Working within axes—axes along which certain textual fragments recur in my writing in different lights over the years, as though rebuking me for not being able to master them—of the unsayable, the unformulable, the esoteric, and haunted by philosophy's violence and by an obscure fascination with its tone, I find it perhaps not surprising that fragments from discussions, often from moments of their breaking up, and often pertaining to matters of authority, or tradition, or discipline, persist uncomfortably in my memory. The reasons for this persistence of conversational fragments evidently go beyond their manifest content, as though they contain some orientation for me that I cannot quite follow.

I had meant to leave room here to recount a variety of such moments; their voices can be famous or quite anonymous. Since there is time for just one, I describe a moment containing, apart from mine indirectly, two voices directly, from the discussion period after one of the seminar talks I had given as a Fellow of the Whitney Humanities Center in the spring of 1983, attended by about two dozen faculty members and graduate students divided between philosophy and the study of literature. In that day's presentation I had begun detailing the kind of reading in Emerson that seemed to me the reward of taking his texts as those of an exacting thinker, in particular showing his development of what seem clear and advanced theories of language and thinking and writing and reading that apply to, and so are verified in, his own texts. One of the philosophers present in the discussion eventually came to say, "But I have always assumed that Emerson was a second-rate mind," and his tone manifested my failure to have given him cause to think again. I managed some words to the effect that that is what I had assumed also until, a few years earlier, I began to learn otherwise. I do not believe that I discourage abnormally easily, but at that moment I let this attempt to repress Emerson bully me, and my proposal that he is a site from which to assess features of the split in the inheritance of philosophy seemed to me one more ridiculous gesture. The discussion faded to an end. The last public words of the occasion, as we were each gathering ourselves to leave, were those of Paul de Man, who turned his formidable smile my way and announced, "Stanley, the Yale Philosophy Department has come through for you."

In my state I found the remark shocking, without quite knowing how to take it. Did it mean that the refusal of the Emerson point was exactly what my text had predicted, hence that it had been confirmed? But how could I accept, except cynically, that the prediction was bound to come true, no matter what my intervention had been? Or did it mean that no one would believe the stake in the refusal of Emerson without witnessing it, and perhaps further that having located a precise point of cultural repression I should keep after it until the resistance is effectively interpreted? But would this have meant that Paul de Man had sensed an affinity with my philosophical resistance against philosophy's resistance, even some recognition of—some willingness for his work to question itself about—his own lack of success with Yale's Philosophy Department, and indeed with the discipline of philosophy generally as represented in the major departments of philosophy in the English-speaking tradition? And how similar was my own lack of success in those precincts?

Having opened these remarks by invoking the idea of the voice of authority and the hands of tradition, I close them with a response and a question con-

cerning what I suppose to be the most famous text that depicts the receiving
of an inheritance, specifically, Isaac's settling of his doubts (about the identity of the first son to present himself for his blessing) by his remark that "the
voice is Jacob's voice, but the hands are the hands of Esau." I ask why blind
Isaac accepted the testimony of the disguised hands rather than that of the
undisguised voice—that is, I ask what my fantasm is of this scene. And I find,
as I ask, that I do not believe Isaac discounted the voice but that he meant
Jacob to have the blessing. This may be understood any number of ways: that
Isaac was guided not by Rebecca's trick but by her desire; that he wished to
throw the tradition of handing the blessing to the firstborn into confusion;
that he had no answer to Esau's sensible question, "Hast thou but one blessing,
my father?", and did not want to show this to Jacob. Registering the issue of
the blindness of tradition, and of the economy of power and impotence in
patriarchal tradition's handing itself on, I am interested to note, here as elsewhere, that it is the woman's voice that is shown to control the men's. My
question becomes: Is it humanism, more or less undefined, speaking in me
(at least one of my remembered voices accuses me of this), that now wishes
to regard Rebecca's secret actions as representing the condition of esotericism
in the transferring of authority? Does this idea mask the condition of actual
women, locked into positions of the manipulation as opposed to the exercise
of power? But mightn't it equally call for the revelation of the condition? Or
grant that the idea suggests an Oedipal interpretation of the fear of the
woman's voice—does this suggest that esotericism is as inescapable as castration anxiety? What it suggests to me is that our ability to speak to one another as human beings should neither be faked nor be postponed by uncontested metaphysics; and that since the overcoming of the split within
philosophy, and that between philosophy and what Hegel calls unphilosophy,
is not to be anticipated, what we have to say to one another must be said in
the meantime.

Who Disappoints Whom?
Allan Bloom at Harvard

In 1987, Allan Bloom, then a relatively unknown conservative philosophy professor at the University of Chicago, published a book called *The Closing of the
American Mind: How Higher Education Has Failed Democracy and Impoverished
the Souls of Today's Students*. The book quickly became a bestseller. Bloom
argued that the humanities as they were being taught in higher education,
and, in particular, in academic philosophy, had failed contemporary students,
instilling in them various prejudices instead of teaching them how to think.
Suddenly in great demand as a guest lecturer, Bloom was in 1988 invited to
give a talk—entitled "The Attack on Reason"—at the Harvard Kennedy
School, and Cavell was invited to serve as a respondent. Cavell published this
response in the journal *Critical Inquiry* in 1989.

———————————

CAN ONE CONCEIVE SOMETHING TO SAY about Allan Bloom's
view of America and the American university that he hasn't already heard?
Setting aside the perhaps undiscussable differences in what we each saw in
our students in the 1960s, I find two regions in which Bloom's experience and
mine differ systematically that are specific and clear enough to be stated briefly,
perhaps usefully: first, our experience of the position of philosophy in the intellectual economy we were presented with in the two decades prior to the
1960s; second, our experience of the modern and the popular in the arts. My

———————————

A version of this essay was published as "Who Disappoints Whom?" *Critical Inquiry* 15, no. 3 (1989):
606–610.

citing of these differences can only prove worthwhile, however, against a background of agreement I find with his work over the centrality of a cluster of issues, of which I specify five: a first agreement concerns the illustriousness (in Emerson's sense, which includes illustrativeness) of the university in the life of a democracy; a second concerns the irreplaceability of Great Books—what Thoreau calls scriptures—in (let's call it) a humanistic education; a third concerns the unaware imbibing of European thought by a chronically unprepared American constitution—a condition that is as live for us, or should be, as when Emerson was founding American thinking by demonstrating his knack of inheriting, by transfiguring, European philosophy; a fourth moment of agreement concerns the goal of a democratic university education as keeping open the idea of philosophy as a way of life, call it the life of the mind, a name for which might be Moral Perfectionism (Bloom speaks of the longing for completeness, Emerson speaks instead of a capacity for partiality, and of the courage to become—both see in the goal a desire for the world's human possibilities, and both are aware that the aspiration is always threatening to turn into debased narcissism or foolish imitation); a fifth sense of my agreement with Bloom concerns the threat that a discourse about such issues, such as the prose fashioned in Bloom's book (manifestly the product of a lifetime of reading and of a devotion to teaching), is becoming unintelligible to the culture that has produced it, and not alone to the young (in my experience, less to them than to others).

The first region of difference I cite is that of our experience on entering the university in the 1940s and then teaching in the 1950s. Bloom describes his first look at the "popularization of German philosophy in the United States"—yielding, for example, ideas of value relativism and value positing—as follows:

> When I came to the University of Chicago in the mid-forties, . . .
> terms like "value judgement" were fresh, confined to an elite and
> promising special insight. There were great expectations in the social
> sciences that a new era was beginning in which man and society
> would be understood better than they had ever been understood before. The academic character of the philosophy departments, with
> their tired and tiresome methodology and positivism, had caused
> people interested in the perennial and live questions about man to migrate to the social sciences. There were two writers who dominated
> and generated real enthusiasm—Freud and Weber.[1]

Entering comparable philosophy departments in the late forties, after an undergraduate major in music, I seemed to see something quite different— that the popularization of German-speaking positivism (linking up with certain strains in native pragmatism) was absorbing the intellectual conscience of a significant face of social science (as well as of academic psychology, along with absorbing morality and religion and the arts), creating a climate in which the question is not whether value positing can express a dedication to the life of the mind, but whether judgments of value can be said to have any intellectual content at all; and in which intelligence is expressed not in discussing which the most interesting writers are and how most strongly to be challenged by them, but in which the reading of texts—*any* writing, great books or small—has something like the status of a hobby in comparison with the serious business of analyzing and solving problems.

But that is philosophy too, however unhappy certain dimensions of this version of it. The *distrust* of reading is half of the philosophical spirit. A devotion to thinking by reading—however great the books in question—will not count, in my corner of things, as a philosophical devotion, unless it knows at each moment how to distrust reading. Emerson's and Thoreau's cautions against the reading of books reveal no intellectual innocence but their philosophical seasoning. The highest instance of this half of the philosophical spirit in the opening half of the present century is Wittgenstein, Heidegger's exact contemporary and I suppose his philosophical equal, at least. The fact of this division of the philosophical spirit—roughly equatable with the split between the English-speaking and the German-speaking traditions of philosophy—is for me the dominant condition of the possibility of philosophy now, the signal opportunity of philosophizing in this nation in particular. The tradition represented in Heidegger's thought functions according to the myth of having read essentially everything; that in Wittgenstein's thought, according to the myth of having read essentially nothing.

I do not say that a philosophical distrust of reading is the same as the refusal or incomprehension of reading, which Bloom so deplores in recent American students. What I suggest is that the persistent unwillingness of American culture to recognize the split in the spirit of philosophy has incomparably more to do with the present failings of the American university than anything our students did in the 1960s. (Some I knew best were indeed taking it upon themselves to bridge or splint this split. They still are.)

It is, I think, Bloom's dismissal of the importance of the American university's drastic reception of positivism, and his neglect of Wittgenstein's counterpoise at once to positivism and Heidegger's achievement, that allows Bloom to burlesque the significance of Thomas Kuhn's *Structure of Scientific Revolutions* and of John Rawls's *A Theory of Justice*. Kuhn's book—whatever its shortcomings (say in providing an epistemology for the concept of a world and of the change of a world), and however much its fame has overshadowed its teaching (so that it is cited as in support of relativism and even of irrationality)—did more than any other text to weaken the hold of a positivist / pragmatist verificationist picture of scientific progress on the academic imagination. And whatever one's misgivings about Rawls's book (for example, in its treatment of Moral Perfectionism), Bloom's idea of Rawls as "writing hundreds of pages to persuade men, and proposing a scheme of government that would force them, not to despise anyone" (p. 30) is too wild for fun. Rawls is trying to make plain and common—I do not doubt that Bloom recognizes this, but then what is at stake in denying it—the proposition that our despising someone is not a ground for depriving him of liberty or of his deal of equality. It is a proposition Utilitarianism was unable to make plain; and in doing more than any other work to challenge the reign of Utilitarianism in academic moral philosophy, Rawls at the same time has made the reading of what Bloom calls old books imperative for moral philosophers.

It would not become one with my commitments to fail to mention a second region of difference between Bloom's experience and mine, that containing phenomena of movie-viewing and of music as vehicles of or challenges to philosophy in these years. I confine myself to one of Bloom's passing observations: "In the Soviet Union they are dependent on operas from the bad old days, because tyranny prevents artistic expression; we are dependent on the same operas, because the thirsts that produced artistic need have been slaked" (p. 233). As elsewhere I am uncertain of the attitude in these words. Is Bloom claiming that no significant operas have been or are being composed in America, or that the recognized masterpieces in this medium written, say, since 1917, receive too few performances on these shores? Apart from citing details this apparent call for more culture, or for more genuine culture, sounds like a general grudge against the modern—something confirmed in Bloom's remarks about abstract painting (p. 63); and in his description of Louis Armstrong "belt[ing] out" Kurt Weill (p. 151) (a description that accords Armstrong none of his virtuosic irony nor any capacity to comprehend and challenge Weill's pathos); and in those pages in which he takes Woody Allen's *Zelig* to represent the world of cinema and then reads the film as a popularization of German philosophy rather than recognizing it as a direct engagement with

Emerson's madly underinterpreted problematic of conformity and self-reliance, against which Allen proposes a study of the relation between character and actor in the medium of film.

No doubt there has been a shift in our institutions of performance; in part this is a function of the American university's having become a center and sustainer of the arts. Let us grant that opera does not play the social role it did in the bad old days. On what ground does Bloom regret this—if he does? He cites Plato's theory of music to lament the young's absorption of rock music. But I do not have to remind the translator of Rousseau as well as of Plato that Plato's theory of music would at least as surely condemn the representations of *Don Giovanni* and of *Falstaff*.

I wonder what Bloom would think of the proposition—justified theoretically to my mind and suggested thematically in movies from *Mr. Deeds Goes to Town* in 1936 to last year's *Moonstruck*—that opera has not mostly died, but mostly has become film, that film is our opera. That the majority of films are largely worthless is irrelevant—so are the majority of books. That no film is as good as *Don Giovanni* or *Falstaff* is also irrelevant—very little of anything is that good. The point of this speculation is that the relation between low and high culture—their access to one another—is definitively different in America from their relation in Europe, a fact ungraspable by, for example, Theodor Adorno. As is the difference in America in the relation between philosophy and literature. These can seem—they can be—vulgar confusions. I find them also, and increasingly, untold encouragements.

A parting word about Bloom's vision of the young with their Walkmans on, which he reads as deafening them to "what the great tradition has to say" (p. 81). It may be so. But maybe it is to be read as their blocking out our opinions and explanations of what they listen to. I do not, on the whole, share their pleasures here. I take it that I am, on the whole, not meant to, meant not to. The young, on this reading, feel that there are times and places in which, in their solitude, they are not answerable to others.

Just like us.

Preface to the Italian Edition
of *The Claim of Reason*

The Claim of Reason (1979) was translated into Italian by Barbara Agnese under the title *La riscoperta dell'ordinario: La filosofia, lo scetticismo, il tragico* (Rome: Carocci Editore, 2001). The Italian translation omits part 3 of the original edition, which is on moral philosophy. We present here the original English text of the preface Cavell wrote for that book. His manuscript is dated January 13, 2001, just a week earlier than his draft preface to the present volume.

IF I NOTE THAT THE EARLIEST material of *The Claim of Reason* reaches back to my doctoral dissertation, submitted to Harvard University and defended in 1961, I must add that I had come late to philosophy, and that the period of my Ph.D. candidacy (roughly the first half of the 1950s) was one of a confusion of philosophical voices in America—later versions of logical positivism were predominant, sometimes incorporating elements of pragmatism, but confronted by the recent publication of Wittgenstein's *Philosophical Investigations,* and by a talented wave of philosophy from Oxford (marked primarily, for me, by the innovations of J. L. Austin), and by rumors of Heidegger (often gathered from the pages of Sartre's existentialism)—and my dissertation, further delayed by, if essentially profiting from, the lectures I was giving in my first years as a teacher of philosophy at Berkeley, did not disguise the intellectual crises I continued to experience. Over the years, while publishing other books, on classical American as well as on current European philosophy, and on literature and cinema, I periodically revised and extended the dissertation, still for a long time motivated in relation to my pedagogical commitments after returning to teach permanently at Harvard. By the time I offered the revised work for publication it contained in various ways about three-fourths of the pages or paragraphs or sentences or phrases of the original dissertation and it had doubled in size, largely because of the addition of its longest, concluding part, part 4, little of which had been envisioned in the original dissertation.

The Claim of Reason was first published in 1979, and everything I have written after its appearance, as well as much before its appearance, is in some way indebted to it, both to the interpretation of such matters as the Wittgensteinian event in philosophy, or of the question of the relation of philosophy and literature—epitomized in its claim that something like the skepticism of Descartes (not alone that of Montaigne, which is a well-known source) is to be found explored in Shakespearean tragedy—as well as to the undisguised struggle in its writing, in which its unpredictable part 4 allows itself literary license to follow the problems of philosophy beyond the forms of academic decorum and reference tolerable in a dissertation. Indeed what seems to have taught me to consider the work finished, which means to accept that its guiding motivations had been sufficiently exposed if not exhausted, was exactly that this concluding part no longer bore an orderly relation to pedagogy. Certain readers of the book have accordingly declared that *The Claim of Reason* is really two books, an academically more or less proper study (in parts 1 through 3) of problems of knowledge and morality and (in part 4) a sequel which proceeds in effect by questioning the limitations or necessities of that propriety. But I trust that it is more generally recognized by those in sympathy with the work that its two sides, or its outward and its inward motions, are meant for each other.

Because the exigencies of the book's publication in Italian has demanded some shortening of a very long book, and since its relatively self-contained part 3, namely its four chapters concentrated on moral philosophy, seemed the obvious candidate for omission, I want to indicate what role those omitted chapters play in the structure and development of the book. The idea of the original dissertation was to show—against the dominant strain of analytical moral philosophy in the English-speaking half of the philosophical world in the 1940s and 1950s (which contain my years in graduate school)—that moral (and aesthetic) judgments do not suffer a lack of rational grounding by comparison with judgments of knowledge, and that to suppose otherwise is a function of a false comparison between moral and epistemological claims. I suppose it to be true enough, as Socrates says to Euthyphro, in Plato's dialogue to which Euthyphro lends his name, that judgments of right and wrong, of the good and the bad, the honorable and the dishonorable, unlike judgments of weight or of length, are liable in ordinary life to a "kind of disagreement that, my friend, causes hatred and anger." In the place of judgments of weight and length, or of what more recent moral philosophers call scientific or cognitive judgments, I took as my foil epistemological judgments concerning the existence and identification of the things of the world (a bed, a piece of wax, a house, a snake, a bird, a cherry, a piece of chalk, a tree); and as cases of moral judgment, in the place of such current instances then as "You ought to keep promises" or "You were wrong to steal money," I took as examples moral crises alluding to texts such as Plato's *Crito,* Sophocles's *Antigone,* George Eliot's *The Mill on the Floss,* E. M. Forster's *Howard's End.* On this basis I argued that since it is natural to assume that the rationality of argument manifested in scientific judgments is a function of the expectation that disputes about them will achieve agreement—that disagreements about weight or length, or about whether metals expand when heated, will be *settled* by measuring or experiment or informal experience, as will disagreements about whether there is a bed in the next room or whether a bird is a goldfinch—and to assume at the same time that it is the capacity for coming to agreement that establishes these practices as (models of, what we mean by) rationality in judgment. The idea of part 3, to the contrary, is that the rationality of moral argument depends not upon agreement in judgment in fact emerging from it (however much the hope of agreement and openness to the possibility of agreement initiates and sustains the argument), but upon the willingness to make ourselves intelligible to one another, which is to say, upon our acceptance of the possibility and necessity of confronting one another with the demands of morality, and the consequent willingness to assume the risks of anger and rebuff and the tolerance to live with, to consent to, various degrees and directions of unsettlement.

This is in general not well understood as an agreement to disagree, but as a recognition of the fact and the value of human separateness and difference—one might think of it as a recognition that our fundamental need for recognition of one another, for addressing one another, goes beyond attempts to get one another to do something, or to choose a particular course of action, hence in a sense, goes beyond, or one might say it comes before, morality.

What happens in part 1 and part 2 is that the preparation of the epistemological measure of judgment with which to approach the rationality of moral judgment showed itself to require more and more steps backward, or further detours into unforeseen avenues, so that they became the bulk of the dissertation. The four chapters on moral philosophy were, I felt, when I came to write them, sufficiently grounded in the way I hoped they would be by what had preceded them, but they so far did not bring out anything like the full, let's say, moral implications of the issues in Wittgenstein's *Investigations* and in skepticism that had been worked out in anticipation of them. By the time part 1 had been revised (finally in 1971, during a sabbatical year), indeed wholly rewritten and expanded (the original part 2 remained quite intact), the consequent demands on part 3 clearly went beyond anything to be thought of as a revision of those chapters. The demand was, so far as I was capable of it, only met by part 4. But that proved to be years away.

What happens in part 4 is that the idea of the moral life as one in which disagreements are amicably settled, or else are amicably enough and rationally tolerated, is superseded. The moral dimension of experience is no longer the subject of a special field of philosophy, but becomes internal to the drive of philosophy as such. One might say that instead of providing the basis for judgments about courses of action philosophy seeks to understand itself as a way of life, as if the need for and difficulties of rational cooperative behavior is, in the academic (as opposed to the more or less popular) intellectual economy of modern societies, the subject of disproportionate attention, compared with the confusions and discomforts of the individual soul's aspiration to find itself at home in the world, or else productively at odds with the home likely to be available to it in the society to which it is born and to which it (unless it is catastrophically unfortunate) consents. This view of philosophy, say of philosophy as the progress of the self to itself, or rather of the perpetual recoil of the self from itself as it stands, I came to call Emersonian perfectionism, commemorating, in a repeated term of this preface, Emerson's description of himself as wishing "to unsettle all things."

Perfectionism is not named (and was largely inexplicit in my mind) as I was composing part 4, but the conditions or imperatives for its exploration are quite visible in retrospect. (The idea of perfectionism, even the word, is evident in the book of mine about a genre of Hollywood film comedy published two years after *The Claim of Reason*, namely *Pursuits of Happiness*, published in Italian in 1999 [Einaudi] under the title *Alla ricerca della felicità*. But the extent to which Emersonianism is expressed in these definitive American films, hence indefinitely far within American cinema, hence society, more generally, was not yet clear to me.)

My explicit interest in the idea of a perfectionist moral outlook took shape out of my study of Wittgenstein's *Philosophical Investigations,* when I came to want a thematic understanding of the intellectual or spiritual fervor often noticed in Wittgenstein's way of writing. Is this to be understood as some kind of literary accident, of negligible philosophical importance? If it were, what could it have meant for Wittgenstein to advise a young friend of his to read the *Investigations* as a religious work? The question became unavoidable for me when I put it together with reading Heidegger's *Being and Time* in a way which takes into the foreground his repeated assertion in that work that it is not to be understood as a work of ethics. Who, one might wish to ask, could mistake that text of Heidegger's as a book of ethics and therefore require a caution against the mistake? Yet that book too places demands on its reader for self-reflection, or self-determination, which is internal to the transformation of the one you find yourself to be, in the world of *Das Man,* into the one who cares authentically about his / her existence. And Heidegger explicitly cites, as if almost in passing, as if its pertinence hardly needs mentioning, the Romantic idea of becoming the one you are (as, by the way, Emerson also cites it). That ethics is in these texts not a separate study means that every utterance and every silence in them are unprotected from moral scrutiny, as if every utterance, or withholding of utterance, marks a confrontation, answers and presses a demand. (Or should. When Emerson announces, in his praise of solitude, that "Every word they say chagrins us," he can be taken as dismayed by the emptiness and laxness of their speech, the sense that they and he do not, as it is said, speak the same language. But he is also calling attention to our habituation to calls upon our attention that are perpetually impertinent and invasive, demanding responses out of all proportion to anyone's desire for the exchanges they invite. It is this cause for mutual contempt that, it seems to me, Heidegger names in contrasting genuine speech with chatter [*Gerede*]. The nonsense that Wittgenstein and J. L. Austin uncover in philosophy may be seen as the most refined, hence the least innocent, versions of the tendency of human speech to emptiness, of the human craving for inconsequence. Austin seemed to dream, as other philosophers have, of finding a cure for this. Wittgenstein is concerned to understand the sources of the craving as well as to cast suspicion on the attempt to cure it once for all rather than day by day.)

But the question arises about the justification for persisting in thinking about Heidegger's call for a transformation away from the everyday and its speech, together with Wittgenstein's call for a return of words to an everyday that never existed, as partaking of a fervor to be understood as moral. It would be the beginning of an answer if it could be made out that perfectionism, of the sort I identify, is essentially if not exclusively motivated as an internal check against the tendency of moral judgment to become moralistic, against, let us say, the tendency of one confronting another morally to fail to examine his / her own standing as moral judge. One might object here that, for example, if abortion is wrong it is wrong, and one who confronts you with this judgment may be right no matter what an examination of his own moral conduct or sensibility may reveal. But moral confrontation—call it the attempt to get another to confront herself or himself—requires a willingness for argument, to demand and to provide intelligibility for one's conduct, including one's motivation in judging, and one's standing as a moral judge is determined by what arguments you are prepared to take, and ask others to take, seriously.

Moralism almost becomes explicit in the chapter in part 3 that takes up an early paper of John Rawls on the topic of moral rules, a paper which precedes by more than a decade his epochal work *A Theory of Justice*. At a pivotal point, Rawls imagines a case in which the player of a game asks for a defining rule of the game to be broken in his favor, something like his asking for an extra penalty kick in soccer on the ground that in his attempt just now his foot slipped. This is meant to clarify the nature of moral rules as rules of institutions or practices which do not allow for exceptions (unless an exception is itself part of a rule). I argue against this idea on the ground that there are precisely no rules in morality that serve the purpose of defining rules for games. Not to know the rules of soccer is not to be competent to judge plays within the game of soccer; this is perhaps no fault of character, and the ignorance can be relieved by instruction in the rules. But if someone tells you that he is asking for another chance to be in moral favor on the ground that his foot slipped, or he was pushed (he agrees that abortion is abhorrent but in this case, given the poverty and age and isolation of the young woman, he could not bring himself to refuse the operation), to defend your negative judgment by citing something like a moral rule is to express a decision not to announce a ruling, and not a decision to cite the rule, but a decision that you and the one you judge are not members of the same moral world. (You do not have to "bring yourself" to refuse an extra penalty kick; the request is incompetent.) I find Rawls's early idea of a moral rule to continue to play an uncomfortably heavy role in his discussion, in *A Theory of Justice*, of social institutions as practices, where a complaint against injustice can be dismissed by saying, from a position that is "above reproach," that the complaint asks for an exception from the principles of justice and is in effect incompetent. Some complaints no doubt are morally incompetent, and tolerably just societies and honest citizens require protection against such charges. But protection requires the willingness to claim, as a matter of judgment, not as a matter of rule, that the communality you share with the one who complains of injustice is, despite your complaint, tolerably just enough, sufficiently just, so that you judge (in effect identifying yourself as speaking for the community) that the other's complaint against it is incompetent, as if he were complaining, and wants redress for the fact, that although his house is comfortable and shelters his family it is not as large as his neighbor's, through no fault of that neighbor. But for you to judge so, to declare in effect that another is morally incompetent, is to put yourself in a position that is not above reproach, but rather one that is exposed to the taint of compromise with injustice, where perhaps too many houses are only better shelter than nothing and too many neighbors who in principle could do something about this discrepancy turn a deaf ear to the complaint. This is not an ignorance that instruction in rules can relieve.

Of course there are ideas of moral perfection that help to further and consolidate an ignorance of injustice, ones which picture the good moral life as one essentially of personal cultivation, intellectual and artistic, even perhaps religious. This is roughly the picture of perfectionism given in *A Theory of Justice,* and my quarrel with it (one that is not with the fundamentals of Rawls's view) is that there is a perfectionism, I call it Emersonian perfectionism, that does not claim exemption from moral community but is rather one that takes exception to that community's insufficient judgment of itself. This view is developed in my book *Conditions Handsome and Unhandsome: The Constitution of Emersonian Perfectionism* (from 1988), which can accordingly be taken to form a new, or delayed, continuation to part 3 of *The Claim of Reason.*

A closing word to mark my pleasure in knowing that *The Claim of Reason* now has the chance to find its breath in Italian. The introduction to *Conditions Handsome and Unhandsome* provides a list of some four dozen examples of classic works of a perfectionist cast, from Plato and Aristotle to Wilde and Ibsen, ending with films, meant to indicate that this cast is not an alternative to particular moral theories but is rather a dimension of human life that no moral theory will be free of. An illustrious example is given by Dante's *Divine Comedy.* I have placed Dante's opening lines recounting the discovery within a dark wood of having lost one's way, or becoming bewildered in the middle of life's journey, with Wittgenstein's image in the *Investigations* of the form of a philosophical problem as discovering that one does not know one's way, and with Thoreau's announcement in the opening lines of *Walden* that he is a sojourner in civilized life, having for the moment returned from a life of awakening in the woods. And the more deeply I become acquainted with these works the more interesting do the connections, and the differences, appear to me. So I am encouraged in my wish to maintain philosophy's difference from its academic neighbors as its moving not from ignorance to learning but from obscurity and fixation to lucidity and motion.

Reflections on Wallace Stevens
at Mount Holyoke

This is a lecture that Cavell gave in 2003 at Mount Holyoke College in Massachusetts, at a meeting commemorating a series of conferences, entitled "Pontigny-en-Amérique," held there during the summers of 1942–1944. These conferences were a continuation in exile of annual events that had been held for decades in France at the Pontigny Abbey. "Pontigny-en-Amérique" brought together leading French and European figures in the arts and sciences, joined by distinguished American writers, thinkers, and artists, for conversations about the future of human civilization in a precarious world. Among the participants were the philosophers Hannah Arendt and Rachel Bespaloff, the poets Marianne Moore and Wallace Stevens, the anthropologist Claude Lévi-Strauss, the linguist Roman Jakobson, the painters Marc Chagall and Robert Motherwell, and the composer Roger Sessions, Cavell's teacher at Berkeley. Cavell discusses the 1942–1944 conferences here and in his autobiography, *Little Did I Know.*

I AM COUNTING ON THE FACT that by the time it has fallen to me to present my remarks on this occasion we will have had sketched for us more of the texture and the details of the event sixty years ago that

A version of this essay was published as "Reflections on Wallace Stevens at Mount Holyoke," in *Artists, Intellectuals, and World War II: The Pontigny Encounters at Mount Holyoke College, 1942–1944,* ed. Christopher Benfey and Karen Remmler (Amherst: University of Massachusetts Press, 2006), 61–79.

we are gathered to commemorate than I have learned in the course of my preparation, on and off these past months, for composing them. It went almost without saying in Christopher Benfey's invitation to me, and in our exchanges about how I might think of my contribution, that I would include reflections on what might have been expected in 1943, from the still moving, wonderfully American, effort, with the nation absorbed in a total and fateful war, to transport the spirit of a signature institution of French high culture to a setting in a characteristic instance of a fine, small New England college. One might even call the event classy, except that this might slight the democratic willingness of its welcome.

Benfey and I touched especially on the question of what might have been gained or been missed in the philosophical voices that had been part of that original effort at Mount Holyoke. The question was inevitable, given the specific suggestion that I might include some response to the text Wallace Stevens prepared for and read at that event, "The Figure of the Youth as Virile Poet," one of the four principal prose texts from Wallace Stevens's hand, each of them directed intensely and explicitly to philosophy, asking it for a response to what he felt himself able and compelled to say about the relation of philosophy and poetry. Benfey and I turned out to share the sense that these texts have still not received a response from philosophers adequate to Stevens's request. The additional suggestion that I might write somewhat autobiographically was, I take it, meant to assure me that I should not suppose I was asked to present myself as a scholar of Wallace Stevens's writing. Indeed, while I have read and in various texts of mine quoted lines of Stevens's poetry, the present occasion is the first on which I have not evaded the impulse actually to attempt something like consecutive responses to reading through the work of this strange, wondrous, often excruciatingly difficult writer.

It is a difficulty rather opposite to that posed in other American writers that Stevens admired and with whom I have spent considerable stretches in recent years in exhilarating contest, above all Emerson and Thoreau. But in writing about them I have been moved to *insist* upon their difficulty, too often finding them quoted as if their sentences are transparent, yielding their significance at a glance, without resistance. My idea is that Emerson and Thoreau characteristically conceal their difficulty, as if to make it seem easier than it is to read and to act better than we do, as they ask us to do. While Stevens will posit ease as an eventuality in taking poetry to our lives, he makes inescapably obvious the initial difficulty in preserving, let us say, our intactness. To recognize and to accompany both our possibilities and our obscurities are, I would say, necessary assists for us.

The autobiographical latitude given me also came, I believe, from the knowledge of the publication roughly a decade ago of conversations with the composer Roger Sessions, another of the greatly distinguished American artists who had accepted an invitation to Pontigny at Mount Holyoke in 1943. In those conversations, Sessions tells an anecdote concerning the world premiere of his first opera, *The Trial of Lucullus,* on a text of Bertolt Brecht, at Berkeley in 1946, in which I figure momentarily but rather superbly as the resourceful clarinet player in the small orchestra for which this marvelous piece is scored, who overcame a crisis in the middle of the opening night's performance, transposing an English horn solo on the clarinet when the English horn suddenly broke down. While I would, the year after graduating from Berkeley, recognize the fact that music was no longer my life, namely that something other that I would eventually learn to call philosophy was what gave my life its drift or gist, the experience of having worked young in the company of an absolutely serious and accomplished artist, whose life and death stake in his art is unstinting and unquestionable, leaves impressions whose powers of orientation and inspiration are undying.

Are such reminiscences to be thought of as marked by anything that happened in South Hadley sixty years ago? But that question is among the motivations of my remarks today, namely the question, What counts as an effect of what happened then and there? Is our commemorative occasion, as it comes to pass over these present days, an effect of it? It seems hard to imagine that these events have been *caused* by that earlier event. Yet I know that having in recent months first learned the bare outlines of the life of Rachel Bespaloff, of whom we will be hearing more tomorrow, has intangibly affected the color and certain emphases of what I have given myself to say now. My image of this gifted intellectual, a Jewish refugee from Eastern Europe through Paris to New York and South Hadley, is affected by its general contrast with the difference in the experiences I continue to imagine of my Jewish family's immigration a generation earlier from Bialystok to Atlanta, remembering reports heard and overheard; and affected most specifically by a detail on her itinerary westward that gave her time to stay for two years in Switzerland to study music with Ernst Bloch.

During my years at Berkeley, Bloch visited there from his home on the coast of Oregon to give a summer class whose ecstatic effect on me was to transform what I conceived that I was meant to do with my life, specifically enabling me to choose the path of philosophy rather than composition when, a few years later, my gradual withdrawal from the life of music precipitated the major intellectual, or spiritual, crisis of my life. There is no counting the

times I have gone over, more recently in writing, my images of those encounters with Bloch—craving to remember every detail of his moods and
ways of moving as he thought, or wrote a progression on the blackboard,
or read from Stanislavsky's book on acting, or from Schumann's criticism,
or played illustrations at the piano, or at a certain moment lapsed into an
irreverent but loving imitation of the manner of recitative Debussy had in-
vented for *Pelléas and Mélisande,* as Bloch described himself and his fellow
music students improvising such ethereal exchanges throughout entire
meals in Paris in 1902, after attending the world premiere of the opera (which
because of Bloch's representation seems as close to me now as it did half a
century ago in Bloch's animated presence). But now my memory is affected
by the question whether anything in this greatly impressionable and expressive man's presentations that summer bore the mark of his experience of the
young Rachel Bespaloff—it was not unusual for him to show that his students
were on his mind, and who more likely among them than a fellow musician
and intellectual and Jew seeking a life in the strangeness of America?—
thereby perhaps conveying an effect that may or may not have made an impression upon me.

I am not speaking about probabilities now but about the question what
human knowledge is that it is at any time based upon such impressions, and
the question what a human life comes to that it is modified by such fitful
things. In classical philosophy, impressions are understood as predictable effects of objects upon my senses. I am interested in the concept of an impression as an experience that a portion of the world unpredictably gives me, in
which it captures my interest, matters to me, or fails to—a product of significance not of causation.

A companion question to that concerning the consequences of the Mount
Holyoke Pontigny event is that of its antecedents—meaning not just empiri-
cally a question concerning who was invited and who attended, but also meant
speculatively as the question concerning who was not invited who might have
been. For example, in responding philosophically, according to my lights, to
passages of Wallace Stevens's writing, I will be invoking the names of Emerson and of Heidegger (as others have) but also of Wittgenstein, implying
that a response cannot match Stevens's zest for the philosophical that is unresponsive to what Emerson and Heidegger and Wittgenstein have urged
about language and the human inhabitation of the world. And yet is it imag-
inable that the philosophical pertinence, even necessity, of these figures could
have appropriately been invoked at Mount Holyoke in 1943? If we agree that

in some obvious sense they could not have been, but agree that they have become philosophically pertinent, even indispensable, then how are we to think about what a culture is, and what its change is? Are we to think of it as out of synchrony with itself, or as maintaining a polysynchrony? And would we want it otherwise?

Let's imagine briefly how or by whom each of these figures might have been handed around the table then in South Hadley. Stevens himself might of course have invoked Emerson, but evidently he could not have envisaged a response from Emerson as assuring his own philosophical pertinence, or his protection against the mastery of philosophy, since he could not count on Emerson as a philosopher—and neither can, still today, most philosophers. As for Wittgenstein, one of his early pupils, Alice Ambrose, one of the two to whom in the academic year 1934–35 Wittgenstein had dictated what came to be called the Brown Book (from which the opening and further extended passages of Wittgenstein's *Philosophical Investigations* ten years later can be seen to be derived) had begun a long lifetime of teaching down the road at Smith College in 1937. But in 1943 that philosophical material was still some ten years away from publication and still quite secure in its state of esotericism. At Mount Holyoke, Jean Wahl already possessed a knowledge of Heidegger's work (Wahl is reported to have joked with students of his at the Sorbonne, before he was arrested and imprisoned by the Gestapo, that the Germans might take kindly to those whom they know are studying Heidegger), and Rachel Bespaloff had published an early essay on Heidegger, but it seems doubtful that they spoke of Heidegger's work on that occasion. Another philosopher present then at Mount Holyoke was Suzanne Langer, who had been a student of Ernst Cassirer's. Cassirer had left Germany for Scandinavia soon after Hitler's rise to power, moved to Yale in 1940, and died suddenly in New York in 1943. I do not know whether Langer would have been present at a fateful conference in Davos, Switzerland, in 1929, at which a confrontation had been arranged between Cassirer and Heidegger, both offering assessments of the achievement of Kant in the history of philosophy; but she would certainly have known that Heidegger was widely thought to have been victorious in that confrontation (Cassirer himself is said to have had that impression), which can be said to have meant the defeat in Germany of the classical humanistic, scholarly reading of the history of philosophy that Heidegger had contempt for, and to have left Heidegger the most advanced philosophical voice in Germany. (Emmanuel Levinas was one of the students present at this conference, who reported in an interview more than sixty years later that at the end of the conference the group of students in attendance composed and performed a skit in which Levinas, because of his shock of light hair, was cast as Cassirer, and in which Cassirer was shown up as the goat of the encounter with Heidegger. Levinas added to his report that he still felt wrong about having been carried away by the proceedings.)

Another student witness present at that Davos conference was Rudolf Carnap, one of whose most influential polemical papers will take the form of an attack on Heidegger as the very type of the purveyor of metaphysical meaninglessness that the school of logical positivism, of which Carnap became the most fruitful founder, was meant to uproot.[1] With the emigration of Carnap and other key figures of the new movement from Vienna and Berlin to the United States at the beginning of the 1940s, logical positivism became, by the time I entered graduate school to begin the study of philosophy in 1948, the dominant avant-garde of the field, and while it is today no longer seriously uncontested, what we might call its style—call this the part of it that shows—remains dominant in what is called analytical philosophy, still the dominant mode of philosophizing in most of the major departments of philosophy in the United States. In fact positivism's influence through the 1950s and 1960s was felt throughout large stretches of the humanities and the social sciences in North American academic life. That it could have achieved this prominence is marked by the well-recognized fact that the migration to North America of intellectuals from central Europe, unlike the rescue and transportation of intellectual refugees from France, began soon after the event of Hitler's ascendance to power and, continuing throughout the years leading up to the outbreak of World War II, took root in American university culture. The only comparably massive effect on that culture in my lifetime was caused by the reception of French thought (so-called post-structuralism) beginning in the late 1960s. But while this later reception served to transform studies in literary and cultural theory, it has had only marginal effects within the professional study of philosophy. We are still working these things out.

Stevens quotes, in his essay "Imagination as Value," from 1948, even pits against each other, passages both from Cassirer's *Essay on Man* and from A. J. Ayer's *Language, Truth, and Logic,* the latter the book from which most people learned the version of what they would know as logical positivism (it remains indeed one of the most successful philosophy textbooks ever written, with sales of over a million copies, and continuing). Heartened by Cassirer's praise of the imagination, in its role as illuminating reality metaphysically—explicitly the obsessive topic of Stevens in his prose writings—Stevens wonders whether, in his words, "we [will] escape destruction at the hands of the logical positivists."

How much Stevens knew of the work of Heidegger remains, so far as I am aware, still uncertain. Frank Kermode, in an admiring essay from the early 1980s, in which he quite unqualifiedly locates Heidegger's interpretations of the poetry of Hölderlin as the revelatory site for an understanding of Stevens's achievement, notes that Stevens had tried to obtain a copy of a French translation of Heidegger's Hölderlin essays from his French bookseller—which strikes me as expressing a wish to keep his curiosity about Heidegger a secret, as Stevens seems to have kept, or protected, so many of his curiosities. Without evidence that Stevens knew Heidegger's writing, Kermode has to content himself with saying that Stevens just did somehow know the truths Heidegger elicited from reading Hölderlin.[2] Professor William Flesch tells me that Stevens had discovered in a French journal an essay by Maurice Blanchot on Heidegger's Hölderlin interpretation. Neither Kermode nor Flesch has, to my knowledge, said whether Stevens sought out anyone with whom to discuss Heidegger's work. Here I think of a moment in (section XXII of) Stevens's long poem "An Ordinary Evening in New Haven," which runs: "Professor Eucalyptus said, 'The search / For reality is as momentous as / The search for god.' It is the philosopher's search." As part of responding to Stevens's appeal to philosophy I would love to know whether Stevens would have recognized in this quotation from Professor Eucalyptus an allusion to Heidegger, since, with the term "Being" substituted for the term "reality," the assertion could be an epigraph for Heidegger's work, especially the later work, which would I think have interested Stevens more than *Being and Time*. If this were initially plausible, it could get a touch of confirmation on considering that the Greek roots of the term *eucalyptus* suggest the beneficence of something that is hidden or covered: this is not a bad rendering of what Heidegger finds in the Greek for "truth"—*aletheia*—which Heidegger reads, not uncontroversially, as giving the sense of uncovering something concealed. It is not controversial to recognize that Stevens unendingly returns to questions or scrupulosities of truth, and of the truth, and of a truth. There are other reasons for suggesting the presence of Heidegger hereabouts, to which I shall come back. (But unlike Cassirer, Heidegger never taught in New Haven.)

I have heard that it was assumed among students of literature of a certain period at Yale (my informant studied there in the late 1970s) that the name Professor Eucalyptus referred to Professor Paul Weiss, perhaps the most prominent of the few philosophers from the United States to appear at Mount

Holyoke in 1943, who was professor of philosophy at Yale from the late 1940s through the 1960s. The assumption of this identification is natural enough concerning a reference apparently to a professor of philosophy in a poem with New Haven in the title, and there would have been scholars of literature at Yale, and specifically of modern poetry, who would have been in a position to verify this. Yet I like what Stevens's New Haven professor is reported to have said about the search for reality and so I hope the attribution is wrong, or unnecessarily exclusive. In the last essay Stevens composed, called "A Collect of Philosophy" (written some years after Stevens's participation in the Pontigny commemoration, and published posthumously), Paul Weiss is cited as among those who had responded to Stevens's question concerning the poetic nature of philosophical concepts, and Weiss is part of the sad story concerning the publication, or non-publication, of that essay. After hearing Stevens read it at Yale, Weiss invited him to publish it in the philosophy journal he edited, the *Review of Metaphysics,* but on receiving it, and after consultation with others, turned it down as more suitable for a literary journal. Weiss is reported—in *Parts of a World: An Oral Biography,* put together in 1985 by Peter Brazeau—to have said that he wrote a courteous letter of rejection to Stevens and was therefore surprised to learn that Stevens had notwithstanding been hurt by it.[3]

It is quite true that, as Weiss and his colleagues agreed, the piece must be thought by professional philosophers to be in various ways naïve, perhaps above all in the sources Stevens cites for his philosophical examples; one of the sources is a history of philosophy for students. Naturally professors as well as artists have, and are entitled to have, their pride, but one can think of courses of action more imaginative than explaining to Wallace Stevens, having invited his contribution, that what he writes is literature and therefore not appropriate to a philosophical enterprise. But perhaps it was too late for that. When Stevens had written to Weiss asking, as he often asked others, for examples of poetic philosophical concepts, Weiss had obliged him by supplying a list of encapsulated philosophical theories associated with great names in the history of the subject—entries one might imagine are suitable for a student's history of philosophy—quite as if it was obvious what Stevens was asking for, obvious what, we might say after Stevens, would suffice.

But it is no more obvious what Stevens was asking for than it is obvious what Stevens's poetry calls for in coming to terms with it. The search for philosophy can make an alarmingly sophisticated and private person say unclear, naïve things, things he himself may not quite mean. But can that itself not be said? The naïve thing in this encounter was shared, I think, by both sides, namely the assumption that Stevens's questions about the poetry of philosophy could be answered without speaking either poetically or philosophically.

Alerted by the complexities suggested in these juxtapositions of characters and these fragments of narratives, let me begin proposing some more consecutive, if still initial, responses to episodes in Stevens's search, sometimes in poetry (that is, by example) and sometimes in prose (that is, by theory), for the poetic register of philosophy.[4]

Take a case Stevens offers in that rejected paper of his, where he speaks of the poetic arising within non-poetic circumstances. He says: "According to the traditional views of sensory perception, we do not see the world immediately but only as the result of a process of seeing and after the completion of that process, that is to say, we never see the world except the moment after."[5] Philosophers I grew up with would surely have questioned the formulation "seeing the world only the moment after." For example it may be asked *what* it is that the moment of seeing comes after. If you answer, "After seeing," then you owe an explanation of the paradox or contradiction in saying that you see only after you see. If, again, you answer, "After the conditions of seeing are satisfied," then you seem to have uttered the banality that you see only when you can see. But suppose, as is not unlikely, that Stevens was speaking poetry. Carnap, in the influential paper of his I alluded to earlier, "The Elimination of Metaphysics through Logical Analysis of Language," from 1932, declares his readiness to grant that metaphysics, while scientifically or cognitively meaningless, may be understood and accepted as poetry, which accordingly means, in a form that makes no cognitive claims upon the world. Carnap's example is, it happens, a passage of Heidegger's, from his *What Is Metaphysics?*, of 1929, the year of the Davos conference. The passage contains the notorious phrase "The Nothing nothings," but Carnap does not go on actually to give a reading of the passage on the basis of the claim that it may be poetry. Whereas it seems clear enough about Stevens's poetry that it makes repeated and tenacious claims for poetry as an understanding of the world, of our lives in the world. To whom are we to listen? Who are we to listen?

In his first book of poems, *Harmonium*, from 1923, in "Thirteen Ways of Looking at a Blackbird," Stevens had said: "I do not know which to prefer, / The beauty of inflections / Or the beauty of innuendoes, / The blackbird whistling / Or just after." This seems to warrant the reaction Stevens expresses to the idea he came upon years later about seeing things the moment after, or say not at first, or at once. (Philosophers have variously found that we do not see things immediately, by which they have meant roughly that we see them, at best, mediately or indirectly. When my teacher J. L. Austin—more famous now for his invention of the theory of the performativity of language—claimed to have shown that the idea that we are fated to see objects indirectly is an empty idea, he went on to insist this meant that the idea that we are fated to see them directly is equally empty. To understand why philosophers are led to sum up our relation to the world in either of these ways was not something Austin had patience for; it was a principal cause that led him to an impatience altogether with what had come to be called philosophy.) Stevens's late reaction to the perpetual lateness of perception is that the idea "instantly changes the face of the world," and it may strike one that the blackbird's turns had already signaled how easy it is for us to miss the experience of the world's arrivals and of its departures, its inflections and innuendoes, as if the world naturally keeps the face of its beauty partially turned from us.

Modern philosophy has generally attempted, unless it has accepted, or merely dismissed, an irreducible skepticism, to overcome some sense of a gap or barrier between human perception and the world (unless reassured by the perpetual intervention of God, as in Descartes or in Berkeley), by proposing, as Kant did, that the way humankind necessarily organizes its perceptions necessarily reveals what we understand as the world we know, or, as philosophers in response to Kant's proposal did, by positing a new form of human intuition or immediacy. What Stevens seems eventually to come to in his poetic idea that perception is not blocked or interrupted but that it comes just after, that it is late, is the thought that the way to overcome the gap in what Professor Eucalyptus calls the search for reality lies in finding how to appear to reality early, earlier than philosophers now imagine to be possible, in what Stevens calls, in "An Ordinary Evening in New Haven" (XXII), an "original earliness"—to get to objects, to get before objects, before they are given to us or dictated to us; or before, we might say, the division hardens between objects and subjects, or between outside and inside.

My invocation of modern philosophical skepticism as an intellectual environment in which to assess Stevens's search for reality is no doubt a function of my own preoccupation with the threat of skepticism as posing the underlying task of Wittgenstein's *Philosophical Investigations,* the text of the twentieth century that more than any other has served to convince me that philosophy remains alive to issues of modern life that concern me most. When Wallace Stevens writes, again in "An Ordinary Evening," "the theory / Of poetry is the theory of life" (XXVIII), and implies perpetually that poetry is the imagination of life on earth and that failing to imagine one's life is a failure in living it, I take him to be responding to the threat of skepticism more clearly than, or as the condition of, the loss of metaphysics, although metaphysics more explicitly enters his prose articulations of his position. But I am not here trying to prove an epistemological priority in his work.

Yet to indicate Stevens's seriousness and diligence in, let's say, theorizing about knowledge, I note that the short poem he places at the end of his *Collected Poems,* a poem to which he gives as its title the motto "Not Ideas about the Thing but the Thing Itself," ends with the claim, "It was like / A new knowledge of reality." Here Stevens is not content, as he was in his initial assessment of the lateness of perception, to conclude that we are confined to a knowledge of what is always past. He is now rather occupied with the conviction that what we perceive—instanced by the cry of a bird and the coming of the sun—comes from outside the mind. This poem consists of six three-line stanzas, of which the opening stanza runs as follows: "At the earliest ending of winter, / In March, a scrawny cry from outside / Seemed like a sound in his mind." I note that half of the poem's stanzas contain the idea of being early or coming before or preceding, and another includes his giving himself assurance that he is not asleep, not dreaming. Stevens names Descartes, and I assume also alludes to him, in his poetry. In "Notes toward a Supreme Fiction" we find: "I have not but I am and as I am, I am", which I understand to say, roughly: Nothing I possess, including my body, proves that I exist; but I since I can think, or say in my mind "I am," it follows that I am. This is substantially one formulation Descartes gives to his cogito ergo sum argument. And I take it as uncontroversial that Stevens's citing here the possibility that I am dreaming what is real is meant in this context to invoke a relation to philosophical skepticism concerning the existence of the world.

I do not know whether Stevens knew that in the preface to the second edition of *The Critique of Pure Reason,* Kant characterizes the issue of skepticism as Stevens does here, not as turning on a distinction between subjectivity and objectivity or between the mental and the material or between appearance and reality but on that between being inside or outside the mind. Kant says there: "It still remains a scandal to philosophy and to human reason in general that the existence of things outside us . . . must be accepted merely on *faith,* and that if anyone thinks good to doubt their existence, we are unable to counter his doubts by any satisfactory proof." I imagine that it would have pleased Stevens to know that Heidegger will respond to Kant's idea of the scandal of skepticism by remarking that the real philosophical scandal is the idea that the answer to skepticism requires a proof. An implication of Heidegger's retort is that seeking a proof merely perpetuates the skeptical attitude, or in any case makes the existence of the world, as surely as it has made God's existence, hostage to the fate of human constructions, inherently open to collapse.

A further implication may be that a permanently valuable response to skepticism will be one that traces the circumstances of human life and thought that make skepticism possible, perhaps necessary, and exemplifies the resources of that life that overcomes skepticism, or shows it to be a habitable, even welcome, moment of human existence. If so, Stevens to my mind enters a claim to have made, in his body of poetry, a distinctively valuable contribution to that task, most patently perhaps in his encouragement to raise the question why philosophers choose the examples they do, Descartes taking the case of his sitting before the fire, Kant that of a drifting boat, Bishop Berkeley that of a cherry, Heidegger of a tree, G. E. Moore that of a human hand, countless academic epistemologists of the twentieth century taking those of a piece of chalk or of a pen—never anything like, as in Stevens, the scrawny cry of a bird before daylight, and not just the colossal sun but the distant coming on of the sun. Acknowledging that Stevens's promptings here might be consequential philosophically will no doubt require being prompted to a willingness somewhat to re-conceive our received ideas of poetry and of philosophy, a willingness some of my favorite philosophers of the past century and a half have shown, notably—beyond Wittgenstein—Emerson, hence Nietzsche, hence Heidegger.

Stevens's interpretation of human perception as late, as happening the moment after, hence as suggesting a poetic counter-action directed to making something happen the moment before, would link up remarkably with a work Heidegger was preparing the year before the one my remarks principally commemorate today, namely in 1942 in Freiburg, on a major text of Hölderlin's, the hymn on the Ister River.[6] I might not have become impressed by this connection between Stevens and Heidegger had I not several years ago published an essay that works through a continuously surprising web of relations between what Heidegger calls Hölderlin's poetizing of this river and Thoreau's philosophizing, let's call it, of his woodland lake Walden.[7]

Passing by such matters as Heidegger and Thoreau both requiring of philosophy that it be a matter of awakening, and their both understanding their respective bodies of water as preparing the earth for human habitation, and both emphasizing the construction of a hearth, and both detecting the pervasiveness of mourning (or melancholy) related to the learning of remaining patiently near or next to the origin of life, and their both taking the marking out of paths as signs of destinies (something Heidegger takes to unify a people, something Thoreau takes as a cue to rebuke himself), let's focus simply on the three-word opening line of the Ister hymn (a poem of roughly 70 comparably short lines): "Now come, fire," a line to which Heidegger devotes the opening pages of his text on the poem. He says of the line, addressed to the rising of the sun, that it is a call (the concept of calling is thematic in *Walden*) and, Heidegger continues, "The call says: we, the ones thus calling, are ready. And something else is also concealed in such calling out: we are ready and are so only because we are called by the coming fire itself." That is, we are there before the sun arrives; awakening must happen thus earlier.

Thoreau is still more explicit. Early in the first chapter of *Walden,* in introducing himself by "attempting to tell" how he has "desired to spend" his life (one attempt he describes as "trying to hear what was in the wind"), he lists the work of "[anticipating], not the sunrise and the dawn merely, but, if possible Nature herself!" Later in that paragraph Thoreau concedes: "It is true, I never assisted the sun materially in his rising, but, doubt not, it was of the last importance only to be present at it." To "assist" at a social event—for example, a theater performance—is precisely an old-fashioned term for making oneself present, or attending. An importance of Thoreau's observation, as elsewhere, is his demonstrating that he can make sunrise a communal event even when what is called religion has forgotten how. This kind of remembrance is something Wallace Stevens requires of poetry, as he names the very idea of God to be the responsibility of poetry. Thoreau's work of anticipating is something he thematizes as being early, and earlier, and earliest.

So *Walden* is a source from which Stevens may be thought to have acquired truths characteristic of Heidegger's work, ones indeed outstripping that work on Hölderlin. I do not know whether it is materially provable that Stevens read Thoreau, but it is enough that there is no doubt of his reading Emerson, which would have sufficed in this region. A favorite quotation of Nietzsche's from Emerson's essay "Circles" speaks of "another dawn risen on mid-noon," which, however, was derived from Milton and is to be found also in Wordsworth's *Prelude*. The difference here is that Emerson is not picturing awakening as an anticipation, but the basic affinity is the perception that an inner dawn is not given to us by the bare fact of the rising sun. More specific to Emerson is the idea of closing the skeptical distance between mind and reality through the concept of what is *near*. (Thoreau's variation is to speak of what is happening at all times *next* to us.)

In Emerson's great essay "Experience" he says: "I cannot get it nearer to me," having identified his experience of the being of the world with his grief over the death of his young son. I have argued in other contexts that Emerson's implication is that, through mourning, and patience, we can reverse skepticism and let the world come nearer to us. This is figured in what happens in Stevens's late poem "The World as Meditation," where Penelope, wondering whether it is Ulysses or is the sun lifting over the eastern horizon, notes that "the warmth of the sun / On her pillow" means that it is only one more material day, hence "She would talk a little to herself as she combed her hair, / Repeating his name with its patient syllables, / Never forgetting him that kept coming constantly so near." In accepting this account of keeping near reality, living with it, as opposed to claiming coincidence or immediacy with it, of the patience the human creature has to learn in its relation to the world it cares for, accepting the active patience that philosophical skepticism construes as an intellectual puzzle to be solved, be put to rest, I accept the poem as a successful celebration of a happy marriage, that understands it to be an epic event. It may then be taken as an answer to Kant's taunting philosophy with leaving the existence of things outside of us at the mercy of faith rather than settled by a proof.

The knack of the answer is to render faith as faithfulness, as daily as the coming of the sun, obscured or not. Stevens refers to such an accomplishment in his conjecture, near the end of "Notes toward a Supreme Fiction," which runs: "Perhaps, / The man-hero is not the exceptional monster, / But he that of repetition is most master," precisely the mastery that faithfulness requires. There is a prominent interpretation of "The World as Meditation" that takes it to be Stevens's confession of a failed marriage, in which case the implication of the "barbarous strength" the poem attributes to faithfulness would become a recipe for spiritual torture, hopeless distance, the dully tantalized world as hell. It is a thought not beyond Stevens, but not, I think, in this poem.

In the concluding paragraph of "Experience" Emerson announces what will become one of Wallace Stevens's most repetitive motives or motifs, namely to "realize his world," and two paragraphs earlier Emerson provides instruction in this process that has various echoes for us. Emerson says: "I am and I have; but I do not get, and when I have fancied I had gotten anything, I found I did not." "To find the real" is how Stevens comparably puts things in "Notes toward a Supreme Fiction," in the section preceding that from which I earlier cited the line "I have not but I am and as I am, I am." The contradiction between Emerson's "I am and I have" and Stevens's "I have not but I am" is canceled as it turns out that what Stevens's says he has is "No need, am happy, forget needs' golden hand, / Am satisfied" (what he has is respite). And when in that same essay of Emerson's we find the claim "Thus inevitably does the universe wear our color," I must hear this as asserting jointly both sides of Stevens's perpetual oscillation between claiming for poetry that it is, and that it is not, the construction, or abstraction, of the individual poet. Of course Emerson draws the implication of his observation by seeing "every object fall into the subject itself"; but what his words actually say is that the universe jousts for our attention and approval. This double sense of "our color," as idiosyncratically or (as Stevens just might have said) idiotically ours and at the same time worn publicly, seems to me a useful way to think of Stevens's punctual signature bursts of color adjectives across his surfaces, from early blackbirds flying in a green light and a rose rabbi and a dream of red weather to a blue guitar and the azury centre of time.

Before looking for a place to stop, remembering that one of the incitements to these beads of philosophy I have strung along was the name and the saying of Professor Eucalyptus that measures the search for reality by the search for God, I pause to voice my sense that so particular a name as eucalyptus (others trees are content with names such as elm, pine, maple, cedar, oak, fir, spruce, beech, birch) is too particular to be confined to a given professor. I take the name, referring to a tree some of whose species bear a leaf that is aromatic and yields an oil used medicinally, as being used by Stevens to refer, somewhat ruefully, not necessarily exclusively, to himself. That the eucalyptus leaf's properties are here held in check by the title Professor is an effect equally pertinent to a streak in Stevens, who likes to include pronouncements in his poetry (he collects them separately under the term "Adagia," adages), such as "We seek / Nothing beyond reality" ("An Ordinary Evening," IX). Is this fact of isolated pronouncement less important than that what goes on to happen in this poem is not what we would expect to happen in a treatise of philosophical puzzlement? Noting that Eucalyptus is related to the term Apocalypse, meaning the uncovering or revelation of what is hidden, and letting this send us back to the connection with Heidegger's conception of truth as *a-letheia,* I cite again Emerson's "Experience," which opens by depicting us as finding ourselves waking on a stair, stairs below and above us, where, as we re-enter existence, "the Genius stands at the door and gives us the lethe to drink [but] mixed the cup too strongly, and we cannot shake off the lethargy now at noonday" (the term "lethargy" making explicit the state induced by drinking from the river Lethe).

And Emerson's essay "Experience" explicitly challenges the philosopher's idea of experience to be found in Kant and in the classical empiricists (Emerson characterizes the idea as a "paltry empiricism," an impoverishment of experience), implicitly resisting Kant's metaphysical, fixed separation of the two worlds Kant perceives humankind to live in, the world of sense and the world of intellect, and Emerson explicitly rejects the despair of what Kant had already called "realizing his world" (a formulation critical for both Emerson and Stevens), a despair fated by a paltry empiricism. Stevens is surely moving similarly when he speaks, in the "Figure of the Youth" essay, of poetry as "destroy[ing] the false imagination." A parallel I cannot doubt was in Stevens's ear when he thus speaks of the poet's destructiveness, I find in a passage from Emerson's essay "Fate," in his saying: "We should be crushed by the atmosphere, but for the reaction of the air within the body. . . . If there be omnipotence in the stroke, there is omnipotence of recoil." Stevens casts this thought slightly differently, within his own philosophical palette, when at the end of the essay written the year earlier than the "Figure of the Youth," namely "The Noble Rider and the Sound of Words," he says: "It is a violence from within that protects us from a violence without. It is the imagination pressing back against the pressure of reality." But Stevens speaks for himself, or rather for poetry, as Emerson had spoken for his prose, when he claims for this violence, with modest exorbitance, that it "helps us to live our lives."

I must try, before having done, some brief answer to the most obvious two cruxes posed in the essay "The Figure of the Youth as Virile Poet," first the title insistence on the poet as a young male, second the repeatedly invoked "sister of the minotaur," to whom, as a new muse, Stevens early confides that he no longer believes "that there is a mystic muse," which is only, he goes on to say, "another of the monsters I had for nurse, whom I have wasted." He declares to her that he is part of the real and hears only the strength of his own speech. Then at the close he again asks this apparently non-mystical and monstrous muse to hear him, who knows that he is part of the real, but beyond this to recognize him as part of the unreal—that is, as part of what is still to be realized, hence to be fictionalized—and to guide him to the truth of the imagination, which he cannot reach by the strength of his speech alone, but which requires "exchanges of speech in which your words are mine, mine yours."

About the first crux, the young male, I note only what is clear on the surface, that he needs to be violent in a male way (virile) because the burden of the past, from which he needs liberation (poetry is always of the present), has been an affair of males; and also because he needs to attract and withstand the indispensable recognition and guidance of a female monster. (The figure of the old poet Stevens figures as a tramp, having, I imagine, given away all the intelligence he had to give; no match for a minotaur's sister.) To say more then depends on following the second crux, concerning who or what this monster / muse is. I shall just try looking at the idea that she is monstrous because, as Stevens puts it earlier, this "muse of [the young poet's] own" is "still half-beast and somehow more than human." (I will assume, though it is not certain, that this rules out her being one of the minotaur's well-known half-sisters, Ariadne or Phaedra. I am here following the thought that Stevens is conjuring an unheard-of female minotaur, a domesticator of the maze, the world and its words, not a rescuer from it.)

I find Emerson a further help here, in his articulation of the intersection of the subjective and the objective, or perhaps I can say of their collusion, where he observes, "We but half express ourselves," which I understand, however else, to imply that the other half of our expression is in the hands of language, which is never wholly ours. I hear a version of this in Stevens where, instead of, as in Emerson, a Genius is standing at the door, Stevens places an Angel "seen for a moment standing in the door" who announces that "in my sight, you see earth again, cleared of its . . . man-locked set, / And, in my hearing, you hear its tragic drone." The figure who announces this (in the poem "Angel Surrounded by Paysans," which concludes *The Auroras of Autumn*) identifies himself as "a man of the mind," and as "The necessary angel of earth," describing himself as "only half a figure of a sort, / A figure half seen" who offers "meanings said / By repetitions of half-meanings." So whereas the sister of the minotaur—another half-figure of a sort, a figure of halves—can be invoked and asked to make her words ours and ours hers, the Angel who offers to make his sight and his hearing ours, can only be awaited and glimpsed, like all that goes unseen, unheard, unimagined, unrealized, unsaid. The poet is the one who knows how to invoke and to await these appearances.

There is no question now of pursuing how Stevens's location of the human as moving between minotaur and angel compares with Aristotle's location of us as neither beasts nor gods, or with Pascal's location of us as between beasts and angels, or with Kant's somewhat different location of us as neither (purely) beasts nor angels. I have been led to emphasize the figures in Stevens as representing moments in which, primarily in my efforts to come to terms with Wittgenstein's *Philosophical Investigations,* I have recurred to the idea that in philosophizing we wish to escape our humanity—our finitude—from above or from below, a wish I have also expressed as the all but inescapable wish of the human to become inhuman, as if to accept monstrousness would be to escape the perpetual knowledge of our disappointments, the maze of infinite desires in finite circumstances.

In each of the appeals Stevens addresses to philosophy there is, to my mind, a false step that helps ensure he will emerge unsatisfied. The error comes out in the opening sentence of his preface to the prose texts in the volume *The Necessary Angel.* In that preface he says: "One function of the poet at any time is to discover by his own thought and feeling what seems to him to be poetry at that time." What Stevens will not conceive is that the philosopher may have a comparable function of discovery, as if for Stevens philosophy, in its otherness, is a fixed, oracular structure and those who speak for it are in possession of an authority that goes beyond what they are able to articulate out of their own experience and practice and wit on each occasion of being stopped to think.

I end with one more link between Stevens and Emerson, glancing at a moment in each at which the right to speak is staked against the mortal dangers and the injustices of their times. Emerson, with shocking intent, deflects imagined charges against his neglect of the poor by claiming in effect that he means his writing to serve the poor in the way he is best fit to serve. And Stevens, in the ambience of World War II, appends to his manifesto "Notes toward a Supreme Fiction" stanzas addressed to a soldier in which he claims the poet is joined in a war of the mind that never ends and that depends on his, on the soldier's, war. These stanzas include the words "The soldier is poor without the poet's lines." So Emerson and Stevens thus each subject their work to an extreme test—call it the test of maintaining the truth of the nation even when the nation is mobilized in maintaining its existence. Presumably they do this to alert us, their readers, that, in taking up their words, we each subject ourselves to judging their survival of this test, hence to the test's reflected judgment of us; we judge that we be judged. This was true in 1943, as it was in Emerson's 1843 and the years after, as it is in 2003.

Foreword to *Qu'est-ce que la philosophie américaine?*

In the 1980s, Cavell entered a period of great productivity, writing intensively on the subject of what he called moral perfectionism. In addition to a number of original essays on Emerson intended for a volume called *Here and There* but ultimately published elsewhere, Cavell produced *In Quest of the Ordinary* (1988), *This New Yet Unapproachable America* (1989), and *Conditions Handsome and Unhandsome* (1990) in a span of less than ten years. The latter two were translated by Sandra Laugier and published in 1991 and 1993, respectively, by Éditions de l'éclat; they were republished by Éditions Gallimard in 2009, together with several other of Cavell's essays on Emerson, under the title *Qu'est-ce que la philosophie américaine?* We present here the original English text of the foreword Cavell wrote for that book.

IT IS WONDERFUL TO KNOW THAT THE FIRST of my Emerson explorations to have been translated into French are to be reissued, and together, under the renowned Gallimard imprint. My gratitude goes out as well to Michel Valensi and Jean-Pierre Cometti of Éditions de l'éclat for taking a chance on their initial French translations.

The interactions of these texts not only afford a realization of all my work on Emerson, but, dispersed among them, exemplify my best efforts to show Emerson's responses to central texts and terms of philosophy to be sufficiently powerful that they put into question what is, and what is to be called, philosophy (a task of questioning that central philosophy must be expected to pick up). Such, at any rate has been my claim since experiencing, comparatively late in my philosophical life, the continuous precision of Emerson's thinking, so regularly found by his negligent countrymen to be intellectually ambitious beyond his means. I hope I am right to see in these texts of mine Emerson's force making itself felt in the way I read Wittgenstein and even Shakespeare and film.

My pleasure in this publication is secured in knowing that my words have been translated by my friends Sandra Laugier, whom I have known since her post-graduate year spent in Harvard's department of philosophy a quarter of a century ago, and her classmate from their time at the École Normale, Christian Fournier. Their combination of philosophical and literary experience continues to astound me after countless conversations over the years, in Paris and in Boston, as does their subtlety with the English language and their depth of interest in American culture. Their informed care with my texts is understandably an inspiration to me.

It is familiar that resourceful translations may teach writers something further about what they have set down. Turning through the pages of my texts and their translations in preparing to compose a few introductory thoughts to the present publication, my eye fell on words quoted on an early page of my essay "Emerson's Constitutional Amending" ("Les amendements d'Emerson à la Constitution des États-Unis") where in one of my many efforts to capture the perpetually surprising richness of Emerson's prose, I was led to cite the following passage from Emerson's essay "On Emancipation in the British West Indies": "Language must be raked, the secrets of the slaughter-houses and infamous holes that cannot front the day, must be ransacked, to tell what negro-slavery has been." I was glad in being reminded of what I go on to say there, but I found that I was also disappointed in it. I felt that the violence of Emerson's horror in the fact of slavery is not sufficiently responded to in what I go on to consider. I turned to the appearance of my quoted Emerson sentence in French to find this: "Il faut fouiller le fin fond du langage, piller les secrets des abattoirs et des trous infâmes qui ne sauraient soutenir la lumière du jour, pour dire ce qu'a été l'esclavage des Nègres." This seemed to me, in my mood then, to translate faithfully my new sense of disappointment, but in this new guise I seemed to recognize the cause of my feeling. "Fouiller le fin fond" clearly gives the sense of exhaustiveness and detail Emerson craves in discovering the sense, and implication, of the words he calls upon to tell what he knows of slavery, something, I note, that he does not claim to have achieved. But there is a further sense in play, one Emerson may be said to have achieved.

What I had insufficiently responded to is brought out in the translation of "rake" by "fouiller." Of course this is not necessarily wrong. Yet even adding "le fin fond" does not distinguish raking from the ensuing "ransacking" ("piller"); both imply the thoroughness or exhaustiveness in a detailed search. But the sense of excavation in "fouiller" misses the literal work of a rake—a long-handled implement, either of bamboo or of wood and iron, each ending in lined teeth, the bamboo version used typically in heaping together fallen leaves or cut grass, the version with iron teeth used more pertinently to loosen a stretch of clumpy earth or, turning the rake over, to smooth the stretch. And beyond the familiar idea of a set of lights raking the sky or a building in order to scan it, for celebration or for trouble, there is in the raking motion an image of scratching or scraping, in direct contrast to the sense of digging for depth in excavating as with picks and shovels, namely a contrasting sense of staying at and disturbing a surface.

And here I find the sense of violence I missed in my earlier published reading of Emerson's sentence. It is the sense of reading the phrase "language must be raked" as announcing language's capacity to rake and at the same time its suffering itself to be raked, raked of course by itself (how else?), scratched and scraped throughout, marred, turned aside or upside down, punished, surprised by itself, by its pain, yet throughout courteously, sociably stifling its sobs. Being philosophy it must not claim to know what all others are in a position to know. And being philosophy it turns perpetually upon itself.—If this does not at once seem what Emerson's twists and turns betoken, one might deliberately try raking it in this light. At random I find: "For all men live by truth, and stand in need of expression. In love, in art, in avarice, in politics, in labor, in games, we study to utter our painful secret" (from Emerson's "The Poet"). I could wish that I had seen this clearly and steadily when I first wrote my piece in question. I am very glad to have the occasion to say it now, in gratitude.

Speaking of occasion, something has now struck me belatedly about what I earlier described as my eye falling on the passage from Emerson that I then quote to reinterpret. I now imagine that I had been guided to this moment by vibrations from the recurring waves of ecstasy in coming to understand as solemn fact that my horribly scarred but madly aspiring nation has elected a black man—this black man—as its president. The depth of promise in what has happened keeps on unfolding in its implications. Our joy—constitutional and Constitutional—underscores the knowledge of how depressed the mood of the country has been (as it has presented itself to me) these past eight years.

For me, I do not guess for how many others, the sense of America as living under the curse and the remains of slavery periodically invades my consciousness. (I have thought sometimes that this was the cause of my prose sounding melancholy to me, for no immediate reason that I could see.) That curse is now lifted. What remains now is the ordinary, daily work of establishing the justice and liberty and general welfare that our Constitution names in its opening and defining call for "a more perfect union."

If Emerson is the name of a writer who showed me that, and perhaps how, to allow myself the freedom to follow my expression wherever it asks to go, France is the name of the longest sustained culture of intellectuality we have, creating the imagination of a public ready to struggle in the streets and in the press for departures in ideas and in the arts to be known and possessed. In a passage of from "Self-Reliance" that has more than once caught my attention, Emerson writes: "I would write on the lintels of the door-post *Whim*. I hope it is somewhat better than whim at last, but we cannot spend the day in explanation." (On the second page of Wittgenstein's *Investigations,* still in its opening section: "Explanations come to an end somewhere.") I like to imagine that in my American land of immigrants the very promise in diversity holds open the possibility of an audience for what Emerson, in his case, modestly calls whim—sometimes I suppose translatable as "caprice"—and bravely enough imagined himself to be inscribing its expression, say its invitation, on the outside, indeed the entrance, to his house in progress.

PART III | Music

An Understanding
with Music

This lecture was delivered at an outreach panel at the American Musicological Society in October 1998. It is Cavell's first explicit, focused return to the subject of music after his 1967 essay "Music Discomposed." Here he follows up on the analyses of opera in *A Pitch of Philosophy* (1994), discussing Gary Tomlinson's *Music in Renaissance Magic: Toward a Historiography of Others* (1993) and Michel Poizat's *The Angel's Cry: Beyond the Pleasure Principle in Opera* (1992).[1] Cavell thus begins what became a cycle of new writings on music, stressing the continuity of music and speech. "Being sung to or played for," he writes, "is as natural to our form of life as being spoken to."

INVITED TO SAY FOR SOME TWENTY MINUTES how the work I do in a certain manner of philosophy, and the work of studying the nature and cultures of music, might bear upon one another, I shall explicitly make myself the subject of a banal experiment, something like one more characteristically conducted in unawareness, namely, to read certain passages out of two recent texts from a profession not mine, not subject to professional evaluation by me, and to report on my initial difficulties in pursuing the understanding of them. The texts, commended to me by musicologist acquaintances, are Gary Tomlinson's *Music in Renaissance Magic: Toward a Historiography of Others* and Michel Poizat's *The Angel's Cry: Beyond the Pleasure Principle in Opera*. Both appeared, or came my way, after I had delivered a set of three lectures in 1992, published as *A Pitch of Philosophy,* the last of which consists of an account, partly autobiographical and partly philosophical, of my encountering opera in my intellectual adventures. Both texts clearly lie across my path here. Do I know how to be guided by them?

While each is rich in its range of reference, they could hardly differ more in their intellectual textures: Tomlinson's scholarship, in the claims he makes about music in the Renaissance and the musical scholarship it has attracted, sets for itself high standards of scrupulousness; Poizat's learning is marked, one could say, by unscrupulousness in a certain French manner, in his claims to articulate his passion for his subject. In approaching them here I note two features or touches they share, one pervasive, one quite momentary, that put me on guard. The pervasive feature is their each appealing throughout, as the steadiest basis for their theorizing, to citations from a major, not to say magic, name in that onslaught of French thought over the past thirty years that has changed the face of American academic life (outside the natural sciences), in Tomlinson's case to Michel Foucault, in Poizat's case to Jacques Lacan. The momentary touch is their each referring once to J. L. Austin's discovery of the performative utterance, and each by way of quoting someone else's view of Austin (in Tomlinson's case, the anthropologist Stanley Tambiah, in Poizat's case the literary / cultural theorist Shoshana Felman).

My guardedness on these points comes from their exposing issues in my sense of embattlement within my professional field of philosophy. In the dispensation of Anglo-American analytical philosophy (as contrasted with the German-French continuation, or discontinuation, of metaphysics), within which I was trained and so many of my students over the decades have mostly or initially been trained, figures such as Foucault and Lacan play essentially no role, unless it is a negative one: to raise the name of their work is invariably to incur suspicion, which perhaps by now has some chance of being allayed. So much the worse for Anglo-American philosophizing, you may say—and I say so too, in part; but I cannot deny what makes this profession suspicious of the other shore of philosophy, I mean the genuine intellectual successes of analytical philosophy.

Among my favorite of its successes is precisely the work of J. L. Austin, while at the same time the body of his work (where it has not become part of, so to speak, conventional philosophical wisdom) is largely neglected in its detail in contemporary analytical philosophizing. It was primarily Austin's work that kept me in graduate school, that in effect allowed me to convert my despair of philosophy into a new form of interest in it. I have characterized that work, along with the practice of the later Wittgenstein, as accomplishing the return of the human voice to philosophy, that is, providing methodical ways of outlining the suppression of voice chronic in philosophy, most particularly in that strain of thinking philosophy calls modern skepticism, beginning famously with Descartes. It is as a response to the suppression of voice that my desire to think about opera, as the Western institution dedicated to, let's say, the celebration of the voice, presented itself to me. (This might be viewed, adapting a phrase of Walter Benjamin's, as an effort to make the phenomenon of opera part of the history of philosophy.) This thought was prepared by my having followed out a reading of Shakespearean tragedy according to which, in the generation preceding that of Descartes, Shakespeare's great tragedies incorporate the full consequences of skepticism's surmise that—as I might put the matter—at the moment our language is finding its most sublime expressiveness (in Hamlet, Othello, Lear, Macbeth), language has become insufficient to name and secure our shared knowledge of the existence of the world and of I and others in it.

Struck by the link of the first decade of the seventeenth century as the time of the major tragedies and as a locus for plotting the birth of opera, how could I not be struck further by Gary Tomlinson's discussion of Monteverdi's participation in the shift from magical speech in music to musical representation of speech (p. 242), particularly in its pertinence to the shift in presenting "characters speaking in song" (p. 244) and to "new relations of language and the world" (ibid.). But do I understand this shift?—especially in its claim to be affirming a historiography of others, one that asks (as Foucault is cited to express it): "What does it mean, no longer being able to think a certain thought?" (p. 247). Tomlinson, for good reason, wants to second an emphasis on the incompleteness of the understanding of another, to preserve the mystery of the other against hegemonic pretensions to mastery. But is it clear how Foucault's picture of, let's say, incommensurable *breaks* in a history, that is, within one culture, applies in thinking about the issue of otherness generally, other persons, other cultures?

I take Wittgenstein's *Philosophical Investigations* to represent the discovery of the other for philosophy in its analytical dispensation, the most enabling philosophical discussion in that mode to investigate the matter of skeptical doubts of the existence of others, or as I put the matter, of the human wish to deny the humanity of others (hence of oneself). Now does it make sense in general to frame the question of my knowledge of another soul, as it were the existence of another body possessed of a consciousness like mine, as one in which I *no longer* know or understand an other, can no longer think the thought of an other, as if there has been a *break* between us? (And does it matter whether the one in question is my friend, a stranger on the street, or the first I encounter after a shipwreck?) It might very well make a contribution to the problem, for example in suggesting that the question of the other *arises* only when I find, or impose, a break between us. But then the preservation of mystery in the position of the other may well not be an issue of Foucauldian conditions of possibility. The break in question may lie in me, without my surmising that my conditions of possibility differ from yours; our sameness contributes to the anguish.

And if I am to see the incompleteness in my understanding, how hard must I have tried to understand? Austin's idea of the performative utterance—in which to say something is to do something—is found by Tomlinson to fail to capture, as it were, the reality of the world of Renaissance magic (p. 248), amounting, following Tambiah, to Malinowski's compromised perception that "though magic may be a false technical act it is a true social act" (p. 249). But Austin's performatives are not false technical acts; they do not, in general, fail to make something happen. (How they may specifically, in particular contexts, fail in their desired effect it is a principal goal of Austin's theory to specify.) They are also, in the dimension Austin favors (that of an utterance's illocutionary force) free of any suspicion of magic. (Austin would have been horrified to suppose otherwise).

Yet there is derivable from Austin's theory of the performative utterance, at a place Austin notices but hastily abandons, a theory of what I call passionate utterance, of the ways in which the interest in language is not primarily in what I do with it as in what I suffer from it. This is where I should like to claim the interest in what Austin calls perlocutionary force lies. And it strikes me that it is the perlocutionary form of force that, so construed, works *like* magic, in the specific sense of producing true technical acts: the other is, as an effect of my words, wounded, embarrassed, intimidated, fascinated, terrified, horrified, exalted, seduced. It was in having to think about the effects of opera's singing that I was two or three years ago drawn to go over a longstanding dissatisfaction with a critical transition in Austin's *How To Do Things with Words* and hit upon the derivation of passionate utterance.[2]

So what—I ask myself—is my problem? Why not present, for example, this theory to further public view, along with its welcome association to a history of magic, and let people take it or leave it alone? Why expect that everyone who touches my old teacher Austin's work should either know it in its sumptuous detail and implication or else not be interested in considering it further? Well, of course I am here working myself up to a plan eventually to make something more public, but the worry for me at the moment is not whether I am understood (I hope I am doing the best my minutes here permit) but whether I understand, or know how to limit my understanding of, texts whose concerns I share.

Michel Poizat's preface to *The Angel's Cry* heads directly into the question of understanding, featuring a quotation from Levi-Strauss, which I give in part:

> There would be no music if language had not preceded it and if music did not continue to depend on it, as it were, through a privative connection. Music is language without meaning: this being so, it is understandable that the listener, who is first and foremost a subject with the gift of speech, should feel himself irresistibly compelled to make up for the absent sense, just as someone who has lost a limb imagines that he still possesses it through the sensations present in the stump.

To which Poizat responds: "Is it perhaps this primordial act of separation that opera speaks of, letting us know that it is paid for with suffering? And is it perhaps in the nostalgia for a paradisiacal unity of preseparation that the opera lover's ecstasy resides?"

Whatever Levi-Strauss's stake, in his story of myth, in such an idea of music's "separating off from language," Poizat's use of the idea, or fantasy, of the relation of the present separation of music and language to a preseparative unity seems quite isomorphic with Tomlinson's proposal, or reaffirmation, of a state—critical for the birth of opera—of a musical and linguistic magical harmony prior to one of representative distance. But apart from Tomlinson's denial of purity to these states, he gives impressive historical evidence for characterizing them specifically and assigning dates to them, whereas Poizat's hypothesis of a primordial connection relies elsewhere than evidence for its conviction, presumably upon a more or less unspoken theory of the psychic development of singing as stretching between speech and the cry, under the demand for pleasure and for an enjoyment beyond pleasure, linked with the identification of this beyond in moments across the history of opera.

There seems little hope that such an idea will help understand why opera arises when and where it does, to which Tomlinson's findings are so pertinent. This aside, while I am sympathetic to Poizat's project of characterizing the operatic voice, and find certain agreeable coincidences with proposals of mine in the lecture on opera I mentioned (ones concerning the loss of voice or the deprivation of voice, and the significance of its being the woman's voice that we desire to hear and desire to still, and the isolation of the voice as an object unlocatable or unpredictable as from a particular body), so many matters in this book of intuitions strike me as unintuitive. For example, in taking the cry as the epitome of opera's expressiveness, the final anguish that transcends both language and music to reach an expression of pure voice, Poizat recalls (without actually mentioning, so far as I recall) Nietzsche's *Birth of Tragedy,* but negates its experience of the cry as the suffering of individuation, that is of finite existence, of which music allows the expression, as if we should without such expression suffocate from our words, buried alive. So that music can be said, in retrospect, to anticipate, or re-enact, the expressive work of language. And then the presence of the cry in opera, taken as a somewhat less unearthly gesture (less a culmination of expressiveness than an exhaustion from it, or from it, a despair of the demand for it) may receive a more plausible explication as letting opera's condition of possibility declare itself, that in it speaking is replaced by singing—considering that a cry is, as it were, between speaking and singing, that it represents itself, that in it the distinction between singer and character is overcome. (This distinction is not overcome in cases when what singing represents is itself someone singing; here the actor / singer and the character / singer are as distinct as ever.)

I head toward a close by letting Levi-Strauss's formulation of music as "language without meaning" prompt a further thought, or meta-thought, about the sublime issue of meaning in music. Why take this formula to imply that music lacks something, as in Levi-Strauss's fantasm of the phantom limb? Evidently he is not suggesting that music is like an uninterpreted formal language (which is, as it were, content to remain uninterpreted). Mightn't one feel either?: Feel meaning is more essential—if there are degrees of the essential— to music than a limb is to a body; or feel: music lacks meaning the way the night lacks the sun, it's what music *is.*

It is the familiar, almost unnoticeable metaphor of music as a language that perhaps forces the idea of meaning as essential to it. So let's try to capture the insight in Levi-Strauss's formulation by changing the name "language" to "system of communication." (Wittgenstein does this in the second section of *Philosophical Investigations* where he does not wish to beg the question of whether a pair of what he calls builders, who possess what we would call only four words, can be imagined to be *speaking* to one another and understanding one another, as opposed, say, to responding as animals to a signal.) The system of communication called music would be the antithesis of this primitive language, music existing in the absolutely sophisticated state in which un-derstanding is endless, in which everything that happens is to be taken as significant, and nothing comes, or need come, as an isolated or incontest-able meaning. (We could say that the instance of music defeats the idea of a certain *theory* of meaning, the one Wittgenstein seeks to defeat as expressed in the opening paragraph of *Philosophical Investigations,* according to which every word has a meaning which is the object that it refers to.)

It is, I think, to convey a sense for (or give a sense to) understanding without meaning, that Wittgenstein notes—and it is the same Wittgenstein who asks "How can anyone understand my thoughts who does not know what music has meant in my life?"—who notes in the *Investigations* (§ 541), "Understanding a sentence is much more akin to understanding a theme in music than one may think." One implication is that sentences too do not acquire their sig-nificance by adding up meanings of their constituents; another implication is that while you may "explain the meaning" of a sentence or of a theme by accenting it differently or rephrasing it or by comparing one with another, you will be doing definitively different things in the different cases. You are, for example, unlikely to illuminate a sentence by reading it backwards, whereas this may precisely and uniquely explain a musical theme; while you may il-luminate either a sentence or a theme by delivering it more softly or more slowly, or by making yourself describe the frame of mind in which it is announced.

Far from taking the lack of meaning as like losing a limb, one might see the possibility of understanding without meaning as redemptive, like losing one's chains. I am thinking of Walter Benjamin's startling observation, in his *Origin of German Tragic Drama,* that in what he understands as the Baroque, "meaning has its home in written language. And the spoken word is only af-flicted by meaning, so to speak, as if by an inescapable disease; it breaks off in the middle of the process of resounding, and the damming up of the feeling, which was ready to pour forth, provokes mourning. Here meaning is encoun-tered . . . as the reason for mournfulness" (p. 209). This is one of various for-mulations, in a founding text of our concept of the modern, in which phi-losophy sees the human, particularly the modern subject, as condemned to meaning, the victim of expression, a victim of others either because, as in Freud's image, "self-betrayal oozes out of every pore," and we lack the possi-bility of privacy, or because, as in Emerson's outcry, "Every word they say cha-grins us" (a perception, in an American accent, more familiar from Kierkegaard and Heidegger), as if language says what nobody any longer means, and we lack the possibility of publicness. In such experiences I find the cue for opera, for a voice ready to demand the recognition of others and capable of judging the world.

Go back for an instant to my saying that we "may" in various ways seek to explain our understanding of a sentence or theme, say by semanticizing a motif, or by evoking its mood, or by tracing its formal connections. You may—I should like to—insist that what any of these procedures do is precisely to explain the meaning. But then of course I owe an explanation of what I am calling meaning and understanding and explaining. And suppose it turns out that what you are "explaining" is why something is as it is and moreover, perhaps, why you want it that way. Wanting is internally related to intending, or desiring to meaning. A certain emphasis on meaning may disguise this complicity. So then there is also the implication not alone of possibility but of responsibility in showing understanding. Understanding without meaning suggests a particular form of communication, of revelation, one in which the demand for expression is put to the test (a matter that should open up anew, as in Wittgenstein's work, the concept of expression). To say that music puts expression to the test is to ask wherein lies my conviction in my own understanding if I cannot justify it to others (which is not the same as *convincing* others). This idea of understanding without meaning (as it were intensifying a moment in Wittgenstein's sense of understanding sentences) is rather the reverse of what, I believe, "ineffability" is taken generally to imply, namely not something unexpressible just in words but something beyond expression as such. The claim in the instance of music is, on the contrary, that expression has (in principle) occurred, in principle perfectly; it is merely the responsibility of each of its recipients to come to terms with his or her experience. This is a demand that music, perhaps first among the arts, shares with philosophy, as I care about it most.

In one of his characteristic gestures, Wittgenstein voices a fruitful aesthetic tip: "Don't take it as a matter of course, but as a remarkable fact, that pictures and fictitious narratives give us pleasure, occupy our minds" (§ 524). Noting the absence of music in Wittgenstein's instances here, I was in effect just now suggesting that we not take it as a matter of course, but as a remarkable fact, that music gives so many human beings so much pleasure, occupies their minds, over so much of their lives, with so little need or demand for explanation, quite as if being sung to or played for is as natural to our form of life as being spoken to.

Kivy on *Idomeneo*

This talk is the only known comment by Cavell on the work of the musicologist Peter Kivy. It was a response to Kivy's lecture "Why Does *Idomeneo* Have a Happy Ending?" given at the annual meeting of the American Society for Aesthetics in 1999, and more generally to Kivy's celebrated book on opera, *Osmin's Rage: Philosophical Reflections on Opera, Drama, and Text* (1988).

I APPLAUD PETER KIVY'S PROJECT MEANT to rehabilitate an understanding and appreciation of a major genre of drama, *opera serie,* what he calls music-made drama. And the larger effort of which that is part, worked out in his *Osmin's Rage,* is one that anyone interested in opera, philosophers or otherwise, must take seriously into account. All I shall do in my few minutes here is to raise a few questions, and suggest alternative routes of response to those presented in his present paper, "Why Does *Idomeneo* Have a Happy Ending?" In their unprotected brevity, my proposals may sound more provocative than they should. But that may all the better serve here to break the ice into a free discussion of *Idomeneo,* epitomized in what we have just been treated to in performance.

Kivy says this:

> In order to believe in the characters that people the *opera serie*, the roman emperors, the Greek heroes, the magicians and knights in armor, with their super-heated, destructive, and self-destructive passions; more important, in order to appreciate why they express their passions musically in the way they do, we must understand, and

accept as a premise of the *opera serie* world, the theory of the emotions upon which the whole thing is predicated. That theory—argued at length in *Osmin's Rage*—is Descartes's influential discourse on psychology, *The Passions of the Soul*. . . . To understand the Cartesian psychology is to understand why the *opera serie* seems so out of tune with *our* psychological reality but is yet in complete musical accord with psychological reality as it was perceived by the Baroque composers.

But immediately, do we think that in order to believe in the characters that people Shakespeare's histories and romances—kings, heroes, magicians, knights in armor—and understand why they express themselves poetically in the way they do, we have to believe in a psychology of the four humours contemporary with Shakespeare? Does, for example, the great quartet we heard performed from *Idomeneo* strike us as "out of tune with our psychological reality"? Surely I am not alone in finding its projection of isolation even in the grip of common suffering—with its surges of longing for recognition and resolution—to be drop-dead convincing. (I feel quite sure that Peter Kivy agrees with this.)

What accordingly seems to need explanation—rather than our contemporary out-of-tuneness with a work such as *Idomeneo* (the first of the sequence of Mozart's great operas)—is the sense that Mozart's psychology, or "psychological reality," is so far ahead of a leading philosophical *theory* of the passions contemporary with it, such as Descartes's. (Perhaps not ahead of what certain theologians had articulated—Augustine or Luther, for example.) Psychological outstripping is familiarly what one feels about Shakespeare's texts, which is doubtless why there is an impulse to compare the corpus of the major operas of Mozart with the achievement of that associated with the name of Shakespeare. Then why *Idomeneo* is less performed than the other Mozart operas must be a function of various other histories—of theatrical fashion, of the evolution of opera companies, of artistic achievement, etc.

Now put this puzzle (of psychological anachronism and relative nonperformance) together with Kivy's further claims that "absolute music [viz., where there is no verbal text] . . . is a pure 'syntactic' structure—a 'syntax' without a semantics" and that "expressive properties . . . have become part of music's 'syntactic' structure" and that "things happen in opera [so massive a thing as a happy end happens] because pure musical 'syntax' requires [it]" and that "music always trumps for Mozart. The overwhelming musicality of *Idomeneo* . . . is in such perfect synchrony in the dramatic and emotional reality of the Cartesian psychology that it constitutes drama-made music at its highest level." Without denying that for Mozart music trumps (though we do not yet know why it wants or has to trump, which would perhaps be to know why Mozart craved to write operas), how we are to measure its synchrony with the dramatic and emotional reality of Cartesian psychology— presumably as manifested in the action and words of *Idomeneo*—*apart* from the music? If the words are designated (and choosing them will be sufficient cause of their being designated) as a libretto, then reading or performing them without their eventual music may prove variously interesting, ranging from the ludicrous to the curiously moving, but to say the music "trumps" its effect is contentious (unless it marks a particular moment): the music "sets" the words. And, on the other hand, if the words have an established life of their own (as in the case of Maeterlinck's *Pelléas and Mélisande,* which Debussy set virtually without alteration), then the idea of trumping is again contentious, requiring specific justification, implying that the music overcomes some expected specific effect within the play (which may be true, but is not an inevitable relation between music and words), or perhaps that with the music the play remains successful and without it not.

Let us ask: Is it part of the dramatic and emotional reality of Cartesian psychology that it assumes individual passions to be perfectly expressible? What the characters of *Idomeneo* incessantly speak about—do I mean what they sing about?—is the sense of their being *unable* to express themselves, either because what they have to reveal is psychologically or socially unacceptable (requiring too appalling a confession of guilt, or of love, or of vengefulness) or because a conflict of passions, which is tearing apart the soul, exceeds the bounds of the expressible. If then we say that the drama is about the terror of inexpressiveness (an interpretation I give to a strain of Wittgenstein's *Investigations*), say it is a fantasy of being buried alive in the body (not something quite unprompted perhaps by Cartesian metaphysics), then we might look to Mozart's music to express *that* terror, an anxiety of inexpressiveness. Is anxiety accounted for in Descartes's psychology? It seems very familiar, even fundamental, to Pascal's theology.

As an example of the soul torn with conflict and anxiety, I propose a well-known crux from Elettra's first aria (it was her last aria that was performed for us), which is prompted by a recitative in which she reports hearing of the death of her protector Idomeneo. In the ensuing aria, a rage aria to end all rages, Elettra recognizes that she feels all the Furies of Hades in her heart. The aria is in binary sonata form, which, at its center, leads to an expectation of a return to the tonic key, in this case the key of D minor. But here, instead, there is a modulation (if you can call it that—it is rather a straight *plunge*) into C minor, a whole tone lower.

I propose one question and one suggestion about this rejected expectation.

Is there a clear sense to be given to the idea that this (structural) plunge of key is a "syntactic requirement" of the music? It seems, on the contrary, an inspired *flouting* of something we might have described as a syntactic requirement. Beckmesser would surely disapprove of the liberty taken. And do we not just as surely crave some explanation for it? (An explanation in terms of harmonic procedure will explain perhaps how Mozart *prepared* for the surprise—by an ambiguous sustained augmented sixth chord—but it does not explain why *this* is what he prepared for, what it is he *wanted,* and teaches us to want. If we are to call such an explanation "syntactic," we will have to call the explanation we crave "semantic.")

Here is one suggested line of investigation. The drop of tonality—like other musical descents—is often, conventionally, understandable as signaling a lowering of spirits. If we grant this in the present case—we would have to do some listening—then the question becomes: Why has Mozart, in what is for all the world an aria of rage, centered a key change suggesting melancholy (a change into a key, moreover, which recurs at the end of the aria as that of the ensuing storm)? What relation between rage and melancholy may Mozart (which is to say, this music) be said here to propose?

A possibility is the thought that rage in response to disparagement, or abandonment, will turn into self-disparagement or self-abandonment; which is more or less Freud's view of melancholia—particularly pertinent in the history (and the psychology) of the disparagement of women.

Then a further line of investigation would take up a thought from Walter Benjamin's analysis in *The Origin of German Tragic Drama*—a text currently pursuing me in its pertinence to opera. Benjamin's text identifies melancholy as the presiding tone of Baroque tragedy, where melancholy bears precisely on the question of expression I have wished to raise, namely that of expressing an anxiety of inexpressiveness. It is specifically Benjamin's claim that the plays of mourning he considers form allegories of a time and place in which there is a crisis of meaning. A time and place in which, as Benjamin more or less puts the matter, we have become victims of meaning, of the effort to mean; so that the very fact of speech, of the obligation to speak, to make ourselves intelligible, is a cause of melancholy. But a crisis of speech and meaning sounds to me like a cue for opera—for its medium as a study of speaking, as it were, by replacing it, magnifying it, through singing.

Philosophy and the Unheard

This is the text of a lecture Cavell gave on Arnold Schoenberg's chamber music, in 1999, at a Harvard conference in honor of the music critic, theorist, and composer David Lewin. Cavell here returns to the topic of dodeca-phonic (twelve-tone) music for the first time since his 1967 essay "Music Discomposed," again addressing Wittgenstein's hostility to modern music.

THE HAPPY FORTUNE IN THE INVITATION to me to participate in this celebratory weekend I assign mainly to two facts of my life. First, its formative intellectual or spiritual crisis, leading me to dedicate myself to the study of philosophy, was the discovery that music was no longer my life's work, something that became undisguisable from myself the year after I grad-uated with a major in music from the University of California at Berkeley. Second, while I have written very little explicitly about music over the ensuing decades, I have known for most of that time that something I have demanded from philosophy was an understanding precisely of what I had sought in music, and in the understanding of music, of what demanded that reclama-tion of experience, of the capacity for being moved, which called out for, and sustained, an accounting as lucid as the music I loved. It was in returning to Berkeley a decade later to begin a lifetime of teaching that this recognition of music, let's say, as a figure for the mind in its most perfected relation to

A version of this essay was published as "Philosophy and the Unheard," in *"Music of My Future": The Schoenberg Quartets and Trio,* ed. Reinhold Brinkmann and Christoph Wolff, Isham Library Pa-pers 5, Harvard Publications in Music 20 (Cambridge, MA: Harvard University Department of Music, 2000; distr. by Harvard University Press), 175–183.

itself, or to its wishes for itself, was confirmed for me (contrary to so much in the formation of professional philosophy in those years) in the conversations and in the musical analysis classes of two colleagues and friends there—sometimes the three of us together—whose passion for music expressed itself in such different as well as in such similar forms, I mean those of Seymour Shifrin and of David Lewin. Whatever bouts of intellectual loneliness I may since then have been tempted to, have been attended by the memory of those scenes of instruction—sublime instances of tracking the work that art does, of the rigor and the beauty one looks and listens for.

It was in that same period that I discovered, after some years of resistance to it, the liberation in the teaching of Wittgenstein's later work, centered in his *Philosophical Investigations*. I was not exactly surprised to learn eventually of Wittgenstein's remark, "Who can understand my philosophical work who does not know what music has meant in my life?" but it makes me wonder the harder why he actually says so little about music. He does, it is true, say a few things; for example in the *Investigations* there is this: "Understanding a sentence is much more akin to understanding a theme in music than one may think" (§ 527).[1] Perhaps the reason Wittgenstein surmises one may avoid this thought is that one imagines the understanding of a sentence to be a matter of understanding and combining the meanings of its constituent words, and these in turn to be a matter of knowing what objects they refer to. A pervasive purpose of the work of the *Investigations* is to trace and to awaken, as if from a trance, each of the interminable consequences of what Wittgenstein calls this primitive picture of human language, and its hold upon philosophical thought. So that the very invocation of the understanding of a musical theme as a guide to philosophical understanding, among the reorientations in this traumatic breakthrough of philosophical imagination, call it the promise of an understanding without meanings, is a utopian glimpse of a new, or undiscovered, relation to language, to its sources in the world, to its means of expression.

The strangeness of Wittgenstein's power, if that is what it is, is tied to the abruptness of his difference from the expected sound of philosophy, say of its pitch sequences (within which, of some fascination for the Schoenbergian ambience of this weekend, the idea of a series, as in the instance of following a rule, plays a notorious role), manifested in the apparent poverty of Wittgenstein's philosophical means. He describes what he does in the *Investigations* as "returning words from their metaphysical to their everyday use"—hardly, it would seem, the stuff of trauma, until perhaps we notice how often modern philosophical advance, or the claim to it, turns not on seeking to re-fute or to continue its past but on wishing to turn its back upon philosophy's past, and then see that Wittgenstein's unheard-of directness in this dissocia-tion is nevertheless in service of philosophy's perpetual discovery of the strangeness of our lives to ourselves—a discovery that reaches from at least the cave in Plato's *Republic*, through the entrance to the dark wood at the opening of *The Divine Comedy*, to the antics of self-torture that Thoreau per-ceives in his fellow inhabitants of Concord, to the couch in Freud's study. The first three images (cave, dark wood, self-torture) are meant as figures of our everyday lives; the last (the couch) is a new response to that life; all demand of us a journey. In Wittgenstein's album (a title he gives to his *Investigations*), the topics of understanding, meaning, sentence, rule, privacy, consciousness, and so forth, are bound up with a vision of the human as caught between a sense of inexpressiveness suggesting suffocation and a sense of uncontrollable expressiveness threatening exposure.

May such a formulation be seen as an initial Wittgensteinian response to the work of Schoenberg—his older, equally displaced compatriot—even knowing that Wittgenstein in person shunned most forms of modernism in the arts and in modern intellectual life generally? I report being struck, re-reading in Schoenberg's letters to prepare for the mood of this weekend, at how punctual and fervent Schoenberg's recurrence is to the wish for, or the despair of, his music's being understood. But the various instances intersect somewhat oddly. In 1926 he writes, "To me it matters more that people should understand my work than that they should take an interest in it."[2] Is this because an interest may be based on an illusory understanding, for example, on an account of what the twelve-tone system is in the absence of the capacity for judging its successes? Later in his life Schoenberg expresses his gratifica-tion in being shown that his "music can speak distinctly to a musician, that he can know and understand me without explanation." Naturally I think here of a fundamental methodological remark in Wittgenstein's *Investigations* (§ 109), that "there must not be anything hypothetical in our considerations. We must do away with all explanation"[3]—in favor of a certain form of what he calls a perspicuous presentation of philosophical material. Earlier Schoenberg had written to Kandinsky: "I forgot, it's no use arguing because of course I won't be listened to; because there is no will to understand, but only one not to hear what the other says."[4] Instead of requiring a "will to understand," Wittgenstein speaks of philosophical problems as kept in place by "an urge to misunderstand" (§ 103), namely to misunderstand what for Wittgenstein should be closest to us, our every word. It is only fitting that Schoenberg should link understanding with hearing; and since he speaks of a composer's responsibility both to performers and to audiences, we have to ask how one may prove (if only to oneself) that one does hear apart from demonstrating it in performance, where communicative virtue depends upon virtuosity, a sparsely distributed property.

If it is in Beethoven that music most famously comes to take on its terrorist aspect, causing anxiety over whether one hears what is happening, it is in Schoenberg that this anxiety reaches its purest pitch, seeming to offer nothing unless it provides everything. In confronting it, each is abandoned to his or her conscience to tell whether to go on with it. This strikes me as a description of an effect of philosophy as well, as it matters most to me, which also chronically creates an anxiety in proving that one understands. Conceivably for this reason modern philosophers who are moved to think recurrently about music tend to regard it as an image of or an inspiration to the philosophical task, hence to appeal to music for its representation of an idea fundamental to their thought, which they may well sense they have otherwise failed to realize unmistakably in their philosophical prose. I think here, beyond the instance of Wittgenstein, of Schopenhauer's sense of the world as will, of course of Nietzsche's perception of the union of the Dionysian and the Apollonian, of the philosopher Ernst Bloch's sense of sustaining hope in the imagination of Utopia, examples that surely lie behind Theodor Adorno's interpretation of Schoenberg's intervention in the history of music (and secondarily of Stravinsky's) in his *Philosophy of Modern Music.*[5]

I do not know what standing Adorno's views have with thinking musicians these days. Charles Rosen in his 1977 Modern Masters book on Schoenberg does not cite Adorno, and in the preface to its 1996 reprinting Rosen mentions Adorno only to dismiss his treatment of Stravinsky as disgraceful and of Schoenberg as unconvincing.[6] But among intellectually inclined nonmusicians it is my impression that Adorno remains a dominating presence in the image of what a philosophy of music may be. Before taking very brief steps into two of Adorno's texts I am glad to recall some sound advice offered by Carl Dahlhaus in his collection *Schoenberg and the New Music,* in which Adorno's is by far the most frequently cited name (except for the names of Wagner and of Schoenberg). Dahlhaus's advice is that "we should only call upon philosophy if it proves impossible to proceed without its help."[7] The soundness of the advice is that philosophy, to be helpful, must always be called upon— it must not seek to have the first, any more than the last, word, to get you to

listen to it. It should first show that it can listen. But the difficulty with Dahlhaus's advice is that it is bound to come too late; by the time we call upon
philosophy we have already subjected ourselves to its forces, turned ourselves
into philosophers. Then it is up to each of us to find our way to intelligibility.

Is there a more extreme example of an artist attempting to make himself
intelligible than Schoenberg, in his music no less than in his theoretical works?
And, as I have had occasion to say about philosophical ambition, someone
whose motive is absolute veracity is likely to be very hard to understand.

The young David Lewin, in a remarkable discussion of act I, scene 1 of
Moses and Aron, opens with some general remarks, which begin with the observation: "The dramatic idea of the work hinges on the paradoxical nature
of God: the *Unvorstellbares* [unrepresentable] that commands itself to be *vor-
gestellt* [represented]."[8] What Lewin goes on to propose is that "the musical
metaphor that reflects (or better defines) the dramatic idea is the nature of
the twelve-tone row and system as 'musical idea' in Schoenberg's terminology.
The 'row' or 'the musical idea' is not a concrete and specific musical subject
or object to be presented for once and for all as referential in sounds and time;
it is, rather, an abstraction that manifests itself everywhere ('allgegenwärtiger')
in the work. . . . It remains unrealized and unfulfilled until it is manifested
and communicated . . . by means of material sounds . . . in all its manifold
potentialities. . . . God demands that His order be communicated to the Volk.
Yet how can they be taught to love and understand the immaterial and Unvorstellbares (the true musical experience)?"[9] When Lewin alertly qualifies
the idea of the musical idea of the row as defining the dramatic idea, he
throws the intellectual burden of understanding these sublime matters all but
entirely upon the work of the music, which he thereupon undertakes to
articulate. But this does not deny, it may be taken to assert, that the idea of
representing the unrepresentable in all its manifold potentialities has itself
innumerable manifestations (Moses' stammer, for example, or the burning
bush), which the musical may contest or confirm.

It is when Adorno interprets what he calls Webern's "fetishism of the row"
as (still) maintaining dialectical force that Adorno has recourse to the idea of
expressing the inexpressible. He amplifies this claim by saying: "One aspect
of the situation is that twelve-tone music, by force of its mere correctness, re-
sists subjective expression. The other important aspect is that the right of the
subject itself to expression [i.e., the right to expression of the individual consciousness in late capitalism] declines. . . . It has become so isolated that it can
hardly seriously hope for anyone who may still understand it. . . . Its melan-

choly disappearance is the purest expression of its terrified and distrustful withdrawal. . . . However, it remains incapable of expressing the inexpressible as truth."[10]

Three more sentences from Adorno will help underscore how his intellectual allegiances allow him, or demand from him, formulations that in moments are close and are yet immeasurably far from those I have cited from David Lewin. Adorno continues: "The possibility of music itself has become uncertain. . . . That certain freedom, into which it undertook to transform its anarchistic condition, was converted in the very hands of this music into a metaphor of the world against which it raises its protest. . . . To a certain degree it places itself at the disposal of the world-spirit which is, after all, not world-logic. . . . [But] the decline of art in a false order is itself false. Its truth is the denial of the submissiveness to which its central principle . . . has driven it."[11] It is in Adorno's efforts to express or to portray as it were the experience of this crisis of expression (as if music now speaks only of speechlessness) that his book is punctuated with notations of loneliness, melancholy, withdrawal, despondency, anxiety, shock, and at the same time declares the continuing impossibility or denial of one's own experience. But the full credibility of this effort—whose importance I should not wish to be neglected—depends upon a fuller trust or interest in Adorno's clarity of experience together with his articulation of it in a further Hegelian process of concepts, than I find I can quite lend to it. Is there some alternative philosophical path through which to explore what I am calling this crisis of expression?

Adorno's characteristic appeal to the negative in his dialectical opposition to the present ("The decline of art in a false order is itself false," which I take to say: the apparent decline of art has something in it which opposes decline) is something that, it seems to me, Thomas Mann had particular trouble with, for all the usefulness Adorno's manuscript on Schoenberg may have had for him in composing *Doctor Faustus*. Adorno writes, in his extraordinarily admiring "Toward a Portrait of Thomas Mann" (1962), of an encounter in which he describes himself as rebelling against the way Mann proposed, in the ending of his book, to describe the composer Leverkühn's last work, his Faust oratorio. "I found," he reports himself saying to Mann, "the heavily laden pages too positive, too unbrokenly theological in relation to the structure not only of the *Lamentation of Dr. Faustus* but of the novel as a whole. They seemed to lack what the crucial passage required, the power of determinate negation as the only permissible figure of the Other. . . . Two days later [after a dinner to which the Adornos had been invited by the Manns] . . .

the author . . . read, clearly excited, the new conclusion which he had written in the meantime. We could not hide how moved we were."[12] It is true that the published version of that passage (I assume it now constitutes the last pages of chapter 46)—even without the chance to compare it with its former draft—seems to revel in negations, beginning with the "revocation," in the oratorio's competition with the Beethoven Ninth, of vocal jubilation, and climaxing with the "deliberate reversal of the 'Watch with me' of Geth-semane," Christ's offer of shared suffering leading to what Faust now rejects as a false salvation. But in the next paragraph, the last of this late chapter, the narrator of Mann's *Dr. Faustus,* in describing the "hope beyond hopelessness" of the oratorio's concluding sound, comes to plead with his reader: "Listen with me." Is this transfiguration of the Gethsemane "Watch with me" from the visible into the ineluctable modality of the audible, endowing unheard music with the power of redemptive suffering—is this transfiguration a match in good faith for philosophy's negations? Adorno reports that he was openly moved. But by what? With what right? Was it by the dramatized effective-ness of dialectic's negation, or was it by an artist's attestation of art's con-testing at once of religion and of philosophy? Mann's narration, if one grants its success here, has, as we used to say, "earned" its conclusion, morally, artis-tically, intellectually. Does dialectic provide an explanation of what earning it consists in? Is this what the injunction means, that we are to believe *in order to* understand? Whom does one believe?

In conjunction with David Lewin's account of the communicability of the omnipresence of the idea or row, I go back for a moment to Wittgenstein's unpredictable *Investigations,* specifically to its claim that in his break with phi-losophy, more specifically with his own past, Wittgenstein continues to follow the aim of logical investigation—the urge to understand the basis, or essence, of everything empirical—but now not by moving to a new language but by turning ourselves to understand what is already in plain view, retrieving the ordinary from the metaphysical. Or rather this ordinary will seem to have been already in plain view when we determine what will constitute under-standing what we are precisely fated to pass by, which in practice begins with the realization that we do not understand (and yet we are obedient enough to be mastered by) the basis upon which we speak as we do, our responsive-ness to the world in what Wittgenstein calls our everyday language, our ini-tial tongue—the same old words, the same old tones. Philosophy is to liberate us—without renouncing our speech—from the false intensities, the falsely conceived dissonances, that philosophy and convention drive us to impose upon ourselves (which are already measures of renouncing). We must recognize the ordinary world of our constructions and of our destructions to be as mysterious (Freud says uncanny, finding a new familiar in place of an old; so, more or less, does Heidegger)—as mysterious as the things of faith once were.

My suggestion is that the Schoenbergian idea of the row with its unforeseen yet pervasive consequences is a serviceable image of the Wittgensteinian idea of grammar and its elaboration of criteria of judgment, which shadow our expressions and which reveal pervasive yet unforeseen conditions of our existence, specifically in its illumination of our finite standing as one in which there is no complete vision of the possibilities of our understanding—no total revelation as it were—but in which the assumption of each of our assertions and retractions, in its specific manifestations in time and place, is to be worked through, discovering, so to speak, for each case its unconscious row.

If this allegory of the *Investigations* through Schoenbergian practice is illuminating, then one may be encouraged to reflect further on why, as I have variously sketched the question, the philosophical subject of the *Investigations,* the modern ego entangled in its expressions of desire (Wittgenstein speaks both of our urge to understand as well as of our equally pressing urge to misunderstand), is specifically characterized by Wittgenstein in its moments of torment, sickness, strangeness, self-destructiveness, perversity, suffocation, and lostness. If these qualities rhyme with ones that musicians call upon to notate their experience of Schoenberg's expressiveness (Charles Rosen, claiming for Schoenberg's music that it "is among the most expressive ever written"—and not just in the period of its expressionism—specifies the qualities he hears as anxiety, anguish, horror, terror, violence, as well as charm), then it may well be in the paths and grounding of Wittgenstein's *Investigations* that we can learn a new responsibility with such concepts.

But is this a way to envision what a philosophy of music should be, one which is itself illuminated by musical procedure? It seems to me—to begin with—a promising way to keep open the question where and how we must claim to understand, and where and how we must prepare ourselves not to.

I conclude by citing a source for the appeal to, or the demand for, understanding cast both as hope and as despair, a source surely known to all the figures I have invoked here, namely Friedrich Schlegel's great romantic essay "On Incomprehensibility." Having introduced almost at once what he calls the fascinating question whether the communication of ideas is actually possible, Schlegel soon announces: "Now, it is a peculiarity of mine that

I absolutely detest incomprehension, not only the incomprehension of the uncomprehending but even more the incomprehension of the comprehending." I note for our interest on this occasion that in appending a poem of his to conclude his essay, Schlegel expresses the wish that a composer will set it to music. The inspiration of this essay, and I would even say, of this wish, come to me, to close my circle of proposals for this day, by way of Ralph Waldo Emerson's once monstrously famous essay "Self-Reliance," which I take as in general a meditation on human understanding (notably of the relation of inspiration to communication, or of what he calls intuition to tuition), and (since we know Emerson read Schlegel) specifically on Schlegel's questioning of understanding, as Emerson relates anecdotes of understanding and misunderstanding to ones concerning standing and standing for; and he includes, in his working through, the idea of following the standard of what he calls the true man, where standard's standing is that of providing a measure but may also pick up, as a flag, the overtone or image of a page turning in a true book. Such readings take Emerson into regions and rigors of thinking that he of course is not normally asked, nor generally granted, the power to reach, but I find his achievements to be lucid and provocative music to my ears.

24

Impressions of Revolution

Beginning in 1990, Cavell regularly attended the Bard Music Festival, an annual two-week classical music festival held during the month of August on the campus of Bard College, Annandale-on-Hudson, New York, and he participated in symposia organized during the festivals. The 2000 festival was dedicated to "Beethoven and His World," and it featured a panel, "Revolution and the Arts," that was chaired by Michael P. Steinberg and included Cavell along with Scott Burnham, Tabetha Ewing, Joseph Kerman, Carol J. Ockman, and Charles Rosen. This piece is the text of Cavell's contribution and the only place in his work in which he discusses "revolutionary" in reference to Beethoven's oeuvre.

THE TITLE OF OUR PANEL MAY, and I suppose is meant to, be taken variously: as the question of the role of the arts, or of an individual art, within or as an expression of a political or cultural revolution; or taken as the question of revolution within an individual art, or within the conception of art in general; or, further, taken as posing the question whether there is some illuminating relation to be discerned between these dimensions of revolution. For example, given that our title has been assigned as part of a festival concentrated on the figure of Beethoven, does it make sense, would it be illuminating, to say that Beethoven's celebration of, or desire to capture

A version of this essay was published as "Impressions of Revolution," *Musical Quarterly* 85, no. 2 (2001): 264–273. Cavell's version contained page numbers for quotations within the text, which the editors have retained; we have also added most of the endnotes that appeared in the published version.

the significance of, the event or aftermath of the French Revolution required or resulted in a revolutionary discovery within his musical thinking, within what he asked of his art; and / or vice versa, that what he asked of his art determined or conditioned his finding it possible or necessary to respond to that event of his world. An analogous reversible question of sense in relation to the French Revolution may be raised concerning two other monsters of accomplishment born the same year as Beethoven, ones, that is to say, who turned nineteen the year the Bastille was stormed and approached thirty when Napoleon (a year older than they) became consul. I am thinking of course of Hegel and of Wordsworth. What would we have to understand in order to understand such claims of a revolution in response to a revolution?

Do we, for example, understand the differences we must have in mind to speak seriously of certain developments within the history of science, and certain within philosophy, and certain within the individual arts, all as revolutions, or even as revolutionary—where speaking "seriously" (as I judge we nowadays would take it) means speaking of such events as on a par with the consequential events amounting to a political revolution within a nation. But Hannah Arendt, in her book *On Revolution,* argues that we have not grasped essential articulations of the concept even in this primary or "serious" application. The fundamental error she points to is the identification of our paradigm revolutions (the American, the French, and the Russian) with the necessity of violence, an identification which serves to identify the aim of revolution exclusively with liberation and to neglect the equally essential aim of establishing a realm, or constitution, of freedom.[1] It follows from this articulation that the only revolution of these three that even partially succeeded in its double aim was the American, the only one whose revolutionary leaders survived intact to help establish and guide a new realm, dedicated to liberty and justice for all; and it is the one whose events are least known to the world, coming to pass in a place whose arts (apart from the political, and its discourse) were insufficiently developed to convey its experience to the world, so unlike the cases of France and of Russia. (This was notably no longer true, with respect to the art of literature, by the time of the second American revolution, the Civil War.)

Arendt's argument is detailed and wide ranging, but is that effort pertinent to the purposes of thinking about revolution and the arts, anyway revolutions within the arts, since we know—do we not—that the use of the concept of revolution in artistic contexts is merely metaphorical, suggesting hardly more than the sense of a big change? But the work that more than any other has

put the concept of revolution on our intellectual and cultural agenda in recent decades has been Thomas Kuhn's *Structure of Scientific Revolutions,* and
the historical events he is accounting for are at least as remote, apparently,
from political events as innovations within the arts are apt to be, and his use
of the term revolution, however controversial it is for some, does not seem to
be metaphorical. Kuhn uses the idea of revolutionary scientific change to
name historical states of science in crisis, in contrast with states of what he
perceives to be normal science, the alternation of which states has characterized the history of science since, say, Copernicus. Kuhn's way of understanding
the distinction between normal and revolutionary science is pictured in his
wildly famous use of the idea of the paradigm shift, according to which normal
science makes progress cumulatively, and interestingly, by means of shared
paradigms, of concept and of practice, in contrast with science in crisis, where
progress, or continuation, requires nonlinear, paradigm-shifting reconception.
Now this is something like the reverse of the way, for example, Charles Rosen,
in his celebrated book *The Classical Style,* understands the changes, big and
small, making up the discoveries of sonata practice or texture. There the development of the classical style is perceived as the history of individual masters of this practice (who may have encountered something like crises and
revolutionary discoveries within their individual developments), in contrast
with those, call them the producers of normal music, who, in using some
selection of musical paradigms cumulatively, without requiring their stylistic
signature upon them, contribute perhaps to the history of a cultural period
but not to an account of the development of the art of music. Indeed, on
Rosen's view in that early book, the idea that sonata form is a stable paradigm whose correct use produces interesting music is one that occurs only
with the deterioration of sonata practice, an academic description of a practice academicized.[2]

Of course it does not follow from this claim that there is no place for the
concept of revolution in the arts, only that we have to rethink the concept in
order to get the best of it. A surprising (to me) consequence for Rosen in *The
Classical Style* is that developments in musical style that he calls revolutionary
precede Beethoven (markedly, beyond the establishment of sonata practice
itself, in Mozart's discovery in that practice of the path to organizing the action of permanent opera), and succeed Beethoven (notably, in the emergence
of romanticism in music), whereas Beethoven himself "remained within" the
classical dispensation.[3] Rosen uses the Schumann *Fantasy* as a touchstone for
the shift from the classical to the romantic style in music, a break with the

increasingly subtle motivic dramas created with the establishment of vying tonal centers, invoking instead an emotionality, a prolongation of theme, and a rhythmic propulsion that is more characteristic of the baroque than of the classical period. I try to imagine the plight of composers of this new period who could not imagine, could not hear for themselves, the kind of drama of, let us say, musical suspense that could be achieved by withholding the root position of the tonic until the last moment of a movement, and went on casting ideas into sonata formulas. The world had changed behind their backs, violence had been done to their craft.

Now, violence and irreversible change are criteria of the concept of the revolutionary as Kuhn defines it for science. (And they seem to satisfy Hannah Arendt's two-phase definition of a movement for liberation followed by a movement toward a new constitution of freedom.) Galileo's conflict over the motion of the earth with the Aristotelian scientists of the church is, I suppose, the most celebrated example here. Kuhn describes this crisis of reconceptualization as defining what he calls "a different world," an incommensurable departure from a former world of assumption, concept, and practice. (Some inhabitants of the former world will survive in the later, some will not.) Many philosophers remain unconvinced that Kuhn succeeded in making this idea clear, and if not in the case of science, then what hope is there of making it clear in the case of the arts, for which the application of the Kuhnian distinction between the revolutionary and the normal is shaky to begin with? The only answer could be that one finds something in such ideas that demands of one to try to make it clear. In this, each must speak for himself or herself.

Here I invoke my own sense of having lived through intellectual transformations in my professional lifetime of teaching in philosophy departments that I judge to manifest fair versions of the violence and irreversibility that the concept of revolution speaks of. In each case new reputations were made and old ones broken, some who were disheartened were young enough to leave the field for another, others were, in exchange, attracted to enter it, and in each case the new constitution demanded and received careful monitoring in everything from the preparation of term papers and Ph.D. dissertations to success in securing the most favored, or any, teaching positions. My teacher J. L. Austin identified his work on what he called ordinary language, and specifically in relation to his discovery of the performative utterance, as part of a continuing revolution, in part self-devouring, in philosophy. Wittgenstein did not speak of revolution but instead one time pictured his work as "replacing" philosophy and another time spoke of the history of philosophy as having a "kink" in it. But again this is perhaps of limited interest in thinking of the arts, since philosophy has contained, throughout its modern history, illustrious names who have associated themselves with a call for revolution in philosophy, mostly in response to the revolution establishing the New Science of the late sixteenth and early seventeenth centuries, perhaps the most famous response being that of Kant, who compared his reconception of the a priori in human knowledge, systematized in *The Critique of Pure Reason,* with Copernicus's revolution in reconceiving the origin of the nonviolent revolutions of the heavenly bodies.

But even if we were in control of an idea of revolution as political and cultural change, and of revolution as a form of philosophical and scientific and artistic change, we would still lack an answer to the question I proposed to address, namely, what we would have to understand in order to understand a composer, Beethoven, for example, or Mozart in the great operas, as producing a revolution in response to a revolution. I proceed to a digression and conclude with some proposals.

The digression is to mention a recent publication which at a certain stage in assembling my thoughts for this occasion I imagined, impractically as it turned out, would occupy the bulk of my time, I mean the art historian T. J. Clark's *Farewell to an Idea.* The idea to which it seeks farewell is modernism, whose definition Clark takes as a continuous part of his task to elaborate and refine and which represents most generally the sense of the history of painting since the French Revolution as a succession of revolutionary shocks each tied with an idea, or an event associated with the idea, of socialism, of arguments concerning some new aspiration for a public life of productive exchange. Paradoxically, the artistic changes so produced claim increasing liberation from reference, or mimetic faithfulness, to the world, and from deference to a public, and instead reflect an insistence on the practices of the making of art to be of sufficient interest to sustain the cultural importance of art—an idea which has taken many banal forms, many of which Clark cites, but which in the attentive, extensive detail Clark devotes to works of David, Seurat, Pissarro, Malevich, Picasso, Pollock, and so on, takes on a surprising and anguished cast. The one sentence I cannot forgo mentioning here occurs at the end of a long chapter reconsidering the manner and the ideas he finds in David's portrait of the assassinated Marat—the writing arm of the revolutionary figure just gone limp over the side of his bathtub—a manner and ideas which Clark finds in elaborate detail to be at play in the painting's initial public showing as part of a Jacobin demonstration in the summer of 1793. The closing moments of this chapter raise the wonder of "what might have been involved for bourgeois individuals—what kinds of inventiveness, what sources of knowledge and ignorance—when they began to represent those whose labor they commanded," whereupon Clark declares: "Beethoven for me is David's brother. I imagine the *Sabines* dancing . . . to the last movement of the Seventh Symphony. And Marat agonizing to the closing bars of the Fifth."[4] Perhaps Clark has in mind Beethoven's contradictory attitudes toward the members of his public—both disdaining them and projecting their salvation. Something Clark does not consider is whether such pieces of Beethoven, comparable in depth and stature to the David painting, can be imagined as an active part of a comparable political demonstration.

Of the fantasm of Marat agonizing at the closing measures of the Fifth, I ask whether Clark, whose book is about something at an end, is hearing in those famous repetitive assertions of the tonic triad and pitch an exultant anguish at the *question* of an ending, at whether, so to speak, there is, and what it would mean if there is not, an assured victory of the tonic. Is to hammer a conclusion into a question a revolutionary departure? What level of agreement might we expect over the meaningfulness of such a question? The thought puts me in mind of the considerable agreement, at some unmeasured level, about certain aims of Beethoven's art among notable experts on the subject.

Compare this from Carl Dahlhaus's book on Beethoven from 1987 (p. 16): "The revolutionary stance of the 'Eroica' has never been denied: in the inner chronology of world history the [heroic style of the] work cries out to be back-dated to 1789,"[5] with this from Reinhold Brinkmann, addressing the *Eroica* in the volume associated with this festival (p. 21): "The orchestra as allegory of the Revolution is what this symphony aims for at the end of the first movement: 'the lava of revolution flows' here too, but as an idea, as a musical idea."[6] Add to these Maynard Solomon's claim, from his *Beethoven Essays* (p. 22): "The Ninth Symphony may also be taken as an emblem of the idealism of Beethoven's youth, when he was enflamed by what he called the 'fever of the Revolution,'" and down the page he takes the Ninth's "unprecedentedly complex use of . . . the web of forecasts, reminiscences, and other denotational devices [to be] the hallmark of a profoundly modernist perspective."[7] Adorno, characteristically, finds a more threatening tone for his intervention: "If we listen to Beethoven and do not hear anything of the revolutionary bourgeoisie—not the echo of its slogans, the need to realize them, the cry for that totality, to which reason and freedom are to have their warrant—we understand Beethoven no better than does the listener who cannot follow his pieces' purely musical content, the inner history that happens to their themes" (*Introduction to the Sociology of Music*).[8] The implication of all is, it seems to me, that the political revolution required, as the condition for its musical expression, a revolutionary turn within the art of music. But does this not beg the question of how, and whether, it is sensible to attribute meaning to music, or of some power of musical mimesis either undetermined or patently banal?

What was Adorno attempting in the fragments of his put together as his posthumous *Beethoven: The Philosophy of Music,* in which he, as we might almost put it, declares that Hegel is for him Beethoven's brother?[9] If the identification of Beethoven-like and Hegel-like transformations or negations of motives or ideas or tonalities could be managed convincingly, an immediate yield would be the possibility of relating Hegel's perpetual translations of history into his philosophical concepts—most famously the event of Napoleon—to analogous translations expressed in music's own abstractions and concretions, and individualities and totalities, and origins and endings, and departures and detours and arrivals, and distances and intimacies, and negations and syntheses. Apart from all this, we are nowadays more accustomed, I believe, to the call for something like cultural significance from the interpretation of works in both the elevated and the popular arts of music. But, in what I have read and heard, the call tends to be combative or defensive, and the response to it suspicious.

If the defensiveness and suspiciousness are to be got beyond, then I imagine that musicians and philosophers will have to spend considerably more time together than they have become used to. This would betoken a little critical revolution on its own. I cannot speak so without some tiny suggestion of something new they might talk about (beyond old sore spots concerning intention, expression, form, etc.). Assuming that they will have to talk about what they want of history and that Walter Benjamin is likely to make an entrance, I quote a passage from Benjamin's *Origin of German Tragic Drama* of particular pertinence to old preoccupations of my own. "The spoken word is only afflicted by meaning . . . ; it breaks off . . . and the damming up of the feeling, which was ready to pour forth, provokes mourning. Meaning is encountered . . . as the reason for mournfulness" (p. 209). Benjamin goes on to observe that "The phonetic tension with speech in the language of the seventeenth century leads directly to music" (p. 211).[10] I conceive that what Benjamin records as a tension in language is a manifestation of what in my work appears as the inexpressiveness that fuels skeptical doubt and despair.

A direct way of coming at this idea is to say that music allows the achieving of understanding without meaning, that is to say, without the articulation of individual acts of reference on which intelligibility is classically thought to depend. That words have meanings by being the names of things is the theory of meaning which Wittgenstein's *Investigations* opens by sketching and continues by tracing its seemingly endless implications, in each case, to self-extinction.

An indirect way I have pursued is to consider that the opening decade of the seventeenth century marks the achievement of Shakespeare's great tragedies and of the invention of opera, events which bespeak a crisis in the expressiveness and referentiality of speech, articulated philosophically in the following generation in Descartes's *Meditations,* in the form of a new discovery of skepticism and a new stake in defeating it, another essential moment that plays an original, or revolutionary, role in Wittgenstein's *Investigations.* Since I find Wittgenstein's sense of skepticism to be keyed to his depiction of philosophy's suspicion of speech as prompting its chronic desire to empty speech of meaning, as if to shun responsibility for what is meant, I am naturally drawn to Benjamin's speaking of baroque tragedy's discovery (as he puts it) of something new, an empty world (p. 139)—in which no action or work is more or less significant than any other.

But if the idea of "understanding without meaning" is to do real work, then we will have to specify the range of procedures that would *show* understanding—harmonic and motivic analysis, Schenkerian representation, semanticization, narrativizing, reading characteristic affects, performing—and articulate both why we want to, and how it is possible to, relate this apparent motley of procedures to something like addressing meaning, when so obviously whatever meaning they discover is so different from knowing or discovering the meaning of a word or a sentence in speech. Surely nothing less would explain what is at stake that is sufficient to cause the radical distrust between those who crave an account of meaning and those who wish to protect music from such invasion. (Surely neither side fails to see what the other sees? This sort of impasse is perennially philosophy's cue.)

Both sides were well represented in the session last week on Meaning and Interpretation during the discussion of a panelist's claim that a late moment in the Funeral March of the *Eroica* is interpretable as a ticking clock, suggesting that time is running, running out. Suppose I respond by saying, the sound is too low and labored to be heard, as claimed, as tick / tock; it strikes me as closer to rob / rub, more say like a labored heartbeat, suggesting life running out. I would hardly regard this as an incompatible suggestion; on the contrary, the fact that both seem to me apt implies that they are to be thought of not as discoveries but as *impressions* and *assignments* of meaning. The philosophical task here then becomes one of showing that this reformulation is not an evasion of the question of meaning in music, but constitutes the beginning of an answer to the question, or to a reformulation of it.

Here it should be recalled how often philosophers have wished to cast impressions as the ground of knowledge. I take it to be the same concept in play here, no doubt modified. The modification is explicit in Emerson's "Experience," where he can (should, I think) be read in effect as criticizing the empiricists for using the concept of impression mechanistically, aping science without being a science, instead of asking what it is that impresses us, makes an impression upon us, truly matters to us. For *that* is what philosophy wants, or should want, to know. Then the question becomes: What is music, or art, that it invites such assignments or investments? (And the answer to this question should help uncover the point of calling music and painting, etc. "languages.") How do the arts show, or remind us, or expand our horizons, so that we see, or remember, or learn, what truly matters to us?—as though without them we build our knowledge of our place in the world on the basis of sensory deprivation, starving our desires. (We can further think of this state as our suffering from object deprivation. I might call this skepticism. Marx's perception of commodification and Heidegger's of the deconditioning of things [in "Das Ding"] propose versions of it.)

Maynard Solomon, insisting, surely correctly, on the essential multiplicity of assignable narratives to a stretch or juncture of music, speaks of music as providing a "nuclear design standing for an infinity of related designs" (p. 13). But this idea risks obscuring what we want to explain, namely our need for such assignments and the possibility of our agreement in proposing them. It is at such an intellectual crossroads that Wittgenstein speaks of freeing ourselves from the idea of universals as explaining the application of the same concept to different things by appealing to a metaphysical something they must have in common (a something that makes a thing a table, or that constitutes expecting someone to tea, or that renders a piece somber), and instead to speak of different instances as linked by a family resemblance, in which no instance is the ancestor of all the others. The nature of our agreement in speech is a matter about which Wittgenstein has revolutionary things to say in his treatment of skepticism, and in particular, it is in this regard that he observes, "Understanding a sentence is much more like understanding a theme in music than one might believe" (§ 527).[11]

What is at stake here I could perhaps summarize or epitomize this way: The emptiness of the world discovered in the melancholy of baroque tragedy is to be filled by music, conceived as its willingness to accept assignments of meaning and its power to transcend all its assignments. This might remind us that music is the latest (except, I would add, for film) of the great arts to develop, I mean to achieve the emotional, intellectual, and cultural range and reticulation of its sister arts in the Western world. The implication is that this development of music, coinciding roughly with the rise of modern philosophy, as, say, in Descartes and Locke, is itself more revolutionary than any subsequent change within it or within any political event of which it could be said to form a part.

A Scale of Eternity

This essay was presented as a talk at the 2002 Bard Music Festival, as part of a panel discussion entitled "Images of Gustav Mahler." It was published in French in 2003 in the journal *Rue Descartes* in a special issue edited by Antonia Soulez on music and the philosophy of language. Cavell effects a rapprochement between Wittgenstein and Mahler, a composer whose work Wittgenstein disliked, and who was lauded by Theodor Adorno as the composer of the "breakthrough." To Cavell's ear, some works of Mahler, in the search for "greatness," evoke the fear of suffocation and inexpressiveness that is expressed in Wittgenstein's *Philosophical Investigations*.

GUSTAV MAHLER'S WORK WAS ALWAYS LATE, appearing as it did after the time in which symphonic writing of his ambition was called for. And if late works are ones in which an artist takes his eternal leave of the world of his work—or of the world in which he worked—his last works ought to bear what knowledge he had of farewells.

It was a fact well known to Mahler's friends that he was recurrently ambivalent, let's call it, about providing a program for his works. I propose to take this ambivalence not as a personal quirk of his own, caught up in passing fashions, but as an expression of an internal quality Mahler knew in his music, as if the life of music, as it revealed itself to him, had suffered a Cassandra-like

Versions of this essay were published as "Les degrés de l'éternité," trans. Christian Fournier, *Rue Descartes* no. 39 (2003): 102–108 (in French), and as "A Scale of Eternity: Gustav Mahler and the Autobiographical," in *Late Thoughts: Reflections on Artists and Composers at Work,* ed. Karen Painter and Thomas Crow (Los Angeles: Getty Research Institute, 2006), 207–215.

fate, blessed with a perfect capacity for telling or expressing the truth, and cursed with the fate of forever being misunderstood. If so, music may be understandable as coming to express a condition that had overtaken language, human speech, as such, a condition I call skepticism, a new form of which is widely held to emerge at the origin of modern philosophy in Descartes, hence in Hume, and hence in the persistent dispensation of Kant. But if language as such has for some reason become compromised in its powers of reference and expression—so that, like the prisoners in Plato's Cave, we cannot assure ourselves of the difference between illusion and reality, in that sense never quite know what we are saying—how can words satisfy us in our descriptions of our experience of music, which itself reflects the condition or fate of human speech? This seems to me a question worth occupying something to be called a philosophy of music.

I begin my exploratory remarks today with some thoughts and themes worked out in my reading over the years of Wittgenstein's *Philosophical Investigations,* where Wittgenstein can be found to say, "Understanding a sentence lies nearer than one thinks to what is ordinarily called understanding a musical theme."[1] Wittgenstein does next to nothing further explicitly with this thought. But let us take it to mean, whatever else, that understanding a sentence is hearing the music that shapes its life—as opposed to the ancient and persistent philosophical theory that Wittgenstein's *Investigations* as a whole can be said to undertake to disentangle, namely that understanding a sentence is knowing the meanings, namely the references, of its individual words. Then Wittgenstein's remark comparing a sentence with a musical theme plays a role uncannily similar, to my mind, to Mahler's repeated gloss on his music that extends beyond the particular movement that prompted it (the Scherzo of the Second Symphony): "When you awake from a melancholy dream and again have to face this . . . never resting, never to be understood hustle and bustle of life, [it] may seem dreadful to you, like the gyrations of the dancing figures in a bright and illuminated ballroom into which you look from a distance in the dark night outside the window, without hearing the music that goes with it. Then life seems senseless to you, the world distorted and mad."[2] This casts, in return, an accurately lurid light on the way Wittgenstein takes philosophers, succumbing to the temptation to metaphysics or false transcendence or skepticism, to torture human speech, to madden human encounter, unable or unwilling to imagine, to participate in—to hear the music of—the dense contexts within which speech makes its specific sense.

But there is a more tangible or historical reason for my invocation of the word of the later Wittgenstein on this occasion, namely his usefulness as a figure from which to measure my responses, so far as I have come to recognize and find words for them, both to Mahler's music, and to Theodor Adorno's book on that music. Adorno is by far the thinker most often referred to in the vast *Mahler Companion* (1999),[3] and he is, like it or not, the thinker of his generation, extending to the present, who has most successfully made a claim to have presented a philosophy of music. So one, like myself, who must consider what such a claim amounts to, can hardly avoid taking him up on it.

In the full and complex opening canvas that Leon Botstein provides to set the Viennese background against which the events of the texts of the *Companion* largely unfold, he notes Wittgenstein's expression of his belief that Mahler's music is worthless, Wittgenstein taking the side of Karl Kraus and Adolf Loos largely against the sensibility of the Secessionists.[4] Yet in Wittgenstein's antipathy—expressed each of the three times Mahler is named in the collection of excerpts from Wittgenstein's Notebooks translated under the title *Culture and Value*—I seem to sense a certain identification of himself with Mahler (facilitated surely, and obscurely, by similarities of cultural origins).[5] Wittgenstein observes: "One ought to put such comparisons [namely, of one's work with the achievements of the heroic past of music, and, I add, of philosophy] right out of one's mind. For if conditions nowadays are really so different from what they once were that one cannot even compare the *genre* one's work belongs to with that of earlier works, then one can't compare them in respect of value either. I myself continually make the mistake I'm referring to."[6] Wittgenstein once referred to his relation to the past of philosophy by saying that his work *replaces* philosophy; and once by saying that history has a kink in it. The relation to Mahler lies not alone in the fact of implied doubts—and compensating ecstasies—about the value of his own work, but in the radicality of the doubt, the invention of or participation in a new term of criticism, that of worthlessness, a sense of personal failure in not reaching the greatness of one's enterprise, where greatness has lost its measure. This loss of measure is one feature of the modernism of these figures, which sometimes takes the form of an uncertainty over whether their work is conservative or radically progressive. Mahler's crisis over his sense of undermined greatness, which led him to consult Freud, is well known, and I will come back to it.

A fear of inexpressiveness or suffocation, and a twin fear of uncontrollable expressiveness and exposure, are fundamental to my reading of Wittgenstein's *Investigations*. They are concepts, I find, that seem to be called for in my experience of Mahler, as are such associated, characteristic concepts in Wittgenstein's *Investigations* as that of the ordinary or everyday, call it the banal, as the method and goal of philosophizing; of becoming lost to the world; of the figure of the child, more pervasive in Wittgenstein's *Philosophical Investigations* than perhaps in any other philosophical work I know; of the torment in human restlessness, of threats of madness, and of the dream of peace; of being held captive by an image; of an urge to misunderstand; of understanding as knowing how to go on; of a yearning for transcendence, expressed as a relentless craving for purity of thought, for an ideal outside of which one cannot breathe; of the idea of how we call things as revealing their nature, an idea pervasive in the *Investigations* and epitomized in the collection of notebook entries when he remarks "Animals come when their names are called. Just like human beings."[7] Yet another is the concept of walking as part, like talking, of what Wittgenstein calls the natural history of the human.

Out of a myriad of connections here with themes (I trust this is plain) familiarly invoked in association with Mahler, I mention the attractive calls of birds in his portraits of nature's demands for our attention, and of the menacing horn calls that at any time provide reminders of human ceremony, as if nature and society are threats to each other; and I think of Adorno's noting that the whole first movement of Mahler's Ninth Symphony, which Adorno calls Mahler's masterpiece, is "inclined to one-measure beginnings; in them the delivery is slightly impeded, as by the constricted breathing of the narrator." In the next sentence he ties this image to the "almost labored one-measure steps of the narrative [that] carry the burden of the symphony's momentum at the start of the Funeral March like a coffin in a slow cortège."[8] Adorno is here seeking as it were to derive intellectually Mahler's direction at this point in the score, "Like a labored cortège." But how does the connection of a difficulty in breathing with the gait of a funeral march capture the experience in Mahler's "masterpiece"? Is it a general reminder of mortality, or is it, as in Wittgenstein, the threatened failure of an ideal, a certain hysteria in the face of loss?

Adorno says nothing further, as I recall, about breathing; as for marching, though he notes that it is not enough to relate Mahler's obsession with marches to his childhood memories, he conceptualizes the march as collective walking. But first, this does not distinguish marches—whether military, funeral, or protest, from sightseeing tramps through the countryside, parades between acts along the paths of an opera house, or holiday window shopping; second, and more important, while Adorno speaks, surely correctly, of the march rhythm as "carrying us along," implying that being moved along is an issue with this music, he at the same time makes being moved along, and hence perhaps being moved at all, essentially a function of our response as an audience in the plural (which perhaps seems fully true only of the problematic Eighth Symphony).[9] Whereas walking (as, for example, implied as early as the *Songs of a Wayfarer,* in each stanza of which the wanderer, with his unshakable companions love and sorrow, pictures himself walking alone), serves otherwise to single us out individually as the music's object, or its other, and to get us to think of walking, strolling, wandering, as the signal gait of the human, invoking the idea of human life as an unsurveyable path. (I should confess that I have been increasingly startled to find the image of walking, in connection with the conditions of thinking, recurrent in philosophical writing, from Plato and Aristotle, to Rousseau and Emerson and Nietzsche and Kierkegaard, as well as in Wittgenstein and in Heidegger.)

The issue of knowing how to go on, to walk, how to continue from an obscure beginning, is an obvious question for one whose fate, like Mahler's, as many of his commentators say in one way or another, was to inherit the symphonic tradition (as a conductor) without finding (as a composer) the established formal conditions, let's call them, of that tradition to be useable or tolerable—for example, tonal stability, balance of themes, repetition. One can see as an allegory of what may seem a pure problem of compositional technique, the spiritual crisis which is said to have brought Mahler to seek Freud's counsel, namely, as reported in Ernest Jones' biography of Freud, Mahler's sense that "his music had always been prevented from achieving the highest rank through the noblest passages, those inspired by the most profound emotions, being spoilt by the intrusion of some commonplace melody."[10] I assume that Adorno is taking a cue, or confirmation, from this report in positing "breakthrough" (a term for "intrusion") as one of three "essential genres in [Mahler's] idea of form" (along with suspension and fulfillment).[11] I have found, so far, that I do not know what weight to attach to Adorno's concept of breakthrough (it seems to fit anything from a change of key to an overall sense of fragmentariness). But if I think here of Wittgenstein's revolution, or kink, in philosophy, as letting the commonplace, or say the banal, break into the mood of philosophizing (as well, as is expected of philosophy from its beginning, demanding that philosophizing break into the spell of the commonplace), and recognize that in Wittgenstein these are two faces of philosophy attempting to recognize each other, then I feel I might turn to Mahler's works as contributions to thinking about philosophy's self-encounter.

Something similar is true of Adorno's use of Hegel's concept of "the course of the world" (*Weltlauf*), which is what is broken through. Adorno finds that Mahler's "aimlessly circling, irresistible movements, the perpetual motion of his music, are always images of the world's course."[12] Now the section of Hegel's *Phenomenology* that initiates the concept of "the course of the world" also interprets this world as "the mind sure of itself and ever on the alert,"[13] which is, however, dialectically a false or partial assurance and alertness to the goodness of the world, and which reflects this phase of encounter with the world in its restlessness or bustle, what in the *Wunderhorn* text of Mahler's Fourth Symphony is called "worldly turmoil" (*weltlich' Getümmel*).[14] Adorno's instinct in this appeal to Hegel strikes me as accurate, but in my half of the philosophical world (hence in half of my philosophical mind) the working out of this instinct in terms of Hegel's text would represent questionable currency, even if my pockets were lined with it. Hence my recourse is to focus here on the aspect of the mind in its restlessness, which, while not precisely named in Wittgenstein's *Investigations* is, as I see it, everywhere implied in its idea of philosophy's apparently interminable effort to bring its own turmoil to a point of peace, or rest (*Ruhe*).

The question on my mind is not so much, or not yet, whether such philosophical ideas are rationally and fruitfully brought to the understanding of music, but rather the prior question whether I understand myself in wanting, and assigning, such connections. Since I cannot sensibly take Wittgenstein further now, I shall close by calling attention to two further texts whose bearing on Mahler's world (and indeed on Wittgenstein's) I have found useful and not seen cited in what I have been reading in the realm of Mahler commentary (or Wittgenstein commentary), and then giving an illustration of what I had in mind by speaking of Mahler's works as contributions to thinking, namely about what philosophy is thinking about.

The first text I adduce deals with the fundamental matter in human existence of repetition. Not everyone finds Freud's speculations in *Beyond the Pleasure Principle* intellectually palatable, but to my mind they starkly illuminate and are illuminated by Mahler's variously reported experience of, let's say, stultification in repetition. The role of repetition, or rather the compulsion to repeat, is in Freud's text critical to his taking the step of postulating a death instinct in struggle with what he calls the erotic instinct in forms of life. It leads to Freud's conception of human instinct, or drive, not as an impulsion to growth and development but as an irreducible attempt to return to a previous, quiescent state. Freud invokes a biological theory to the effect that all organic substance attempts to return to its inorganic state, namely to death, but in the human, the erotic drive, having invested and elaborated itself in the objects in the world, engages itself in what Freud calls a *detour* (the thing, it would seem, philosophy and religion have interpreted as a path) that is comprehensible as a quest for one's own death, one that, as it were, would make sense of the singularity of one's life.[15] I have to say that this idea of detour seems to me at least as plausible a mark of Mahler's preoccupation with death, as expressed in his music, as any other I have come upon, surely as specific to his music (perhaps to music more generally) as the idea of breakthrough. (I note that there are admirers of the world of Mahler's music who might shun the extravagance of such thoughts of Freud's, while yet they permit themselves the description of their experience of, say, Mahler's Third Symphony as a depiction of the world of organic nature arising out of the world of the inorganic.)

The second text I adduce is William Empson's *Some Versions of Pastoral,* one of the permanent works of criticism to have emerged in the period of literary New Criticism (before and after World War II) and to have become swamped by the costly, however necessary, reception of French / German theory over the past several decades. Empson there extends the classical idea of the genre of the pastoral, through Shakespeare, Marvell, and Milton to include works such as *The Beggar's Opera* and *Alice in Wonderland,* understanding these works as expressing the human intuition of what Empson calls (and what Adorno calls) "the insufficiency of existence" (an idea they evidently both take from Hegel),[16] marking the unappeasable human dissatisfaction with each of its dispensations, the condition I called human restlessness.

The pair of examples I offer of Mahler's taking on philosophy's self-encounter are the following. I assume it is well recognized that after Mahler's most famous case of eternal resolution or irresolution at the end of *The Song of the Earth*—the voice iterating a descent in whole steps from the third to the second to the first degree of its home scale, then, as if thinking better of ending, going back to the descent from the third to the second, and twice as it were declining to descend to the home degree—Mahler's ensuing piece, the first movement of the Ninth Symphony, opens in effect by re-raising the question of the whole step descent from the mediant, and again, at the end of the movement, the principal voice declines the final step, declines as it were to rest in peace. Now there is the following difference between these pianissimo farewells. In the Ninth Symphony, other voices at the end sound the home pitch, only not within the register of the principal (oboe) voice. (So the question is opened for us to determine the significance of the fact of *register* in such works, an issue hardly unfamiliar in Mahler's originality of orchestration.) In *The Song of the Earth,* the home degree is also reached in other, orchestral, voices, this time in a register two octaves lower rather than two octaves higher, and this time with a further small difference. Again a harp, in a slow, rising arpeggio outlining the home triad, is the only moving thing in this whole world. But this time, in *The Song of the Earth,* the resolving pitch, within the register of the woman's voice, is not altogether avoided. Its occurrence there was more painful than that. The harp touches that tone on the weakest, last beat of the penultimate bar of change, and then, in tempo, moves on the final downbeat, away one last time to the median step of the scale. So yearning turns in a heartbeat into memory.

Suppose we say of the end of the opening movement of the Ninth, where the leading voice's home pitch, in its own register, is altogether avoided, something Walter Benjamin quotes more than once from Kafka: "There is hope, an infinite amount of hope—but not for us."[17] (Not in our own register.) And then say of the end of *The Song of the Earth,* where the pitch in its register is touched upon and left, in words of Nietzsche, that his eternity has been cut short, to an instant, existing as the moment of a glance. Then we shall have to ask what the relation is of such words to what we have experienced of this music. If we say they are the afterlife of such work, two questions arise. What if the experience has passed us by, as surely it sometimes will, on a given performance? And what if this is the only afterlife we are given to know?

Epilogue

Bon Voyage

Cavell wrote these brief remarks for the *Harvard Radcliffe Yearbook* in 1997 on the occasion of his retirement, addressing graduating students and reflecting on his own intellectual journey.

THE LAST THREE OF MY five years in Harvard's Ph.D. program in philosophy were spent in the luxuriousness of a Harvard Junior Fellowship, as follows: in the first eighteen months I composed the opening half of a projected doctoral dissertation; in the next four months I discarded that project (primarily because of work I was doing with the philosopher J. L. Austin, visiting from Oxford as William James Lecturer for 1955–1956); in the last twelve months I undertook to see during the daylight hours every notable building and painting in Western Europe and during the evening hours to attend every opera produced within reach of that progress. So that by the time I made my way back to Berkeley to take up an assistant professorship (I had spent my undergraduate years there as a music major) I felt wholly unprepared to say anything systematic about what I thought philosophy was, or had become.

How could I enter a classroom to teach, when I felt I was the one most in need of being taught?—unless, perhaps, my colleagues and my students would

First published in the *Harvard Radcliffe Yearbook* no. 361 (1997), p. 70.

turn out to be sources of instruction, and unless, somehow, I could myself teach courses that I had always wanted to take.

To tell the senses and degrees in which these possibilities materialized, continuing at Harvard when I returned here to teach permanently in 1963, would be to tell much of my intellectual life. One of the experiences most decisive in this adventure was my realization—early in the years of teaching in Harvard's old General Education program (Humanities 5) and continuing in my contribution later to the Core Curriculum (Moral Reasoning 34)—that the population of a large Harvard class in the humanities, mostly consisting of undergraduates but with the section persons in attendance, along with graduate students from various departments wishing to collect further images for a kind of teaching their futures might hold in store, and along further with the interspersing of visitors, scholars and others, that a Harvard auditorium draws, constituted as perfect a set of occasions for the public exploration of great philosophical texts of our tradition (eventually including literary texts and films) as I could wish to imagine. I had the feeling that in such a forum, extending through the season of a spring or a fall, what I most had it at heart to say about these works that I love, if articulated clearly and fervently enough, with no withholding, time permitting, of any suggested nuance or complexity at my command, would be fully understood and assessed with intelligence and good will. No comparable experience has had a greater effect on my quest for a sound of philosophical prose that I could place conviction in, nor has been more heartening to it.

Since this is also a last year at Harvard for me, I welcome this public chance to give a graduating class my thanks, extend to you my congratulations, and to wish you bon voyage.

Appendix

Draft Preface to *Here and There*

Cavell drafted this preface to *Here and There* following several exchanges with Alan Thomas at the University of Chicago Press. At the time, the table of contents included three additional sections—one on Shakespeare, one with prefaces to editions and translations of *The Claim of Reason,* and one that consisted of a group of interviews along with the memoir on Austin. In this preface, however, Cavell only discusses the parts that are found in the present edition—Departures, Assignments, and Music—and its brevity was intentional. "I should think the introduction to this volume will be brief, mostly describing the organization of the essays and my general sense of departures and arrivals" (letter to Alan Thomas, December 23, 2000).

GATHERED IN THIS PLACE from here and there are the pieces of work, concentrated within recent years but in a few cases going back to the 1980s, that I find worth rescuing either from oblivion or from the evanescence or specialization of their original locations of publication and that fit neither with the collection of my work on film outside the books dedicated to it nor as part of the shorter volume made of a sequence of pieces on vicissitudes of praise (concerning the likes of Shakespeare, Henry James, and Fred Astaire) that are to appear in the same season. The groupings of the present volume are anything but mysterious in intention. Only the first two require any explanation beyond their titles.

The opening section, "Departures," puts together mostly the longer texts involved, which lay out the general lines of my interests that are mainly new, or newly explicit, and that I expect to motivate further work. The second section, "Assignments," are short responses to requests of various kinds from often unexpected quarters of a kind that retirement from teaching has given me more freedom to accept than I have been used to. Some are promissory notes to myself that I will take an idea further. Some are meant to project a line of interest that I may never find time or occasion to pursue to an extent that matches the degree of my sense of its importance, but that, even in its brief materialization, creates an effect that puts the whole of my efforts in a somewhat different light. The group whose emergence most surprised me I guess is that of the four pieces on music. Music is as old among my cultural practices as reading words or telling time, but except for a pair of forays in my first book, I have until quite recently avoided the issue.

The idea of a here with a there as sites of philosophy, namely as suggesting measures of distance between different philosophical projects, but as a sense or measure of the task within each project, became explicit in a comparatively recent essay of mine on the aesthetics of Wittgenstein's *Philosophical Investigations,* where the ordinary in which we exist and from which we philosophize, and the fervor of aspiration with and toward which we philosophize, are pictured as near and far shores between which the river of philosophy has to take and modify its way. It is the peculiarity of this river that it is incessantly tempted to deny the necessity of one or other of its shores.

BROOKLINE
JANUARY 2001

Notes

EDITORS' INTRODUCTION

1. Cavell uses in some places the slightly longer main title *Both Here and There*. But in a table of contents for the book drawn up in 1999, as well as in a December 23, 2000, email message, he employs the briefer title *Here and There*.

2. The text of the draft preface is provided in full in the Appendix to this book. In this passage, Cavell refers to his article "The *Investigations'* Everyday Aesthetics of Itself," in John Gibson and Wolfgang Huemer, eds., *The Literary Wittgenstein* (London: Routledge, 2004), 21–33. The main passage he has in mind reads:

   How shall we place the farther shore of perspicuousness, the literary? Let us say it is, alluding to Kant, a standpoint from which to see the methods of the *Investigations,* their leading words home, undoing the charms of metaphysics, a perspective apart from which there is no pressing issue of spiritual fervor, whether felt as religious, moral, or aesthetic. Standpoint implies an alternative, a competing standpoint, a near shore. For professional philosophers this shore is that of philosophical "problems"—in the Preface to *Philosophical Investigations* Wittgenstein lists them as "[*subjects such as*] the concepts of meaning, of understanding, of a proposition, of logic, the foundations of mathematics, states of consciousness, and other things." Without this shore, the *Investigations* would not press upon, and not belong in, an academic philosophical curriculum. Because of the farther shore, its belonging is, and should be, uneasy. (26)

3. Cavell, *The Claim of Reason: Wittgenstein, Skepticism, Morality, and Tragedy* (Oxford: Oxford University Press, 1979), 3.

4. Cavell, *Must We Mean What We Say? A Book of Essays* (New York: Charles Scribner's Sons, 1969), xxix.

5. There are respects in which Cavell's book *Themes Out of School: Effects and Causes* (Chicago: University of Chicago Press, 1984) bears a similarity to the project of *Here and*

There, in bringing together occasional essays on American culture. Cavell explains in his preface to *Themes* (p. xiii) that he wanted to "line up" essays—especially on film—that "in their freer, or more various, formats . . . bear the *effect* of" the monographs he had recently completed, namely, *The Claim of Reason* and *Pursuits of Happiness: The Hollywood Comedy of Remarriage* (Cambridge, MA: Harvard University Press, 1981).

6. From unpublished email messages to Alan Thomas, director of the University of Chicago Press, August 9, 1999, and December 12, 2000.

7. Cavell, *Disowning Knowledge: In Seven Plays of Shakespeare* (Cambridge: Cambridge University Press, 2003) (enlarged edition of *Disowning Knowledge: In Six Plays of Shakespeare*, 1987).

8. Cavell, *Emerson's Transcendental Etudes,* ed. David Justin Hodge (Stanford: Stanford University Press, 2003). David Justin Hodge changed his name to David LaRocca in 2005 and has edited several works on Cavell since that time, including *Inheriting Stanley Cavell: Memories, Dreams, Reflections* (New York: Bloomsbury Academic, 2020); *The Thought of Stanley Cavell and Cinema: Turning Anew to the Ontology of Film a Half-Century after* The World Viewed (New York: Bloomsbury Academic, 2020); and *Movies with Stanley Cavell in Mind* (New York: Bloomsbury Academic, 2021).

9. *Cavell on Film,* ed. William Rothman (Albany: State University of New York Press, 2005).

10. Cavell, *Philosophy the Day after Tomorrow* (Cambridge, MA: Harvard University Press, 2006).

11. Cavell, *Little Did I Know: Excerpts from Memory* (Stanford, CA: Stanford University Press, 2010).

12. We did not include the essays on film that appear in the various draft tables of contents that Cavell left behind. All of his writings on film up to 2002, except for those that appear in his own books on film, are collected in *Cavell on Film.*

13. J. L. Austin, *How to Do Things with Words,* 2nd ed. (Cambridge, MA: Harvard University Press, 1975).

14. For Cavell's account of the effects Austin's visit had on him, see also *Little Did I Know,* esp. 306, 318–319, and 322, and this volume's Epilogue.

15. Cavell, *Little Did I Know,* 372.

16. Cavell, "The Availability of Wittgenstein's Later Philosophy," in *Must We Mean What We Say?* 52. Expanded versions of this passage appear in Chapters 2 ("The World as Things") and 3 ("The Division of Talent").

17. See the Prologue and Chapters 1, 2, 3, 16, 17, 18, 19, 20.

18. Cavell, *The Claim of Reason,* 178.

19. See esp. "Knowing and Acknowledging," in *Must We Mean What We Say?* and part 4 of *The Claim of Reason.*

20. Cavell, *The Claim of Reason,* xxii–xxiii.

21. See *Disowning Knowledge: In Six Plays of Shakespeare*.

22. Cavell, *The Claim of Reason*, esp. 47.

23. On film, see *Pursuits of Happiness*; *Contesting Tears: The Hollywood Melodrama of the Unknown Woman* (Chicago: University of Chicago Press, 1987); and *Cities of Words: Pedagogical Letters on a Register of the Moral Life* (Cambridge, MA: Harvard University Press, 2004).

24. In *The Claim of Reason*, *The World Viewed* (New York: Viking, 1971), and, remarkably, *The Senses of Walden* (New York: Viking, 1972), Emerson's name rarely appears. But in 1978, having completed *The Claim of Reason*, Cavell wrote "Thinking of Emerson" and then "An Emerson Mood," essays on Emerson that were published in the expanded edition of *The Senses of Walden* (Chicago: University of Chicago Press, 1980). See, e.g., 128 and 135–136.

25. See also *Conditions Handsome and Unhandsome: The Constitution of Emersonian Perfectionism* (Chicago: University of Chicago Press, 1990), esp. chap. 1. Cavell was already developing the idea of what he would later call moral perfectionism in the essays on Emerson that were published in the 1980 expanded edition of *The Senses of Walden*. See, e.g., 128 and 135–136.

26. *This New Yet Unapproachable America: Lectures after Emerson after Wittgenstein* (Albuquerque, NM: Living Batch Press, 1989) and *Conditions Handsome and Unhandsome* were translated and published in French, in 1991 and 1993, respectively, and were republished together in 2009.

27. *Qu'est-ce que la philosophie américaine?* brings together French translations of *This New Yet Unapproachable America*, *Conditions Handsome and Unhandsome*, and the essay "Emerson's Constitutional Amending."

28. See in the present volume Chapters 1, 2, 14, and the chapters on music in Part 3, esp. Chapters 23 and 24. See also "The Uncanniness of the Ordinary," in *In Quest of the Ordinary: Lines of Skepticism and Romanticism* (Chicago: University of Chicago Press, 1988).

29. This includes Chapter 4 ("To Place Wittgenstein"), which in a 2000 table of contents Cavell situated within the section he labeled "Assignments," and the memoir-like Chapter 5 ("Notes after Austin"), which Cavell initially placed in a section, not otherwise represented in the current book, that he called "Interviews and a Memoir." The reenactment of ordinary language philosophy in *Here and There* is present not only in Chapters 4–5 but throughout the volume, for example, in "The Division of Talent" (Chapter 3) and in "Finding Words" (Chapter 9).

30. Cavell published a book with the same title: *Philosophy the Day after Tomorrow* (Cambridge, MA: Belknap Press of Harvard University Press, 2005).

31. See also Cavell's account of the tragedy of the repeated loss of his childhood collections of things like bottle caps, collections his mother regarded as "clear clutter"; *Little Did I Know*, 38.

32. See also Chapter 8 ("Signals and Affinities"). In 2005, Cavell published "The World as Things" as the last chapter of his collection *Philosophy the Day after Tomorrow,* 236–282. But Cavell doesn't mention it in his preface, and it would not be unreasonable to speculate that he placed it there because he thought he would not bring out *Here and There.*

33. Later Cavell would make this point in reference to the work of Jacques Derrida in particular, declaring that Derrida "seems to insist on the pathos of the philosophical view of language that he combats." *A Pitch of Philosophy: Autobiographical Exercises* (Cambridge, MA: Harvard University Press, 1994), 72.

34. See esp. *A Pitch of Philosophy,* chap. 2. Cavell is concerned with his relationship to poststructuralism more generally in a couple of the shorter pieces in the present book: Chapters 16 (foreword to Northrop Frye, *A Natural Perspective*) and 17 ("Who Disappoints Whom? Allan Bloom at Harvard").

35. Cavell retired from teaching at Harvard in 1997.

36. For Cavell's remarks on his own psychoanalysis, see *Little Did I Know,* 108 and 452. He started to follow a certification program but was dismissed; *Little Did I Know,* 512–513.

37. See Stephen Mulhall's introduction to *The Cavell Reader* (Oxford: Blackwell, 1996), esp. 12–13.

38. This death takes the form of living with radical skepticism, madness, obtuseness. See Chapters 6, 10, and 12.

39. For some notable recent contributions to anthropology that show Cavell's influence, together with Wittgenstein's, see Andrew Brandel and Marco Motta, eds., *Living with Concepts: Anthropology in the Grip of Reality* (New York: Fordham University Press, 2020); Veena Das, *Life and Words: Violence and the Descent into the Ordinary* (Berkeley: University of California Press, 2007); Veena Das, *Textures of the Ordinary: Doing Anthropology after Wittgenstein* (New York: Fordham University Press, 2020); Veena Das et al., *The Ground Between: Anthropologists Engage Philosophy* (Durham, NC: Duke University Press, 2015).

40. *Les Voix de la raison* (Paris: Le Seuil, 1996), 12 (preface to the French edition of *The Claim of Reason*). Cavell meant to include this preface in *Here and There,* together with the preface to the Italian edition, but except for brief additions, it is close to the preface to the English first edition (1979).

41. *Les Voix de la raison,* 12. Cavell was intensely interested in the international circulation of philosophy, as in the meetings at Mount Holyoke College, in 1942–1944, that brought together American and European intellectuals and artists in exile. See Chapter 19 ("Reflections on Wallace Stevens at Mount Holyoke") and *Little Did I Know,* 184.

42. See also the February 7, 2002, interview "A Philosopher Goes to the Movies," part of a Berkeley-based "Conversations with History" series (https://www.youtube.com/watch?v=eIIKqEl8xEw), in which Cavell discusses the crisis of finding that music is no longer his life's work at 13:15; and see *Little Did I Know,* 187, 225, and 284.

43. *Little Did I Know,* 185.

44. *Philosophical Investigations,* §527. Cavell cites this passage in Chapters 23, 24, and 25.

45. Cavell published a version of his Harvard lectures as *Cities of Words.*

CHAPTER 2. THE WORLD AS THINGS

1. Krzysztof Pomian, *Collectors and Curiosities: Paris and Venice, 1500–1800,* trans. Elizabeth Wiles-Portier (Cambridge: Polity Press; Cambridge, Mass.: Blackwell, 1990).

2. See Jean Baudrillard, "The System of Collecting," in *The Cultures of Collecting,* ed. John Elsner and Roger Cardinal (Cambridge, Mass.: Harvard University Press, 1994); Pomian, *Collectors and Curiosities;* Susan Stewart, "Death and Life, in That Order, in the Works of Charles Willson Peale," in *The Cultures of Collecting;* Robert Opie, "'Unless you do these crazy things . . .': An Interview with Robert Opie," in ibid.; Philip Fisher, *Making and Effacing Art* (Cambridge, Mass.: Harvard University Press, 1997); Michel Foucault. *The Order of Things: An Archaeology of the Human Sciences* (New York: Vintage Books, 1994; 1966).

3. See James Clifford, *The Predicament of Culture* (Cambridge, Mass.: Harvard University Press, 1988).

4. Ludwig Wittgenstein, *Philosophical Investigations,* trans. Elizabeth Anscombe, 3d ed. (Oxford: Blackwell, 1958; 1953), §1.

5. Wittgenstein, *Philosophical Investigations,* §1.

6. Ludwig Wittgenstein, *Tractatus logico-philosophicus,* trans. D. F. Pears and B. F. McGuinness, 2d ed. (London: Routledge & Kegan Paul, 1961; 1921), p. 149.

7. Baudrillard, "The System of Collecting," in *The Cultures of Collecting,* p. 12.

8. Wittgenstein, *Philosophical Investigations,* § 65, 66, 67.

9. Martin Heidegger, "The Thing," in *Poetry, Language, Thought,* trans. Albert Hofstadter (New York: Harper & Row, 1975; 1971), p. 165.

10. Heidegger, "The Thing," pp. 165, 166.

11. Heidegger, "The Thing," p. 174.

12. Heidegger, "The Thing," p. 171.

13. Wittgenstein, *Philosophical Investigations,* §317.

14. Wittgenstein, *Philosophical Investigations,* §373.

15. Heidegger, "Building Dwelling Thinking," in *Poetry, Language, Thought,* p. 146.

16. Michael Fried, *Three American Painters: Kenneth Noland, Jules Olitski, Frank Stella,* exh. cat. (Cambridge, Mass.: Fogg Art Museum, 1965).

17. W. V. Quine, *Pursuit of Truth* (Cambridge, Mass.: Harvard University Press, 1990).

18. Walter Benjamin, *Charles Baudelaire: A Lyric Poet in the Era of High Capitalism,* trans. Harry Zohn (London: Verso, 1983), pp. 168–69.

19. Benjamin, *Charles Baudelaire,* p. 172.

20. David Hume, *A Treatise of Human Nature,* ed. L. A. Selby-Bigge, vol. I, iv (Oxford: Oxford University Press, 1951), p. 252.

21. Hume, *Treatise*, p. 269.

22. Hume, *Treatise*, p. 269.

23. Hume, *Treatise*, p. 252.

24. Hume, *Treatise*, p. 253.

25. Hume, *Treatise*, p. 251.

26. Hume, *Treatise*, p. xx.

27. See Mieke Bal, "Telling Objects: A Narrative Perspective on Collecting," in *The Cultures of Collecting;* Stewart, "Death and Life"; Fisher, *Making and Effacing Art.*

28. See Norton Batkin, "Conceptualizing the History of the Contemporary Museum: On Foucault and Benjamin," *Philosophical Topics,* vol. 25, no. 1 (spring 1997).

29. Immanuel Kant, *Critique of Judgment,* trans. J. H. Bernard (New York: Hafner Press, 1951; 1790).

30. Benjamin, *The Origin of German Tragic Drama,* trans. John Osborne (London: NLB, 1977).

31. Georg Simmel, "The Metropolis and Mental Life," in *On Individuality and Social Forms,* ed. Donald N. Levine, trans. Edward A. Shils (Chicago: University of Chicago Press, 1971), pp. 329, 330.

32. Simmel, "Metropolis," p. 324.

33. Benjamin, "Eduard Fuchs, Collector and Historian," in *One-Way Streets and Other Writings,* trans. Edmund Jephcott and Kingsley Shorter (London and New York: Verso, 1997), sec. 3.

34. Ralph Waldo Emerson, "History," in *Essays and Lectures,* ed. Joel Porte (New York: Library of America, 1983).

35. Sigmund Freud, *Civilization and Its Discontents,* ed. and trans. James Strachey, vol. 21 (London: Hogarth Press, 1961), pp. 142–143.

36. Jacques Lacan, *The Ethics of Psychoanalysis,* Seminar VII (1959–60), trans. Dennis Porter (New York: Norton, 1992).

37. Baudrillard, "The System of Collecting," p. 24.

38. John Forrester, "Collector, Naturalist, Surrealist," in *Dispatches from the Freud Wars* (Cambridge, Mass.: Harvard University Press, 1997), pp. 107–37.

39. For a good introduction to Winnicott's work, see Adam Phillips, *Winnicott* (Cambridge, Mass.: Harvard University Press, 1988).

40. Wittgenstein, *Philosophical Investigations,* § 183.

41. Lacan, *The Ethics of Psychoanalysis,* p. 114.

42. See, for example, Melanie Klein, *Envy and Gratitude* (New York: Free Press, 1984).

43. John Rawls, *A Theory of Justice* (Cambridge, Mass.: Harvard University Press, 1971), p. 442.

44. Christine Korsgaard, "The Reasons We Can Share: An Attack on the Distinction between Agent-relative and Agent-neutral Values," in *Creating the Kingdom of Ends* (Cambridge and New York: Cambridge University Press, 1996), pp. 275–310.

45. Dave Hickey, *Air Guitar: Essays on Art and Democracy* (Los Angeles: Art Issues Press, 1997), p. 16.

46. Hickey, *Air Guitar*, p. 23.

47. Stanley Cavell, *Must We Mean What We Say? A Book of Essays* (Cambridge and New York: Cambridge University Press, 1976; 1969), p. 52.

48. Klein, *Envy and Gratitude*.

49. Marc Shell, *Art and Money* (Chicago: University of Chicago Press, 1995).

50. See Fried, "Art and Objecthood" (1967), in *Art and Objecthood* (Chicago: Chicago University Press, 1998); Clement Greenberg, "Modernist Painting" (1960) and "After Abstract Expressionism" (1962), in *Modernism with a Vengeance,* vol. 4, *The Collected Essays and Criticism,* ed. John O'Brian (Chicago: University of Chicago Press, 1993).

51. Heidegger, "The Thing," p. 166.

52. Heidegger, "The Thing," pp. 168ff. Subsequent quotations in this paragraph are from p. 181.

53. Cavell, "Finding as Founding," in *This New Yet Unapproachable America: Lectures after Emerson after Wittgenstein* (Albuquerque, N.M.: Living Batch Press, 1989).

54. William Rubin, *Dada, Surrealism and Their Heritage,* exh. cat. (New York: Museum of Modern Art, 1968).

55. Cavell, *The World Viewed: Reflections of the Ontology of Film* (Cambridge, Mass., and London: Harvard University Press, 1979; 1971).

56. Cavell, *The Senses of Walden* (Chicago: University of Chicago Press, 1992; 1972), pp. 100–104.

57. Cavell, *The World Viewed,* p. 115.

58. Heidegger, "The Origin of the Work of Art," pp. 25, 72.

59. See, for example, Stephen Melville, *Philosophy beside Itself: On Deconstruction and Modernism,* Theory and History of Literature, vol. 27 (Minneapolis, 1986).

60. Thomas S. Kuhn, *The Structure of Scientific Revolutions,* 3d ed. (Chicago: University of Chicago Press, 1996; 1962).

61. Pomian, *Collectors and Curiosities,* for example, p. 44.

62. Foucault, *The Order of Things,* p. 131.

63. Lee Rust Brown, *The Emerson Museum: Practical Romanticism and the Pursuit of the Whole* (Cambridge, Mass.: Harvard University Press, 1997).

64. Emerson, *The Journals and Miscellaneous Notebooks of Ralph Waldo Emerson,* vol. 4, ed. Alfred R. Ferguson (Cambridge, Mass.: Belknap Press, 1964; 1832–34), entry for July 13, 1833.

65. Emerson, *Journals,* vol. 4, entry for July 13, 1833.

66. Emerson, "Self-Reliance," in *Essays, and Essays: Second Series* (Columbus: Merritt, 1969; 1844; 1849), p. 50.

67. Emerson, "The American Scholar," "Fate," "Divinity School Address," "Circles," and "Experience," in *Essays and Lectures.*

68. Emerson, "Experience."

69. Henry David Thoreau, *Walden*, ed. Walter Harding (New York: Washington Square Press, 1970; 1854), chap. 1, "Economy," passim.

70. Thoreau, *Walden*, p. 43.

71. Susan Howe, "Sorting Facts; or Nineteen Ways of Looking at Marker," in *Beyond Document: Essays on Non-Fiction Film*, ed. Charles Warren (Wesleyan University Press, 1996).

72. Wittgenstein, *Philosophical Investigations*, § 133.

73. Stewart, "Death and Life," p. 204; Forrester, "Collector, Naturalist, Surrealist," p. 107.

74. Wittgenstein, *Philosophical Investigations*, § 116.

75. Opie, "'Unless you do these crazy things. . . .'"

76. Thoreau, *Walden*, p. 39.

77. Thoreau, *Walden*, p. 50.

78. Thoreau, *Walden*, p. 50.

79. Sei Shonagon, *The Pillow Book*, trans. Ivan Morris (New York: Columbia University Press, 1991).

80. John Locke, *The Second Treatise of Government*, in *Locke's Two Treatises of Government*, ed. Peter Laslett, 2d ed. (Cambridge: Cambridge University Press, 1967), chap. V. sec. 27, p. 306.

81. Thoreau, *Walden*, p. 141.

82. Benjamin, "Theses on the Philosophy of History," in *Illuminations: Essays and Reflections*, ed. Hannah Arendt, trans. Harry Zohn (New York: Schocken Books, 1969), p. 256.

83. Heidegger, *What Is Called Thinking?*, trans. J. Glenn Gray (New York: Harper and Row, 1968; 1951–52), pp. 200ff.

84. Wittgenstein, *Philosopical Investigations*, §124.

85. Wittgenstein, *Philosopical Investigations*, §108.

86. Wittgenstein, *Philosopical Investigations*, §524.

CHAPTER 3. THE DIVISION OF TALENT

1. See W. Jackson Bate, "The Crisis in English Studies," *Harvard Magazine* 85 (Sept.–Oct. 1982): 46–53.

2. See Stanley Fish, "Profession Despise Thyself: Fear and Self-Loathing in Literary Studies," *Critical Inquiry* 10 (Dec. 1983): 349–64.

3. See Steven Knapp and Walter Benn Michaels, "Against Theory," *Critical Inquiry* 8 (Summer 1982): 723–42; all further references to this work, abbreviated "AT," will be included in the text.

4. See Stanley Cavell, "Music Discomposed" and "A Matter of Meaning It," *Must We Mean What We Say?: A Book of Essays* (Cambridge, 1969), pp. 180–212 and 213–37, respectively, and W. K. Wimsatt and Monroe C. Beardsley, "The Intentional Fallacy," in Wimsatt, *The Verbal Icon: Studies in the Meaning of Poetry* (Lexington, Ky., 1954), pp. 3–18.

5. On reading the responses to Knapp and Michaels printed in *Critical Inquiry,* I see that William C. Dowling takes exception to their identity thesis on grounds certain of which are similar to mine, if on a more theoretical plane (see "Intentionless Meaning," *Critical Inquiry* 9 [June 1983]: 784–89).

6. See Paul de Man, "Reply to Raymond Geuss," *Critical Inquiry* 10 (Dec. 1983): 383–90; all further references to this work, abbreviated "RRG," will be included in the text. See also de Man, "Sign and Symbol in Hegel's Aesthetics," *Critical Inquiry* 8 (Summer 1982): 761–75.

7. Raymond Geuss, "A Response to Paul de Man," *Critical Inquiry* 10 (Dec. 1983): 381.

8. I have said more about this in "Politics as Opposed to What?," in *The Politics of Interpretation,* ed. W. J. T. Mitchell (Chicago, 1983), pp. 186–92.

9. See Jacques Derrida, "The Principle of Reason: The University in the Eyes of Its Pupils," trans. Catherine Porter and Edward P. Morris, *Diacritics* 13 (Fall 1983): 3–20; all further references to this work, abbreviated "PR," will be included in the text.

10. Ralph Waldo Emerson, *Nature, "Nature," Addresses, and Lectures* (Cambridge, Mass., 1979), p. 18.

11. Cavell, *The Senses of "Walden"* (New York, 1972), p. 5.

12. William Howarth, "On Reading *Walden,*" *Thoreau Quarterly* 14 (Summer-Fall 1982): 140 n. 4.

13. Henry David Thoreau, *Walden* (New York, 1960), p. 58 (chap. 2, par. 21); and see Cavell, *The Senses of "Walden,"* pp. 93–95.

14. Cavell, "The Availability of Wittgenstein's Later Philosophy," *Must We Mean What We Say?,* p. 52.

15. See Cavell, *The Claim of Reason: Wittgenstein, Skepticism, Morality, and Tragedy* (Oxford, 1979).

16. That certain details of deconstruction may be located against certain details of skepticism as I have mapped them in *The Claim of Reason* is an idea that Michael Fischer of the University of New Mexico has begun working out surprisingly and systematically. As part of our correspondence on this issue, I sent Professor Fischer a copy of the text I read to the Association of Departments of English, and it was his response to that text that more than anything else prompted me to compose this postscript.

17. See J. L. Austin, "Ifs and Cans" and "Pretending," *Philosophical Papers,* ed. J. O. Urmson and G. J. Warnock, 3d ed. (Oxford, 1979), pp. 230–32 and 271.

CHAPTER 6. SILENCES NOISES VOICES

1. Ludwig Wittgenstein, *Philosophical Investigations,* 3d ed., ed. G. E. M. Anscombe and R. Rhees, trans. G. E. M. Anscombe (Oxford: Basil Blackwell and Mott, 1958; 1st edition 1953).

2. "Notes and Afterthoughts on the Opening of Wittgenstein's *Investigations*," in Cavell, *Philosophical Passages: Wittgenstein, Emerson, Austin* (Cambridge, Mass.: Blackwell, 1995), pp. 125–186.

3. *A Pitch of Philosophy* (Cambridge, Mass.: Harvard University Press, 1995).

4. "Fragment of an Analysis of a Case of Hysteria," in *The Standard Edition of the Complete Psychological Works of Sigmund Freud*, ed. and trans. James Strachey et al. (London: Hogarth Press, 1957–1966), vol. 7, pp. 77–78.

5. "The Freudian Thing," in *Écrits: A Selection*, trans. Alan Sheridan (New York: Norton, 1955).

CHAPTER 7. BENJAMIN AND WITTGENSTEIN

1. See *Walter Benjamin's Philosophy: Destruction and Experience*, ed. Andrew Benjamin and Peter Osborne (London, 1994); *Benjamin: Philosophy, Aesthetics, History*, ed. Gary Smith (Chicago, 1989); and Walter Benjamin, *Illuminations*, trans. Harry Zohn, ed. Hannah Arendt (New York, 1969).

2. See Benjamin, letter to Gershom Scholem, 17 Apr. 1931, *The Correspondence of Walter Benjamin, 1892–1940*, trans. Manfred R. Jacobson and Evelyn M. Jacobson, ed. Scholem and Theodor W. Adorno (Chicago, 1994), p. 378.

3. Benjamin, "Program for a Proletarian Children's Theater," in *The Weimar Republic Sourcebook*, trans. Don Reneau et al., ed. Anton Kaes, Martin Jay, and Edward Dimendberg (Berkeley, 1994), p. 233.

4. See Jeffrey Mehlman, *Walter Benjamin for Children: An Essay on His Radio Years* (Chicago, 1993).

5. See Ludwig Wittgenstein, *Philosophical Investigations*, 3d ed., trans. G. E. M. Anscombe (London, 1958), for example, §47; hereafter abbreviated *PI*.

6. See Benjamin, "Karl Kraus," *Reflections: Essays, Aphorisms, Autobiographical Writings*, trans. Edmund Jephcott, ed. Peter Demetz (New York, 1978), pp. 239–73.

7. Benjamin, *The Origin of German Tragic Drama*, trans. John Osborne (1977; London, 1985), p. 155; hereafter abbreviated *OG*; see also p. 158.

8. See Martin Heidegger, "Language," *Poetry, Language, Thought*, trans. Albert Hofstadter, ed. J. Glenn Gray (New York, 1975), pp. 194–95.

9. See Beatrice Hanssen, *Walter Benjamin's Other History: Of Stones, Animals, Human Beings, and Angels* (Berkeley, 1997).

10. Benjamin, "Franz Kafka: On the Tenth Anniversary of His Death," *Illuminations*, p. 122.

11. Benjamin, "The Concept of Criticism in German Romanticism," trans. David Lachterman, Howard Eiland, and Ian Belfour, *Selected Writings, 1913–1926*, ed. Marcus Bullock and Michael W. Jennings (Cambridge, Mass., 1996), p. 179.

12. Ibid., pp. 152, 159.

13. Benjamin, "Goethe's Elective Affinities," trans. Stanley Corngold, *Selected Writings, 1913–1926*, pp. 300, 301.

14. Benjamin, "On Language as Such and on the Language of Man," trans. Jephcott, *Selected Writings, 1913–1926*, p. 72.

15. Winfried Menninghaus, who organized the Yale conference, commented to me after my talk that Benjamin was in fact interested in nonsense, construing (if I understood) the freedom from sense in fairy tales as a rescue from the dictation of sense in myth. I am not prepared now to speak to this. Nor can I now derive the tuition from a theme from the *Trauerspiel* book that to my ear captures the intuition in my tendency to characterize the skeptic as wishing to escape the responsibility for meaning his words; I refer to Benjamin's claim that, in the baroque antithesis of sound and meaning, "meaning is encountered, and will continue to be encountered as the reason for mournfulness" (*OG*, p. 209).

16. Benjamin, "Theses on the Philosophy of History," *Illuminations*, p. 258.

17. Ralph Waldo Emerson, "Self-Reliance," *Essays and Lectures*, ed. Joel Porte (New York, 1983), p. 264.

18. Emerson, "New England Reformers," *Essays and Lectures*, p. 600.

19. Benjamin, "Goethe's Elective Affinities," p. 356.

20. Emerson, "Experience," *Essays and Lectures*, p. 492.

21. William Shakespeare, *Henry VIII*, in *The Riverside Shakespeare*, ed. G. Blakemore Evans et al. (Boston, 1974), 5.1.135–37, p. 1011.

CHAPTER 10. WELCOMING JEAN LAPLANCHE

1. *Editors' note:* The work referred to is *Jean Laplanche: Seduction, Translation and the Drives: A Dossier*, ed. John Fletcher and Martin Stanton (London: Institute of Contemporary Arts, 1992).

2. *Jean Laplanche*, p. 210.

CHAPTER 11. ON A PSYCHOANALYTICAL RESPONSE TO FAULKNER'S FORM

1. Gilbert J. Rose, *Between Couch and Piano: Psychoanalysis, Music, Art and Neuroscience* (London: Routledge, 2004).

2. William Faulkner, *Light in August* (Harmondsworth: Penguin, 1960).

CHAPTER 12. NOTES MOSTLY ABOUT EMPATHY

1. J. L. Austin, "Other Minds," in *Logic and Language*, ed. Anthony Flew, 2nd series (Oxford: Basil Blackwell & Mott, 1953), 152.

CHAPTER 15. FOREWORD TO NORTHROP FRYE, *A NATURAL PERSPECTIVE*

1. I note with thanks that the foreword was improved by suggestions from Steven Affeldt, Nancy Bauer, and James Conant.

CHAPTER 16. IN THE MEANTIME

1. Stanley Cavell, *Must We Mean What We Say?: A Book of Essays* (Cambridge and New York: Cambridge University Press, 1976), 21 n. 19.
2. Cavell, *Must We Mean What We Say?*, 36 n. 31.
3. Jacques Derrida, *Margins of Philosophy* (Chicago: University of Chicago Press, 1982), 123.
4. See Derrida, "The Ends of Man," in *Margins*, 109–136.

CHAPTER 17. WHO DISAPPOINTS WHOM? ALLAN BLOOM AT HARVARD

1. Allan Bloom, *The Closing of the American Mind: How Higher Education Has Failed Democracy and Impoverished the Souls of Today's Students* (New York, 1987), p. 148; hereafter cited by page number.

CHAPTER 19. REFLECTIONS ON WALLACE STEVENS AT MOUNT HOLYOKE

1. Rudolf Carnap, "The Elimination of Metaphysics through Logical Analysis of Language," in *Logical Positivism*, ed. A. J. Ayer (Glencoe, Ill.: Free Press, 1959).
2. Frank Kermode, "Dwelling Poetically in Connecticut," in *Pieces of My Mind* (New York: Farrar, Straus and Giroux, 2003).
3. Peter Brazeau, *Parts of a World: Wallace Stevens Remembered* (San Francisco: North Point, 1985), 214.
4. I am conscious of having been helped by the literary-critical writing of Helen Vendler, and of Laura Quinney, and by a late essay of Randall Jarrell: Helen Vendler, "Stevens' Secrecies," in *Wallace Stevens: Words Chosen Out of Desire* (Knoxville: University of Tennessee Press, 1984), 44–60; Laura Quinney, *Poetics of Disappointment* (Charlottesville: University Press of Virginia, 1999); Randall Jarrell, "Reflections on Wallace Stevens," in *No Other Book: Selected Essays*, ed. Brad Leithauser (New York: HarperCollins, 1999), 112–22.
5. Wallace Stevens, *Opus Posthumous*, ed. Samuel French Morse (New York: Knopf, 1957), 190.
6. Martin Heidegger, *Hölderlin's Hymn "The Ister,"* trans. William McNeill and Julia Davis (Bloomington: Indiana University Press, 1996).

7. Stanley Cavell, "Thoreau Thinks of Ponds, Heidegger of Rivers," in *Philosophy the Day after Tomorrow* (Cambridge, Mass.: Harvard University Press, 2005), 213–35. An earlier version appeared in *Appropriating Heidegger,* ed. James E. Faulconer and Mark A. Wrathhall (Cambridge: Cambridge University Press, 2000), 30–49.

CHAPTER 21. AN UNDERSTANDING WITH MUSIC

1. *Editors' note:* Page citations within the essay are to the following works: Walter Benjamin, *The Origin of German Tragic Drama,* trans. J. Osborne (London: Verso, 1998); Michel Poizat, *The Angel's Cry: Beyond the Pleasure Principle in Opera* (Ithaca: Cornell University Press, 1992); and Gary Tomlinson, *Music in Renaissance Magic: Toward a Historiography of Others* (Chicago: Chicago University Press, 1993).
2. The first, highly compressed presentation of the derivation of passionate utterance was given in an address to the American Philosophical Association in December 1996; it was printed in the Association's *Proceedings and Addresses,* vol. 71, no. 2, November 1997. See pages 28–31.

CHAPTER 23. PHILOSOPHY AND THE UNHEARD

1. Ludwig Wittgenstein, *Philosophical Investigations,* trans. G. E. M. Anscombe (Oxford: Basil Blackwell, 1968), 143.
2. Schoenberg to Max Butting, 4 February 1926, in Arnold Schoenberg, *Letters,* ed. Erwin Stein, trans. Eithne Wilkins and Ernst Kaiser (Berkeley: University of California Press, 1987), 118.
3. Wittgenstein, *Philosophical Investigations,* 47.
4. Schoenberg to Wassily Kandinsky, 4 May 1923, in Arnold Schoenberg, *Letters,* 93.
5. Theodor Adorno, *Philosophy of Modern Music,* trans. Anne G. Mitchell and Wesley V. Blomster (New York: Seabury Press, 1973).
6. Charles Rosen, *Arnold Schoenberg* (Chicago: University of Chicago Press, 1996), viii.
7. Carl Dahlhaus, *Schoenberg and the New Music,* trans. Derrick Puffett and Alfred Clayton (Cambridge: Cambridge University Press, 1987), 275.
8. David Lewin, "*Moses und Aron:* Some General Remarks, and Analytic Notes for Act I, Scene I," *Perspectives of New Music* 6 (fall–winter 1967): 1.
9. Lewin, "*Moses und Aron.*"
10. Adorno, *Philosophy of Modern Music,* 112.
11. Adorno, *Philosophy of Modern Music,* 112–113.
12. Theodor Adorno, "Toward a Portrait of Thomas Mann," in *Notes to Literature,* vol. 2, ed. Rolf Tiedemann, trans. Shierry Weber Nicholson (New York: Columbia University Press, 1992), 17–18.

CHAPTER 24. IMPRESSIONS OF REVOLUTION

1. Hannah Arendt, *On Revolution* (New York: Viking, 1965).

2. Thomas Kuhn, *The Structure of Scientific Revolutions* (Chicago: Chicago University Press, 1962); and Charles Rosen, *The Classical Style: Haydn, Mozart, Beethoven* (New York: Viking, 1971), esp. the opening pages of chap. 2, "Theories of Form."

3. Rosen, *Classical Style,* 385.

4. T. J. Clark, *Farewell to an Idea: Episodes from a History of Modernism* (New Haven, Conn.: Yale University Press, 1999), 52.

5. Carl Dahlhaus, *Ludwig van Beethoven: Approaches to His Music,* trans. Mary Whittall (Oxford: Clarendon Press, 1991).

6. Reinhold Brinkmann, "In the Time of the *Eroica,*" in *Beethoven and His World,* ed. Scott Burnham and Michael P. Steinberg (Princeton, N.J.: Princeton University Press, 2000).

7. Maynard Solomon, *Beethoven Essays* (Cambridge, Mass.: Harvard University Press, 1988).

8. Theodor W. Adorno, *Introduction to the Sociology of Music,* trans. E. B. Ashton (New York: Seabury Press, 1976), 62.

9. Theodor W. Adorno, *Beethoven: The Philosophy of Music,* ed. Rolf Tiedemann, trans. Edmund Jephcott (Stanford: Stanford University Press, 1998), 10, 210. "In a similar sense to that in which there is only Hegelian philosophy, in the history of music there is only Beethoven" (10).

10. Walter Benjamin, *The Origins of German Tragic Drama,* trans. John Osborne (London: NLB, 1977).

11. Ludwig Wittgenstein, *Philosophical Investigations,* trans. G. E. M. Anscombe (Oxford: Basil Blackwell, 1958).

CHAPTER 25. A SCALE OF ETERNITY

1. Ludwig Wittgenstein, *Philosophical Investigations: The German Text, with a Revised English Translation,* trans. G. E. M. Anscombe, 3rd ed. (Oxford: Blackwell, 2001), § 527.

2. A reworded amalgamation of sentences from two letters of Mahler's, as presented in Constantine Floros, *Gustav Mahler: The Symphonies,* trans. Vernon Wicker (Aldershot, England: Scolar, 1993), 63.

3. Donald Mitchell and Andrew Nicholson, eds., *The Mahler Companion* (Oxford: Oxford Univ. Press, 1999).

4. Leon Botstein, "Gustav Mahler's Vienna," in Donald Mitchell and Andrew Nicholson, eds., *The Mahler Companion* (Oxford: Oxford Univ. Press, 1999), 34.

5. Wittgenstein's notebooks have been translated under the title *Culture and Value,* ed. Georg Herick von Wright and Heidi Nyman, trans. Peter Winch, 2nd ed. (Oxford: Blackwell, 1980), 20, 38, 67.

6. Wittgenstein, *Culture and Value* (note 5), 67.

7. Wittgenstein, *Culture and Value* (note 5), 67.

8. Theodor W. Adorno, *Mahler: A Musical Physiognomy,* trans. Edmund Jephcott (Chicago: Univ. of Chicago Press, 1991), 155.

9. Theodor W. Adorno, "Marginalia on Mahler," in *idem, Essays on Music,* ed. Richard Leppert, trans. Susan H. Gillespie (Berkeley: Univ. of California Press, 2002), 617.

10. Ernest Jones, *The Life and Work of Sigmund Freud* (New York: Basic, 1953–57), 2:80.

11. Adorno, *Mahler* (note 8), 41.

12. Adorno, *Mahler* (note 8), 6.

13. G. W. F. Hegel, "Virtue and the Course of the World," in *idem, The Phenomenology of Mind,* trans. and ed. J. B. Baillie, 2nd ed., rev. and corr. (London: George Allen & Unwin, 1931), 408, 410.

14. Adorno, *Mahler* (note 8), 6.

15. Sigmund Freud, *Beyond the Pleasure Principle,* in *idem, The Standard Edition of the Complete Psychological Works of Sigmund Freud,* vol. 18, (1920–1922): *Beyond the Pleasure Principle, Group Psychology, and Other Works,* ed. James Strachey (London: Hogarth, 1960), 7–44.

16. William Empson, *Some Versions of Pastoral* (London: Hogarth, 1986); and Adorno, *Mahler* (note 8), 129.

17. Walter Benjamin, "Franz Kafka," in *Illuminations,* ed. Hannah Arendt, trans. Harry Zohn (New York: Schocken, 1969), 116. Benjamin identifies the source of this remark as from "a conversation which Max Brod has related."

Editors' Acknowledgments

This volume would not have been possible without help from many people. We are especially grateful to Cathleen Cavell, Stanley Cavell's widow and literary executor, for trusting us with this project, giving us access to materials Cavell left behind, providing us with essential guidance on the contents of the *Nachlass*, and trusting us to do the editing work. We are deeply indebted to Norton Batkin, Rachel Cavell, David Cavell, and Benjamin Cavell for assisting us in understanding the context for some of the pieces included here. We appreciatively acknowledge the efforts of Eric Ritter, who, in organizing materials in Cavell's study, uncovered several different versions of a table of contents for *Here and There: Sites of Philosophy*, as well as Cavell's correspondence about the project with Alan Thomas at the University of Chicago Press, and who provided us with copies of a number of the essays included here. We also thank Arnold Davidson and Byron Davies for helpful conversations and advice.

We began work on this volume with Lindsay Waters at Harvard University Press shortly, as it happened, before he announced his retirement in late 2020. We are grateful for Lindsay's support and generous advice, and we feel very lucky to have been able to continue the work at HUP with Emily Silk, who, together with her colleagues Louise Robbins, Melissa Rodman, and Olivia Woods, along with Mary Ribesky, of Westchester Publishing Services, made the process of completing it more efficient and enjoyable than we had imagined was possible.

We owe thanks to Cayla Clinkenbeard for her ingenuity and thoughtfulness in tracking down information about the published versions of a number of chapters; to Margaret Smith and Carmen Hendershott at NYU, Allen Jones at the New School, and Rachel Greenhaus at the Harvard University Archives for their research and investigative assistance; to Alexandre Gefen for his invaluable support and help with all things digital; to Tara Mastrelli for helping to prepare the final manuscript for publication and for tactfully contributing to the editing process, calling our attention to unseen issues; to Stephen Mulhall for a wonderfully insightful and useful set of comments on a draft of our editors' introduction.

Stanley Cavell's philosophical practice began and ended with the question of what human beings, including philosophers, have taken to be of importance. He regarded the philosophers' obsessions with knowledge as a symptom of our avoidance of acknowledging our own and others' humanity—what Wittgenstein called "the pivot of our real need." In this context, it is important to note that had Cavell lived to put the finishing touches on this book, he would have dedicated it to his youngest and deeply beloved grandchild, Josephine Ava Cavell.

Index

Leibniz, Gottfried Wilhelm von, 85, 174

lethargy, 237–238

Levinas, Emmanuel, 227–228

Lévi-Strauss, Claude, 251–252

Lewin, David, 260–261, 264–266

liberation, 22–23, 40, 70, 89, 96, 198, 239, 261, 270–278

Life and Death in Psychoanalysis (Laplanche), 154

Life and Words (Das), 10, 187–192

Light in August (Faulkner), 158–163

literary studies: Benjamin's place in, 9; Derrida and, 8, 74–88, 127, 201–209, 296n33; ordinary language and, 107–108; philosophy's relation to, 72–92, 126–127, 194–200, 201–209, 214, 216, 223–240; psychoanalysis and, 139, 158–163, 195–196

Little Did I Know (Cavell), 9, 11

Locke, John, 69, 278

logical positivism, 8, 82, 101–102, 120–121, 127–130, 178, 182, 194, 201–205, 215, 228–229, 231

Logische Aufbau der Welt (Carnap), 15

Loos, Adolf, 281

love, 29–31, 128–129

Lovejoy, Arthur, 198

magic, 249–251

Mahler, Gustav, 12, 279–286

Mahler Companion, 281

Mann, Thomas, 265

Marker, Chris, 65–66, 69

marriage, 128–129, 236

Marvell, Andrew, 286

Marx, Karl, 42, 69, 147, 277

meaning: collecting and, 36; impressions and, 277; intention and, 76–78; music and, 11–12, 251–253, 275; understanding and, 247–254, 260–261, 267, 275–277; use as, 95

measuring, 1, 16, 22, 39, 55, 57–58

Meditations (Descartes), 173–174, 276

Mehlmann, Jeffrey, 122

melancholy, 28, 51, 57, 98, 122–126, 131, 207, 243–244, 258–259, 264–265, 275–276, 278

melodramas, 2, 133, 143

Melville, Herman, 135

Melville, Stephen, 60

memory, 34, 44, 65

Menninghaus, Winfried, 303n15

metaphilosophy, 97

Michaels, Walter Benn, 76–78

Miller, J. Hillis, 87–88

Mill on the Floss, The (Eliot), 217

Milton, John, 235, 286

modern, the: Benjamin and, 133–34, 137; Bloom on, 210–214; *Philosophical Investigations* as, 97; philosophical unrepresentability and, 23–24; revolution and, 273; Simmel on, 51–52; skepticism and, 165–166, 173–174; tradition and, 5–6, 121; Wittgenstein and, 260–268

"Modernist Painting" (Greenberg), 57

Montaigne, Michel de, 67, 115, 216

Moonstruck (film), 214

Moore, G. E., 234

moralism, 160, 167, 220

moral perfectionism, 6–7, 12–13, 129, 145–146, 206–207, 211, 213, 216–221, 295n25

Moral Reasoning, 34, 288

Moses and Aron (Lewin), 264

mourning, 51, 122–123, 131, 236, 253, 275–276